FRENCH THE EASY WAY

BOOK 2

by

CHRISTOPHER KENDRIS

B.S., M.S., Columbia University
in the City of New York
M.A., Ph.D., Northwestern University
in Evanston, Illinois
Diplômé, Faculté des Lettres, Université de Paris
(en Sorbonne)

Department of Foreign Languages
MONT PLEASANT PUBLIC HIGH SCHOOL
The City School District of
Schenectady, New York

BARRON'S EDUCATIONAL SERIES, INC.

New York • London • Toronto • Sydney

Printed in 1987

© Copyright 1983 by Barron's Educational Series, Inc.

All inquiries should be addressed to:
Barron's Educational Series, Inc.
250 Wireless Boulevard
Hauppauge, New York 11788

Library of Congress Catalog Card No. 82-1634

International Standard Book No. 0-8120-2505-9

Library of Congress Cataloging in Publication Data (Revised)
(Revised for vol. 2)

Kendris, Christopher.
  French the easy way.

  Includes index.
  Summary: Presents fundamentals of French grammar
for high school and college students who are familiar with basic
elements of the French language.
  1. French language—Grammar—1950–
[1. French language—Grammar] I. Title.
PC2112.K396   448.2′421   82-1634
ISBN 0-8120-2505-9 (set)

PRINTED IN THE UNITED STATES OF AMERICA
789   410   9876

For my lovely wife Yolanda, my two sons Alex and Ted,
my daughter-in-law Tina McMaster Kendris, my two grandsons
Alexander Bryan and Daniel Patrick Christopher.

With all my love

CONTENTS

PART II: FIVE PRACTICE TESTS

This is the second of two books. It is intended for you if you have begun to study French either in school, in college, at home on your own, or with a private tutor.

Book 2 of this new EASY WAY series is a continuation of French 1 with an emphasis on intermediate and advanced language, including a complete and thorough review of beginning French.

If I have inadvertently omitted any points in French grammar, vocabulary, and idiomatic expressions you think are important, please write to me, care of the publisher of this book, so that I may include them in the next edition.

ABOUT THE AUTHOR

Christopher Kendris has worked as interpreter and translator for the U.S. State Department at the American Embassy in Paris.

Dr. Kendris earned his B.S. and M.S. degrees at Columbia University in the City of New York, where he held a New York State scholarship, and his M.A. and Ph.D. degrees at Northwestern University in Evanston, Illinois. He also earned two diplomas with *Mention très Honorable* at the Université de Paris (en Sorbonne), Faculté des Lettres, École Supérieure de Préparation et de Perfectionnement des Professeurs de Français à l'Étranger, and at the Institut de Phonétique, Paris.

He has taught French at the College of The University of Chicago as visiting summer lecturer and at Northwestern University, where he held a Teaching Assistantship and Tutorial Fellowship for four years. He has also taught at Colby College, Duke University, Rutgers—the State University of New Jersey, and the State University of New York at Albany. He was Chairman of the Foreign Languages Department at Farmingdale High School, where he was also a teacher of French and Spanish. He is the author of numerous school and college books, workbooks, dictionaries, and other language aids. Among his most popular works are *201, 301,* and *501 French Verbs Fully Conjugated in All the Tenses; 201, 301,* and *501 Spanish Verbs Fully Conjugated in All the Tenses* (with special features); *French Now!* (Level One textbook and workbook); *How to Prepare for the College Board Achievement Test in French; How to Prepare for the College Board Achievement Test in Spanish; French Composition, a Practical Guide;* and two workbooks, *Beginning to Write in French* and *Beginning to Write in Spanish*—all of which have been issued by this publisher. He also wrote the English version of Maurice Grevisse's *Le français correct,* published under the title *Correct French,* also issued by this publisher.

Dr. Kendris is listed in *Contemporary Authors* and *Directory of American Scholars.*

INTRODUCTION

This book is intended for you if you have at least some knowledge of the basic elements of the French language. You can improve what you may already know of French grammar if you study this book 20 minutes every day starting at the beginning.

You can review by yourself what you have studied, what you have not studied too thoroughly in the past, or what you have forgotten in French 1, 2, and 3 because this book contains all the fundamentals generally presented in those three levels.

The main points in French grammar in this book are arranged in a § decimal system for quick and easy reference. If you want to review French pronouns, for example (of which there are several different kinds), the Index in the back tells you in what § (section) you can find them with examples that illustrate them in French and English.

Do you feel you need to refresh your memory of direct and indirect object pronouns? Turn to the Index and look up the § number for the entry *pronouns*. The section number is given as **§29.—§29.53.** In that section of the book, you will find all the French pronouns that you need to know for mastery.

Maybe you do not know a noun from a pronoun, a possessive adjective from a possessive pronoun. In that case, look up the different parts of speech in the Index, or look up a particular French word. For example, you may not know that **meilleur** (which means *better*) is an adjective and that **mieux** (which also means *better*) is an adverb. If you do not know when to use which of these two words, look up **meilleur** and **mieux** in the Index for the § reference. I include in the Index many key words in French which are usually troublesome for English-speaking students learning the French language.

Do you know the difference in use between **dans** and **en**, both of which mean *in*? Look up those two words in the Index and you will find that in **§16.** an explanation is given with examples in French and English.

You say you can't unhook French verbs yet?! Look up the entry *verbs* in the Index and it will send you to different sections of this book where you can get a better picture of what they are all about. See, for example, **§39.30—§39.32** where I diagram French sentences so that you can get a better picture of how a verb and other elements in a sentence function. Read, in particular, **§39.86** where I present a comparison of meanings and uses of French verb tenses and moods as related to English verb tenses and moods.

Do you know that the verb **devoir** has special meanings in different tenses? The Index, under the entry **devoir**, refers you to **§17.** and I give you examples of its uses.

Do you understand clearly the correct word order of elements in a French sentence? Look up the entry *word order of elements in a French sentence* in the Index. In **§42.**, I give you summaries of word order of elements in different kinds of sentences in French with examples.

When I give you examples in French, I frequently give the English translation. Nevertheless, there is a French-English vocabulary in the back for your use.

Browse through the Index. You may stumble on something that will arouse your curiosity. The Index has been compiled to help you find efficiently and quickly what you need to know. If you study this book every day, you should score high on the grammar section of standardized tests given to students in schools, to students entering college, and to graduate students who are preparing to take placement, proficiency, qualifying, and validating tests in French.

If I have inadvertently omitted any point in French grammar which you think is important, please write to me care of the publisher of this book so that it may be included in the next edition.

CHRISTOPHER KENDRIS

ABBREVIATIONS USED IN THIS BOOK

adj. adjective

adv. adverb, adverbial

ant. anterior

art. article

aux. auxiliary (helping)

cond. conditional

conj. conjunction

def. definite

dem. *or* **demons.** demonstrative

dir. direct

disj. disjunctive

e.g. for example

f. *or* **fem.** feminine

ff and the following

fut. future

i.e. that is, that is to say

imper. imperative

imperf. imperfect

indef. indefinite

indic. indicative

indir. indirect

inf. infinitive

m. *or* **masc.** masculine

n. noun

obj. object

p. page

par. paragraph

part. participle

perf. perfect

pers. person

pl. plural

plup. pluperfect

poss. possessive

prep. preposition

pres. present

pron. pronoun

qqch quelque chose (something)

qqn quelqu'un (someone)

refl. reflexive

s. *or* **sing.** singular

subj. subjunctive

v. verb

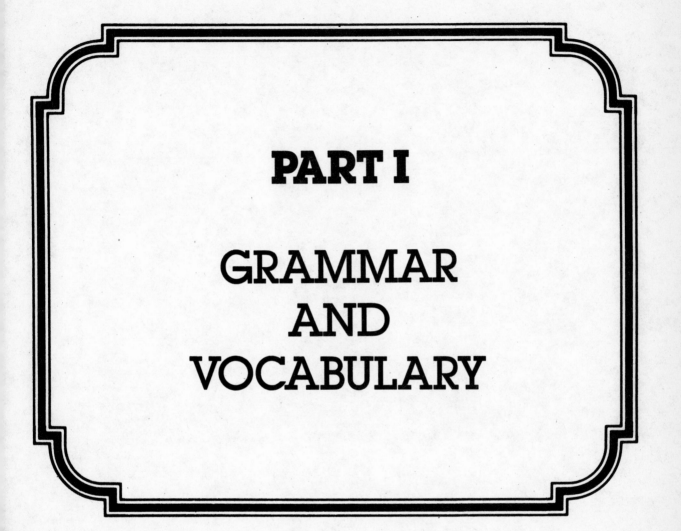

PART I

GRAMMAR
AND
VOCABULARY

GRAMMAR AND VOCABULARY

A § decimal system has been used in this book so that you may quickly find the reference to a particular point in grammar when you use the index. For example, if you look up the entry *adjectives* in the index, you will find the reference given as §1.

§1. ADJECTIVES

§1.1 Agreement

An adjective normally agrees in gender (feminine or masculine) and number (singular or plural) with the noun or pronoun it modifies. An adjective is a word that describes a noun or a pronoun.

EXAMPLES:

Alexandre et Théodore sont beaux et intelligents / Alexander and Theodore are handsome and intelligent.

Yolande est belle / Yolanda is beautiful.

Janine et Monique sont belles / Janine and Monique are beautiful.

Hélène et Simone sont actives / Helen and Simone are active.

Anne est jolie / Anne is pretty.

Michel est beau / Michael is handsome.

C'est un bel arbre / It's a beautiful tree.

Ils sont amusants / They are funny.

Je ne vois aucun taxi / I don't see any taxi.

Je ne connais aucune dame dans cette salle / I don't know any lady in this room.

Voulez-vous un autre livre? / Do you want another book?

Aimeriez-vous une autre pâtisserie? / Would you like another pastry?

Chaque garçon est présent / Every boy is present.

Chaque jeune fille est présente / Every girl is present.

Josiane est ici depuis quelque temps / Josiane has been here for some time.

Valentine est absente depuis quelques semaines / Valentine has been absent for a few weeks.

§1.2 Comparison

§1.3

Of the same degree: **aussi . . . que** (as . . . as)
Of a lesser degree: **moins . . . que** (less . . . than)
Of a higher degree: **plus . . . que** (more . . . than)

EXAMPLES:

Janine est aussi grande que Monique / Janine is as tall as Monique.

Monique est moins intelligente que Janine / Monique is less intelligent than Janine.

Janine est plus jolie que Monique / Janine is prettier than Monique.

§1.4

Aussi . . . que becomes **si . . . que** in a negative sentence.

EXAMPLE: **Robert n'est pas si grand que Joseph** / Robert is not as (so) tall as Joseph.

§1.5

The comparison of the adj. *bad* is: **mauvais, pire, le pire**

EXAMPLES:

Ce crayon est mauvais / This pencil is bad.

Ce crayon est pire que l'autre / This pencil is worse than the other.

Ce crayon est le pire / This pencil is the worst.

§1.6

Plus que (more than) becomes **plus de** + a number.

EXAMPLES:

Il a plus de cinquante ans / He is more than fifty years old.

Je lui ai donné plus de cent dollars / I gave him (her) more than one hundred dollars.

§1.7 Demonstrative

A demonstrative adj. is used to point out something or someone. They are:

GENDER	SINGULAR	PLURAL	*English meaning* S.	PL.
Masculine	**ce, cet**	**ces**	this or that	these or those
Feminine	**cette**	**ces**	this or that	these or those

EXAMPLES:

Ce garçon est beau / This boy is handsome.

Cet arbre est beau / This tree is beautiful.

Cette femme est belle / This woman is beautiful.

Ces hommes sont beaux / These men are handsome.

Ces livres sont beaux / These books are beautiful.

Ces dames sont belles / These ladies are beautiful.

§1.8

If you wish to make a contrast between *this* and *that* or *these* and *those*, add **–ci** (this, these) or **–là** (that, those) to the noun with a hyphen.

EXAMPLES:

Ce garçon-ci est plus fort que ce garçon-là / This boy is stronger than that boy.

Cette jeune fille-ci est plus jolie que cette jeune fille-là / This girl is prettier than that girl.

Ces livres-ci sont plus beaux que ces livres-là / These books are more beautiful than those books.

§1.9

The form **cet** is used in front of a masc. sing. noun or adj. beginning with a vowel or silent *h*: **cet arbre, cet homme, cet énorme bâtiment.**

If there is more than one noun, a demonstrative adj. must be used in front of each noun: **cette dame et ce monsieur.**

§1.10 Descriptive

A descriptive adj. is a word that describes a noun or pronoun: **une belle maison, un beau livre, un bel arbre, une jolie dame.**

§1.11 Formation of feminine singular

(a) The fem. sing. of an adj. is normally formed by adding **e** to the masc. sing. adj.: joli / jolie; présent / présente; grand / grande

(b) If a masc. sing. adj. already ends in **e**, the fem. sing. is the same form: aimable / aimable; énorme / énorme; faible / faible

(c) Some fem. sing. forms are irregular. If a masc. sing. adj. ends in **c**, change to **que** for the fem.; **er** to **ère**; **f** to **ve**; **g** to **gue**; **x** to **se**.

EXAMPLES:

public / publique; premier / première; actif / active; long / longue; heureux / heureuse

(d) Some masc. sing. adjectives double the final consonant before adding **e** to form the feminine.

EXAMPLES:

ancien / ancienne; bas / basse; bon / bonne; cruel / cruelle; gentil / gentille; muet / muette; quel / quelle

(e) The following fem. sing. adjectives were formed from the irregular masc. sing. forms:

MASC. SING. IN FRONT OF A MASC. SING. NOUN BEGINNING WITH A CONSONANT	IRREG. MASC. SING. IN FRONT OF A MASC. SING. NOUN BEGINNING WITH A VOWEL OR SILENT *H*	FEM. SING.
beau / beautiful, handsome	**bel**	**belle**
fou / crazy	**fol**	**folle**
mou / soft	**mol**	**molle**
nouveau / new	**nouvel**	**nouvelle**
vieux / old	**vieil**	**vieille**

(f) Finally, there are some common masc. sing. adjectives which have irregular forms in the fem. sing. and they do not fall into any particular category like those above.

EXAMPLES:
> **blanc** / **blanche**; **complet** / **complète**; **doux** / **douce**; **faux** / **fausse**; **favori** / **favorite**; **frais** / **fraîche**; **sec** / **sèche**

§1.12   Interrogative

The adj. **quel** is generally regarded as interrogative because it is frequently used in a question. Its forms are: **quel, quelle, quels, quelles.**

EXAMPLES:
> **Quel livre voulez-vous?** / Which book do you want?
> **Quel est votre nom?** / What is your name?
>
> **Quelle heure est-il?** / What time is it?
> **Quelle est votre adresse?** / What is your address?
>
> **Quels sont les mois de l'année?** / What are the months of the year?
> **Quelles sont les saisons?** / What are the seasons?

§1.13   The adj. **quel** is also used in exclamations without the indef. art. **un** or **une**.

EXAMPLES:
> **Quel garçon!** / What a boy!
> **Quelle jeune fille!** / What a girl!

§1.14   Formation of plural

(a) The plural is normally formed by adding **s** to the masc. or fem. sing.: bon / bons; bonne / bonnes; joli / jolis; jolie / jolies

(b) If the masc. sing. already ends in **s** or **x**, it remains the same in the masc. pl.: gris / gris; heureux / heureux

(c) If a masc. sing. adj. ends in **al**, it changes to **aux**: égal / égaux; principal / principaux

(d) If a masc. sing. adj. ends in **eau**, it changes to **eaux**: nouveau / nouveaux

§1.15   Position

(a) In French, most descriptive adjectives are placed *after* the noun; *e.g.,* colors, nationality, religion: **une robe blanche, un fromage français, un garçon français, une femme catholique.**

(b) An adj. of nationality is not capitalized but a noun indicating nationality is capitalized: **un Américain, une Américaine, un Français, une Française.**

(c) Here are some common short adjectives that generally are placed in front of the noun: **un autre livre, un bel arbre, un beau cadeau, un bon dîner, chaque jour, un gros livre, une jeune dame, une jolie maison, une petite table, plusieurs amis, un vieil homme, le premier rang, quelques bonbons, un tel garçon, toute la journée.**

(d) Some adjectives change in meaning, depending on whether the adj. is in front of the noun or after it.

EXAMPLES:

la semaine dernière last week	**la dernière semaine** the last (final) week
ma robe propre my clean dress	**ma propre robe** my own dress
une femme brave a brave woman	**une brave femme** a fine woman
le même moment the same moment	**le moment même** the very moment
un livre cher an expensive book	**un cher ami** a dear friend

§1.16   Possessive

Masculine			
SINGULAR		PLURAL	
mon livre	my book	**mes livres**	my books
ton stylo	your pen	**tes stylos**	your pens
son ballon	his (her, its) balloon	**ses ballons**	his (her, its) balloons
notre parapluie	our umbrella	**nos parapluies**	our umbrellas
votre sandwich	your sandwich	**vos sandwichs**	your sandwiches
leur gâteau	their cake	**leurs gâteaux**	their cakes

Feminine			
SINGULAR		PLURAL	
ma robe	my dress	**mes robes**	my dresses
ta jaquette	your jacket	**tes jaquettes**	your jackets
sa balle	his (her, its) ball	**ses balles**	his (her, its) balls
notre maison	our house	**nos maisons**	our houses
votre voiture	your car	**vos voitures**	your cars
leur soeur	their sister	**leurs soeurs**	their sisters

(a) A possessive adjective agrees in gender and number *with the noun* it modifies, *not with the possessor.*

(b) Some possessive adjectives do not agree with the gender of the noun *in the singular.* They are all the same, whether in front of a masculine or feminine singular noun: **notre, votre, leur.**

(c) Some possessive adjectives do not agree with the gender of the noun *in the plural.* They are all the same, whether in front of a masculine or feminine plural noun: **mes, tes, ses, nos, vos, leurs.**

(d) What you have to be aware of are the following possessive adjectives: **mon** or **ma, ton** or **ta, son** or **sa.**

(e) In front of a *feminine singular noun* beginning with a vowel or silent *h,* the masculine singular forms are used: **mon, ton, son**—instead of **ma, ta, sa:**

mon adresse	my address	**son** amie	his (or her) friend
ton opinion	your opinion	**mon** habitude	my habit (custom)

(f) Since **son, sa** and **ses** can mean *his* or *her*, you may add **à lui** or **à elle** to make the meaning clear:

sa maison à lui	his house	**son livre à elle**	her book
sa maison à elle	her house	**ses livres à lui**	his books
son livre à lui	his book	**ses livres à elle**	her books

(g) If there is more than one noun, a possessive adjective must be used in front of each noun: **ma mère et mon père, mon livre et mon cahier**.

§1.17 Superlative

(a) It is formed by placing the appropriate def. art. (**le, la, les**) in front of the comparative: **Joséphine est la plus jolie jeune fille de la classe** / Josephine is the prettiest girl in the class.

(b) If the adj. normally follows the noun, the def. art. must be used twice—in front of the noun and in front of the superlative: **Monsieur Hibou fut le président le plus sage de la nation** / Mr. Hibou was the wisest president of the nation.

(c) After a superlative, the prep. **de** is normally used (*not* dans) to express *in*: **Pierre est le plus beau garçon de la classe** / Peter is the most handsome boy in the class. This **de** is sometimes translated into English as *of* or *on*: **le plus actif de l'équipe** / the most active on the team.

(d) If more than one comparative or superlative is expressed, each is repeated: **Marie est la plus intelligente et la plus sérieuse de l'école**.

§1.18 Adjectives used in an adverbial sense

An adj. used as an adverb does not normally change in form: **Cette rose sent bon.**

§1.19 With parts of the body and clothing

(a) When using the verb **avoir**, the def. art. is normally used with parts of the body, not the possessive adjective: **Henri a les mains sales; Simone a les cheveux roux.**

(b) When using a reflexive verb, the def. art. is normally used, not the possessive adjective: **Paulette s'est lavé les cheveux** / Paulette washed her hair.

(c) The def. art. is used instead of the poss. adj. when referring to parts of the body or clothing if it is clear who the possessor is: **Henri tient le livre dans la main** / Henry is holding the book in his hand; **Je mets le chapeau sur la tête** / I am putting my hat on my head.

§1.20 Summary of irregular comparative and superlative adjectives

ADJECTIVE (MASC.)	COMPARATIVE	SUPERLATIVE
bon, *good*	**meilleur,** *better*	**le meilleur,** *(the) best*
mauvais, *bad*	**plus mauvais,** *worse*	**le plus mauvais,** *(the) worst*
petit, *small*	**pire,** *worse*	**le pire,** *(the) worst*
	plus petit, *smaller (in size)*	**le plus petit,** *(the) smallest*
	moindre, *less (in importance)*	**le moindre,** *(the) least*

§2. ADVERBS

§2.1 Comparative and Superlative

ADVERB	COMPARATIVE	SUPERLATIVE
vite (quickly)	**plus vite (que)** *more quickly (than)* *faster (than)*	**le plus vite** *(the) most quickly* *(the) fastest*
	moins vite (que) *less quickly (than)*	**le moins vite** *(the) least quickly*
	aussi vite (que) *as quickly (as)* *as fast (as)*	

EXAMPLES:

Arlette parle plus vite que Marie-France / Arlette talks faster than Marie-France.

Madame Legrange parle moins vite que Madame Duval / Madame Legrange talks less quickly than Madame Duval.

Monsieur Bernard parle aussi vite que Monsieur Claude / Mr. Bernard talks as fast as Mr. Claude.

Madame Durocher parle le plus vite tandis que Madame Milot parle le moins vite / Madame Durocher talks the fastest whereas Madame Milot talks the least quickly.

§2.2 **Aussi . . . que** becomes **si . . . que** in a negative sentence.

EXAMPLE: **Justin ne parle pas si vite que Justine** / Justin does not talk as (so) fast as Justine.

§2.3 Common adverbs irregular in the comparative and superlative

ADVERB	COMPARATIVE	SUPERLATIVE
bien, (well)	**mieux** (better)	**le mieux** (best, the best)
beaucoup (much)	**plus** (more)	**le plus** (most, the most)
mal (badly)	**plus mal** (worse) **pis** (worse)	**le plus mal** (worst, the worst) **le pis** (worst, the worst)
peu (little)	**moins** (less)	**le moins bien** (the worst)

EXAMPLES:

Pierre travaille bien, Henri travaille mieux que Robert, et Georges travaille le mieux.

Marie étudie beaucoup, Paulette étudie plus que Marie, et Henriette étudie le plus.

§2.4 Formation

§2.5

First, you must know that an adverb is a word that modifies a verb, an adjective, or another adverb: **Lily chante bien, Robert est vraiment intelligent, et Christine récite ses leçons fort bien.**

§2.6

There are many adverbs in French that do not have to be formed from another word; for example: **bien, mal, vite, combien, comment, pourquoi, où.**

§2.7

There are many other adverbs that are formed. The usual way is to add the suffix **-ment** to the masc. sing. form of an adj. whose last letter is a vowel; for example: **probable / probablement, poli / poliment, vrai / vraiment.**

§2.8 The suffix **-ment** is added to the fem. sing. form if the masc. sing. ends in a consonant; for example: **affreux / affreuse / affreusement; seul / seule / seulement; amer / amère / amèrement; franc / franche / franchement.**

§2.9 The ending **-ment** is equivalent to the English ending **-ly: lent / lente / lentement** (slow / slowly).

§2.10 Some adjectives that end in **-ant** or **-ent** become adverbs by changing **-ant** to **-amment** and **-ent** to **-emment: innocent / innocemment; constant / constamment; récent / récemment.**

§2.11 Some adverbs take **é** instead of **e** before adding **-ment: profond / profondément; confus / confusément; précis / précisément.**

§2.12 The adj. **gentil** becomes **gentiment** as an adverb and **bref** becomes **brièvement.**

§2.13 **Interrogative**
Some common interrogative adverbs are: **comment, combien, pourquoi, quand, où.**

> EXAMPLES:
> **Comment allez-vous? Combien coûte ce livre? Pourquoi partez-vous? Quand arriverez-vous? Où allez-vous?** / How are you? How much does this book cost? Why are you leaving? When will you arrive? Where are you going?

§2.14 **Of quantity**
Some adverbial expressions of quantity are: **beaucoup de, assez de, peu de, trop de, plus de.** With these, no article is used: **peu de sucre, beaucoup de travail, assez de temps, trop de lait.**

§2.15 **Position**

> 1. David aime **beaucoup** les chocolats / David likes chocolates *a lot.*
> 2. Paulette a parlé **distinctement** / Paulette spoke *distinctly.*
> 3. Julie a **bien** parlé / Julie spoke *well.*

(a) In French, an adverb ordinarily *follows* the simple verb it modifies, as in the first model sentence in the above box.

(b) If a verb is compound, as in the **passé composé** (model sentence 2 above), the adverb generally *follows* the past participle if it is a long adverb. The adverb **distinctement** is long. Some exceptions: **certainement, complètement,** and **probablement** are usually placed between the helping verb and the past participle: **Elle est probablement partie, Il a complètement fini le travail.**

(c) If a verb is compound, as in the **passé composé** (model sentence 3 above), short common adverbs (like **beaucoup, bien, déjà, encore, mal, mieux, souvent, toujours**) ordinarily precede the past participle; in other words, may be placed between the helping verb and the past participle.

(d) For emphasis, an adverb may be placed at the beginning of a sentence: **Malheureusement, Suzanne est déjà partie.**

§3. ANTONYMS

One very good way to increase your French vocabulary is to think of an antonym (opposite meaning) or synonym (similar meaning) for every word in French that you already know. Of course, there is no antonym or synonym for all words in the French language—nor in English. But you should, at least, wonder what the possible antonyms and synonyms are of French words. For example, stop and think: What is the antonym of **aller**? The antonym of **jamais**? A synonym of **erreur**?

§3.1   **Here are some simple antonyms which you certainly ought to know:**

absent, absente *adj.*, absent / **présent, présente** *adj.*, present

acheter *v.*, to buy / **vendre** *v.*, to sell

agréable *adj.*, pleasant, agreeable / **désagréable** *adj.*, unpleasant, disagreeable

aimable *adj.*, kind / **méchant, méchante** *adj.*, mean, nasty

aller *v.*, to go / **venir** *v.*, to come

ami, amie *n.*, friend / **ennemi, ennemie** *n.*, enemy

s'amuser *refl.v.*, to enjoy oneself, to have a good time / **s'ennuyer** *refl.v.*, to be bored

ancien, ancienne *adj.*, old, ancient / **nouveau, nouvel, nouvelle** *adj.*, new

avant *prep.*, before / **après** *prep.*, after

bas, basse *adj.*, low / **haut, haute** *adj.*, high

beau, bel, belle *adj.*, beautiful, handsome / **laid, laide** *adj.*, ugly

beaucoup (de) *adv.*, much, many / **peu (de)** *adv.*, little, some

beauté *n.f.*, beauty / **laideur** *n.f.*, ugliness

bête *adj.*, stupid / **intelligent, intelligente** *adj.*, intelligent

blanc, blanche *adj.*, white / **noir, noire** *adj.*, black

bon, bonne *adj.*, good / **mauvais, mauvaise** *adj.*, bad

bonheur *n.m.*, happiness / **malheur** *n.m.*, unhappiness

chaud, chaude *adj.*, hot, warm / **froid, froide** *adj.*, cold

cher, chère *adj.*, expensive / **bon marché** cheap

content, contente *adj.*, glad, pleased / **mécontent, mécontente** *adj.*, displeased

court, courte *adj.*, short / **long, longue** *adj.*, long

debout *adv.*, standing / **assis, assise** *adj.*, seated, sitting

dedans *adv.*, inside / **dehors** *adv.*, outside

demander *v.*, to ask / **répondre** *v.*, to reply

dernier, dernière *adj.*, last / **premier, première** *adj.*, first

derrière *adv.*, *prep.*, behind, in back of / **devant** *adv.*, *prep.*, in front of

dessous *adv.*, *prep.*, below, underneath / **dessus** *adv.*, *prep.*, above, over

différent, différente *adj.*, different / **même** *adj.*, same

difficile *adj.*, difficult / **facile** *adj.*, easy

domestique *adj.*, domestic / **sauvage** *adj.*, wild

donner *v.*, to give / **recevoir** *v.*, to receive

droite *n.f.*, right / **gauche** *n.f.*, left

emprunter *v.*, to borrow / **prêter** *v.*, to lend

entrer (dans) *v.*, to enter (in, into) / **sortir (de)** *v.*, to go out (of, from)

est *n.m.*, East / **ouest** *n.m.*, West

étroit, étroite *adj.*, narrow / **large** *adj.*, wide

faible *adj.*, weak / **fort, forte** *adj.*, strong

fermer *v.*, to close / **ouvrir** *v.*, to open

fin *n.f.*, end / **commencement** *n.m.*, beginning

finir *v.*, to finish / **commencer** *v.*, to begin; **se mettre à** *v.*, to begin + inf.

gagner *v.*, to win / **perdre** *v.*, to lose

gai, gaie *adj.*, gay, happy / **triste** *adj.*, sad

grand, grande *adj.*, large, tall, big / **petit, petite** *adj.*, small, little

gros, grosse *adj.*, fat / **maigre** *adj.*, thin

grossier, grossière *adj.*, coarse, impolite / **poli, polie** *adj.*, polite

heureux, heureuse *adj.*, happy / **malheureux, malheureuse** *adj.*, unhappy

hier *adv.*, yesterday / **demain** *adv.*, tomorrow

homme *n.m.*, man / **femme** *n.f.*, woman

ici *adv.*, here / **là** *adv.*, there

inutile *adj.*, useless / **utile** *adj.*, useful

jamais *adv.*, never / **toujours** *adv.*, always

jeune *adj.*, young / **vieux, vieil, vieille** *adj.*, old

jeune fille *n.f.*, girl / **garçon** *n.m.*, boy

jeunesse *n.f.*, youth / **vieillesse** *n.f.*, old age

joli, jolie *adj.*, pretty / **laid, laide** *adj.*, ugly

jour *n.m.*, day / **nuit** *n.f.*, night

léger, légère *adj.*, light / **lourd, lourde** *adj.*, heavy

lendemain *n.m.*, the next (following) day / **veille** *n.f.*, the eve (evening before)

lentement *adv.*, slowly / **vite** *adv.*, quickly

mal *adv.*, badly / **bien** *adv.*, well

mari *n.m.*, husband / **femme** *n.f.*, wife

matin *n.m.*, morning / **soir** *n.m.*, evening

mer *n.f.*, sea / **ciel** *n.m.*, sky

midi *n.m.*, noon / **minuit** *n.m.*, midnight

moderne *adj.*, modern / **ancien, ancienne** *adj.*, ancient, old

moins *adv.*, less / **plus** *adv.*, more

monter *v.*, to go up / **descendre** *v.*, to go down

né, née *adj.*, *past part.*, born / **mort, morte** *adj.*, *past part.*, died, dead

nord *n.m.*, North / **sud** *n.m.*, South

nouveau, nouvel, nouvelle *adj.*, new / **vieux, vieil, vieille** *adj.*, old

obéir (à) *v.*, to obey / **désobéir (à)** *v.*, to disobey

ôter *v.*, to remove, to take off / **mettre** *v.*, to put, to put on

oui *adv.*, yes / **non** *adv.*, no

paix *n.f.*, peace / **guerre** *n.f.*, war

paraître *v.*, to appear / **disparaître** *v.*, to disappear

paresseux, paresseuse *adj.*, lazy / **diligent, diligente** *adj.*, diligent

partir *v.*, to leave / **arriver** *v.*, to arrive

pauvre *adj.*, poor / **riche** *adj.*, rich

perdre *v.*, to lose / **trouver** *v.*, to find

plancher *n.m.*, floor / **plafond** *n.m.*, ceiling

plein, pleine *adj.*, full / **vide** *adj.*, empty

poli, polie *adj.*, polite / **impoli, impolie** *adj.*, impolite possible *adj.*, possible / **impossible** *adj.*, impossible

prendre *v.*, to take / **donner** *v.*, to give

près (de) *adv.*, *prep.*, near / **loin (de)** *adv.*, *prep.*, far (from)

propre *adj.*, clean / **sale** *adj.*, dirty

quelque chose *pron.*, something / **rien** *pron.*, nothing

quelqu'un *pron.*, someone, somebody / **personne** *pron.*, nobody, no one

question *n.f.*, question / **réponse** *n.f.*, answer, reply, response

refuser *v.*, to refuse / **accepter** *v.*, to accept

reine *n.f.*, queen / **roi** *n.m.*, king

réussir (à) *v.*, to succeed (at, in) / **échouer (à)** *v.*, to fail (at, in)

rire *v.*, to laugh / **pleurer** *v.*, to cry, to weep

sans *prep.*, without / **avec** *prep.*, with

silence *n.m.*, silence / **bruit** *n.m.*, noise

soleil *n.m.*, sun / **lune** *n.f.*, moon

souvent *adv.*, often / **rarement** *adv.*, rarely

sur *prep.*, on / **sous** *prep.*, under

sûr, sûre *adj.*, sure, certain / **incertain, incertaine** *adj.*, unsure, uncertain

terre *n.f.*, earth, land / **ciel** *n.m.*, sky

tôt *adv.*, early / **tard** *adv.*, late

travailler *v.*, to work / **jouer** *v.*, to play

travailleur, travailleuse *adj.*, diligent, hardworking / **paresseux, paresseuse** *adj.*, lazy

vie *n.f.*, life / **mort** *n.f.*, death

ville *n.f.*, city / **campagne** *n.f.*, country(side)

vivre *v.*, to live / **mourir** *v.*, to die

vrai, vraie *adj.*, true / **faux, fausse** *adj.*, false

§3.2   Now try these antonyms. They are not so simple as the others:

abolir *v.*, to abolish / **conserver** *v.*, to preserve, to conserve

accuser *v.*, to accuse / **justifier** *v.*, to justify

adresse *n.f.*, *skill* / **maladresse** *n.f.*, clumsiness

aider *v.*, to help / **nuire** *v.*, to harm

aisé *adj.*, easy / **difficile** *adj.*, difficult

allonger *v.*, to lengthen / **abréger** *v.*, to shorten

attrayant, attrayante *adj.*, attractive / **repoussant, repoussante** *adj.*, repulsive

avare *adj.*, stingy, miserly / **dépensier, dépensière** *adj.*, thriftless, extravagant

barbare *adj.*, savage, barbarous / **civilisé, civilisée** *adj.*, civilized

bavard, bavarde *adj.*, talkative / **taciturne** *adj.*, quiet, taciturn

bénir *v.*, to bless / **maudire** *v.*, to curse

bonté *n.f.*, goodness / **méchanceté** *n.f.*, wickedness

cadet, cadette *n.*, younger, youngest / **aîné, aînée** *n.*, older, oldest

calmer *v.*, to calm / **agiter** *v.*, **exciter** *v.*, to excite

chaleureux, chaleureuse *adj.*, warm / **froid, froide** *adj.*, cold

chauffer *v.*, to heat, to warm up / **refroidir** *v.*, to cool, to cool off

condamner *v.*, to condemn / **absoudre** *v.*, to absolve

confiance *n.f.*, confidence / **méfiance** *n.f.*, distrust

créer *v.*, to create / **détruire** *v.*, to destroy

dépenser *v.*, to spend / **économiser** *v.*, to save

déplaisant, déplaisante *adj.*, unpleasant / **agréable** *adj.*, pleasant, agreeable

descendre *v.*, to go down, to descend / **monter** *v.*, to go up, to ascend

diminuer *v.*, to lessen, to diminish / **augmenter** *v.*, to increase, to augment

divertissant, divertissante *adj.*, amusing, diverting / **ennuyant, ennuyante; ennuyeux, ennuyeuse** *adj.*, annoying

éclaircir *v.*, to light up / **obscurcir** *v.*, to darken

effrayant, effrayante *adj.*, frightening / **rassurant, rassurante** *adj.*, reassuring

élever *v.*, to raise / **abaisser** *v.*, to lower

(s')éloigner *v.*, to separate, to withdraw / **(se) rapprocher** *v.*, to draw near

embonpoint *n.m.*, stoutness, plumpness / **maigreur** *n.f.*, leanness, thinness

épouvanter *v.*, to frighten / **rassurer** *v.*, to reassure

facultatif, facultative *adj.*, optional / **obligatoire** *adj.*, obligatory, mandatory

fainéant, fainéante *adj.*, lazy / **diligent, diligente** *adj.*, industrious

femelle *n.f.*, female / **mâle** *n.m.*, male

gaspiller *v.*, to waste / **économiser** *v.*, to save

gratuit *adj.*, free / **coûteux** *adj.*, costly

(s')habiller *v.*, to dress / **(se)déshabiller** *v.*, to undress

haïr *v.*, to hate / **aimer** *v.*, to like, to love

humble *adj.*, humble / **orgueilleux, orgueilleuse** *adj.*, proud

humide *adj.*, damp / **sec, sèche** *adj.*, dry

inférieur, inférieure *adj.*, lower / **supérieur, supérieure** *adj.*, upper

innocent, innocente *adj.*, innocent / **coupable** *adj.*, guilty

introduire *v.*, to show in / **expulser** *v.*, to expel

joie *n.f.*, joy / **tristesse** *n.f.*, sadness

lâche *adj.*, cowardly / **brave** *adj.*, brave

liberté *n.f.*, liberty / **esclavage** *n.m.*, slavery

louange *n.f.*, praise / **blâme** *n.m.*, blame, disapproval

mensonge *n.m.*, lie, falsehood / **vérité** *n.f.*, truth

mépriser *v.*, to scorn / **estimer** *v.*, to esteem

nain *n.m.*, dwarf / **géant** *n.m.*, giant

négliger *v.*, to neglect / **soigner** *v.*, to care for

ouverture *n.f.*, opening / **fermeture** *n.f.*, closing
pair *adj.*, even / **impair** *adj.*, odd
paresse *n.f.*, laziness / **travail** *n.m.*, work
pauvreté *n.f.*, poverty / **richesse** *n.f.*, wealth, riches
peine *n.f.*, trouble, pain, hardship / **plaisir** *n.m.*, pleasure
plat, plate *adj.*, flat / **montagneux, montagneuse** *adj.*, mountainous
récolter *v.*, to harvest / **semer** *v.*, to sow

reconnaissant, reconnaissante *adj.*, grateful / **ingrat, ingrate** *adj.*, ungrateful
remplir *v.*, to fill / **vider** *v.*, to empty
retour *n.m.*, return / **départ** *n.m.*, departure
sécher *v.*, to dry / **mouiller** *v.*, to dampen, to wet
souple *adj.*, flexible / **raide** *adj.*, stiff
vacarme *n.m.*, uproar, tumult / **silence** *n.m.*, silence
vitesse *n.f.*, speed / **lenteur** *n.f.*, slowness

§4. ARTICLES

§4.1 Definite article

§4.2 There are four definite articles in French and they all mean *the*: **le, la, l'**, and **les**: **le livre, la leçon, l'encre, les crayons.**

§4.3 The definite article is used:

(a) In front of each noun even if there is more than one noun stated, which is not always done in English: **J'ai le livre et le cahier** / I have the book and notebook.

(b) With a noun when you make a general statement: **J'aime le café** / I like coffee; **J'aime l'été** / I like summer; **La vie est belle** / Life is beautiful; **La France est belle** / France is beautiful.

(c) With a noun of weight or measure to express *a, an, per*: **dix francs la livre** / ten francs a pound; **dix francs la douzaine** / ten francs a dozen (per dozen).

(d) In front of a noun indicating a profession, rank, adjective, or title followed by the name of the person: **Le professeur Poulin est absent aujourd'hui** / Professor Poulin is absent today; **La reine Elisabeth est belle** / Queen Elizabeth is beautiful.

But in direct address (when talking directly to the person and you mention the rank, profession, *etc.*), do not use the def. art.: **Bonjour, docteur Sétout** / Hello, Doctor Sétout.

(e) With the name of a language: **J'étudie le français** / I am studying French.

But do not use the def. art. after the verb **parler** when the name of the language is immediately after a form of **parler**: **Je parle français** / I speak French.

Also, do not use the def. art. if the name of a language is immediately after the prep. **en**: **J'écris en français** / I am writing in French.

Also, do not use the def. art. after the prep. **de** in an adjective phrase: **J'ai mon livre de français** / I have my French book.

(f) With the days of the week when you want to indicate an action which is habitually repeated: **Le samedi je vais au cinéma** / On Saturdays I go to the movies.

(g) With parts of the body or articles of clothing if the possessor is clearly stated: **Janine a les cheveux noirs** / Janine's hair is black; **Je mets le chapeau sur la tête** / I am putting my hat on my head.

(h) With the following expressions indicating segments of the day: **l'après-midi** / in the afternoon; **le matin** / in the morning; **le soir** / in the evening.

(i) With common expressions, for example: **à l'école** / to school, in school; **à la maison** / at home; **à l'église** / to church, in church; **la semaine dernière** / last week; **l'année dernière** / last year: **Je suis allé à l'école la semaine dernière** / I went to school last week.

(j) With a proper name that is described: **J'aime le vieux Paris** / I like old (the old section of) Paris.

(k) With the prep. **dans** + the name of a country or continent modified by an adjective: **dans la France méridionale** / in southern France; **dans l'Amérique du Nord** / in North America.

(l) With the prep. **de** + the name of a country or continent modified by an adjective: **de la France méridionale** / from southern France; **de l'Amérique du Nord** / from North America.

(m) With the prep. **à** (which combines to **au** or **aux**) in front of the name of a country which is masc.: **Je vais au Canada** / I am going to Canada; **Madame Dufy va aux Etats-Unis** / Madame Dufy is going to the United States.

(n) With the prep. **de** (which combines to **du** or **des**) in front of the name of a country which is masc.: **du Portugal** / from Portugal; **du Mexique** / from Mexico; **des Etats-Unis** / from the United States.

(o) With the family names in the plural, in which case the spelling of the family name does not change: **Je vais chez les Milot** / I am going to the Milots.

(p) With certain idiomatic expressions, such as: **la plupart de** / most of: **La plupart des jeunes filles dans cette école sont jolies** / Most of the girls in this school are pretty.

(q) With the prep. **de** + a common noun to indicate possession: **le livre du garçon** / the boy's book; **les livres des garçons** / the boys' books.

(r) Contraction of the definite article with **à** and **de**:

When the prep. **à** or **de** is in front of the def. art., it contracts as follows:

à + le > au: Je vais au Canada; Je parle au garçon.
à + les > aux: Je vais aux grands magasins.
de + le > du: Je viens du restaurant.
de + les > des: Je viens des grands magasins.

There is no change with **l'** or **la: Je vais à l'aéroport; Je vais à la campagne; Je viens de l'école; Je viens de la bibliothèque.**

(s) Use the def. art. with the partitive in the affirmative: **J'ai du café, J'ai de l'argent, J'ai des amis.**

§4.4   **The definite article is not used:**

(a) In direct address: **Bonjour, docteur Leduc.**

(b) After the verb **parler** when the name of the language is right after a form of **parler: Je parle français.**

(c) After the prep. **en: Nous écrivons en français.** Exceptions: **en l'air** / in the air; **en l'absence de** / in the absence of; **en l'honneur de** / in honor of.

(d) After the prep. **de** in an adjective phrase: **J'aime mon livre de français; Madame Harris est professeur de français.**

(e) With the days of the week when you want to indicate only a particular day: **Samedi je vais au cinéma** / On Saturday I am going to the movies

(f) With a feminine country and continents when you use **en** to mean *at* or *to*: **Je vais en France, en Angleterre, en Allemagne, et à beaucoup d'autres pays en Europe. J'irai aussi en Australie, en Asie, et en Amérique.**

(g) With a feminine country and continents when you use **de** to mean *of* or *from*: **Paul vient de France, les Armstrong viennent d'Australie, et Hilda vient d'Allemagne.**

(h) With most cities: **à Paris, à New York; de Londres, de Montréal, de Toronto.**

(i) With a noun in apposition: **Paul, fils du professeur Leblanc, est très aimable; Washington, capitale des Etats-Unis, est une belle ville.**

(j) With titles of monarchs: **Louis Seize (Louis XVI)** / Louis the Sixteenth.

(k) With the partitive in the negative or with an adjective: **Je n'ai pas de café; Je n'ai pas d'argent; J'ai de bons amis.** BUT you do use the def. art. with the affirmative partitive: **J'ai du café; J'ai de l'argent; J'ai des amis.**

(l) Do not use the def. art. with the prep. **sans** or with the construction **ne . . . ni . . . ni . . .**: **Je n'ai ni papier ni stylo; Il est parti sans argent; C'est une maison sans enfants.**

(m) Do not use the def. art. with certain expressions of quantity that take **de: beaucoup de, trop de, combien de, peu de, plus de, assez de: J'ai beaucoup de livres; j'ai trop de devoirs; j'ai peu de sucre; j'ai plus d'amis que vous; j'ai assez de devoirs.**

(n) Do not use the def. art. with the prep. **avec** when the noun after it is abstract: **Jean-Luc parle avec enthousiasme.**

§4.5   Indefinite article

§4.6   The indefinite articles are: **un** (meaning *a* or *an*) and **une** (meaning *a* or *an*); the plural is ordinarily **des: J'ai un frère** / I have a brother; **J'ai une soeur** / I have a sister; **J'ai une pomme** / I have an apple; **J'ai un oncle** / I have an uncle; **J'ai des frères, des soeurs, des oncles, des tantes, et des amis** / I have brothers, sisters, uncles, aunts, and friends.

§4.7   **The indefinite article is used:**

(a) When you want to say *a* or *an*. They are also used as a numeral to mean *one*: **un livre** / a book or one book; **une orange** / an orange or one orange. If you want to make it clear that you mean *one*, you may use *seul* or *seule* after *un* or *une*: **J'ai un seul livre** / I have one book; **J'ai une seule amie** / I have one girl friend.

(b) In front of each noun in a series, which we do not always do in English: **J'ai un cahier, un crayon, et une gomme** / I have a notebook, pencil, and eraser. This use is the same for the definite article in a series of nouns. See above §4.3 **(a)**.

(c) The plural of **un** or **une**, which is **des**, is the same as the plural of the partitive in the affirmative: **J'ai des livres, des cahiers, et des crayons** / I have (some) books, (some) notebooks, and (some) pencils. See Partitive, in §25. and §25.1 farther on.

(d) With **C'est** or **Ce sont** with or without an adjective: **C'est un docteur** / He's a doctor; **C'est un mauvais docteur** / He's a bad doctor; **Ce sont des étudiants** / They are students. **C'est une infirmière** / She's a nurse; **C'est une bonne femme auteur** / She is a good author. In the negative, too, with **c'est** or **ce sont**, keep the indef. art.: **Ce n'est pas un bon dentiste** / He is not a good dentist.

§4.8   **The indefinite article is not used:**

(a) With **cent** and **mille: J'ai cent dollars** / I have a hundred dollars; **J'ai mille dollars** / I have a thousand dollars.

(b) With **il est, ils sont, elle est, elles sont** + an unmodified noun of nationality, profession, or religion: **Elle est professeur** / She is a professor; **Il est catholique** / He is (a) Catholic; **Elle est Française** / She is French; **Madame Duby est poète** / Madame Duby is a poet; **Elle est actrice** / She's an actress.

BUT you do use the indef. art. if you use an adjective: **Madame Duby est une bonne poète** (*or* **une bonne poétesse**).

(c) When you use **quel** in an exclamation: **Quelle femme!** / What a woman! **Quel homme!** / What a man!

(d) When you use **que de** + a noun in an exclamation: **Que de problèmes!** / How many problems!

(e) With negations, particularly with the verb **avoir: Avez-vous un livre? Non, je n'ai pas de livre** / Have you a book? No, I don't have a book (any book). See also Partitive, §25. and §25.1 farther on.

§5. CAUSATIVE (CAUSAL) FAIRE

§5.1   The construction **faire** + **inf.** means to have something done by someone. The causative **faire** can be in any tense but it must be followed by an infinitive.

Examples with nouns and pronouns as direct and indirect objects:

(a) **Madame Smith fait travailler ses élèves dans la classe de français** / Mrs. Smith makes her students work in French class *or* Mrs. Smith has her students work in French class.

In this example, the direct obj. is the noun **élèves** and it is placed right after the infinitive.

(b) **Madame Smith les fait travailler dans la classe de français** / Mrs. Smith makes them work (has them work) in French class.

In this example, the direct obj. is the pronoun **les**, referring to **les élèves**. It is placed in front of the verb form of **faire**, where it logically belongs. The dir. obj. here is a person.

(c) **Madame Smith fait lire la phrase** / Mrs. Smith is having the sentence read *or* Mrs. Smith has the sentence read.

In this example, the direct obj. is the noun **phrase** and it is placed right after the infinitive, as in (a) above.

(d) **Madame Smith la fait lire** / Mrs. Smith is having it read.

In this example, the direct obj. is the pronoun **la**, referring to **la phrase**. It is placed in front of the verb form of **faire**, where it logically belongs. This is like (b) above but here we have a thing as dir. obj. In (a) and (b) above, the dir. obj. is a person.

(e) **Madame Smith fait travailler Anne dans la classe de français** / Mrs. Smith makes Anne work (has Anne work) in the French class.

In this example, the dir. obj. is a noun, **Anne**, who is a person. It is placed right after the infinitive, where it logically belongs. This example is like §5.1 (a) above. The dir. obj. in that example is in the plural; this example is in the singular, but both examples have persons as direct object.

(f) **Madame Smith fait lire Anne** / Mrs. Smith makes Anne read (has Anne read). This example is like §5.1 (a) above.

(g) **Madame Smith fait lire la phrase** / Mrs. Smith is having the sentence read *or* Mrs. Smith has the sentence read. This example is identical to §5.1 (c) above.

(h) Now, watch this carefully:

Madame Smith fait lire la phrase à Anne / Mrs. Smith is having Anne read the sentence OR: Mrs. Smith is having the sentence read by Anne.

When you have two objects—a thing and a person—the thing is the direct object and the person is the indirect object.

(i) And now, note this carefully:

Madame Smith la fait lire à Anne / Mrs. Smith is having Anne read it OR Mrs. Smith is having it read by Anne.

The thing (**la**, meaning **la lettre**) is the direct object and the person is the indir. obj.— **à Anne**.

(j) And finally, both objects (the direct and the indirect) are both pronouns:

Madame Smith la lui fait lire / Mrs. Smith is having her read it OR Mrs. Smith is having it read by her.

Note that double object pronouns in the **causative faire** construction are always objects of the verb form of **faire**, not the infinitive that follows. The dir. obj. is usually the thing and the indir. obj. is usually the person.

(k) **Madame Smith les leur fait écrire** / Mrs. Smith is having them write them OR Mrs. Smith is having them written by them.

(l) In a compound tense, such as the **passé composé**, never make an agreement on the past participle **fait** in a **causative faire** sentence with a preceding direct object.

Madame Smith les leur a fait écrire / Mrs. Smith had them write them OR Mrs. Smith had them written by them.

(m) In some cases with a **causative faire** construction, the prep. **à** can mean *to* or *by*. In such a case, use **par** to make the thought clear.

EXAMPLES:

J'ai fait envoyer la lettre à mon père / I had the letter sent *to* my father OR: I had the letter sent *by* my father.

If you mean that you had the letter sent *by* your father, then say: **J'ai fait envoyer la lettre par mon père.** The use of **par** avoids ambiguity.

Otherwise, **J'ai fait envoyer la lettre à mon père** has the meaning: I had the letter sent (BY SOMEBODY) to my father.

§6. C'EST + ADJ. + À + INF. OR IL EST + ADJ. + DE + INF.

§6.1 C'est + adj. + à + inf.

(a) **C'est difficile à faire** / It is difficult to do.

Use this construction when the thing that is difficult to do *has already been mentioned* and it is not mentioned in the sentence where this construction is used.

EXAMPLES:

Le devoir pour demain est difficile, n'est-ce pas? / The homework for tomorrow is difficult, isn't it?

Oui, c'est difficile à faire / Yes, it (what was just mentioned) is difficult to do.

J'aimerais faire une blouse / I would like to make a blouse. **C'est facile à faire! Je vais vous montrer** / It's easy to do! I'll show you.

§6.2 Il est + adj. + de + inf.

(a) **Il est impossible de lire ce gros livre en une heure** / It is impossible to read this thick book within one hour.

Use this construction when the thing that is impossible (or difficult, or easy, or any adjective) to do is mentioned in the same sentence at the same time.

§7. CONJUNCTIONS AND CONJUNCTIVE LOCUTIONS

§7.1 A conjunction is a word that connects words, phrases, clauses or sentences, *e.g.,* and, but, or, because / **et, mais, ou, parce que.**

§7.2 Certain conjunctions that introduce a clause require the subjunctive mood of the verb in that clause. See **Subjunctive** in **§35.1** farther on to know what those conjunctions are.

§7.3 Here are some conjunctions that you certainly ought to know. Some require the subjunctive and they are discussed under the entry **Subjunctive** in **§35.1** farther on.

à moins que / unless	**dès que** / as soon as
afin que / in order that, so that	**donc** / therefore
aussitôt que / as soon as	**en même temps que** / at the same time as
avant que / before	**et** / and
bien que / although	**jusqu'à ce que** / until
car / for	**lorsque** / when, at the time when
comme / as, since	**maintenant que** / now that
de crainte que / for fear that	**mais** / but
de peur que / for fear that	**ou** / or
de sorte que / so that, in such a way that	**parce que** / because
depuis que / since	**pendant le temps que** / while

pendant que / while
pour que / in order that
pourvu que / provided that
puisque / since
quand / when

que / that
quoi que / whatever, no matter what
quoique / although
si / if
tandis que / while, whereas

§7.4 Here are some that are not used as commonly as those above but you ought to be familiar with them because they are often used in the reading comprehension passages on standardized tests. Some of them require the subjunctive and they are discussed under the entry **Subjunctive** in **§35.1** farther on.

à ce que / that, according to, according to what
à mesure que / as, in proportion as
à présent que / now that
à proportion que / as, in proportion as
ainsi que / as, as well as, just as
alors même que / even when, even though
alors que / while, as, just as, when, whereas
après que / after
au cas où / in case, in case that, in the event when, in the event that
au cas que / in case, in case that, in the event when, in the event that
au commencement que / at (in) the beginning when
au début que / at (in) the beginning when
autant que / as much as, as far as, as near as
autre chose que / other than
autre que / other than
car en effet / for in fact
cependant (que) / while, however, yet, nevertheless
d'après ce que / according to, from what
d'autant plus que / all the more . . . as, doubly so . . . as
d'autant que / the more so as, all the more so because
de façon que / so that, in a way that, in such a way that
de la même façon que / in the same way that
de manière que / so that, in a way that, in such a way that

de même que / as . . . , so, as well as, the same as, just as
de telle sorte que / so that, in such a way that, in a way that
en admettant que / admitting that
en cas que / in case, in the case that, in the event that
en ce temps où / at this time when, at that time when
en sorte que / in such a way that, so that, in a way that
en supposant que / supposing that
en tant que / as (like)
encore que / although
malgré que / though, although [Prefer to use **bien que**]
plutôt que / rather than
pour autant que / as much as, as far as [Prefer to use **autant que**]
quand même / even if
sans que / without
si tant est que / if indeed
sinon / if not, otherwise
soit que . . . ou que / whether . . . (or) whether, either . . . or
soit que . . . soit que / whether . . . whether
surtout que / especially because
tant il y a que / the fact remains that
tant que / as long as, as far as

§8. DATES, DAYS, MONTHS, SEASONS

§8.1 **Dates**

You ought to know the following expressions:

(a) **Quelle est la date aujourd'hui?** / What's the date today?
Quel jour du mois est-ce aujourd'hui? / What's the date today?
Quel jour du mois sommes-nous aujourd'hui? / What's the date today?

C'est aujourd'hui le premier octobre / Today is October first.
C'est aujourd'hui le deux novembre / Today is November second.

(b) **Quel jour de la semaine est-ce aujourd'hui?** / What day of the week is it today?

C'est lundi / It's Monday.
C'est aujourd'hui mardi / Today is Tuesday.

(c) **Quand êtes-vous né(e)?** / When were you born?
Je suis né(e) le dix-neuf juin, mil neuf cent soixante-cinq / I was born on June 19, 1965.

§8.2   **Days**

The days of the week, which are all masc., are:

dimanche, lundi, mardi, mercredi, jeudi, vendredi, samedi
Sunday, Monday, Tuesday, Wednesday, Thursday, Friday, Saturday

In French, the days of the week are written in small letters, although in some French business letters and in French newspapers you will sometimes see them written with the first letter capitalized.

§8.3   **Months**

The months of the year, which are all masc., are:

janvier, février, mars, avril, mai, juin, juillet, août,
January, February, March, April, May, June, July, August,

septembre, octobre, novembre, décembre
September, October, November, December

In French, the months of the year are customarily written in small letters, although in some French business letters and in French newspapers you will sometimes see them written with the first letter capitalized.

To say *in* + the name of the month, use **en**: **en janvier, en février**; or: **au mois de janvier, au mois de février** / in the month of January . . .

§8.4   **Seasons**

The seasons of the year, which are all masc., are:

le printemps, l'été, l'automne, l'hiver
spring, summer, fall, winter

To say *in* + the name of the season, use **en**, except with **printemps**: **au printemps, en été, en automne, en hiver** / in spring, in summer . . .

§9.   **TELLING TIME**

§9.1   **Time expressions you ought to know:**

(a) **Quelle heure est-il?** / What time is it?
(b) **Il est une heure** / It is one o'clock.
(c) **Il est une heure dix** / It is ten minutes after one.
(d) **Il est une heure et quart** / It is a quarter after one.
(e) **Il est deux heures et demie** / It is half past two; it is two thirty.
(f) **Il est trois heures moins vingt** / It is twenty minutes to three.
(g) **Il est trois heures moins un quart** / It is a quarter to three.
(h) **Il est midi** / It is noon.
(i) **Il est minuit** / It is midnight.
(j) **à quelle heure?** / at what time?
(k) **à une heure** / at one o'clock.
(l) **à une heure précise** / at exactly one o'clock.
(m) **à deux heures précises** / at exactly two o'clock.
(n) **à neuf heures du matin** / at nine in the morning.
(o) **à trois heures de l'après-midi** / at three in the afternoon.
(p) **à dix heures du soir** / at ten in the evening.
(q) **à l'heure** / on time.
(r) **à temps** / in time.
(s) **vers trois heures** / around three o'clock; about three o'clock.
(t) **un quart d'heure** / a quarter of an hour; a quarter hour.
(u) **une demi-heure** / a half hour.
(v) **Il est midi et demi** / It is twelve thirty; It is half past twelve (noon).
(w) **Il est minuit et demi** / It is twelve thirty; It is half past twelve (midnight).

§9.2   **Note the following remarks:**

(a) In telling time, **Il est** is used plus the hour, whether it is one or more than one, *e.g.,* **Il est une heure, Il est deux heures.**

(b) If the time is *after* the hour, state the hour, then the minutes, *e.g.,* **Il est une heure dix.**

(c) The conjunction **et** is used with **quart** after the hour and with **demi** or **demie**, *e.g.,* **Il est une heure et quart; Il est une heure et demie; Il est midi et demi.**

(d) The masc. form **demi** is used after a masc. noun, *e.g.,* **Il est midi et demi.** The fem. form **demie** is used after a fem. noun, *e.g.,* **Il est deux heures et demie.**

(e) **Demi** remains **demi** when *before* a fem. or masc. noun and it is joined to the noun with a hyphen, *e.g.,* **une demi-heure.**

(f) If the time expressed is *before* the hour, **moins** is used, *e.g.,* **Il est trois heures moins vingt**.

(g) A quarter *after* the hour is **et quart**; a quarter *to* the hour is **moins le quart.**

(h) To express A.M. use **du matin**; to express P.M. use **de l'après-midi** if the time is in the afternoon, or **du soir** if in the evening.

§9.3   **Note another way to tell time, which is official time used by the French government on radio and TV, in railroad and bus stations, and at airports:**

(a) It is the 24-hour system around the clock.

(b) In this system, **quart** and **demi** or **demie** are not used. **Moins** and **et** are not used.

(c) When you hear or see the stated time, subtract 12 from the number that you hear or see. If the number is less than 12, it is A.M. time, except for **24 heures**, which is midnight; **zéro heure** is also midnight.

EXAMPLES:
 Il est treize heures / It is 1:00 P.M.
 Il est quinze heures / It is 3:00 P.M.
 Il est vingt heures trente / It is 8:30 P.M.
 Il est vingt-quatre heures / It is midnight.
 Il est zéro heure / It is midnight.
 Il est seize heures trente / It is 4:30 P.M.
 Il est dix-huit heures quinze / It is 6:15 P.M.
 Il est vingt heures quarante-cinq / It is 8:45 P.M.
 Il est vingt-deux heures cinquante / It is 10:50 P.M.

(d) The abbreviation for **heure** or **heures** is **h.**

EXAMPLES:
 Il est 20 h. 20 / It is 8:20 P.M.
 Il est 15 h. 50 / It is 3:50 P.M.
 Il est 23 h. 30 / It is 11:30 P.M.

§10.   DEPUIS

§10.1   **With the present indicative tense**

When an action of some sort began in the past and is still going on in the present, use the present tense with **depuis** + the length of time:

 Je travaille dans ce bureau depuis trois ans.
 I have been working in this office for three years.
 J'habite cette maison depuis quinze ans.
 I have been living in this house for fifteen years.
 Je suis malade depuis une semaine.
 I have been sick for one week.

§10.2   With the imperfect indicative tense

When an action of some sort began in the past and continued up to another point in the past, which you are telling about, use the imperfect indicative tense with **depuis** + the length of time:

J'attendais l'autobus depuis vingt minutes quand il est arrivé / I had been waiting for the bus for twenty minutes when it arrived.

Je travaillais dans ce bureau-là depuis trois ans quand j'ai trouvé un autre emploi dans un autre bureau / I had been working in that office for three years when I found another job in another office.

§10.3   Depuis in a question

§10.4   Depuis combien de temps

(a) **Depuis combien de temps attendez-vous l'autobus?** / How long have you been waiting for the bus?

J'attends l'autobus depuis vingt minutes / I have been waiting for the bus for twenty minutes.

NOTE: When you use **depuis combien de temps** in your question, you expect the other person to tell you how long, how much time—how many minutes, how many hours, how many days, weeks, months, years.

(b) **Depuis combien de temps travailliez-vous dans ce bureau-là quand vous avez trouvé un autre emploi dans un autre bureau?** / How long had you been working in that office when you found another job in another office?

Je travaillais dans ce bureau-là depuis trois ans quand j'ai trouvé un autre emploi dans un autre bureau / I had been working in that office for three years when I found another job in another office.

§10.5   Depuis quand

(a) **Depuis quand habitez-vous cet appartement?** / Since when have you been living in this apartment?

J'habite cet appartement depuis le premier septembre / I have been living in this apartment since September first.

NOTE: When you use **depuis quand** in your question, you expect the other person to tell you since what particular point in time in the past—a particular day, a date, a particular month; in other words, since *when*, not *how long*.

(b) **Depuis quand êtes-vous malade?** / Since when have you been sick?
Je suis malade depuis samedi / I have been sick since Saturday.

(c) **Depuis quand habitiez-vous l'appartement quand vous avez déménagé?** / Since when had you been living in the apartment when you moved?

J'habitais l'appartement depuis le premier avril 1985 quand j'ai déménagé / I had been living in the apartment since April first, 1985 when I moved.

§11.   IL Y A + LENGTH OF TIME + QUE; VOICI + LENGTH OF TIME + QUE; VOILÀ + LENGTH OF TIME + QUE

§11.1   These expressions in questions and answers

§11.2

(a) **Combien de temps y a-t-il que vous attendez l'autobus?** / How long have you been waiting for the bus?

Il y a vingt minutes que j'attends l'autobus / I have been waiting for the bus for twenty minutes.

Voici vingt minutes que je l'attends / I have been waiting for it for twenty minutes.

Voilà vingt minutes que je l'attends / I have been waiting for it for twenty minutes.

NOTE: When you use these expressions, you generally use them at the beginning of your answer + the verb.

When you use the **depuis** construction, the verb comes first: **J'attends l'autobus depuis vingt minutes.**

§11.3   (b) **Combien de temps y avait-il que vous attendiez l'autobus?** / How long had you been waiting for the bus?

Il y avait vingt minutes que j'attendais l'autobus / I had been waiting for the bus for twenty minutes (understood: when it finally arrived).

§12.   IL Y A + LENGTH OF TIME

§12.1   **Il y a + length of time** means *ago*. Do not use **que** in this construction as in the above examples in §11. because the meaning is entirely different.

EXAMPLES:

Madame Martin est partie il y a une heure / Mrs. Martin left an hour ago.
L'autobus est arrivé il y a vingt minutes / The bus arrived twenty minutes ago.

§13.   IL Y A AND IL Y AVAIT

§13.1   **Il y a** alone means *there is* or *there are* when you are merely making a statement.

EXAMPLES:

Il y a vingt élèves dans cette classe / There are twenty students in this class.
Il y a une mouche dans la soupe / There is a fly in the soup.

§13.2   **Il y avait** alone means *there was* or *there were* when you are merely making a statement.

EXAMPLES:

Il y avait vingt élèves dans cette classe / There were (used to be) twenty students in this class.
Il y avait deux mouches dans la soupe / There were two flies in the soup.

§14.   VOICI AND VOILÀ

§14.1   These two expressions are used to point out someone or something.

EXAMPLES:

Voici un taxi! / Here's a taxi!
Voilà un taxi là-bas! / There's a taxi over there!
Voici ma carte d'identité et voilà mon passeport / Here's my I.D. card and there's my passport.
Voici mon père et voilà ma mère / Here's my father and there's my mother.

§15.   PENDANT AND POUR

§15.1   **Pendant** (during, for) and **pour** (for) are not used in the **depuis** construction explained in §10. above nor in the other types of constructions explained in §11. above.

§15.2   **In the present tense**

Combien de temps étudiez-vous chaque soir? / How long do you study every evening?

J'étudie une heure chaque soir OR **J'étudie pendant une heure chaque soir** / I study one hour each night OR I study for one hour each night.

§15.3   **In the passé composé**

Combien de temps êtes-vous resté(e) à Paris? / How long did you stay in Paris?

Je suis resté(e) à Paris deux semaines OR **Je suis resté(e) à Paris pendant deux semaines** / I stayed in Paris two weeks OR I stayed in Paris for two weeks.

§15.4   **In the future**

Combien de temps resterez-vous à Paris? / How long will you stay in Paris?

J'y resterai pour deux semaines / I will stay there for two weeks. OR: **J'y resterai deux semaines** / I will stay there two weeks.

§16.   DANS AND EN + A LENGTH OF TIME

§16.1   These two prepositions mean *in* but each is used in a different sense.

§16.2   **Dans** + a length of time indicates that something will happen at the end of that length of time: **Le docteur va venir dans une demi-heure** / The doctor will come in a half hour (*i.e.*, at the end of a half hour).

§16.3   If by *in* you mean at the end of that length of time, use **dans**.

§16.4   **Dans** and a duration of time can be at the beginning of the sentence or at the end of it and future time is ordinarily implied.

§16.5   **En** + a length of time indicates that something happened or will happen at any time *within* that length of time.

§16.6   EXAMPLES:
Robert a fait cela en une heure / Robert did that in (within) an (one) hour.
Robert fera cela en une heure / Robert will do that in (within) an (one) hour.

§16.7   BUT: **Robert fera cela dans une heure** / Robert will do that in (at the end of) an (one) hour.

§16.8   AND NOTE: **Le docteur va venir dans une heure** / The doctor will come in (at the end of) one hour.
Le docteur va venir en une heure / The doctor is going to come in (within) one hour (*i.e.*, at any time before the hour is up).
Le docteur est venu en une heure / The doctor came in (within) an hour. OR: **En une heure, le docteur est venu** / In (within) one hour, the doctor came.

In this last example, I think you know enough French by now to feel that it would sound wrong to use **dans** instead of **en**. Why? Because **dans** generally implies only future time and **en** implies either past or future.

§17.   DEVOIR

The verb **devoir** has special uses and different meanings in different tenses. For the complete conjug of **devoir,** as well as other commonly used verbs, see §40.1 farther on.

§17.1   **Present tense**

EXAMPLES:
Je dois étudier / I have to study / I must study / I am supposed to study.
Il doit être fou! / He must be crazy / He's probably crazy!
Mon oncle doit avoir quatre-vingts ans / My uncle must be 80 years old / My uncle is probably 80 years old.

§17.2   **Imperfect tense**

EXAMPLES:
Je devais étudier / I had to study / I was supposed to study.

Quand j'étais à l'école, je devais toujours étudier / When I was in school, I always used to have to study.

Ma mère devait avoir quatre-vingts ans quand elle est morte / My mother was probably 80 years old when she died. OR: My mother must have been 80 years old when she died.

§17.3 Future

EXAMPLES:

Je devrai étudier / I will have to study.

Nous devrons faire le travail ce soir / We will have to do the work this evening.

§17.4 Conditional

EXAMPLES:

Je devrais étudier / I ought to study OR I should study.

Vous devriez étudier plus souvent / You ought to study more often / You should study more often.

§17.5 Passé composé

EXAMPLES:

Je ne suis pas allé(e) au cinéma parce que j'ai dû étudier / I did not go to the movies because I had to study.

J'ai dû prendre l'autobus parce qu'il n'y avait pas de train à cette heure-là / I had to take the bus because there was no train at that hour.

Robert n'est pas ici / Robert is not here.

Il a dû partir / He must have left / He has probably left / He had to leave / He has had to leave.

§17.6 Conditional Perfect

EXAMPLES:

J'aurais dû étudier! / I should have studied / I ought to have studied!

Vous auriez dû me dire la vérité / You should have told me the truth / You ought to have told me the truth.

§17.7 With a direct or indirect object there is still another meaning.

EXAMPLES:

Je dois de l'argent / I owe some money.

Je le lui dois / I owe it to him (*or* to her).

§18. ENVERS AND VERS

§18.1 **Envers** is used in a figurative sense in the meaning of *with regard to* someone, *with respect to* someone, *for* someone or *for* something.

EXAMPLES:

Je montre beaucoup de respect envers les vieilles personnes / I show a lot of respect toward old persons.

Je ne montre aucun respect envers un criminel / I show no respect toward a criminal.

§18.2 **Vers** also means *toward* but in a physical sense, in the direction of, as well as in a figurative sense.

EXAMPLES:

Pourquoi allez-vous vers la porte? / Why are you going toward the door?

Je vais partir vers trois heures / I am going to leave toward (around) three o'clock.

J'ai quitté le cinéma vers la fin du film / I left the movies toward the end of the film.

Il va vers elle / He is going toward her.

Il dirige ses paroles vers la vérité / He is directing his words toward the truth.

§19. FALLOIR

§19.1 **Falloir** is an impersonal verb, which means that it is used only in the 3rd pers. sing. (**il** form) in all the tenses; its primary meaning is *to be necessary*. **Falloir** is conjugated fully in all the tenses and moods in §40.1.

§19.2 EXAMPLES:

Il faut étudier pour avoir de bonnes notes / It is necessary to study in order to have good grades.

Faut-il le faire tout de suite? / Is it necessary to do it at once?

Oui, il le faut / Yes, it is (understood: necessary to do it).

In this example, notice the use of the neuter direct object **le**; it is needed to show emphasis and to complete the thought.

Il faut être honnête / It is necessary to be honest OR: One must be honest.

IN THE NEGATIVE: **Il ne faut pas être malhonnête** / One must not be dishonest.

Note that **il faut** in the negative means *one must not*.

Il ne faut pas fumer dans l'école / One must not smoke in school.

Il faut de l'argent pour voyager / One needs money to travel.

Note that with a direct object (**de l'argent**) **il faut** means *one needs*.

J'ai besoin d'acheter un livre qui coûte dix francs. / J'ai cinq francs et il me faut encore la moitié, cinq francs.

I need to buy a book that costs ten francs. I have five francs and half (of the amount) is lacking, five francs.

Note that here the meaning is *to need* in the sense of *to lack*.

Il faut que je fasse mes devoirs / I must do my assignments.

Here, note that **il faut que** + a new clause requires the verb in the new clause to be in the subjunctive. See **§35.6.**

Il me faut étudier / I must study.

Il lui faut un ami / He *or* she needs a friend.

Note that when you use **falloir**, as in this example, you need to use the indirect object for the person and the direct object for the thing.

Il me le faut / I need it (in the sense that *it is lacking to me*).

§20. IDIOMS, INCLUDING VERBAL, IDIOMATIC, COMMON, AND USEFUL EXPRESSIONS

§20.1 The entries that follow have been arranged by key word.

§20.2 **With À**

à with (a descriptive characteristic); **Qui est le monsieur à la barbe noire?** / Who is the gentleman with the black beard?

à bicyclette by bicycle, on a bicycle

à bientôt so long, see you soon

à cause de on account of, because of

à cette heure at this time, at the present moment

à cheval on horseback

à côté de beside, next to

à demain until tomorrow, see you tomorrow

à demi half, halfway, by halves

à droite at (on, to) the right

à fond thoroughly

à force de by dint of

à gauche at (on, to) the left

à haute voix   aloud, out loud, in a loud voice
à jamais   forever
à l'école   at (in, to) school
à l'étranger   abroad, overseas
à l'heure   on time
à l'instant   instantly
à l'occasion   on the occasion
à la bonne heure!   good! fine! swell!
à la campagne   at (in, to) the country(side)
à la fin   at last, finally
à la fois   at the same time
à la légère   lightly
à la main   in one's hand, by hand
à la maison   at home
à la mode   fashionable, in style, in fashion, in vogue
à la page deux   on page two
à la queue leu leu   one after the other (like wolves)
à la radio   on the radio
à la recherche de   in search of
à la renverse   backwards
à la télé   on TV
à malin, malin et demi   set a thief to catch a thief
à merveille   marvelously, wonderfully
à moitié   half, in half
à mon avis   in my opinion
à nous deux, à nous trois   together
à part   aside
à partir de   beginning with
à pas de loup   silently, quietly
à peine   hardly, scarcely
à peu près   approximately, about, nearly
à pied   on foot
à plus tard   see you later
à plusieurs reprises   several times
à présent   now, at present
à propos   by the way
à propos de   about, with reference to, concerning
à quelle heure?   at what time?
à qui est ce livre?   whose is this book?
à quoi bon?   what's the use?
à sa portée   within one's reach
à ses propres yeux   in one's own eyes
à son gré   to one's liking

à temps   in time
à tour de rôle   in turn
à tout à l'heure   see you in a little while
à tout prix   at any cost
à travers   across, through
à tue-tête   at the top of one's voice, as loud as possible
à vélo   on a bike
à voix basse   in a low voice, softly
à volonté   at will, willingly
à vrai dire   to tell the truth
à vue d'oeil   visibly
adresser la parole à   to speak to
agir à la légère   to act thoughtlessly
aller à pied   to walk (to go on foot)
avoir à   to have to, to be obliged to
avoir mal à   to have a pain or ache in
c'est-à-dire   that is, that is to say
de temps à autre   from time to time, occasionally
donner à manger à   to feed
donner congé à   to grant leave to
donner rendez-vous à qqn   to make an appointment with someone
dormir à la belle étoile   to sleep outdoors
fermer à clef   to lock
grâce à   thanks to
jouer à   to play (a game or sport)
laid à faire peur   frightfully ugly
monter à cheval   to go horseback riding
ne pas tarder à   not to be long (late) in
peu à peu   little by little
pleuvoir à verse   to rain hard
quant à   as for
quelque chose à + inf.   something + inf.
savoir à quoi s'en tenir   to know what one is to believe
tête-à-tête   personal, private conversation
tomber à la renverse   to fall backward
tout à coup   suddenly
tout à fait   completely, quite
tout à l'heure   a little while ago, in a little while
venir à bout de + inf.   to manage, to succeed + inf.
ventre à terre   at full speed
vis-à-vis   opposite

§20.3   With AU

au bas de   at the bottom of
au besoin   if need be, if necessary
au bout de   at the end of, at the tip of
au contraire   on the contrary
au courant   in the "know", informed
au début   at (in) the beginning
au-dessous de   below, beneath
au-dessus de   above, over
au fait   as a matter of fact

au fond de   in the bottom of
au fur et à mesure   simultaneously and proportionately
au haut de   at the top of
au lieu de   instead of
au loin   in the distance, from afar
au milieu de   in the middle of
au moins   at least
au pied de   at the foot of

au printemps in the spring
au revoir good-bye
au sous-sol in the basement
au sujet de about, concerning
au téléphone on the telephone
café au lait coffee light with milk

fermer au verrou to bolt
mettre au courant de to inform about
rire au nez to laugh in someone's face
rosbif au jus roastbeef with gravy (natural juice)

§20.4 With AUX

aux dépens at the expense
aux pommes frites with French fries
être aux écoutes to be on the watch, to eavesdrop

rire aux éclats to roar with laughter
sauter aux yeux to be evident, self evident

§20.5 With ALLER

aller to feel (health); **Comment allez-vous?**
aller à to be becoming, to fit, to suit; **Cette robe lui va bien** / This dress suits her fine; **Sa barbe ne lui va pas** / His beard does not look good on him.
aller à la pêche to go fishing
aller à la rencontre de qqn to go to meet someone

aller à pied to walk, to go on foot
aller au-devant de qqn to go to meet someone
aller au fond des choses to get to the bottom of things
aller chercher to go get
allons donc! nonsense! come on, now!

§20.6 With AVOIR

avoir . . . ans to be . . . years old; **Quel âge avez-vous? J'ai dix-sept ans.**
avoir à + inf. to have to, to be obliged to + inf.
avoir affaire à qqn to deal with someone
avoir beau + inf. to be useless + inf., to do something in vain; **Vous avez beau parler; je ne vous écoute pas** / You are talking in vain; I am not listening to you.
avoir besoin de to need, to have need of
avoir bonne mine to look well, to look good (persons)
avoir chaud to be (feel) warm (persons)
avoir congé to have a day off, a holiday
avoir de la chance to be lucky
avoir de quoi + inf. to have the material, means, enough + inf.; **As-tu de quoi manger?** / Have you something (enough) to eat?
avoir des nouvelles to receive news, to hear (from someone)
avoir du savoir-faire to have tact
avoir du savoir-vivre to have good manners, etiquette
avoir envie de + inf. to feel like, to have a desire to
avoir faim to be (feel) hungry
avoir froid to be (feel) cold (persons)
avoir hâte to be in a hurry
avoir honte to be ashamed, to feel ashamed
avoir l'air + adj. to seem, to appear, to look + adj.; **Vous avez l'air malade** / You look sick.

avoir l'air de + inf. to appear + inf.; **Vous avez l'air d'être malade** / You appear to be sick.
avoir l'habitude de + inf. to be accustomed to, to be in the habit of; **J'ai l'habitude de faire mes devoirs avant le dîner** / I'm in the habit of doing my homework before dinner.
avoir l'idée de + inf. to have a notion + inf.
avoir l'intention de + inf. to intend + inf.
avoir l'occasion de + inf. to have the opportunity + inf.
avoir l'oeil au guet to be on the look-out, on the watch
avoir la bonté de + inf. to have the kindness + inf.
avoir la langue bien pendue to have the gift of gab
avoir la parole to have the floor (to speak)
avoir le coeur gros to be heartbroken
avoir le temps de + inf. to have (the) time + inf.
avoir lieu to take place
avoir mal to feel sick
avoir mal à + (place where it hurts) to have a pain or ache in . . . ; **J'ai mal à la jambe** / My leg hurts; **J'ai mal au dos** / My back hurts; **J'ai mal au cou** / I have a pain in the neck.
avoir mauvaise mine to look ill, not to look well
avoir peine à + inf. to have difficulty in + pres. part.
avoir peur de to be afraid of

avoir pitié de   to take pity on
avoir raison   to be right (persons)
avoir soif   to be thirsty
avoir sommeil   to be sleepy
avoir son mot à dire   to have one's way
avoir tort   to be wrong (persons)
avoir une faim de loup   to be starving
en avoir marre   to be fed up, to be bored stiff,
to be sick and tired of something; **J'en ai marre!** / I'm fed up! I can't stand it!
en avoir par-dessus la tête   to have enough of it, to be sick and tired of it; **J'en ai par-dessus la tête!** / I've had it up to here!
en avoir plein le dos   to be sick and tired of it; **J'en ai plein le dos!** / I'm sick and tired of it!

§20.7   With BAS

au bas de   at the bottom of
en bas   downstairs, below
là-bas   over there

A bas les devoirs!   Down with homework!
parler tout bas   to speak very softly
de haut en bas   from top to bottom

§20.8   With BIEN

bien des   many; **Roger a bien des amis** / Roger has many friends.
bien entendu   of course

dire du bien de   to speak well of
être bien aise   to be very glad, happy
tant bien que mal   rather badly, so-so

§20.9   With BON

à quoi bon?   what's the use?
bon gré, mal gré   willing or not, willy nilly
bon marché   cheap, at a low price
bon pour qqn   good to someone, kind to someone

de bon appétit   with good appetite, heartily
de bon coeur   gladly, willingly
savoir bon gré à qqn   to be thankful, grateful to someone

§20.10   With ÇA

çà et là   here and there
Ça m'est égal   It makes no difference to me.
comme ci, comme ça   so-so

Ça va?   Is everything okay?
C'est comme ça!   That's how it is!
Pas de ça!   None of that!

§20.11   With CELA

Cela est égal   It's all the same; It doesn't matter / It makes no difference.
Cela m'est égal   It doesn't matter to me / It's all the same to me.
Cela n'importe   That doesn't matter.
Cela ne fait rien   That makes no difference.
Cela ne lui va pas   That doesn't suit her or him.

Cela ne sert à rien   That serves no purpose.
Cela ne vous regarde pas   That's none of your business.
malgré cela   in spite of that
malgré tout cela   in spite of all that
Que veut dire cela?   What does that mean?
Qu'est-ce qui s'est passé? / What happened?

§20.12   With CE, C'EST, EST-CE

c'est-à-dire   that is, that is to say
C'est aujourd'hui lundi   Today is Monday.
C'est dommage   It's a pity / It's too bad.
C'est entendu   It's understood / It's agreed / All right / O.K.
C'est épatant!   It's wonderful! / That's wonderful!

C'est trop fort!   That's just too much!
n'est-ce pas?   isn't that so? / isn't it? *etc.*
Qu'est-ce que c'est?   What is it?
Quel jour est-ce aujourd'hui?   What day is it today? **C'est lundi** / It's Monday.

§20.13   With D'

comme d'habitude   as usual
d'abord   at first
d'accord   okay, agreed
d'ailleurs   besides, moreover
d'aujourd'hui en huit   a week from today
d'avance   in advance, beforehand

d'habitude   ordinarily, usually, generally
d'ici longtemps   for a long time to come
d'ordinaire   ordinarily, usually, generally
changer d'avis   to change one's opinion, one's mind
tout d'un coup   all of a sudden

§20.14   With DE

afin de + inf.   in order + inf.
au haut de   at the top of
autour de   around
avant de + inf.   before + pres. part.
changer de train   to change trains; **changer de vêtements** / to change clothes, *etc.*
combien de   how much, how many
de bon appétit   with good appetite, heartily
de bon coeur   gladly, willingly
de bonne heure   early
de cette façon   in this way
de façon à + inf.   so as + inf.
de jour en jour   from day to day
de l'autre côté de   on the other side of
de la part de   on behalf of, from
de mon côté   for my part, as far as I am concerned
de nouveau   again
de parti pris   on purpose, deliberately
de plus   furthermore
de plus en plus   more and more
de quelle couleur . . . ?   what color . . . ?
de quoi + inf.   something, enough + inf.; **de quoi écrire** / something to write with; **de quoi manger** / something or enough to eat; **de quoi vivre** / something or enough to live on
de rien   you're welcome, don't mention it
de rigueur   required, obligatory
de son mieux   one's best
de suite   one after another, in succession
de temps à autre   from time to time, occasionally
de temps en temps   from time to time, occasionally
de toutes ses forces   with all one's might, strenuously
du côté de   in the direction of, toward
éclater de rire   to burst out laughing

en face de   opposite
entendre parler de   to hear about
et ainsi de suite   and so on and so forth
être de retour   to be back
être en train de   to be in the act of, to be in the process of
être temps de + inf.   to be time + inf.
faire semblant de + inf.   to pretend + inf.
faute de   for lack of, for want of
féliciter qqn de qqch   to congratulate someone for something
Il n'y a pas de quoi!   You're welcome!
jamais de la vie   never in one's life, never! out of the question!
jouer de   to play (a musical instrument)
le long de   along
manquer de + inf.   to fail to, to almost do something; **J'ai manqué de tomber** / I almost fell; **Victor a manqué de venir** / Victor failed to come.
mettre de côté   to lay aside, to save
pas de mal!   no harm!
pas de moyen   no way
pour comble de malheur   to make matters worse
près de   near
quelque chose de + adj.   something + adj.; **J'ai bu quelque chose de bon!** / I drank something good!
Quoi de neuf?   What's new?
Rien de neuf!   Nothing's new!
tout de même   all the same
tout de suite   immediately, at once
venir de + inf.   to have just done something; **Je viens de manger** / I have just eaten / I just ate; **Guillaume vient de sortir** / William has just gone out.

§20.15   With DU

dire du bien de qqn   to speak well of someone
dire du mal de qqn   to speak ill of someone
donner du chagrin à qqn   to give someone grief
du côté de   in the direction of, toward
du matin au soir   from morning until night

du moins   at least
du reste   besides, in addition, furthermore
montrer du doigt   to point out, to show, to indicate by pointing
pas du tout   not at all

§20.16   With EN

de jour en jour   from day to day
de temps en temps   from time to time
en anglais, en français, *etc.*   in English, in French, *etc.*
en arrière   backwards, to the rear, behind
en automne, en hiver, en été   in the fall, in winter, in summer
en automobile   by car
en avion   by plane

en avoir marre   to be fed up, to be bored stiff, to be sick and tired of something; **J'en ai marre!** / I'm fed up! / I've had it!
en avoir par-dessus la tête   to have had it up to here; **J'en ai par-dessus la tête!** / I've had it up to here!
en avoir plein le dos   to be sick and tired of something
en bas   downstairs, below

en bateau by boat

en bois, en pierre, en + some material made of wood, of stone, *etc.*

en chemin de fer by train

en dessous (de) underneath

en dessus (de) above, on top, over

en effet in fact, indeed, yes indeed, as a matter of fact

en face de opposite

en faire autant to do the same, to do as much

en famille as a family

en haut upstairs, above

en huit jours in a week

en même temps at the same time

en plein air in the open air, outdoors

en quinze jours in two weeks

en retard late, not on time

en tout cas in any case, at any rate

en toute hâte with all possible speed, haste

en ville downtown, in (at, to) town

En voilà assez! Enough of that!

en voiture by car; **en voiture!** / all aboard!

en vouloir à qqn to bear a grudge against someone; **Je lui en veux** / I have a grudge against him (her).

être en train de + inf. to be in the act of + pres. part., to be in the process of, to be busy + pres. part.

Je vous en prie I beg you / You're welcome.

mettre en pièces to tear to pieces, to break into pieces

n'en pouvoir plus to be unable to go on any longer, to be exhausted; **Je n'en peux plus /** I can't go on any longer.

voir tout en rose to see the bright side of things, to be optimistic

§20.17 With ÊTRE

être à l'heure to be on time

être à qqn to belong to someone; **Ce livre est à moi** / This book belongs to me.

être à temps to be in time

être au courant de to be informed about

être bien to be comfortable

être bien aise (de) to be very glad, happy (to)

être bien mis (mise) to be well dressed

être d'accord avec to agree with

être dans son assiette to be "right up one's alley"

être de retour to be back

être en état de + inf. to be able + inf.

être en retard to be late, not to be on time

être en train de + inf. to be in the act of + pres. part., to be in the process of, to be busy + pres. part.

être en vacances to be on vacation

être enrhumé to have a cold, to be sick with a cold

être hors de soi to be beside oneself, to be upset, to be furious, to be irritated, annoyed

être le bienvenu (la bienvenue) to be welcomed

être pressé(e) to be in a hurry

être sur le point de + inf. to be about + inf.

être temps de + inf. to be time + inf.

Quelle heure est-il? What time is it? **Il est une heure** / It is one o'clock; **Il est deux heures** / It is two o'clock.

y être to be there, to understand it, to get it; **J'y suis!** / I get it! / I understand it!

Il était une fois . . . Once upon a time there was (there were) . . .

§20.18 With FAIRE

aussitôt dit aussitôt fait; aussitôt dit que fait no sooner said than done

Cela ne fait rien That doesn't matter / That makes no difference.

Comment se fait-il? How come?

en faire autant to do the same, to do as much

faire + inf. to have something done; See **§5.**

faire à sa tête to have one's way

faire attention (à) to pay attention (to)

faire beau to be pleasant, nice weather; (For a list of weather expressions, see **§37.—§37.5**)

faire bon accueil to welcome

faire chaud to be warm (weather); (For a list of weather expressions, see **§37.—§37.5**)

faire d'une pierre deux coups to kill two birds with one stone

faire de l'autostop to hitchhike

faire de la peine à qqn to hurt someone (morally)

faire de son mieux to do one's best

faire des châteaux en Espagne to build castles in the air

faire des emplettes; faire des courses; faire du shopping to do or to go shopping

faire des progrès to make progress

faire du bien à qqn to do good for someone; **Cela lui fera du bien** / That will do her (or him) some good.

faire du vélo to ride a bike

faire exprès to do on purpose

faire face à to oppose

faire faire qqch to have something done or made; **Je me fais faire une robe** / I'm having a dress made (BY SOMEONE) for myself. See also **§5.**

faire froid to be cold (weather); (For a list of weather expressions, see **§37.—§37.5**)

faire jour to be daylight

faire la bête to act like a fool

faire la connaissance de qqn to make the acquaintance of someone, to meet someone for the first time, to become acquainted with someone

faire la cuisine to do the cooking

faire la grasse matinée to sleep late in the morning

faire la malle to pack the trunk

faire la queue to line up, to get in line, to stand in line, to queue up

faire la sourde oreille to turn a deaf ear, to pretend not to hear

faire le ménage to do housework

faire le tour de to take a stroll, to go around

faire les bagages to pack the baggage, luggage

faire les valises to pack the suitcases, valises

faire mal à qqn to hurt, to harm someone

faire mon affaire to suit me, to be just the thing for me

faire nuit to be night(time)

faire part à qqn to inform someone

faire part de qqch à qqn to let someone know about something, to inform, to notify someone of something

faire partie de to be a part of

faire peur à qqn to frighten someone

faire plaisir à qqn to please someone

faire savoir qqch à qqn to inform someone of something

faire semblant de + inf. to pretend + inf.

faire ses adieux to say good-bye

faire ses amitiés à qqn to give one's regards to someone

faire son possible to do one's best

faire suivre le courier to forward mail

faire un tour to go for a stroll

faire un voyage to take a trip

faire une malle to pack a trunk

faire une partie de to play a game of

faire une promenade to take a walk

faire une promenade en voiture to go for a drive

faire une question to ask, to pose a question

faire une visite to pay a visit

faire venir qqn to have someone come; **Il a fait venir le docteur** / He had the doctor come. (See **causative faire** in §5.)

faire venir l'eau à la bouche to make one's mouth water

Faites comme chez vous! Make yourself at home!

Que faire? What is to be done?

Quel temps fait-il? What's the weather like? (See also §37.)

§20.19 With FOIS

à la fois at the same time

encore une fois once more, one more time

Il était une fois . . . Once upon a time there was (there were) . . .

une fois de plus once more, one more time

§20.20 With MIEUX

aimer mieux to prefer, to like better

aller mieux to feel better (person's health); **Etes-vous toujours malade?** / Are you still sick? **Je vais mieux, merci** / I'm feeling better, thank you.

de son mieux one's best

faire de son mieux to do one's best

tant mieux so much the better

valoir mieux to be better (worth more), to be preferable

§20.21 With NON

Je crois que non / I don't think so.

mais non! / of course not!

Non merci! No, thank you!

J'espère bien que non! I hope not!

§20.22 With PAR

par bonheur fortunately

par ci par là here and there

par conséquent consequently, therefore

par exemple for example

par hasard by chance

par ici through here, this way, in this direction

par jour per day, daily

par la fenêtre out the window, through the window

par là through there, that way, in that direction

par malheur unfortunately

par mois per month, monthly

par semaine per week, weekly

par tous les temps in all kinds of weather

apprendre par coeur to learn by heart, to memorize

finir par + inf. to end up by + pres. part.; **Ils ont fini par se marier** / They ended up by getting married.

jeter l'argent par la fenêtre to waste money

§20.23 With PAROLE

adresser la parole à to address, to speak to
avoir la parole to have the floor (to speak)

reprendre la parole to go on speaking, to re-sume speaking

§20.24 With PLAIRE

Plaît-il? What did you say? / Would you repeat that please?

s'il te plaît please (familiar "tu" form)
s'il vous plaît please (polite "vous" form)

§20.25 With PLUS

de plus furthermore, besides, in addition
de plus en plus more and more
n'en pouvoir plus to be exhausted, not to be able to go on any longer; **Je n'en peux plus!** I can't go on any longer!

Plus ça change plus c'est la même chose. The more it changes the more it remains the same.
une fois de plus once more, one more time

§20.26 With PRENDRE

prendre garde de + inf. avoid + pres. part. OR take care not + inf. **Prenez garde de tomber** / Avoid falling; **Prenez garde de ne pas tomber** / Take care not to fall.

prendre le parti de + inf. to decide + inf.
prendre un billet to buy a ticket

§20.27 With QUEL

Quel âge avez-vous? How old are you?
Quel garçon! What a boy!

Quel jour est-ce aujourd'hui? What day is it today?

§20.28 With QUELLE

De quelle couleur est (sont) . . . ? What color is (are) . . . ?
Quelle fille! What a girl!

Quelle heure est-il? What time is it?
Quelle veine! What luck!

§20.29 With QUELQUE CHOSE

quelque chose à + inf. something + inf.; **J'ai quelque chose à lui dire** / I have something to say to him (to her).

quelque chose de + adj. something + adj.; **J'ai quelque chose d'intéressant à vous dire** I have something interesting to tell you (to say to you).

§20.30 With QUOI

à quoi bon? what's the use?
avoir de quoi + inf. to have something (enough) + inf. **Avez-vous de quoi écrire?** Do you have something to write with?

Il n'y a pas de quoi! You're welcome!
Quoi?! What?! (used in an exclamation)
Quoi de neuf? What's new?

§20.31 With RIEN

Cela ne fait rien That doesn't matter.
Cela ne sert à rien That serves no purpose.

de rien you're welcome, don't mention it
Rien de neuf! Nothing's new!

§20.32 With SUR

donner sur to look out upon; **La salle à manger donne sur le jardin** / The dining room looks out on the garden.
dormir sur les deux oreilles to sleep soundly

être sur le point de + inf. to be about to + inf.
sur mesure made to order, custom made (clothing)

§20.33   With TANT

tant bien que mal so-so	**J'ai tant de travail!** I have so much work!
tant mieux so much the better	**Je t'aime tant!** I love you so much!
tant pis so much the worse	**tant de choses** so many things

§20.34   With TOUS

tous deux OR **tous les deux** both (*masc. pl.*)	**tous les matins** every morning
tous les ans every year	**tous les soirs** every evening
tous les jours every day	

§20.35   With TOUT

après tout after all	**tout d'un coup** all of a sudden
en tout cas in any case, at any rate	**tout de même!** all the same! just the same!
malgré tout cela in spite of all that	**tout de suite** immediately, at once, right away
pas du tout not at all	**tout le monde** everybody
tout à coup suddenly	**tout le temps** all the time
tout à fait completely, entirely	**voir tout en rose** to see the bright side of any-
tout à l'heure a little while ago, in a little while	thing, to be optimistic
tout d'abord first of all	

§20.36   With TOUTE

en toute hâte with all possible speed, in great haste	**toutes les deux** OR **toutes deux** both (*fem. pl.*)
toute chose everything	**toutes les nuits** every night
de toutes ses forces with all one's might, strenuously	

§20.37   With Y

il y a + length of time ago; **il y a un mois** a month ago (See also **§12.**)	**Il y avait . . .** There was (there were) . . . ; (See also **§13.**)
il y a there is, there are (See also **§13.**)	**Il n'y a pas de quoi** You're welcome.
	y compris including

§20.38   Verbs with special meanings (See also Verbs, in **§39.—§39.50**).

arriver   to happen; **Qu'est-ce qui est arrivé?** What happened?

avoir   to have something the matter; **Qu'est-ce que vous avez?** / What's the matter with you?

entendre dire que   to hear it said that, to hear tell that; **J'entends dire que Robert s'est marié** / I hear (tell) that Robert got married.

entendre parler de   to hear of, to hear about; **J'ai entendu parler d'un grand changement dans l'administration** / I've heard about a big change in the administration.

envoyer chercher   to send for; **Je vais envoyer chercher le médecin** / I'm going to send for the doctor.

être à qqn   to belong to someone; **Ce livre est à moi** / This book belongs to me.

faillir + inf.   to almost do something; **Le bébé a failli tomber** / The baby almost fell.

mettre   to put on; **Gisèle a mis sa plus jolie robe** / Gisèle put on her prettiest dress.

mettre la table   to set the table

profiter de   to take advantage of

rendre visite à   to pay a visit to

venir à   to happen to; **Si nous venons à nous voir en ville, nous pouvons prendre une tasse de café** / If we happen to see each other downtown, we can have a cup of coffee.

venir de + inf.   to have just done something; **Joseph vient de partir** / Joseph has just left; **Barbara venait de partir quand Françoise est arrivée** / Barbara had just left when Françoise arrived.

§21.   INFINITIVES

§21.1   Definition

In English, an infinitive contains the prep. *to* in front of it: *to give, to finish, to sell.* In French, an infinitive has a certain ending. There are three major types of infinitives in French: 1st type are those that end in **—er** (**donner**); 2nd type, those that end in **—ir** (**finir**); 3rd type, those that end in **—re** (**vendre**). See also §39.86—§39.102.

§21.2 **Negation**

Generally speaking, make an infinitive negative in French merely by placing **ne pas** in front of it: **Je vous dis de ne pas sortir** / I am telling you not to go out.

§21.3 **After a verb of perception**

The infinitive is often used after a verb of perception to express an action that is in progress:

EXAMPLES:

J'entends quelqu'un chanter / I hear somebody singing.
Je vois venir les enfants / I see the children coming.

§21.4 Some common verbs of perception are: **apercevoir** (to perceive), **écouter** (to listen to), **entendre** (to hear), **regarder** (to look at), **sentir** (to feel), **voir** (to see).

§21.5 **Preceded by the prepositions à or de**

There are certain French verbs that take either the prep. **à** or **de** + an inf.

EXAMPLES:

Il commence à pleuvoir / It is beginning to rain.
Je songe à faire un voyage / I am thinking of taking a trip.
Il a cessé de pleuvoir / It has stopped raining.
Je regrette de ne pas avoir le temps d'aller avec vous / I am sorry not to have the time to go with you.

See also §39.42—§39.50.

§21.6 **Avant de and sans + infinitive**

The prepositions **avant de** and **sans** + inf. are expressed in English with the present participle form of a verb.

EXAMPLES:

Sylvie a mangé avant de sortir / Sylvia ate before going out.
André est parti sans dire un mot / Andrew left without saying a word.

Generally speaking, a verb is in the infinitive form in French if there is a preposition immediately before it.

§21.7 **Use of infinitive instead of a verb form**

Generally speaking, an infinitive is used instead of a verb form if the subject in a sentence is the same for the actions expressed in the sentence:

EXAMPLES:

Je veux faire le travail / I want to do the work. BUT if there are two different subjects, you must use a new clause and a new verb form: **Je veux que vous fassiez le travail** I want you to do the work.
Je préfère me coucher tôt / I prefer to go to bed early. BUT WITH TWO DIFFERENT SUBJECTS: **Je préfère que vous vous couchiez tôt** / I prefer that you go to bed early.

§21.8 **Past infinitive**

In French the past infinitive is expressed by using **avoir** or **être** (in the infinitive form) + the past participle of the main verb that is being used. The past participle in French is usually expressed in English by a present participle.

EXAMPLES:

Après avoir quitté la maison, Monsieur et Madame Dubé sont allés au cinéma
After leaving the house, Mr. and Mrs. Dubé went to the movies.
Après être arrivée, Jeanne a téléphoné à sa mère / After arriving, Jeanne telephoned her mother.

In a word, a past infinitive is nothing more than the use of **avoir** or **être** (in the infinitive form) + the past participle of the verb you are expressing. You must be careful to use the appropriate auxiliary (**avoir** or **être**) depending on which one of these two your verb requires. To know if **avoir** or **être** is required, see **§39.25, §39.26ff.**

EXAMPLES:

Il a été déclaré coupable d'avoir volé la bicyclette / He was declared guilty of stealing (of having stolen) the bicycle.

Elle a fait ses excuses d'être arrivée en retard / She apologized for arriving (having arrived) late.

§22. MEILLEUR AND MIEUX

§22.1 **Meilleur** is an adj. and must agree in gender and number with the noun or pronoun it modifies:

EXAMPLES:

Cette pomme est bonne, cette pomme-là est meilleure que celle-ci, et celle-là est la meilleure: This apple is good, that apple is better than this one, and that one is the best.

Ces pommes sont bonnes, ces pommes-là sont meilleures que celles-ci, et celles-là sont les meilleures: These apples are good, those apples are better than these, and those are the best.

§22.2 **Mieux** is an adverb and is invariable (it does not change in form); An adverb modifies a verb, an adjective, or another adverb:

EXAMPLES:

Henri travaille bien, Pierre travaille mieux que Robert, et Guy travaille le mieux: Henry works well, Peter works better than Robert, and Guy works the best.

Marie chante bien, Anne chante mieux que Marie, et Claire chante le mieux: Mary sings well, Anne sings better than Mary, and Claire sings the best.

§23. NOUNS

§23.1 Some nouns have one meaning when masculine and another meaning when feminine. Note the following:

§23.2

NOUN	MASCULINE GENDER MEANING	FEMININE GENDER MEANING
aide	assistant, helper	help, aid
crêpe	crape	thin pancake
critique	critic	criticism
enseigne	ensign	sign, flag
garde	guard, guardian	body of troops, watch
guide	guide, guide book	rein (of horses)
livre	book	pound
manche	handle	sleeve
manoeuvre	laborer	manoeuvring, handling
mémoire	memorandum, report	memory
mode	mode, method	fashion
moule	mould	mussel
office	duty, function	pantry
page	page, messenger	page of a book
pendule	pendulum	clock
physique	physique (one's body)	physics

NOUN	MASCULINE GENDER MEANING	FEMININE GENDER MEANING
poêle	stove	frying pan, skillet
politique	politician	politics
poste	position (job)	mail, post (office)
solde	clearance sale	military pay
somme	nap	sum, amount
tour	turn, trick	tower
trompette	trumpeter	trumpet
vague	uncertainty, vagueness	wave (water)
vapeur	steamer, steamship	steam
vase	vase	mud, slime, sludge
voile	veil	sail

§24.   OUI AND SI

Ordinarily, **oui** is used to mean **yes**. However, **si** is used to mean **yes** in response to a question in the negative.

EXAMPLES:

Aimez-vous le français?—Oui, j'aime le français / Do you like French?—Yes, I like French.

N'aimez-vous pas le français?—Si, j'aime le français / Don't you like French?—Yes, I like French.

§25.   PARTITIVE

Essentially, the plural of the indefinite articles **un** and **une** is **des**. The partitive denotes *a part* of a whole; in other words, *some*. In English, we express the partitive by saying *some* or *any* in front of the noun. In French, we use the following forms in front of the noun:

Masculine singular: **du** or **de l'**
Feminine singular: **de la** or **de l'**
Plural for masc. or fem.: **des**

EXAMPLES:

1. SIMPLE AFFIRMATIVE

J'ai **du** café.	I have *some* coffee.
J'ai **de la** viande.	I have *some* meat.
J'ai **de l'**eau.	I have *some* water.
J'ai **des** bonbons.	I have *some* candy.

2. SIMPLE NEGATIVE

Je n'ai **pas de** café.	I don't have *any* coffee.
Je n'ai **pas de** viande.	I don't have *any* meat.
Je n'ai **pas d'**eau.	I don't have *any* water.
Je n'ai **pas de** bonbons.	I don't have *any* candy.

3. WITH AN ADJECTIVE

J'ai **de jolis** chapeaux.	I have *some* pretty hats.
J'ai **de jolies** robes.	I have *some* pretty dresses.

§25.1   **Note the following:**

(a) Use either **du**, **de la**, **de l'**, or **des** in front of the noun, depending on whether the noun is masc. or fem., sing. or pl. Study the examples in the first box above.

(b) The form **du** is used in front of a masc. sing. noun beginning with a consonant, as in **j'ai du café**. See the first box above.

(c) The form **de la** is used in front of a fem. sing. noun beginning with a consonant, as in **j'ai de la viande**. See the first box above.

(d) The form **de l'** is used in front of a fem. or masc. sing. noun beginning with a vowel or silent *h*, as in **j'ai de l'eau**. See the first box above.

(e) The form **des** is used in front of all plural nouns.

(f) To express *any* in front of a noun, when the verb is negative, use **de** in front of the noun. The noun can be fem. or masc. sing. or pl., but it must begin with a consonant, as in **je n'ai pas de café**. See the second box above.

(g) To express *any* in front of a noun, when the verb is negative, use **d'** in front of the noun. The noun can be fem. or masc., sing. or pl., but it must begin with a vowel or silent *h*, as in **je n'ai pas d'eau**. See the second box above.

(h) When the noun is preceded by an adj., use **de**, as in **j'ai de jolis chapeaux**. See the third box above.

(i) When the noun is preceded by an adverb or noun of quantity or measure, use **de**, as in **j'ai beaucoup de choses, j'ai un sac de pommes**.

(j) When the noun is modified by another noun, use **de**, as in **une école de filles**.

(k) The partitive is not used with **sans** or **ne . . . ni . . . ni**.

EXAMPLES:

J'ai quitté la maison sans argent.
I left the house *without any money*.

Je n'ai ni argent ni billets.
I have *neither* money *nor* tickets.

(l) Use **quelques** and not the partitive when by *some* you mean *a few*, in other words, *not many*:

EXAMPLES:

J'ai quelques amis / I have a few (some) friends.
J'ai quelques bonbons / I have a few (some) candies.

(m) If the adjective and the plural noun are a unit; that is to say, if they usually go together, use **des**, not just plain **de**, because the adjective is considered to be part of the word itself: **jeunes filles** (girls).

EXAMPLES:

Le professeur a *des jeunes filles* intelligentes dans sa classe de français / The professor has intelligent girls in his French class.

J'ai *des petits pois* dans mon assiette / I have some peas in my plate.

Il y a *des jeunes gens* dans cette classe / There are young people in this class.

(n) When the negated verb is **ne . . . que**, meaning *only*, the partitive consists of **de** plus the definite article. Compare the following with the examples in the second box above and comments (f) and (g) above.

EXAMPLES:

Elle ne lit que des livres / She reads only books.
Elle ne mange que des bonbons / She eats only candy.

BUT: **Elle ne lit pas de livres** / She doesn't read any books.
Elle ne mange pas de bonbons / She doesn't eat any candy.

(o) When used, the partitive must be repeated before each noun, which is not done in English:

EXAMPLE:

Ici on vend du papier, de l'encre, et des cahiers.
Here they sell paper, ink, and notebooks.

(p) For the use of the pronoun **en** to take the place of the partitive articles, see **§29.1**.

§26.   PASSIVE VOICE

When verbs are used in the active voice, which is almost all the time, the subject is the doer. However, when the passive voice is used, the subject of the sentence is NOT the doer; the action falls on the subject. The agent (the doer) is sometimes expressed, sometimes not, as is done in English. The passive voice, therefore, is composed of the verb in the passive, which is any tense of **être** + the past participle of the verb you are using to indicate the action performed upon the subject. Since **être** is the verb used in the passive voice, the past participle of your other verb must agree with the subject in gender and number.

EXAMPLES:

Jacqueline a été reçue à l'université / Jacqueline has been accepted at the university.
   (No agent, no doer, is expressed here.)
Jacqueline a été blessée par un camion / Jacqueline was (has been) injured by a truck.
   (Here, the agent—the doer—is expressed.)
Ce livre est écrit par un auteur célèbre / This book is written by a famous author.
Cette composition a été écrite par un jeune élève / This composition was written by a young student.

§26.1   Preposition **de** instead of the preposition **par**

Usually the preposition **de** is used instead of **par** with such verbs as: **aimer, admirer, accompagner, apprécier, voir.**

EXAMPLES:

Jacqueline est aimée de tout le monde / Jacqueline is liked (loved) by everyone.
BUT: Nous avons été suivis par un chien perdu / We were followed by a lost dog.

§26.2   Use of the indefinite pronoun subject **on** instead of the passive voice.

The passive voice is generally avoided if the thought can be expressed in the active voice with **on** as the subject.

EXAMPLES:

On vend de bonnes choses dans ce magasin / Good things are sold in this store.
On parle français ici / French is spoken here.

§26.3   You must avoid using the passive voice with a reflexive verb. Use a reflexive verb with an active subject.

EXAMPLES:

Elle s'appelle Jeanne / She is called Joan.
Comment se prononce ce mot? / How is this word pronounced?

§27.   NE EXPLETIVE

In French, the use of **ne** in front of the verb in the clause introduced by certain conjunctions and some verbs is called **ne explétif**. For years, some American and English grammarians have called this **ne explétif** "pleonastic **ne**" or merely "a pleonasm". This term in English is not entirely accurate.

A pleonasm, in French and English, is the use of an additional word which is not necessary (which is redundant) to express what has already been stated; for example, *to descend downstairs* (**descendre en bas**), *to climb up* (**monter en haut**), *a free gift* (**un cadeau gratuit**).

In English, we have the word *expletive*, which is the best word for the French **explétif**; therefore, in English I refer to the French **ne explétif** as expletive **ne**, not pleonastic **ne**.

An example of an expletive in English grammar is the word *there* used as follows: *There are many books on the desk*; we could easily say *Many books are on the desk*. But when we place the verb *are* in front of the subject *books*, we need to fill out the sentence by beginning it with *There are . . .* ; or even in the singular: *There is one book on the desk*; we could easily say *One book is on the desk*, without the expletive *there*. Another example of an expletive in English is the use of *it*, as in: *It is her obligation to do it*. We could easily say: *Her obligation is to do it*, without the expletive *it*.

All French grammarians do not agree on when to use the **ne explétif** and nowadays most French people do not bother to observe correct usage of this **ne explétif**; the tendency seems to be to ignore it completely or to use it optionally. However:

§27.1 Let me give you examples of when the use of expletive **ne** is required:

§27.2 (a) After a verb or conjunction expressing fear: **Je crains qu'elle ne meure; Je prie de peur qu'elle ne meure.**

§27.3 (b) After the verb **trembler**: **Je tremble qu'elle ne meure.**

§27.4 NOTE that in these two examples, the fear or trembling is about something that may happen: use the expletive **ne**.

§27.5 If the fear or trembling is about something that may NOT happen, use **ne . . . pas** in the result clause: **J'ai peur que mon fils ne soit pas reçu à l'université** / I'm afraid that my son will not be accepted at the university.

§27.6 ALSO NOTE that if the verb of fear or trembling is used in the negative—in other words, you do not fear or tremble about something—there is no need for the expletive **ne**: **Je ne crains pas qu'il vienne** / I am not afraid that he might come; **Je ne tremble pas qu'elle vienne** / I am not trembling that she might come.

§27.7 (c) After the simple conjunction **que** when it is used as a short form to take the place of **à moins que, avant que, de peur que**, or **sans que**: **Partez tout de suite, que je ne vous insulte** / Leave immediately before I insult you. [When these conjunctions are stated in full, only **de peur que** requires the expletive **ne**]

For the use of the subjunctive of the verb in the **que** clause in the above examples, see §35., §35.1, §35.8, §35.9.

§27.8 (d) Generally speaking, at all other times, do not use the expletive **ne** because it is used either optionally or it must not be used. You are safe, therefore, if you use it only in the above cases where it is required.

§28. POUVOIR

The verb **pouvoir** has special uses and special meanings. It is fully conjugated for you farther on in §40.1.

§28.1 **Present tense**
EXAMPLES:
Je ne peux pas sortir aujourd'hui parce que je suis malade / I cannot (am unable to) go out today because I am sick.

Est-ce que je peux entrer? OR **Puis-je entrer?** / May I come in?

Madame Marin peut être malade / Mrs. Marin may be sick.
This use of **pouvoir** suggests a possibility.

Je n'en peux plus / I can't go on any longer.
This use suggests a physical exhaustion.

Il se peut / It is possible.
This use as a reflexive verb suggests a possibility.

Cela ne se peut pas / That can't be done.
This use as a reflexive verb suggests an impossibility.

§28.2   **Conditional**

(a)   **Pourriez-vous me prêter dix francs?** / Could you lend me ten francs?

§28.3   **Conditional Perfect**

(a)   **Auriez-vous pu venir chez moi?** / Could you have come to my place?

(b)   **Ils auraient pu rater le train** / They might have missed the train.

§29.   PRONOUNS

§29.1   **En**

§29.2

The pronoun **en** takes the place of the partitive and serves as a direct object; it can refer to persons or things. See also **§25.ff.**

EXAMPLES:

Avez-vous des frères? / Do you have *any* brothers?
Oui, j'en ai / Yes, I have (some).

Avez-vous de l'argent? Have you *any* money?
Oui, j'en ai / Yes, I have (some).
Non, je n'en ai pas / No, I don't have any.

Donnez-moi des bonbons / Give me *some* candy.
Donnez-m'en / Give me some.
Ne m'en donnez pas / Don't give me any.

§29.3

The past participle of a compound verb does not agree with the preceding dir. obj. **en.**

(a)   **Avez-vous écrit des lettres?** / Did you write any letters?
Oui, j'en ai écrit trois / Yes, I wrote three (of them).

(b)   **Avez-vous rencontré des amis?** / Did you meet any friends?
Oui, j'en ai vu plusieurs / Yes, I saw several (of them).

§29.4   Reflexive verbs that take the prep. **de**

§29.5   Use **en** to take the place of the prep. **de** + a thing.

(a)   **Est-ce que vous vous souvenez de l'adresse?** / Do you remember the address?
Oui, je m'en souviens / Yes, I remember it.

(b)   **Est-ce que vous vous servez des hors-d'oeuvre?** / Are you helping yourself to the hors-d'oeuvre?
Oui, merci, je m'en sers / Yes, thank you, I'm helping myself to some.

§29.6   Do not use **en** to take the place of the prep. **de** + a person. Use the disjunctive pronouns. (See what the disjunctive pronouns are in **§29.22**)

(a)   **Est-ce que vous vous souvenez de cette dame?** / Do you remember this lady?
Oui, je me souviens d'elle / Yes, I remember her.

(b)   **Est-ce que vous vous souvenez de cet homme?** / Do you remember this man?
Oui, je me souviens de lui / Yes, I remember him.

§29.7   **Expressions of quantity**

Use **en** to take the place of **de** + noun and retain the word of quantity.

(a) **Avez-vous beaucoup d'amis?** / Do you have many friends?
Oui, j'en ai beaucoup / Yes, I have many (of them).

(b) **Avez-vous beaucoup de travail?** / Do you have a lot of work?
Oui, j'en ai beaucoup / Yes, I have a lot (of it).

(c) **Madame Paquet a-t-elle mis trop de sel dans le ragoût?** / Did Mrs. Paquet put too much salt in the stew?
Oui, elle en a mis trop dans le ragoût / Yes, she put too much (of it) in the stew.

§29.8   **As an adverbial pronoun of place**, meaning *from there*

Use **en** to take the place of the prep. **de** + the place.

(a) **Est-ce que vous venez de l'école?** / Are you coming from school?
Oui, j'en viens / Yes, I am coming from there.
Non, je n'en viens pas / No, I am not coming from there.

(b) **Est-ce que vous venez des grands magasins?** / Are you coming from the department stores?
Oui, j'en viens / Yes, I am (coming from there).

(c) **Est-ce que vous venez de Paris?** / Are you coming from Paris?
Oui, j'en viens / Yes, I am (coming from there).

§29.9   **Y**

§29.10   Use **y** as a pronoun to serve as an object replacing a prepositional phrase beginning with **à, dans, sur, chez** referring to things, places, or ideas.

(a) **Est-ce que vous pensez à l'examen?** / Are you thinking of the exam?
Oui, j'y pense / Yes, I am (thinking of it).

(b) **Je réponds à la lettre** / I am answering the letter.
J'y réponds / I am answering it.

(c) **Est-ce que vous vous intéressez aux sports?** / Are you interested in sports?
Oui, je m'y intéresse / Yes, I'm interested (in them).

(d) **Est-ce que le livre est dans le tiroir?** / Is the book in the drawer?
Oui, il y est / Yes, it is (there).

(e) **Est-ce que les fleurs sont sur la table?** / Are the flowers on the table?
Oui, elles y sont / Yes, they are (there).

(f) **Est-ce que vous allez chez Pierre?** / Are you going to Pierre's?
Oui, j'y vais / Yes, I am going (there).

(g) **Est-ce que vous irez à Paris?** / Will you go to Paris?
Oui, j'irai / Yes, I will (go).

NOTE that you do not use the adverbial pronoun **y** here because the verb form of **aller** in the future begins with the vowel **i**. Do not say **J'y irai**; say **J'irai**. The same is true of **aller** in the conditional:

(h) **Iriez-vous à Paris si vous aviez le temps?** / Would you go to Paris if you had (the) time?
Oui, j'irais / Yes, I would (go).

§29.11   **Subject pronouns**

§29.12   The subject pronouns are:

	Singular	Plural
1ST PERSON	**je** (I) (*or* **j'**)	**nous** (we)
2ND PERSON	**tu** (you *familiar*)	**vous** (you *polite singular*) & plural
3RD PERSON	**il** (he *or* it) **elle** (she *or* it) **on** (one)	**ils** (they, *masc.pl.*) **elles** (they, *fem.pl.*)

NOTE that the 3rd person sing. subject pronoun **on** has several meanings in English: **On ne sait jamais** / One never knows; You never know; People never know; A person never knows. **On dit que Marie s'est mariée avec Jean** / They say that Mary married John.

§29.13 **Demonstrative pronouns**

§29.14 The demonstrative pronouns are:

	Singular	Plural
MASCULINE	**celui** (the one)	**ceux** (the ones)
FEMININE	**celle** (the one)	**celles** (the ones)

§29.15 They are generally used with the following words after them:

celui de (the one of)
celle de (the one of)
ceux de (the ones of)
celles de (the ones of)
celui-ci (this one, the latter)
celle-ci (this one, the latter)
celui-là (that one, the former)
celle-là (that one, the former)
ceux-ci (these, the latter)
celles-ci (these, the latter)
ceux-là (those, the former)
celles-là (those, the former)
celui qui (the one who, the one that—as subject)
celle qui (the one who, the one that—as subject)

ceux qui (the ones who, the ones that—as subject)
celles qui (the ones who, the ones that—as subject)
celui que (the one who, the one that—as object)
celle que (the one who, the one that—as object)
ceux que (the ones who, the ones that—as object)
celles que (the ones who, the ones that—as object)
celui dont (the one of which)
celle dont (the one of which)
ceux dont (the ones of which)
celles dont (the ones of which)

§ 29.16 EXAMPLES:

J'ai mangé mon gâteau et celui de Pierre / I ate my cake and Peter's.

J'aime beaucoup ma voiture et celle de Jacques / I like my car very much and Jack's.

J'ai mangé mes petits pois et ceux de David / I ate my peas and David's.

J'aime tes jupes et celles de Jeanne / I like your skirts and Joan's.

J'ai deux éclairs; est-ce que tu préfères celui-ci ou celui-là? / I have two eclairs; do you prefer this one or that one?

J'ai deux pommes; est-ce que tu préfères celle-ci ou celle-là? / I have two apples; do you prefer this one or that one?

J'ai quatre crayons; est-ce que tu préfères ceux-ci ou ceux-là? / I have four pencils; do you prefer these or those?

J'ai quatre robes; est-ce que tu préfères celles-ci ou celles-là? / I have four dresses; do you prefer these or those?

Paul et Jean sont frères; celui-ci [the latter, meaning Jean] **est petit et celui-là** [the former, meaning Paul] **est grand** / Paul and John are brothers; the latter is short and the former is tall.

J'ai deux soeurs. Elles s'appellent Anne et Monique. Celle-ci est petite, celle-là est grande / I have two sisters. Their names are Anne and Monique. The latter [meaning Monique] is short; the former [meaning Anne] is tall.

L'homme que vous voyez là-bas est celui qui a gagné le grand prix / The man whom you see over there is the one who won the first prize.

La femme que vous voyez là-bas est celle qui a gagné le grand prix / The woman whom you see over there is the one who won the first prize.

Les hommes que vous voyez là-bas sont ceux qui ont perdu le match / The men whom you see over there are the ones who lost the game.

Les femmes que vous voyez là-bas sont celles qui ont perdu le match / The women whom you see over there are the ones who lost the game.

Celui que vous voyez là-bas est mon frère / The one whom you see over there is my brother.

Celle que vous voyez là-bas est ma soeur / The one whom you see over there is my sister.

Ceux que vous voyez là-bas sont mes frères / The ones whom you see over there are my brothers.

Celles que vous voyez là-bas sont mes soeurs / The ones whom you see over there are my sisters.

Ce livre est celui dont je vous ai parlé hier / This book is the one of which I spoke to you yesterday.

Cette voiture est celle dont je vous ai parlé hier / This car is the one I talked to you about yesterday.

§29.17　**ce or c', ceci, cela, ça**

These are demonstrative pronouns but they are invariable, which means that they do not change in gender and number. They refer to things that are not identified by name and they may refer to an idea or a statement mentioned.

§29.18　EXAMPLES:

C'est vrai / It's true.

Ceci est vrai / This is true; **ceci est faux** / this is false.

Cela est vrai / That is true; **cela est faux** / that is false.

Ça m'intéresse beaucoup / That interests me very much.

Qu'est-ce que c'est que cela? OR **Qu'est-ce que c'est que ça?** / What's that?

NOTE that **ça** is shortened from **cela.**

Qui est à la porte?—C'est Isabelle / Who is at the door? It's Isabelle.

See also **§4.7 (d), §4.8 (b), §6., 6.1, 6.2; §8.1 (a) + (b).** Also, do not forget to consult the index from time to time.

§29.19　**Direct object pronouns**

The direct object pronouns are:

Person		Singular		Plural
1ST	**me** *or* **m'**	me	**nous**	us
2ND	**te** *or* **t'**	you (*familiar*)	**vous**	you (*sing. polite or plural*)
3RD	{**le** *or* **l'**	him, it (*person or thing*)	**les**	them (*persons or things*)
	{**la** *or* **l'**	her, it		

(a) A direct object pronoun takes the place of a direct object noun.

(b) A direct object noun ordinarily comes after the verb, but a direct object pronoun is ordinarily placed *in front of the verb or infinitive.*

(c) The vowel **e** in **me**, **te**, **le** and the vowel **a** in **la** drop and an apostrophe is added if the verb right after it starts with a vowel or silent *h*, *e.g.*, **Je l'aime** (I like him, or I like her, or I like it).

(d) You might say that the direct object "receives" the action of the verb.

(e) Sometimes the direct object pronoun is placed after the verb. This happens in the affirmative imperative:

EXAMPLES:
Faites-le / Do it.
Suivez-moi / Follow me. (NOTE that **me** changes to **moi**)

(f) See my Summaries of word order of elements in French sentences beginning in **§42**.

§29.20 Indirect object pronouns

The indirect object pronouns are:

Person	Singular			Plural	
1ST	**me** *or* **m'**	to me	**nous**	to us
2ND	**te** *or* **t'**	to you (*familiar*)	**vous**	to you (*sing. polite or pl.*)
3RD	**lui**	to him, to her	**leur**	to them

(a) An indirect object pronoun takes the place of an indirect object noun.

(b) You might say that an indirect object "receives" the direct object because it is usually a matter of something "going" to someone; for example, *to me, to you, to him, to her.* Sometimes the *to* is not mentioned in English: *I am giving him the book*; what we really mean to say is, *I am giving the book to him.* Then, too, there are some verbs in French that take an indirect object pronoun because the verb takes the preposition **à** (to); for example, **Je lui réponds** can be translated into English as: *I am answering her (or) him* or, *I am responding to her (or) to him.*

(c) An indirect object pronoun is ordinarily placed *in front of the verb*: **Je vous parle** / I am talking to you.

(d) Sometimes the indirect object pronoun is placed after the verb. This happens in the affirmative imperative:

EXAMPLES:
Parlez-moi / Speak to me. (Note that **me** changes to **moi**)
Parlez-lui / Speak to her (or) Speak to him.

(e) See my Summaries of word order of elements in French sentences, farther on beginning with **§42**.

§29.21 Double object pronouns

To get a picture of what the word order is when you have more than one object pronoun (direct and indirect) in a sentence, see my Summaries of word order of elements in French sentences beginning with **§42**.

§29.22 Disjunctive pronouns

Disjunctive pronouns are also known as tonic pronouns or stressed pronouns. They are:

Person	Singular		Plural	
1ST	**moi**	me *or* I	**nous**	us *or* we
2ND	**toi**	you (*familiar*)	**vous**	you (*formal sing. or pl.*)
3RD	{**soi**	oneself	{**eux**	them, they (*masc.*)
	lui	him *or* he	{**elles**	them, they (*fem.*)
	elle	her *or* she		

A disjunctive pronoun is used:

(a) As object of a preposition:

(1) **Elle parle avec moi** / She is talking with me.
(2) **Nous allons chez eux** / We are going to their house.
(3) **Je pense à lui** / I am thinking of him.
(4) **Je pense toujours à toi** / I always think of you.

(b) In a compound subject or object:

(1) **Eux et leurs amis vont venir chez moi** / They and their friends are going to come to my place (my house).
(2) **Lui et elle sont amoureux** / He and she are in love.
(3) **Je vous connais—toi et lui** / I know you—you and him.
(4) **Oui, je les vois maintenant—lui et elles** / Yes, I see them now—him and them.

(c) For emphasis:

(1) **Moi, je parle bien; lui, il ne parle pas bien** / I speak well; he does not speak well.
(2) **Lui, surtout, est travailleur** / He, especially, is a worker.

(d) To indicate possession with **à** if the verb is **être** and if the subject is a noun, personal pronoun, or a demonstrative pronoun:

(1) **Ce livre est à moi** / This book is mine.
(2) **Je suis à toi** / I am yours.
(3) **Celles-ci sont à eux** / These are theirs.

(e) With **c'est:**

(1) **Qui est à la porte?—C'est moi** / Who is at the door? It's me *or* It is I.
(2) **C'est toi?—C'est moi** / Is it you?—It's me *or* It is I.

(f) With **ce sont** in a statement but not usually in a question:

(1) **Est-ce eux?—Oui, ce sont eux** / Is it they?—Yes, it's they.
(2) **Qui est à la porte? Est-ce Marie et Jeanne?—Oui, ce sont elles** / Who is at the door? Is it Mary and Joan?—Yes, it's they.

(g) With **même** and **mêmes**:

(1) **Est-ce Pierre?—Oui, c'est lui-même** / Is it Peter? Yes, it's he himself.
(2) **Est-ce que vous allez le manger vous-même?** / Are you going to eat it yourself?
(3) **Est-ce qu'ils vont les manger eux-mêmes?** / Are they going to eat them themselves?

(h) When no verb is stated:

(1) **Qui est à l'appareil?—Moi** / Who is on the phone?—Me.
(2) **Qui a brisé le vase?—Eux** / Who broke the vase?—Them *or* They.

NOTE: See my Summaries of word order of elements in French sentences in **§42.ff.**

§29.23 Indefinite pronouns

Some common indefinite pronouns are:

aucun, aucune   not any, not one, none
un autre, une autre   another, another one
Nous autres Français   We French people
Nous autres Américains   We American people
l'un l'autre, l'une l'autre   each other (of only two)
les uns les autres, les unes les autres   one another (more than two)
certains, certaines   certain ones
chacun, chacune   each one
nul, nulle   not one, not any, none
n'importe qui, n'importe quel   anyone
n'importe quoi   anything
on   people, one, they, you, we; **On dit qu'il va pleuvoir** / They say that it's going to rain; **On ne sait jamais** / One never knows; **On aime manger** / People like to eat.
personne   no one, nobody
plusieurs   several; **J'en ai plusieurs** / I have several of them.
quelque chose   something
quelqu'un, quelqu'une   someone, somebody
quelques-uns, quelques-unes   some, a few
quiconque   whoever, whosoever
rien   nothing
soi   oneself; **On est chez soi dans cet hôtel** / People feel at home in this hotel.
tout   all, everything; **Tout est bien qui finit bien** / All is well that ends well.

§29.24   Interrogative pronouns

§29.25   Referring to PERSONS

§29.26   As subject of a verb

(1) **Qui est à l'appareil?** / Who is on the phone?

(2) **Qui est-ce qui est à l'appareil?** / Who is on the phone?

(3) **Lequel des deux garçons va vous voir?** / Which one of the two boys is going to see you?

(4) **Laquelle des deux jeunes filles va vous voir?** / Which one of the two girls is going to see you?

(5) **Lesquels de ces hommes vont faire le travail?** / Which ones of these men are going to do the work?

(6) **Lesquelles de ces femmes vont faire le travail?** / Which ones of these women are going to do the work?

§29.27   As direct object of a verb

(1) **Qui aimez-vous?** / Whom do you love?

(2) **Qui est-ce que vous aimez?** / Whom do you love?

(3) **Qui est-ce qu'elle aime?** / Whom does she love?

(4) **Lequel de ces deux garçons aimez-vous?** / Which one of these two boys do you love?

(5) **Laquelle de ces deux jeunes filles aimez-vous?** / Which one of these two girls do you love?

(6) **Lesquels de ces hommes admirez-vous?** / Which ones of these men do you admire?

(7) **Lesquelles de ces femmes admirez-vous?** / Which ones of these women do you admire?

§29.28   As object of a preposition

(1) **Avec qui allez-vous au cinéma?** / With whom are you going to the movies?

(2) **A qui parlez-vous au téléphone?** / To whom are you talking on the telephone?

NOTE that when the interrogative pronouns **lequel, laquelle, lesquels,** and **lesquelles** are objects of the prepositions **à** or **de**, their forms are:

auquel, à laquelle, auxquels, auxquelles;
duquel, de laquelle, desquels, desquelles

(3) **Auquel de ces deux garçons parlez-vous?** / To which one of these two boys do you talk?

(4) **A laquelle de ces deux jeunes filles parlez-vous?** / To which one of these two girls do you talk?

(5) **Auxquels de ces hommes parlez-vous?** / To which ones of these men do you talk?

(6) **Auxquelles de ces femmes parlez-vous?** / To which ones of these women are you talking?

(7) **Duquel de ces deux garçons parlez-vous?** / About which one of these two boys are you talking?

(8) **De laquelle de ces deux jeunes filles parlez-vous?** / About which one of these two girls are you talking?

(9) **Desquels de ces hommes parlez-vous?** / About which ones of these men are you talking?

(10) **Desquelles de ces femmes parlez-vous?** / About which ones of these women are you talking?

§29.29   **Referring to THINGS**

§29.30   **As subject of a verb**

(1) **Qu'est-ce qui est arrivé?** / What arrived? OR What happened?
   Qu'est-ce qui s'est passé? / What happened?

(2) **Lequel de ces deux trains arrivera le premier?** / Which one of these two trains will arrive first?

(3) **Laquelle de ces deux voitures marche bien?** / Which one of these two cars runs well?

(4) **Lesquels de tous ces trains sont modernes?** / Which ones of all these trains are modern?

(5) **Lesquelles de toutes ces voitures marchent bien?** / Which ones of all these cars run well?

§29.31   **As direct object of a verb**

(1) **Que faites-vous?** / What are you doing?

(2) **Qu'a-t-elle?** / What does she have? OR What's the matter with her?

(3) **Qu'est-ce que vous faites?** / What are you doing?

(4) **Qu'est-ce qu'elle fait?** / What is she doing?

(5) **Lequel de ces deux livres préférez-vous?** / Which one of these two books do you prefer?

(6) **Laquelle de ces voitures préférez-vous?** / Which one of these cars do you prefer?

(7) **Lesquels de ces livres avez-vous écrits?** / Which (ones) of these books did you write?

(8) **Lesquelles de ces pâtisseries avez-vous faites?** / Which (ones) of these pastries did you make?

§29.32   **As object of a preposition**

(1) **Avec quoi écrivez-vous?** / With what are you writing?

(2) **A quoi pensez-vous?** / Of what are you thinking? OR What are you thinking of?

NOTE that the use of **lequel, laquelle, lesquels,** and **lesquelles** referring to things as objects of prepositions is the same as examples (3) through (10) in §29.28 above where they are used referring to persons. The forms are exactly the same when they combine with the prepositions **à** or **de**. For example, compare the example in sentence (7) there with the following: **Duquel de ces livres parlez-vous?** / Of which of these books are you talking? OR About which of these books are you talking OR Which of these books are you talking of (about)?

§29.33   **Neuter pronoun le**
The word **le**, as you know, is the def. art. masc. sing. It is also the dir. obj. masc. sing. That

word is also used as a neuter pronoun and it functions as a dir. obj. referring to an adjective, a phrase, a clause, or a complete statement. It is generally not translated into English, except to mean *it* or *so*:

(1) **Janine est jolie mais Henriette ne l'est pas** / Janine is pretty but Henrietta is not (*i.e.*, pretty).

(2) **Moi, je crois qu'ils vont gagner le match, et vous?—Je le crois aussi** / I think they are going to win the game, and you?—I think so, too.

§29.34 Position of pronouns in a sentence

To get a picture of what the word order is when you have more than one pronoun of any kind in a sentence, see my Summaries of word order of elements in French beginning with **§42.ff.**

§29.35 Possessive pronouns

The possessive pronouns are:

Masculine			
SINGULAR		PLURAL	
le mien	mine	**les miens**	mine
le tien	yours (*familiar*)	**les tiens**	yours (*familiar*)
le sien	his, hers, its	**les siens**	his, hers, its
le nôtre	ours	**les nôtres**	ours
le vôtre	yours	**les vôtres**	yours
le leur	theirs	**les leurs**	theirs
Feminine			
SINGULAR		PLURAL	
la mienne	mine	**les miennes**	mine
la tienne	yours (*familiar*)	**les tiennes**	yours (*familiar*)
la sienne	his, hers, its	**les siennes**	his, hers, its
la nôtre	ours	**les nôtres**	ours
la vôtre	yours	**les vôtres**	yours
la leur	theirs	**les leurs**	theirs

(a) A possessive pronoun takes the place of a possessive adjective + noun: **mon livre** / my book; **le mien** / mine.

(b) A possessive pronoun agrees in gender and number with what it is replacing: **son livre** / his book OR her book; **le sien** / his OR hers.

(c) When the definite articles **le** and **les** are preceded by the prepositions **à** and **de**, they combine in the usual way that you already know: **au mien, aux miens, du mien, des miens.** As you know, **à la** and **de la** remain: **à la mienne, de la mienne, à la sienne, de la sienne,** *etc.*

EXAMPLES:

Paul me parle de ses parents et je lui parle des miens / Paul is talking to me about his parents and I am talking to him about mine.

Je préfère ma voiture à la tienne / I prefer my car to yours.

Je m'intéresse à mes problèmes et aux leurs / I am interested in my problems and in theirs.

(d) The possessive pronouns are used with **être** to emphasize a distinction: **Ce livre-ci est le mien et celui-là est le tien** / This book is mine and that one is yours.

(e) If no distinction is made as to who owns what, use **être** + **à** + disjunctive pronoun: **Ce livre est à lui** / This book is his.

(f) In French, we do not translate word for word such English expressions as *a friend of mine, a book of mine*. Instead of using the possessive pronouns in French, we say *one of my friends, one of my books*, etc.:

un de mes amis / a friend of mine; **un de mes livres** / a book of mine;
une de ses amies / a girl friend of hers OR a girl friend of his;
un de nos amis / a friend of ours.

§29.36 Reflexive pronouns

§29.37 The reflexive pronouns, which are used with reflexive verbs, are: **me, te, se, nous,** and **vous.**

§29.38 The reflexive pronouns in English are: myself, yourself, herself, himself, oneself, itself, ourselves, yourselves, and themselves.

§29.39 To form the present tense of a reflexive verb in a simple affirmative sentence, put the reflexive pronoun in front of the verb: **Je me lave** / I wash myself.

§29.40 A reflexive verb expresses an action that is turned back upon the subject; **Jacqueline se lave tous les jours** / Jacqueline washes herself every day.

§29.41 You must be careful to use the appropriate reflexive pronoun, the one that matches the subject pronoun. You already know the subject pronouns, but here they are again, beside the reflexive pronouns:

Person	Singular	Plural
1ST	**je me lave**	**nous nous lavons**
2ND	**tu te laves**	**vous vous lavez**
3RD	**il se lave** **elle se lave** **on se lave**	**ils se lavent** **elles se lavent**

§29.42 To get a picture of what the word order is when you have more than one pronoun of any kind in a sentence, see my Summaries of word order of elements in French sentences, farther on in this section beginning with **§42.ff.**

§29.43 Relative pronouns

§29.44 A relative pronoun is a word that refers (relates) to an antecedent. An antecedent is something that comes before something; it can be a word, a phrase, a clause which is replaced by a pronoun or some other substitute. Example: *Is it Mary who did that?* In this sentence, *who* is the relative pronoun and *Mary* is the antecedent. Another example, a longer one: *It seems to me that you are wrong, which is what I had suspected right along.* The relative pronoun is *which* and the antecedent is the clause, *that you are wrong.*

§29.45 The common relative pronouns are:

§29.46 **dont** / of whom, of which, whose, whom, which
Voici le livre dont j'ai besoin / Here is the book which I need OR Here is the book of which I have need. (YOU ARE DEALING WITH *avoir besoin* de HERE.)
Monsieur Béry, dont le fils est avocat, est maintenant en France / Mr. Béry, whose son is a lawyer, is now in France.
C'est Monsieur Boucher dont je me méfie / It is Mr. Boucher whom I mistrust. (YOU ARE DEALING WITH *se méfier* de HERE.)

§29.47   **ce dont** / what, of which, that of which

Je ne trouve pas ce dont j'ai besoin / I don't find what I need OR I don't find that of which I have need. (YOU ARE DEALING WITH *avoir besoin* de HERE.) (Here, the antecedent is not stated and **ce *dont*** is needed).

Ce dont vous parlez est absurde / What you are talking about is absurd OR That which you are talking about is absurd. (YOU ARE DEALING WITH *parler* de HERE.)

NOTE that **dont** is used when it refers to persons or things that are clearly specified, when the antecedent is clearly indicated. Use **ce dont** when there is no antecedent clearly specified, when it is indeterminate. Generally, choose **dont** when you have to account for a **de** which is dropped.

§29.48   **ce que** or **ce qu'**   what, that which

Comprenez-vous ce que je vous dis? / Do you understand what I am telling you?

Comprenez-vous ce qu'elle vous dit? / Do you understand what she is saying to you?

Je comprends ce que vous dites et je comprends ce qu'elle dit / I understand what you are saying and I understand what she is saying.

Ce que vous dites est vrai / What you are saying is true OR That which you are saying is true.

NOTE here, too, that **ce que** is used when there is no antecedent clearly stated in the sentence. In the examples given above, we do not know what it is (**ce que c'est**) which was said. The idea here is similar to the use of **ce dont**, except that **dont** is used when you are dealing with the prep. **de** which is dropped—generally speaking—and that **de** is replaced with **dont**. NOTE that **ce que** is a direct object.

§29.49   **ce qui**   what, that which

Ce qui est vrai est vrai / What is true is true OR That which is true is true.

Je ne sais pas ce qui s'est passé / I don't know what happened.

NOTE that **ce qui** is a subject.

§29.50   **lequel** (in all its forms)   which

As a relative pronoun, **lequel** (in its various forms) is used as object of a preposition referring to things. (See also **§29.24** through **§29.32** above)

Est-ce cette porte par laquelle je passe pour trouver le train? / Is it this door through which I go to find the train?

Donnez-moi un autre morceau de papier sur lequel je peux écrire mon adresse / Give me another piece of paper on which I can write my address.

§29.51   **où**   where, in which, on which

Aimez-vous la salle à manger où nous mangeons? / Do you like the dining room where we eat?

Je vais ouvrir le tiroir où j'ai mis l'argent / I am going to open the drawer where I put the money. OR YOU CAN SAY: **Je vais ouvrir le tiroir dans lequel j'ai mis l'argent** / I am going to open the drawer in which I placed the money.

NOTE that in French you can use **où** to mean not only *where*, but sometimes *when*:

Paul est entré au moment où je partais / Paul entered at the moment when I was leaving.

Elle s'est mariée le jour même où son père est mort / She got married on the very day when her father died.

§29.52   **que** or **qu'**   whom, which, that

Le garçon que vous voyez là-bas est mon meilleur ami / The boy whom you see over there is my best friend.

Le livre que vous avez en main est à moi / The book which (OR: that) you have in your hand is mine.

La composition qu'elle a écrite est excellente / The composition which (OR: that) she wrote is excellent.

NOTE: Make a distinction between **que** and **qu'** as a relative pronoun in the examples given above and **que** as a simple conjunction introducing a new clause, as in: **Je sais que vous avez raison** / I know that you are right; **Je pense que la vie est belle** / I think that life is beautiful.

As a relative pronoun, **que** refers to an antecedent which can be a person or a thing. In the above examples the antecedents are: **le garçon, le livre, la composition.**

§29.53   **qui**   who, whom, which, that
         Connais-tu la jeune fille qui parle avec mon frère? / Do you know the girl who is talking with my brother?
         Avez-vous une bicyclette qui marche bien? / Do you have a bicycle that (OR: which) runs well?
         Connais-tu la jeune fille avec qui je parlais tout à l'heure? / Do you know the girl with whom I was talking a little while ago?

NOTE, in the first two examples above, that **qui** is used as a subject for persons and things as a relative pronoun. It is used as object of prepositions, as in the third example, only for persons. For things as objects of prepositions, use the **lequel** forms (see **§29.50**).

§30.   NEGATIONS

The common negations are **ne** + **verb** + any of the following:

§30.1   **aucun, aucune: Je n'ai aucun livre; je n'ai aucune automobile** / I have no book; I have no automobile.
         guère: Paul n'a guère parlé / Paul hardly (scarcely) spoke.
         jamais: François n'étudie jamais / Frank never studies.
         ni . . . ni: Je n'ai ni argent ni billets / I have neither money nor tickets.
         nul, nulle: Je n'en ai nul besoin / I have no need of it; **Je ne vais nulle part** / I'm not going anywhere.
         pas: Je n'ai pas de papier / I haven't any paper OR I don't have any paper OR I have no paper.
         pas du tout: Je ne comprends pas du tout / I do not understand at all.
         personne: Je ne vois personne / I see nobody OR I don't see anybody OR I see no one.
         plus: Mon père ne peut plus travailler / My father can no longer work OR My father can't work any more.
         point: Cet enfant n'a point d'argent / This child has no money at all.
         que: Je n'ai que deux francs / I have only two francs; **Il ne fait que travailler** / He only works.
         rien: Je n'ai rien sur moi / I have nothing on me OR I don't have anything on me.

NOTE that all these negations require **ne** in front of the main verb. Also, note that **aucun, aucune, nul, nulle, personne,** and **rien** can be used as subjects and you still need to use **ne** in front of the verb:

         Aucun n'est présent; aucune n'est présente / Not one is present. **Nul homme n'est parfait; nulle femme n'est parfaite** / No man is perfect; no woman is perfect. **Personne n'est ici** / No one is here. **Rien n'est ici** / Nothing is here.

§31.   SAVOIR

The verb **savoir** has special uses and special meanings.

§31.1   **Present tense**
         EXAMPLES:
         Je sais la réponse / I know the answer.
         Je sais lire en français / I know how to read in French OR: I can read in French.

§31.2   **Conditional**

(a) **Sauriez-vous l'adresse d'un docteur dans ce quartier?** / Would you know the address of a doctor in this neighborhood? OR: Can you tell me the address of a doctor in this area?

(b) **Je ne saurais penser à tout!** / I can't think of everything!

§31.3   **Imperative**

(a) **Sachons-le bien!** / Let's be well aware of it!

(b) **Sachez que votre père vient de mourir** / Be informed that your father has just died.

§32.   SAVOIR AND CONNAÎTRE

The main difference between the meaning of these two verbs in the sense of *to know* is that **connaître** means merely to be acquainted with; for example, to be acquainted with a person, a city, a neighborhood, a country, the title of a book, the works of an author.

EXAMPLES:

Savez-vous la réponse? / Do you know the answer?

Savez-vous l'heure qu'il est? / **Savez-vous quelle heure il est?** / Do you know what time it is?

Connaissez-vous cette dame? / Do you know this lady?

Connaissez-vous Paris? / Do you know Paris?

Connaissez-vous les oeuvres de Proust? / Do you know the works of Proust?

Connaissez-vous ce livre? / Do you know this book?

§33.   ENTENDRE AND COMPRENDRE

The main difference between the meaning of these two verbs is that **entendre** means *to hear* and **comprendre** *to understand*. Sometimes **entendre** can mean *to understand* or *to mean*:

EXAMPLES:

Entendez-vous la musique? / Do you hear the music?

Comprenez-vous la leçon? / Do you understand the lesson?

"M'entends-tu?!" dit la mère à l'enfant. "Ne fais pas cela!" / "Do you understand me?!" says the mother to the child. "Don't do that!"

Je ne comprends pas le docteur Fu Manchu parce qu'il ne parle que chinois / I do not understand Dr. Fu Manchu because he speaks only Chinese.

Qu'entendez-vous par là?? / What do you mean by that?? / What are you insinuating by that remark??

Je comprends vos paroles mais je ne vous entends pas; expliquez-vous, s'il vous plaît / I understand your words but I don't understand you; explain yourself, please.

§34.   SI CLAUSE: A SUMMARY

WHEN THE VERB IN THE SI CLAUSE IS:	THE VERB IN THE MAIN OR RESULT CLAUSE IS:
present indicative	present indicative, or future, or imperative
imperfect indicative	conditional
pluperfect indicative	conditional perfect

§34.1   NOTE: By **si** we mean *if*. Sometimes **si** can mean *whether* and in that case, this summary of what tenses are used with **si** (meaning *if*) does not apply. When **si** means *whether*, there are no restrictions about the tenses. By the way, the sequence of tenses with a **si** clause is the same in English with an *if* clause.

§34.2   EXAMPLES:

Si elle arrive, je pars / If she arrives, I'm leaving.

Si elle arrive, je partirai / If she arrives, I will leave.

Si elle arrive, partez! / If she arrives, leave!

Si Paul étudiait, il recevrait de meilleures notes / If Paul studied, he would receive better grades.

Si Georges avait étudié, il aurait reçu de bonnes notes / If George had studied, he would have received good grades.

§35.   SUBJUNCTIVE

The subjunctive is not a tense; it is a mood, or mode. Usually, when we speak in French or English, we use the indicative mood. We use the subjunctive mood in French for certain reasons. The following are the principal reasons.

§35.1   After certain conjunctions

When the following conjunctions introduce a new clause, the verb in that new clause is normally in the subjunctive mood:

à condition que   on condition that; **Je vous prêterai l'argent à condition que vous me le rendiez le plutôt possible**.

à moins que   unless; **Je pars à six heures précises à moins qu'il (n') y ait un orage.** [Expletive **ne** is optional; see §27.—27.8.]

afin que   in order that, so that; **Je vous explique clairement afin que vous compreniez.**

attendre que   to wait until; **Attendez que je finisse mon dîner.**

au cas que   in case; **Au cas qu'il vienne, je pars tout de suite.**

autant que   **Autant que je le sache . . .** / As far as I know . . .

avant que   before; **Ne me dites rien avant qu'il vienne.** [Expletive **ne** is optional; see §27.—27.8.]

bien que   although; **Bien que Madame Cartier soit malade, elle a toujours bon appétit.**

de crainte que   for fear that; **La mère a dit à sa petite fille de rester dans la maison de crainte qu'elle ne se fasse mal dans la rue.** [Expletive **ne** is required; see §27.—27.8.]

de façon que   so that, in a way that, in such a way that; **Barbara étudie de façon qu'elle puisse réussir.**

de manière que   so that, in a way that, in such a way that; **Joseph travaille dans la salle de classe de manière qu'il puisse réussir.**

de peur que   for fear that; **Je vous dis de rester dans la maison aujourd'hui de peur que vous ne glissiez sur la glace.** [Expletive **ne** is required; see §27.—27.8.]

de sorte que   so that, in a way that, in such a way that; **Nettoyez la chambre de sorte que tout soit propre.**

en attendant que   until; **Nous allons rester ici en attendant qu'elle vienne.**

en cas que   in case, in case that, in the event that; **En cas qu'il vienne, je pars tout de suite.**

jusqu'à ce que   until; **Je vais attendre jusqu'à ce que vous finissiez.**

malgré que   although; **Malgré que Madame Cartier soit malade, elle a toujours bon appétit.** (NOTE: prefer to use **bien que,** as in the example given with **bien que** above on this list)

pour autant que   as far as, as much as; **Pour autant que je me souvienne . . .** / As far as I remember. (NOTE: prefer to use **autant que,** as in the example given with **autant que** above on this list)

pour que   in order that, so that; **Expliquez-vous mieux, s'il vous plaît, pour que je comprenne.**

pourvu que provided that; **Vous pouvez parler librement pourvu que vous me laissiez faire de même.**

que . . . ou non whether . . . or not; **Qu'il vienne ou non, cela m'est égal.**

quoique although; **Quoiqu'il soit vieux, il a l'agilité d'un jeune homme.**

sans que without; **Ne sortez pas sans que je le sache** / Do not leave without my knowing it.

soit que . . . ou que whether . . . or; either . . . or; **Soit qu'elle comprenne ou qu'elle ne comprenne pas, cela m'est égal.**

soit que . . . soit que whether . . . or whether; **Soit que vous le fassiez, soit que vous ne le fassiez pas, cela m'est égal.**

tâcher que to try to, to attempt to; **Tâchez que le bébé soit bien nourri.**

veiller à ce que to see to it that; **Veillez à ce que la porte soit fermée à clef pendant mon absence.**

§35.2 After indefinite expressions

où que wherever; **Où que vous alliez, cela ne m'importe pas.**

quel que whatever; **Je vous aiderai, quelles que soient vos ambitions** / I will help you, whatever your ambitions may be. (NOTE that the appropriate form of **quel** is needed in this indefinite expression because you are dealing with a noun (**ambitions**) and **quel** functions as an adjective)

qui que whoever; **Qui que vous soyez, je ne veux pas vous écouter** / Whoever you are (Whoever you may be), I don't want to listen to you.

quoi que whatever, no matter what; **Quoi que cet homme dise, je ne le crois pas** / No matter what this man says, I do not believe him.

si + adj. + que however; **Si bavarde qu'elle soit, elle ne dit jamais de bêtises** / However talkative she may be, she never says anything stupid.

§35.3 After an indefinite antecedent

See **§29.44** for a brief definition of an antecedent.

The reason why the subjunctive is needed after an indefinite antecedent is that the person or thing desired may possibly not exist; or, if it does exist, you may never find it.

(a) **Je cherche une personne qui soit honnête** / I am looking for a person who is honest.

(b) **Je cherche un appartement qui ne soit pas trop cher** / I am looking for an apartment that is not too expensive.

(c) **Connaissez-vous quelqu'un qui puisse réparer mon téléviseur une fois pour toutes?** / Do you know someone who can repair my TV set once and for all?

(d) **Y a-t-il un élève qui comprenne le subjonctif?** / Is there a student who understands the subjunctive?

BUT IF THE PERSON OR THING YOU ARE LOOKING FOR DOES EXIST, USE THE INDICATIVE MOOD:

(a) **J'ai trouvé une personne qui est honnête.**
(b) **J'ai un appartement qui n'est pas trop cher.**
(c) **Je connais une personne qui peut réparer votre téléviseur.**

§35.4 After a superlative expressing an opinion

Those superlatives expressing an opinion are commonly: **le seul, la seule** (the only), **le premier, la première** (the first), **le dernier, la dernière** (the last), **le plus petit, la plus petite** (the smallest), **le plus grand, la plus grande,** *etc.*

(a) **A mon avis, Marie est la seule étudiante qui comprenne le subjonctif parfaitement.**

(b) **Selon mon opinion, Henriette est la plus jolie élève que j'aie jamais vue.**

§35.5   After **Que**, meaning *let* or *may* to express a wish, an order, a command in the 3rd person singular or plural

   (a) **Qu'il parte!** / Let him leave!

   (b) **Que Dieu nous pardonne!** / May God forgive us! (NOTE that the form *pardonne* is the same in the 3rd pers. subjunctive as in the indicative)

   (c) **Qu'ils s'en aillent!** / Let them go away!
        NOTE that what is understood in front of **Que** here is (**Je veux**) **que** . . .

§35.6   **After certain impersonal expressions**

   c'est dommage que   it's a pity that, it's too bad that; **C'est dommage qu'elle soit morte.**

   il est à souhaiter que   it is to be desired that; **Il est à souhaiter qu'elle soit guérie.**

   il est bizarre que   it is odd that; **Il est bizarre qu'il soit parti sans rien dire.**

   il est bon que   it is good that; **Il est bon que vous restiez au lit.**

   il est convenable que   it is fitting (proper) that; **Il est convenable qu'il vienne me voir.**

   il est douteux que   it is doubtful that; **Il est douteux qu'il soit présent au concert ce soir.**

   il est essentiel que   it is essential that; **Il est essentiel que vous veniez me voir le plus tôt possible.**

   il est étonnant que   it is astonishing that; **Il est étonnant qu'elle soit sortie sans rien dire.**

   il est étrange que   it is strange that; **Il est étrange qu'il n'ait pas répondu à ta lettre.**

   il est faux que   it is false (it is not true) that; **Il est faux que vous ayez vu ma soeur dans ce cabaret.**

   il est heureux que   it is fortunate that; **Il est très heureux que Madame Piquet soit guérie.**

   il est honteux que   it is shameful (a shame) that; **Il est honteux que vous trichiez.**

   il est important que   it is important that; **Il est important que vous arriviez à l'heure.**

   il est impossible que   it is impossible that; **Il est impossible que je sois chez vous avant trois heures.**

   il est juste que   it is right that; **Il est juste que le criminel soit puni pour son crime.**

   il est naturel que   it is natural that; **Il est naturel qu'on ait peur dans un moment dangereux.**

   il est nécessaire que   it is necessary that; **Il est nécessaire que tu finisses la leçon de français avant d'aller au cinéma.**

   il est possible que   it is possible that; **Il est possible que Madame Paquet soit déjà partie.**

   il est rare que   it is rare that; **Il est rare qu'elle sorte.**

   il est regrettable que   it is regrettable that; **Il est regrettable que cet homme riche ait perdu tout au jeu.**

   il est surprenant que   it is surprising that; **Il est surprenant que tu n'aies pas fait ton devoir aujourd'hui.**

   il est temps que   it is time that; **Il est temps que tu fasses tes devoirs tous les jours.**

   il est urgent que   it is urgent that; **Il est urgent que le docteur vienne immédiatement.**

   il faut que   it is necessary that; **Il faut que tu sois ici à neuf heures précises.**

   il importe que   it is important that; **Il importe que tu me dises toute la vérité.**

   il se peut que   it may be that; **Il se peut qu'elle soit sortie.**

   il semble que   it seems that, it appears that; **Il semble que Madame Gervaise soit déjà partie.**

   il suffit que   it is enough that, it suffices that; **Il suffit qu'il soit informé tout simplement.**

   il vaut mieux que   it is better that; **Il vaut mieux que vous soyez présent quand le docteur est ici.**

§35.7   **After the following impersonal expressions** (in English, the subject is *It*) used in the negative or interrogative because they suggest some kind of doubt, uncertainty, hesitation . . .

Il ne me semble pas que . . .	Il ne paraît pas que . . .
Me semble-t-il que . . . ?	Paraît-il que . . . ?
Il n'est pas clair que . . .	Il n'est pas vrai que . . .
Est-il clair que . . . ?	Est-il vrai que . . . ?
Il n'est pas évident que . . .	Il n'est pas sûr que . . .
Est-il évident que . . . ?	Est-il sûr que . . . ?
Il n'est pas certain que . . .	Il n'est pas probable que . . .
Est-il certain que . . . ?	Est-il probable que . . . ?

§35.8   **After certain verbs expressing doubt, emotion, wishing**

aimer que . . .   to like that . . .
aimer mieux que . . .   to prefer that . . .
s'attendre à ce que . . .   to expect that . . .
avoir peur que . . .   to be afraid that . . . [expletive **ne** is required; see §27.—§27.8.]
craindre que . . .   to fear that . . . [expletive **ne** is required; see §27.—§27.8.]
défendre que . . .   to forbid that . . .
désirer que . . .   to desire that . . .
douter que . . .   to doubt that . . .
empêcher que . . .   to prevent that . . .
s'étonner que . . .   to be astonished that . . .
s'étonner de ce que . . .   to be astonished at the fact that . . .
être bien aise que . . .   to be pleased that . . .
être content que . . .   to be glad that . . .
être désolé que . . .   to be distressed that . . .
être étonné que . . .   to be astonished that . . .
être heureux que . . .   to be happy that . . .
être joyeux que . . .   to be joyful that . . .
être malheureux que . . .   to be unhappy that . . .
être ravi que . . .   to be delighted that . . .
être surpris que . . .   to be surprised that . . .
être triste que . . .   to be sad that . . .
exiger que . . .   to demand that . . .
se fâcher que . . .   to be angry that . . .
insister que . . .   to insist that . . .
ordonner que . . .   to order that . . .
préférer que . . .   to prefer that . . .
regretter que . . .   to regret that . . .
souhaiter que . . .   to wish that . . .
tenir à ce que . . .   to insist upon . . .
trembler que . . .   to tremble that . . . [expletive **ne** is required; see §27.—§27.8.]
vouloir que . . .   to want that . . .

§35.9   SOME EXAMPLES:

J'aimerais que vous restiez ici / I would like you to stay here.
J'aime mieux que vous restiez ici / I prefer that you stay here.
Je m'attends à ce qu'elle vienne immédiatement / I expect her to come immediately.
J'ai peur qu'il ne soit malade / I am afraid that he may be sick. [expletive **ne** is required; see §27.—§27.8.]
Je crains qu'elle ne soit gravement malade / I fear that she may be seriously ill. [expletive **ne** is required; see §27.—§27.8.]
Je m'étonne qu'elle ne soit pas venue me voir / I am astonished that she has not come to see me.

Je m'étonne de ce qu'il ne soit pas parti / I am astonished (at the fact that) he has not left.

Ta mère est contente que tu sois heureux / Your mother is glad that you are happy.

Madame Poulet est désolée que son mari ait perdu toute sa fortune / Mrs. Poulet is distressed that her husband has lost his entire fortune.

§35.10   After verbs of believing and thinking, such as **croire**, **penser**, **trouver** (meaning *to think, to have an impression*), and **espérer** when used in the negative OR interrogative but not when both interrogative AND negative . . .

§35.11   EXAMPLES:

Je ne pense pas qu'il soit coupable / I don't think that he is guilty. **Croyez-vous qu'il dise la vérité?** / Do you believe he is telling the truth?

BUT: **Ne croyez-vous pas qu'il dit la vérité?** / Don't you think that he is telling the truth?

Trouvez-vous qu'il y ait beaucoup de crimes dans la société d'aujourd'hui? / Do you find (think) that there are many crimes in today's society?

BUT: **Ne trouvez-vous pas que ce livre est intéressant?** / Don't you think (OR: Don't you find) that this book is interesting?

§36.   VOULOIR

The verb **vouloir,** has special uses and meanings. For the complete conjugation of **vouloir,** as well as other commonly used regular and irregular verbs, see §40. farther on.

§36.1   **Present tense**

(a) **Je veux aller en France** / I want to go to France.

(b) **Je veux bien sortir avec vous ce soir** / I am willing to go out with you this evening.

(c) **Voulez-vous bien vous asseoir, madame?** / Would you be good enough to sit down, madam?

(d) **Que veut dire ce mot?** / What does this word mean?

(e) **Que voulez-vous dire, monsieur?** / What do you mean, sir?

(f) **Qu'est-ce que cela veut dire?** / What does that mean?

(g) **Je lui en veux** / I have a grudge against him. (The idiomatic expression here is **en vouloir à qqn** / to bear a grudge against someone)

§36.2   **Conditional**

(a) **Je voudrais un café-crème, s'il vous plaît** / I would like a coffee with cream, please.

§36.3   **Imperative**

(a) **Veuillez vous asseoir, madame** / Kindly sit down, madam.

(b) **Veuillez accepter mes meilleurs sentiments** / Please accept my best regards.

(NOTE here that **veuillez** is followed by the infinitive form of a verb.)

§37.   WEATHER EXPRESSIONS

Quel temps fait-il? / What's the weather like?

§37.1   (a) With **Il fait** . . .

Il fait beau / The weather is fine; The weather is beautiful.
Il fait beau temps / The weather is beautiful.
Il fait bon / It's nice; It's good.
Il fait brumeux / It's misty.

Il fait chaud / It's warm.
Il fait clair / It is clear.
Il fait de l'orage / It's storming; there is a thunderstorm.
Il fait des éclairs / It is lightning.
Il fait doux / It's mild.
Il fait du soleil / It's sunny. (You can also say: **Il fait soleil.**)
Il fait du tonnerre / It's thundering. (You can also say: **Il tonne.**)
Il fait du vent / It's windy.
Il fait frais / It is cool.
Il fait froid / It's cold.
Il fait glissant / It is slippery.
Il fait humide / It's humid.
Il fait jour / It is daylight.
Il fait lourd / The weather is sultry.
Il fait mauvais / The weather is bad.
Il fait nuit / It is dark.
Il fait sec / It's dry.
Il fait une chaleur épouvantable / It's awfully (frightfully) hot.

§37.2   (b) With **Il fait un temps . . .**

Il fait un temps affreux / The weather is frightful.
Il fait un temps calme / The weather is calm.
Il fait un temps couvert / The weather is cloudy.
Il fait un temps de saison / The weather is seasonal.
Il fait un temps épouvantable / The weather is frightful.
Il fait un temps lourd / It's muggy.
Il fait un temps magnifique / The weather is magnificent.
Il fait un temps pourri / The weather is rotten.
Il fait un temps serein / The weather is serene.
Il fait un temps superbe / The weather is superb.

§37.3   (c) With **Le temps + verb . . .**

Le temps menace / The weather is threatening.
Le temps s'éclaircit / The weather is clearing up.
Le temps se gâte / The weather is getting bad.
Le temps se met au beau / The weather is getting beautiful.
Le temps se met au froid / It's getting cold.
Le temps se radoucit / The weather is getting nice again.
Le temps se rafraîchit / The weather is getting cool.

§37.4   (d) With **Le ciel est . . .**

Le ciel est bleu / The sky is blue.
Le ciel est calme / The sky is calm.
Le ciel est couvert / The sky is cloudy.
Le ciel est gris / The sky is gray.
Le ciel est serein / The sky is serene.

§37.5   (e) With other verbs

Il gèle / It's freezing.
Il grêle / It's hailing.
Il neige / It's snowing.
Il pleut / It's raining.
Il tombe de la grêle / It's hailing.
Il va grêler / It's going to hail.

Il tonne / It's thundering.

Je sors par tous les temps / I go out in all kinds of weather.

Quelle est la prévision de la météo pour aujourd' hui? / What is the weather forecast for today? (OR: **Quelles sont les prévisions de la météo pour aujourd' hui?**)

§38. SYNONYMS

In **§3.** I gave you many antonyms that you ought to know. I suggested that one very good way to increase your French vocabulary is to think of an antonym or synonym for every word in French that you already know or that you come across in your readings.

§38.1 Listed below are some basic synonyms that you certainly ought to know because they are really for review. Do you know one very good way to study them? Let me give you a suggestion. Take a 3 × 5 card and cover the words in English on the right side. Look at the first French line of synonyms. Read them in French out loud. Then give the English meaning aloud. If you do not remember the English meaning, move the 3 × 5 card down so you can see the printed English word or words. Then cover the English again. Then repeat the French words again that are on the left side. Then give the English meaning. If you still do not remember the English meaning, take another peek at the English and start over again. Do this for each line of French synonyms and for the antonyms, too, given in **§3.1** and **§3.2.** What you need to concentrate on is recognizing what the French words mean.

Very frequently, in reading comprehension passages the correct answer is one that contains either a synonym or antonym of the key words in the reading passage. For example, if the key word is **fatigué** in a reading passage and the sentence states that Paul was unable to do something because he was **fatigué**, the correct answer among the multiple choices may be a synonym, for example, **épuisé**; the correct answer may state something like: **Pierre n'a pas pu le faire parce qu'il était épuisé.** Of course, in the reading of the passage you surely understood **fatigué**, but could you recognize **épuisé** as a synonym of that word to spot the correct answer?

§38.2 Here they are; know these.

accoster *v.*, **aborder**	to come up to, to approach
adresse *n.f.*, **habileté**	skill, expertness
aide *n.f.*, **secours** , *n.m.*	aid, help
aimer mieux *v.*, **préférer**	to like better, to prefer
aliment *n.m.*, **nourriture** *n.f.*	food, nourishment
aller *v.*, **se porter**	to feel, to be (health)
aller *v.*, **se rendre**	to go
amas *n.m.*, **tas**	heap, pile
anneau *n.m.*, **bague** *n.f.*	ring (on finger)
arriver *v.*, **se passer**	to happen, to occur
aussitôt que *conj.*, **dès que**	as soon as
auteur *n.m.*, **écrivain**	author, writer
bâtiment *n.m.*, **édifice**	building, edifice
bâtir *v.*, **construire**	to build, to construct
beaucoup de *adv.*, **bien des**	many
besogne *n.f.*, **tâche**	work, piece of work, task
bienveillance *n.f.*, **bonté**	kindness, goodness
bref, brève *adj.*, **court, courte**	brief, short
calepin *n.m.*, **carnet**	memo book, note book
calmer *v.*, **apaiser**	to calm, to appease
casser *v.*, **rompre** *v.*, **briser**	to break
causer *v.*, **parler**	to chat, to talk
centre *n.m.*, **milieu**	center, middle
certain, certaine *adj.*, **sûr, sûre**	certain, sure
cesser *v.*, **arrêter**	to cease, to stop
chagrin *n.m.*, **souci**	sorrow, trouble, care, concern
châtier *v.*, **punir**	to chastise, to punish

chemin *n.m.*, route *n.f.*	road, route
commencer à + *inf.*, *v.* se mettre à	to commence, to begin, to start + inf.
conseil *n.m.*, avis	counsel, advice, opinion
content, contente *adj.*, heureux, heureuse	content, happy
de façon que *conj.*, de manière que	so that, in such a way
décéder *v.*, mourir	to die
dédain *n.m.*, mépris	disdain, scorn
dégoût *n.m.*, répugnance *n.f.*	disgust, repugnance
dérober *v.*, voler	to rob, to steal
désirer *v.*, vouloir	to desire, to want
disputer *v.*, contester	to dispute, to argue, to contest
docteur *n.m.*, médecin	doctor, physician
dorénavant *adv.*, désormais	henceforth, from now on
dur, dure *adj.*, insensible	hard, callous, unfeeling, insensitive
embrasser *v.*, donner un baiser	to embrace, to hug, to give a kiss
employer *v.*, se servir de	to employ, to use, to make use of
éperdu, éperdue *adj.*, agité, agitée	distracted, confused, troubled
épouvanter *v.*, effrayer	to frighten, to terrify, to scare
erreur *n.f.*, faute	error, fault, mistake
espèce *n.f.*, sorte	species, type, kind, sort
essayer de *v.*, tâcher de + inf.	to try, to attempt + inf.
étaler *v.*, exposer	to display, to show, to expose
étrennes *n.f.*, cadeau *n.m.*	Christmas gifts, present, gift
façon *n.f.*, manière	way, manner
fainéant, fainéante *adj.*, paresseux, paresseuse	a do nothing, idler, lazy
fameux, fameuse *adj.*, célèbre	famous, celebrated
fatigué, fatiguée *adj.*, épuisé, épuisée	tired, fatigued, exhausted
favori, favorite *adj.*, préféré, préférée	favorite, preferred
femme *n.f.*, épouse	wife, spouse
fin *n.f.*, bout *n.m.*	end
finir *v.*, terminer	to finish, to end, to terminate
flot *n.m.*, onde *n.f.*	wave (water)
frémir *v.*, trembler	to shiver, to quiver, to tremble
galette *n.f.*, gâteau *n.m.*	cake
gaspiller *v.*, dissiper	to waste, to dissipate
gâter *v.*, abîmer	to spoil, to ruin, to damage
glace *n.f.*, miroir *n.m.*	hand mirror, mirror
grossier, grossière *adj.*, vulgaire	gross, vulgar, cheap, common
habiter *v.*, demeurer	to live (in), to dwell, to inhabit
haïr *v.*, détester	to hate, to detest
image *n.f.*, tableau *n.m.*	image, picture
indiquer *v.*, montrer	to indicate, to show
jadis *adv.*, autrefois	formerly, in times gone by
jeu *n.m.*, divertissement	game, amusement
jeûne *n.m.*, abstinence *n.f.*	fasting, abstinence
labourer *v.*, travailler	to labor, to work
laisser *v.*, permettre	to allow, to permit
las, lasse *adj.*, fatigué, fatiguée	weary, tired
lier *v.*, attacher	to tie, to attach
lieu *n.m.*, endroit	place, spot, location
logis *n.m.*, habitation *n.f.*	lodging, dwelling
lueur *n.f.*, lumière	gleam, light
lutter *v.*, combattre	to struggle, to fight, to combat
maître *n.m.*, instituteur	master, teacher, instructor
maîtresse *n.f.*, institutrice	mistress, teacher, instructor
mari *n.m.*, époux	husband, spouse
mauvais, mauvaise *adj.*, méchant, méchante	bad, mean, nasty
mêler *v.*, mélanger	to mix, to blend
mener *v.*, conduire	to lead, to take (someone)
mignon, mignonne *adj.*, délicat, délicate, gentil, gentille	dainty, delicate, nice

mince *adj.*, grêle	thin, slender, skinny
naïf, naïve *adj.*, ingénu, ingénue	naive, simple, innocent
net, nette *adj.*, propre	neat, clean
noces *n.f.*, mariage *n.m.*	wedding, marriage
oeuvre *n.f.*, travail *n.m.*	work
ombre *n.f.*, obscurité	shade, shadow, darkness
ombrelle *n.f.*, parasol *n.m.*	sunshade, parasol, beach umbrella
oreiller *n.m.*, coussin	pillow (for sleep), cushion
parce que *conj.*, car	because, for
pareil, pareille *adj.*, égal, égale	similar, equivalent, equal
parmi *prep.*, entre	among, between
parole *n.f.*, mot *n.m.*	spoken word, written word
parvenir à *v.*, réussir à	to succeed, to attain
pays *n.m.*, nation *n.f.*	country, nation
pensée *n.f.*, idée	thought, idea
penser *v.*, réfléchir	to think, to reflect
penser à *v.*, songer à	to think of, to dream of
pourtant *adv.*, cependant, néanmoins	however, nevertheless
professeur *n.m.*, maître, maîtresse	professor, teacher
puis *adv.*, ensuite	then, afterwards
quand *conj.*, lorsque	when
quelquefois *adv.*, parfois	sometimes, at times
rameau *n.m.*, branche *n.f.*	branch (tree)
se rappeler *v.*, se souvenir de	to recall, to remember
rater *v.*, échouer	to miss, to fail
récolter *v.*, recueillir	to gather, to collect
rendre *v.*, retourner, aller	to return, to go
rester *v.*, demeurer	to stay, to remain
réussir à *v.*, parvenir à	to succeed, to attain
secours *n.m.*, aide, *n.f.*	help, aid
sérieux, sérieuse *adj.*, grave	serious, grave
seulement *adv.*, ne + verb + que	only
soin *n.m.*, attention *n.f.*	care, attention
soulier *n.m.*, chaussure *n.f.*	shoe, footwear
sud *n.m.*, Midi	south
tout de suite *adv.*, immédiatement	right away, immediately
triste *adj.*, malheureux, malheureuse	sad, unhappy
verser *v.*, répandre	to pour, to spread
vêtements *n.m.*, habits	clothes, clothing
visage *n.m.*, figure *n.f.*	face
vite *adv.*, rapidement	quickly, rapidly

§39.   VERBS

§39.1   Introduction

A verb is where the action is! A verb is a word that expresses an action (like *go, eat, write*) or a state of being (like *think, believe, be*). Tense means time. French and English verb tenses are divided into three main groups of time: past, present and future. A verb tense shows if an action or state of being took place, is taking place or will take place.

French and English verbs are also used in four moods (or modes). Mood has to do with the *way* a person regards an action or a state that he expresses. For example, a person may merely make a statement or ask a question—this is the Indicative Mood, which we use most of the time in French and English. A person may say that he *would do* something if something else were possible or that he *would have done* something if something else had been possible—this is the Conditional Mood. A person may use a verb *in such a way* that he indicates a wish, a fear, a regret, a supposition, or something of this sort—this is the Subjunctive Mood. The Subjunctive

Mood is used in French much more than in English. A person may command that something be done—this is the Imperative Mood.

There are six tenses in English: Present, Past, Future, Present Perfect, Past Perfect, and Future Perfect. The first three are simple tenses. The other three are compound tenses and are based on the simple tenses. In French, however, there are fourteen tenses, seven of which are simple and seven of which are compound.

Beginning with **§39.70ff.** farther on, the tenses and moods are given in French and the equivalent name or names in English are given in parentheses. Although some of the names given in English are not considered to be tenses (for there are only six), they are given for the purpose of identification as they are related to the French names. The comparison includes only the essential points you need to know about the meanings and uses of French verb tenses and moods as related to English usage. I shall use examples to illustrate their meanings and uses.

But first, here are some essential points you need to know about French verbs:

§39.2   Agreement of subject and verb

A subject and verb form must agree in person and number. By *person* is meant 1st, 2nd, or 3rd; by *number* is meant singular or plural. To get a picture of the three persons, see **Subject pronouns, §29.12.** This may seem elementary and obvious to you, but too often students become careless on tests and they neglect to watch for the correct ending of a verb form to agree with the subject in person and number. You must be aware of this.

§39.3   Agreement of subject and reflexive pronoun of a reflexive verb

A subject and reflexive pronoun must agree in person and number. Here, too, students often are careless on tests and neglect to select the proper reflexive pronoun that matches the subject. To get a picture of the correct reflexive pronoun that goes with the subject, according to the person you need (1st, 2nd, or 3rd, singular or plural), see **Reflexive pronouns, §29.36.**

§39.4   Agreement of subject and past participle of an être verb

The past participle of an **être** verb agrees with the subject in gender and number:

Elle est allée au cinéma / She went to the movies / She has gone to the movies.
Elles sont allées au cinéma / They went to the movies / They have gone to the movies.

§39.5   Agreement of preceding reflexive pronoun and past participle of a reflexive verb

Elle s'est lavée / She washed herself.
Elles se sont lavées / They washed themselves.

NOTE that an agreement on the past participle of a reflexive verb is made here with the preceding reflexive pronoun because the pronoun serves as a preceding direct object. But if there is an obvious direct object mentioned, there is no agreement because the reflexive pronoun, in such a case, serves as the indirect object pronoun.

§39.6   No agreement of preceding reflexive pronoun and past participle of a reflexive verb

Elle s'est lavé les mains / She washed her hands.
Elles se sont lavé les mains / They washed their hands.

§39.7

NOTE that there is no agreement on the past participle of a reflexive verb if the preceding reflexive pronoun serves as an indirect object pronoun. How do you know when the reflexive pronoun is a direct object or indirect object? If there is an obvious direct object mentioned, as in these two examples (**les mains**), the reflexive pronoun must be the indirect object pronoun—and we do not make an agreement on a past participle with an indirect object, whether it precedes or follows—ever.

§39.8

NOTE also:

Elles se sont regardées / They looked at each other.

Here, the reflexive pronoun **se** is the preceding direct object. How do you know? There is no other obvious direct object mentioned, so what they looked at was **se** (each other); of course, you have to look at the subject to see what the gender and number is of the reflexive pronoun **se** in the sentence you are dealing with. The action of the verb is reciprocal.

§39.9   This same sentence, **Elles se sont regardées**, might also mean: They looked at themselves. The principle of agreement is still the same. If you mean to say *They looked at each other*, in order to avoid two meanings, add **l'une et l'autre**. If more than two persons, add **les unes les autres**.

§39.10   Remember that the verb **regarder** in French means *to look at* in English, and the prep. *at* is not expressed with **à** in French; it is, you might say, included in the verb—that is why we are dealing with the reflexive pronoun as a direct object here, not an indirect object pronoun.

§39.11   And NOTE:

Elles se sont parlé au téléphone / They talked to each other on the telephone.

Here, the reflexive pronoun **se** is obviously an indirect object pronoun because they spoke *to* each other; **parler à** is what you are dealing with here. And remember that no agreement is made on a past participle with an indirect object. The action of the verb is reciprocal.

§39.12   **Agreement of past participle of an avoir verb with a preceding direct object**

§39.13   The past participle of an **avoir** verb agrees with the preceding direct object (if there is one) in gender and number:

§39.14   **J'ai vu Jeanne au concert** / I saw Joan at the concert.

There is no agreement here on the past participle (**vu**) of this **avoir** verb because there is no preceding direct object. The direct object in this example comes *after* the verb and it is **Jeanne**.

§39.15   **Je l'ai vue au concert** / I saw her at the concert.

There is an agreement on the past participle (**vue**) of this **avoir** verb because there is a preceding direct object, which is **l'** (**la**, with **a** dropped). Agreement is made in gender and number.

§39.16   **J'ai vu les jeunes filles au concert** / I saw the girls at the concert.

There is no agreement here on the past participle (**vu**) of this **avoir** verb because there is no preceding direct object. The direct object in this example comes *after* the verb and it is **les jeunes filles**.

§39.17   **Aimez-vous les fleurs que je vous ai données?** / Do you like the flowers which (*or* that) I gave you?

There is an agreement on the past participle (**données**) of this **avoir** verb because there is a preceding direct object, which is **les fleurs**; the relative pronoun **que** refers to **les fleurs**. Since this noun direct object precedes the verb, we must make an agreement on the past participle in gender and number. A preceding direct object, therefore, can be a pronoun or a noun.

§39.18   **Quels films avez-vous vus?** / What films did you see?

There is an agreement on the past participle (**vus**) of this **avoir** verb because there is a preceding direct object, which is **films**, a masc. pl. noun.

§39.19   **Avez-vous mangé les pâtisseries?** / Did you eat the pastries?

There is no agreement here on the past participle (**mangé**) of this **avoir** verb because there is no preceding direct object. The direct object in this example comes *after* the verb and it is **les pâtisseries**.

§39.20   **Oui, je les ai mangées** / Yes, I ate them.

There is an agreement on the past participle (**mangées**) of this **avoir** verb because there is a preceding direct object, which is **les**, and it refers to something fem., plural, possibly **les pâtisseries**, in §39.19 above.

§39.21   **Avez-vous mangé assez de pâtisseries?** / Did you eat enough pastries?

There is no agreement here on the past participle (**mangé**) of this **avoir** verb because there is no preceding direct object.

§39.22   **Oui, j'en ai mangé assez** / Yes, I ate enough of them.

There is no agreement on the past participle (**mangé**) of this **avoir** verb because the preceding direct object is, in this sentence, the pronoun **en**. We do not normally make an agreement with **en**, whether it precedes or follows. This is an exception.

§39.23   **Formation of past participle**

The past participle is regularly formed from the infinitive:
—**er** ending verbs, drop the —**er** and add **é**: donner, donné
—**ir** ending verbs, drop the —**ir** and add **i**: finir, fini
—**re** ending verbs, drop the —**re** and add **u**: vendre, vendu

§39.24   **Common irregular past participles**

INFINITIVE	PAST PARTICIPLE	INFINITIVE	PAST PARTICIPLE
apprendre	appris	naître	né
asseoir	assis	offrir	offert
avoir	eu	ouvrir	ouvert
boire	bu	paraître	paru
comprendre	compris	permettre	permis
conduire	conduit	plaire	plu
connaître	connu	pleuvoir	plu
construire	construit	pouvoir	pu
courir	couru	prendre	pris
couvrir	couvert	promettre	promis
craindre	craint	recevoir	reçu
croire	cru	revenir	revenu
devenir	devenu	rire	ri
devoir	dû	savoir	su
dire	dit	suivre	suivi
écrire	écrit	taire	tu
être	été	tenir	tenu
faire	fait	valoir	valu
falloir	fallu	venir	venu
lire	lu	vivre	vécu
mettre	mis	voir	vu
mourir	mort	vouloir	voulu

§39.25   **Auxiliary (or Helping) verbs, avoir and être**

The auxiliary verbs (also called *helping verbs*) **avoir and être** are used in any of the tenses + the past participle of the main verb you are using to form any of the compound tenses. You must be careful to choose the proper helping verb with the main verb that you are using. As you know, some verbs take **avoir** and some take **être** to form the compound tenses.

§39.26   Verbs conjugated with avoir or être to form a compound tense

§39.27   (a) Generally speaking, a French verb is conjugated with **avoir** to form a compound tense.

§39.28   (b) All reflexive verbs, such as **se laver**, are conjugated with **être**.

§39.29   (c) The following is a list of common non-reflexive verbs that are conjugated with **être**:

1. **aller** to go /**Elle est allée au cinéma.**
2. **arriver** to arrive /**Elle est arrivée.**
3. ***descendre** to go down, come down
   Elle est descendue vite.
   She came down quickly.
   BUT: ***Elle a descendu la valise.**
   She brought down the suitcase.
4. **devenir** to become /**Elle est devenue docteur.**
5. **entrer** to enter, go in, come in / **Elle est entrée.**
6. ***monter** to go up, come up
   Elle est montée lentement.
   She went up slowly.
   BUT: ***Elle a monté l'escalier.**
   She went up the stairs.
7. **mourir** to die /**Elle est morte.**
8. **naître** to be born /**Elle est née le premier octobre.**
9. **partir** to leave /**Elle est partie.**
10. ***passer** to go by, pass by
    Elle est passée par chez moi.
    She came by my house.

BUT: ***Elle m'a passé le sel.**
She passed me the salt.
AND: ***Elle a passé un examen.**
She took an exam.
11. ***rentrer** to go in again, to return (home)
    Elle est rentrée tôt.
    She returned home early.
    BUT: ***Elle a rentré le chat dans la maison.**
    She brought (took) the cat into the house.
12. **rester** to remain, stay/**Elle est restée chez elle.**
13. **retourner** to return, go back / **Elle est retournée.**
14. **revenir** to come back /**Elle est revenue.**
15. ***sortir** to go out
    Elle est sortie hier soir.
    She went out last night.
    BUT: ***Elle a sorti son mouchoir.**
    She took out her handkerchief.
16. **tomber** to fall /**Elle est tombée.**
17. **venir** to come /**Elle est venue.**

★ Some of these verbs, as noted above, are conjugated with **avoir** *if the verb is used in a transitive sense and has a direct object.*

(d) You must be sure to know the verbs in the above box—even if it means memorizing them!

§39.30   Transitive verbs

A transitive verb is a verb that takes a direct object. Such a verb is called *transitive* because the action passes over and directly affects something or someone in some way:

(a) **Je vois mon ami** / I see my friend.
(b) **Je ferme la fenêtre** / I am closing the window.
(c) **J'ai vu mes amis hier soir au concert** / I saw my friends last night at the concert.
(d) **Avant de sortir, le professeur a fermé les fenêtres de la salle de classe** / Before going out, the professor closed the windows of the classroom.

NOTE that in the above examples, the direct object is a noun in every sentence. Let me diagram them for you so you can see that a transitive verb performs an action that passes over and affects someone or something:

(a)

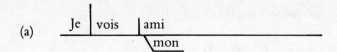

Here, **Je** is the subject; **vois** is the verb; **ami** is the direct object; **mon** is a possessive adjective that modifies **ami**.

(b)

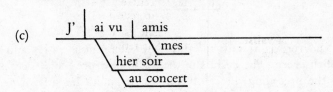

Here, **Je** is the subject; **ferme** is the verb; **fenêtre** is the direct object; **la** is the definite article fem. sing. that modifies **fenêtre**.

(c)

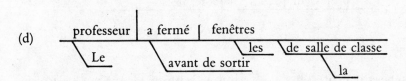

Here, **J'** is the subject; **ai vu** is the verb; **amis** is the direct object; **mes** is a possessive adjective that modifies **amis**; **hier soir** has an adverbial value that tells you *when* the action of the verb took place; **au concert** is an adverbial prepositional phrase that tells you *where* the action of the verb took place; hence, they are placed under the words they are related to.

(d)

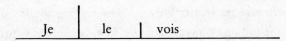

Here, **professeur** is the subject; **le** is the def. art. sing. masc. that modifies it so it is placed under it; **a fermé** is the verb; **avant de sortir** is an adverbial prepositional phrase that tells you *when* the action of the verb took place; **fenêtres** is the direct object; **les** is the def. art. plural that modifies the noun **fenêtres** so it is placed under it because it is related to it; **de la salle de classe** is an adjectival prepositional phrase that describes the noun **fenêtres**; **la** is the def. art. sing. fem. that modifies **salle de classe** and it is placed under it because it is related to it.

§39.31   When the direct object of the verb is a **pronoun**, it is placed **in front of** the verb most of the time; the only time it is placed **after** the verb is in the **affirmative imperative**. To get a picture of the position of pronoun direct objects, see Summaries of word order of elements in French sentences, beginning with §42. farther on.

§39.32   Let me diagram the same sentences above using them with **direct object pronouns** instead of direct object nouns:

(a) **Je le vois** / I see him.

Je	le	vois

The subject is **je**; the verb is **vois**; the direct object pronoun is **le** and it is placed directly in front of the verb.

(b) **Je la ferme** / I am closing it.

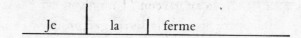

The subject is **je**; the verb is **ferme**; the direct object pronoun is **la** and it is placed directly in front of the verb.

(c) **Je les ai vus hier soir au concert** / I saw them last night at the concert.

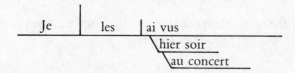

The subject is **je**; the verb is **ai vus**; the direct object pronoun is **les** and it is placed directly in front of the verb. The verb is in the **passé composé** and the past participle (**vus**) agrees with the preceding direct object, **les** (meaning **les amis**) in gender and number which, in this case, is masculine plural.

(d) **Avant de sortir, le professeur les a fermées** / Before leaving, the professor closed them.

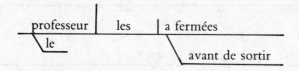

The subject is **professeur**; the verb is **a fermées**; the direct object pronoun is **les** and it is placed directly in front of the verb. The verb is in the **passé composé** and the past participle (**fermées**) agrees with the preceding direct object, **les** (meaning **les fenêtres**) in gender and number which, in this case, is feminine plural.

§39.33   Intransitive verbs

An intransitive verb is a verb that does not take a direct object. Such a verb is called **intransitive** because the action does not pass over and directly affect anyone or anything.

(a) **La maîtresse parle** / The teacher is talking.

(b) **Elle est partie tôt** / She left early.

(c) **Elles sont descendues vite** / They came down quickly.

(d) **Nous sommes montées lentement** / We went up slowly.

An intransitive verb takes an indirect object:

(a) **La maîtresse parle aux élèves** / The teacher is talking to the students.

Here, the indirect object noun is **élèves** because it is preceded by **aux** (to the).

(b) **La maîtresse leur parle** / The teacher is talking to them.

Here, the indirect object is the pronoun **leur**, meaning *to them*.

§39.34   Of course, **a transitive verb** can take an indirect object, too:

(a) **Je donne le livre au garçon** / I am giving the book to the boy.

Here, the direct object is **le livre**; **garçon** is the indirect object because it is indirectly affected and is preceded by **au** (to the).

(b) **Je le lui donne** / I am giving it to him.

Here, the direct object pronoun is **le** (meaning **le livre**) and the indirect object pronoun is **lui** (meaning *to him*).

To get a picture of the position of pronoun direct objects and pronoun indirect objects, see Summaries of word order of elements in French sentences, beginning with **§42.** farther on.

§39.35   Present participle

§39.36   Formation

The present participle is regularly formed in the following way: Take the **"nous"** form of the present indicative tense of the verb you have in mind, drop the ending **—ons** and add **—ant**. That ending is equivalent to **—ing** in English; for example:

chantons, chantant
finissons, finissant
vendons, vendant
mangeons, mangeant
allons, allant
travaillons, travaillant

§39.37   Common irregular present participles

avoir, ayant
être, étant
savoir, sachant

§39.38   En + present participle

The present participle in French is used primarily with the preposition **en**, meaning *on, upon, in, by, while*:

en chantant / while singing
en finissant / upon finishing, on finishing
en vendant / by selling, while selling, upon selling
en mangeant / upon eating, while eating
en voyageant / by traveling
en ayant / on having
en étant / on being, upon being
en sachant / upon knowing

§39.39   The present participle is sometimes used as an adjective:

une jeune fille charmante / a charming girl
un enfant amusant / an amusing child (boy)
une enfant amusante / an amusing child (girl)
des idées étonnantes / astonishing ideas

§39.40   **Table showing derivation of tenses of a verb conjugated with AVOIR**

Infinitif	*Participe Présent*	*Participe Passé*	*Présent de l'Indicatif*	*Passé Simple*
donner	**donnant**	**donné**	**je donne**	**je donnai**

FUTUR	IMPARFAIT DE L'INDICATIF	PASSÉ COMPOSÉ	PRÉSENT DE L'INDICATIF	PASSÉ SIMPLE
donner**ai**	donn**ais**	**ai** donné	donn**e**	donn**ai**
donner**as**	donn**ais**	**as** donné	donn**es**	donn**as**
donner**a**	donn**ait**	**a** donné	donn**e**	donn**a**
donner**ons**	donn**ions**	**avons** donné	donn**ons**	donn**âmes**
donner**ez**	donn**iez**	**avez** donné	donn**ez**	donn**âtes**
donner**ont**	donn**aient**	**ont** donné	donn**ent**	donn**èrent**

CONDITIONNEL		PLUS-QUE-PARFAIT DE L'INDICATIF	IMPÉRATIF	IMPARFAIT DU SUBJONCTIF
donner**ais**		**avais** donné	donn**e**	donn**asse**
donner**ais**		**avais** donné	donn**ons**	donn**asses**
donner**ait**		**avait** donné	donn**ez**	donn**ât**

			PRÉSENT DU SUBJONCTIF	
donner**ions**		**avions** donné	donn**e**	donn**assions**
donner**iez**		**aviez** donné	donn**es**	donn**assiez**
donner**aient**		**avaient** donné	donn**e**	donn**assent**

		PASSÉ ANTÉRIEUR		
		eus donné	donn**ions**	
		eus donné	donn**iez**	
		eut donné	donn**ent**	
		eûmes donné		
		eûtes donné		
		eurent donné		

FUTUR ANTÉRIEUR	CONDITIONNEL PASSÉ	PASSÉ DU SUBJONCTIF	PLUS-QUE-PARFAIT DU SUBJONCTIF
aurai donné	**aurais** donné	**aie** donné	**eusse** donné
auras donné	**aurais** donné	**aies** donné	**eusses** donné
aura donné	**aurait** donné	**ait** donné	**eût** donné
aurons donné	**aurions** donné	**ayons** donné	**eussions** donné
aurez donné	**auriez** donné	**ayez** donné	**eussiez** donné
auront donné	**auraient** donné	**aient** donné	**eussent** donné

§39.41 Table showing derivation of tenses of a verb conjugated with ÊTRE

Infinitif	*Participe Présent*	*Participe Passé*	*Présent de l'Indicatif*	*Passé Simple*
arriver	**arrivant**	**arrivé**	**j'arrive**	**J'arrivai**

FUTUR	IMPARFAIT DE L'INDICATIF	PASSÉ COMPOSÉ	PRÉSENT DE L'INDICATIF	PASSÉ SIMPLE
arriver**ai**	arriv**ais**	**suis** arrivé(e)	arriv**e**	arriv**ai**
arriver**as**	arriv**ais**	**es** arrivé(e)	arriv**es**	arriv**as**
arriver**a**	arriv**ait**	**est** arrivé(e)	arriv**e**	arriv**a**
arriver**ons**	arriv**ions**	**sommes** arrivé(e)s	arriv**ons**	arriv**âmes**
arriver**ez**	arriv**iez**	**êtes** arrivé(e)(s)	arriv**ez**	arriv**âtes**
arriver**ont**	arriv**aient**	**sont** arrivé(e)s	arriv**ent**	arriv**èrent**

CONDITIONNEL		PLUS-QUE-PARFAIT DE L'INDICATIF	IMPÉRATIF	IMPARFAIT DU SUBJONCTIF
arriver**ais**		**étais** arrivé(e)	arriv**e**	arriv**asse**
arriver**ais**		**étais** arrivé(e)	arriv**ons**	arriv**asses**
arriver**ait**		**était** arrivé(e)	arriv**ez**	arriv**ât**

			PRÉSENT DU SUBJONCTIF	
arriver**ions**		**étions** arrivé(e)s	arriv**e**	arriv**assions**
arriver**iez**		**étiez** arrivé(e)(s)	arriv**es**	arriv**assiez**
arriver**aient**		**étaient** arrivé(e)s	arriv**e**	arriv**assent**

		PASSÉ ANTÉRIEUR		
		fus arrivé(e)	arriv**ions**	
		fus arrivé(e)	arriv**iez**	
		fut arrivé(e)	arriv**ent**	
		fûmes arrivé(e)s		
		fûtes arrivé(e)(s)		
		furent arrivé(e)s		

FUTUR ANTÉRIEUR	CONDITIONNEL PASSÉ	PASSÉ DU SUBJONCTIF	PLUS-QUE-PARFAIT DU SUBJONCTIF
serai arrivé(e)	**serais** arrivé(e)	**sois** arrivé(e)	**fusse** arrivé(e)
seras arrivé(e)	**serais** arrivé(e)	**sois** arrivé(e)	**fusses** arrivé(e)
sera arrivé(e)	**serait** arrivé (e)	**soit** arrivé(e)	**fût** arrivé(e)
serons arrivé(e)s	**serions** arrivé(e)s	**soyons** arrivé(e)s	**fussions** arrivé(e)s
serez arrivé(e)(s)	**seriez** arrivé(e)(s)	**soyez** arrivé(e)(s)	**fussiez** arrivé(e)(s)
seront arrivé(e)s	**seraient** arrivé(e)s	**soient** arrivé(e)s	**fussent** arrivé(e)s

§39.42   **Verbs and prepositions**

§39.43   **The following verbs take à + noun**

assister à qqch (**à un assemblage, à une réunion, à un spectacle,** *etc.*) / to attend a gathering, a meeting, a theatrical presentation, *etc.*, or to be present at: **Allez-vous assister à la conférence du professeur Godard?** / Are you going to attend (to be present at) Prof. Godard's lecture? **Oui, je vais y assister** / Yes, I am going to attend it.

demander à qqn / to ask someone: **Demandez à la dame où s'arrête l'autobus** / Ask the lady where the bus stops.

déplaire à qqn / to displease someone, to be displeasing to someone: **Cet homme-là déplaît à ma soeur** / That man is displeasing to my sister; **Cet homme-là lui déplaît** / That man is displeasing to her.

désobéir à qqn / to disobey someone: **Ce chien ne désobéit jamais à son maître** / This dog never disobeys his master; **Il ne lui désobéit jamais** / He never disobeys him.

être à qqn / to belong to someone: **Ce livre est à Victor** / This book belongs to Victor. [NOTE this special possessive meaning when you use **être + à**.]

faire attention à qqn ou à qqch / to pay attention to someone or to something: **Faites attention au professeur** / Pay attention to the professor; **Faites attention aux marches** / Pay attention to the steps.

se fier à qqn / to trust someone: **Je me fie à mes parents** / I trust my parents; **Je me fie à eux** / I trust them.

goûter à qqch / to taste a little, to sample a little something: **Goûtez à ce gâteau; il est délicieux et vous m'en direz des nouvelles** / Taste a little of this cake; it is delicious and you will rave about it; **Goûtez-y!** / Taste it! [**Goûtez-en!** / Taste some (of it)!]

s'habituer à qqn ou à qqch / to get used to someone or something: **Je m'habitue à mon nouveau professeur** / I am getting used to my new teacher; **Je m'habitue à lui** / I am getting used to him; **Je m'habitue à ce travail** / I am getting used to this work; **Je m'y habitue** / I am getting used to it.

s'intéresser à qqn ou à qqch / to be interested in someone or something: **Je m'intéresse aux sports** / I am interested in sports.

jouer à / to play (a game or sport): **Il aime bien jouer à la balle** / He likes to play ball; **Elle aime bien jouer au tennis** / She likes to play tennis.

manquer à qqn / to miss someone (because of an absence): **Vous me manquez** / I miss you; **Ses enfants lui manquent** / He (or She) misses his (or her) children.

se mêler à qqch / to mingle with, to mix with, to join in: **Il se mêle à tous les groupes à l'école** / He mixes with all the groups at school.

nuire à qqn ou à qqch / to harm someone or something: **Ce que vous faites peut nuire à la réputation de votre famille** / What you are doing may harm the reputation of your family.

obéir à qqn / to obey someone: **Une personne honorable obéit à ses parents** / An honorable person obeys his (her) parents.

s'opposer à qqn ou à qqch / to oppose someone or something: **Je m'oppose aux idées du président** / I am opposed to the president's ideas.

penser à qqn ou à qqch / to think of (about) someone or something: **Je pense à mes amis** / I am thinking of my friends; **Je pense à eux** / I am thinking of them; **Je pense à mon travail** / I am thinking about my work; **J'y pense** / I am thinking about it.

plaire à qqn / to please, to be pleasing to someone: **Mon mariage plaît à ma famille** / My marriage pleases my family; **Mon mariage leur plaît** / My marriage pleases them (is pleasing to them).

répondre à qqn ou à qqch / to answer someone or something: **J'ai répondu au professeur** / I answered the teacher; **Je lui ai répondu** / I answered him; **J'ai répondu à la lettre** / I answered the letter; **J'y ai répondu** / I answered it.

résister à qqn ou à qqch / to resist someone or something: **Le criminel a résisté à l'agent de police** / The criminal resisted the police officer.

ressembler à qqn / to resemble someone: **Il ressemble beaucoup à sa mère** / He resembles his mother a lot.

réussir à qqch / to succeed in something; **réussir à un examen** / to pass an examination: **Il a réussi à l'examen** / He passed the exam.

serrer la main à qqn / to shake hands with someone: **Bobby, va serrer la main à la dame** / Bobby, go shake hands with the lady.

survivre à qqn ou à qqch / to survive someone or something: **Il a survécu à l'ouragan** / He survived the hurricane.

téléphoner à qqn / to telephone someone: **Marie a téléphoné à Paul** / Marie telephoned Paul; **Elle lui a téléphoné** / She telephoned him.

§39.44   The following verbs take à + inf.

aider à / to help: **Roger aide son petit frère à faire sa leçon de mathématiques** / Roger is helping his little brother do his math lesson.

aimer à / to like: **J'aime à lire** / I like to read. [NOTE that **aimer à + inf.** is used primarily in literary style; ordinarily, use **aimer + inf.**]

s'amuser à / to amuse oneself, to enjoy, to have fun: **Il y a des élèves qui s'amusent à mettre le professeur en colère** / There are pupils who have fun making the teacher angry.

apprendre à / to learn: **J'apprends à lire** / I am learning to read.

s'apprêter à / to get ready: **Je m'apprête à aller au bal** / I am getting ready to go to the dance.

arriver à / to succeed in: **Jacques arrive à comprendre le subjonctif** / Jack is succeeding in learning the subjunctive.

s'attendre à / to expect: **Je m'attendais à trouver une salle de classe vide** / I was expecting to find an empty classroom.

autoriser à / to authorize, to allow; **Je vous autorise à quitter cette salle de classe tout de suite** / I authorize you to leave this classroom immediately.

avoir à / to have, to be obliged (to do something): **J'ai à faire mes devoirs ce soir** / I have to do my homework tonight.

commencer à / to begin: **Il commence à pleuvoir** / It is beginning to rain. [NOTE that **commencer de + inf.** is also correct.]

consentir à / to consent: **Je consens à venir chez vous après le dîner** / I consent (agree) to come to your house after dinner.

continuer à / to continue: **Je continue à étudier le français** / I am continuing to study French. [NOTE that **continuer de + inf.** is also correct.]

décider qqn à / to persuade someone: **J'ai décidé mon père à me prêter quelques francs** / I persuaded my father to lend me a few francs.

se décider à / to make up one's mind: **Il s'est décidé à l'épouser** / He made up his mind to marry her.

demander à / to ask, to request: **Elle demande à parler** / She asks to speak. [NOTE that here the subjects are the same—she is the one who is asking to speak. If the subjects are different, use **demander de: Je vous demande de parler** / I am asking you to talk.]

encourager à / to encourage: **Je l'ai encouragé à suivre un cours de français** / I encouraged him to take a course in French.

s'engager à / to get oneself around (to doing something): **Je ne peux pas m'engager à accepter ses idées frivoles** / I can't get myself around to accepting his (her) frivolous ideas.

enseigner à / to teach: **Je vous enseigne à lire en français** / I am teaching you to read in French.

s'habituer à / to get used (to): **Je m'habitue à parler français couramment** / I am getting used to speaking French fluently.

hésiter à / to hesitate: **J'hésite à répondre à sa lettre** / I hesitate to reply to her (his) letter.

inviter à / to invite: **Monsieur et Madame Boivin ont invité les Béry à dîner chez eux** / Mr. and Mrs. Boivin invited the Bérys to have dinner at their house.

se mettre à / to begin: **L'enfant se met à rire** / The child is beginning to laugh.

parvenir à / to succeed: **Elle est parvenue à devenir docteur** / She succeeded in becoming a doctor.

persister à / to persist: **Je persiste à croire que cet homme est innocent** / I persist in believing that this man is innocent.

se plaire à / to take pleasure in: **Il se plaît à taquiner ses amis** / He takes pleasure in teasing his friends.

recommencer à / to begin again: **Il recommence à pleuvoir** / It is beginning to rain again.

résister à / to resist: **Je résiste à croire qu'il est malhonnête** / I resist believing that he is dishonest.

réussir à / to succeed in: **Henri a réussi à me convaincre** / Henry succeeded in convincing me.

songer à / to dream, to think: **Elle songe à trouver un millionnaire** / She is dreaming of finding a millionaire.

tarder à / to delay: **Mes amis tardent à venir** / My friends are late in coming.

tenir à / to insist, to be anxious: **Je tiens absolument à voir mon enfant cet instant** / I am very anxious to see my child this instant.

venir à / to happen (to): **Si je viens à voir mes amis en ville, je vous le dirai** / If I happen to see my friends downtown, I will tell you (so).

§39.45   The following verbs take de + noun

s'agir de / to be a question of, to be a matter of: **Il s'agit de l'amour** / It is a matter of love.

s'approcher de / to approach: **La dame s'approche de la porte et elle l'ouvre** / The lady approaches the door and opens it.

changer de / to change: **Je dois changer de train à Paris** / I have to change trains in Paris.

dépendre de / to depend on: **Je veux sortir avec toi mais cela dépend des circonstances** / I want to go out with you but that depends on the circumstances.

douter de / to doubt: **Je doute de la véracité de ce que vous dites** / I doubt the veracity of what you are saying.

se douter de / to suspect: **Je me doute de ses actions** / I suspect his (her) actions.

féliciter de / to congratulate on: **Je vous félicite de vos progrès** / I congratulate you on your progress.

jouer de / to play (a musical instrument): **Je sais jouer du piano** / I know how to play the piano.

jouir de / to enjoy: **Mon père jouit d'une bonne santé** / My father enjoys good health.

manquer de / to lack: **Cette personne manque de politesse** / This person lacks courtesy; **Mon frère manque de bon sens** / My brother lacks common sense.

se méfier de / to distrust, to mistrust, to beware of: **Je me méfie des personnes que je ne connais pas** / I distrust persons whom I do not know.

se moquer de / to make fun of: **Les enfants aiment se moquer d'un singe** / Children like to make fun of a monkey.

s'occuper de / to be busy with: **Madame Boulanger s'occupe de son mari infirme** / Mrs. Boulanger is busy with her disabled husband; **Je m'occupe de mes affaires** / I mind my own business; **Occupez-vous de vos affaires!** / Mind your own business!

partir de / to leave: **Il est parti de la maison à 8 h.** / He left the house at 8 o'clock.

se passer de / to do without: **Je me passe de sel** / I do without salt.

se plaindre de / to complain about: **Il se plaint toujours de son travail** / He always complains about his work.

remercier de / to thank: **Je vous remercie de votre bonté** / I thank you for your kindness. [Use **remercier de** + an abstract noun or + inf.; Use **remercier pour** + a concrete object; *e.g.*, **Je vous remercie pour le cadeau** / I thank you for the present.]

se rendre compte de / to realize: **Je me rends compte de la condition de cette personne** / I realize the condition of this person.

rire de / to laugh at; **Tout le monde rit de cette personne** / Everybody laughs at this person.

se servir de / to employ, to use, to make use of: **Je me sers d'un stylo quand j'écris une lettre** / I use a pen when I write a letter.

se soucier de / to care about, to be concerned about: **Marc se soucie de ses amis** / Marc cares about his friends.

se souvenir de / to remember: **Oui, je me souviens de Gervaise** / Yes, I remember Gervaise; **je me souviens de lui** / I remember him; **Je me souviens d'elle** / I remember her; **Je me souviens de l'été passé** / I remember last summer; **Je m'en souviens** / I remember it.

tenir de / to take after (to resemble): **Julie tient de sa mère** / Julie takes after her mother.

§39.46 Verbs that take de + inf.

s'agir de / to be a question of, to be a matter of: **Il s'agit de faire les devoirs tous les jours** / It is a matter of doing the homework every day.

avoir peur de / to be afraid of: **Le petit garçon a peur de traverser la rue seul** / The little boy is afraid of crossing the street alone.

cesser de / to stop, to cease: **Il a cessé de pleuvoir** / It has stopped raining.

commencer de / to begin: **Il a commencé de pleuvoir** / It has started to rain. [NOTE that **commencer à + inf.** is also correct.]

continuer de / to continue: **Il continue de pleuvoir** / It's still raining OR It's continuing to rain. [NOTE that **continuer à + inf.** is also correct.]

craindre de / to be afraid of, to fear: **La petite fille craint de traverser la rue seule** / The little girl is afraid of crossing the street alone.

décider de / to decide: **J'ai décidé de partir tout de suite** / I decided to leave immediately; **Il a décidé d'acheter la maison** / He decided to buy the house.

demander de / to ask, to request: **Je vous demande de parler** / I am asking you to speak. [NOTE that here the subjects are different: I am asking you to speak; whereas, when the subjects are the same, use **demander à: Elle demande à parler** / She is asking to speak; **Je demande à parler** / I am asking to speak.]

se dépêcher de / to hurry: **Je me suis dépêché de venir chez vous pour vous dire quelque chose** / I hurried to come to your place in order to tell you something.

empêcher de / to keep from, to prevent: **Je vous empêche de sortir** / I prevent you from going out.

s'empresser de / to hurry: **Je m'empresse de venir chez toi** / I am hurrying to come to your place.

essayer de / to try: **J'essaye d'ouvrir la porte mais je ne peux pas** / I'm trying to open the door but I can't.

féliciter de / to congratulate: **On m'a félicité d'avoir gagné le prix** / I was congratulated on having won the prize.

finir de / to finish: **J'ai fini de travailler sur cette composition** / I have finished working on this composition.

gronder de / to scold: **La maîtresse a grondé l'élève d'avoir fait beaucoup de fautes dans le devoir** / The teacher scolded the pupil for having made many errors in the homework.

se hâter de / to hurry: **Je me hâte de venir chez toi** / I am hurrying to come to your house.

manquer de / to neglect to, to fail to, to forget to: **Guy a manqué de compléter sa leçon de français** / Guy neglected to complete his French lesson.

offrir de / to offer: **J'ai offert d'écrire une lettre pour elle** / I offered to write a letter for her.

oublier de / to forget: **J'ai oublié de vous donner la monnaie** / I forgot to give you the change.

persuader de / to persuade: **J'ai persuadé mon père de me prêter quelques francs** / I persuaded my father to lend me a few francs.

prendre garde de / to take care not to: **Prenez garde de tomber** / Be careful not to fall.

prendre le parti de faire qqch / to decide to do something: **Théodore n'a pas hésité à prendre le parti de voter pour elle** / Theodore did not hesitate to decide to vote for her.

prier de / to beg: **Je vous prie d'arrêter** / I beg you to stop.

promettre de / to promise: **J'ai promis de venir chez toi à 8 h.** / I promised to come to your place at 8 o'clock.

refuser de / to refuse: **Je refuse de le croire** / I refuse to believe it.

regretter de / to regret, to be sorry; **Je regrette d'être obligé de vous dire cela** / I am sorry to be obliged to tell you that.

remercier de / to thank: **Je vous remercie d'être venu si vite** / I thank you for coming (having come) so quickly. [Use **remercier de + inf.** or **+ abstract noun.** Use **remercier pour + concrete object.**]

se souvenir de / to remember: **Tu vois? Je me suis souvenu de venir chez toi** / You see? I remembered to come to your house.

tâcher de / to try: **Tâche de finir tes devoirs avant de sortir** / Try to finish your homework before going out.

venir de / to have just (done something): **Je viens de manger** / I have just eaten OR I just ate.

§39.47   The following verbs commonly take à + noun + de + inf.

The model to follow is: **J'ai conseillé à Robert de suivre un cours de français** / I advised Robert to take a course in French.

conseiller à / to advise: **J'ai conseillé à Jeanne de se marier** / I advised Joan to get married.

défendre à / to forbid: **Mon père défend à mon frère de fumer** / My father forbids my brother to smoke.

demander à / to ask, to request: **J'ai demandé à Marie de venir** / I asked Mary to come.

dire à / to say, to tell: **J'ai dit à Charles de venir** / I told Charles to come.

interdire à / to forbid: **Mon père interdit à mon frère de fumer** / My father forbids my brother to smoke.

ordonner à / to order: **J'ai ordonné au chauffeur de ralentir** / I ordered the driver to slow down.

permettre à / to permit: **J'ai permis à l'étudiant de partir quelques minutes avant la fin de la classe** / I permitted the student to leave a few minutes before the end of class.

promettre à / to promise: **J'ai promis à mon ami d'arriver à l'heure** / I promised my friend to arrive on time.

téléphoner à / to telephone: **J'ai téléphoné à Marcel de venir me voir** / I phoned Marcel to come to see me.

§39.48   Verb + other prepositions

commencer par + inf. / to begin by + present participle: **La présidente a commencé par discuter les problèmes de la société** / The president began by discussing the problems in society.

continuer par + inf. / to continue by + pres. part.: **La maîtresse a continué la conférence par lire un poème** / The teacher continued the lecture by reading a poem.

s'entendre avec qqn / to get along with someone

entrer dans + noun / to enter, to go in: **Elle est entrée dans le restaurant** / She went into the restaurant.

être en colère contre qqn / to be angry with someone: **Monsieur Laroche est toujours en colère contre ses voisins** / Mr. Laroche is always angry with his neighbors.

finir par + inf. / to end up by + pres. part.: **Clément a fini par épouser une femme plus âgée que lui** / Clement ended up marrying a woman older than he.

s'incliner devant qqn / to bow to someone: **La princesse s'incline devant la reine** / The princess is bowing to the queen.

insister pour + inf. / to insist on, upon: **J'insiste pour obtenir tous mes droits** / I insist on obtaining all my rights.

se marier avec qqn / to marry someone: **Elle va se marier avec lui** / She is going to marry him.

se mettre en colère / to become angry, upset: **Monsieur Leduc se met en colère facilement** / Mr. Leduc gets angry easily.

se mettre en route / to start out, to set out: **Ils se sont mis en route dès l'aube** / They started out at dawn.

remercier pour + a concrete noun / to thank for: **Je vous remercie pour le joli cadeau** / I thank you for the pretty present. [Remember to use **remercier pour + a concrete object**; use **remercier de + an abstract noun** or **+ inf. Je vous remercie de votre bonté** / I thank you for your kindness; **Je vous remercie d'être venue si vite** / I thank you for coming so quickly.]

§39.49   Verb + NO PREPOSITION + inf.

adorer + inf. / to adore, to love: **Madame Morin adore mettre tous ses bijoux avant de sortir** / Mrs. Morin loves to put on all her jewelry before going out.

aimer + inf. / to like: **J'aime lire** / I like to read. [You may also say: **J'aime à lire**, but **aimer + à + inf.** is used primarily in literary style.]

aimer mieux + inf. / to prefer: **J'aime mieux rester ici** / I prefer to stay here.

aller + inf. / to go: **Je vais faire mes devoirs maintenant** / I am going to do my homework now.

apercevoir + inf. / to perceive: **J'aperçois s'avancer l'ouragan** / I notice the hurricane advancing. [This is a verb of perception. You may also say: **J'aperçois l'ouragan qui s'avance.**]

compter + inf. / to intend: **Je compte aller en France l'été prochain** / I intend to go to France next summer.

croire + inf. / to believe: **Il croit être innocent** / He believes he is innocent.

désirer + inf. / to desire, to wish: **Je désire prendre une tasse de café** / I desire to have a cup of coffee.

devoir + inf. / to have to, ought to: **Je dois faire mes devoirs avant de sortir** / I have to do my homework before going out.

écouter + inf. / to listen to: **J'écoute chanter les enfants** / I am listening to the children singing. [This is a verb of perception. You may also say: **J'écoute les enfants qui chantent.**]

entendre + inf. / to hear: **J'entends chanter les enfants** / I hear the children singing. [This is a verb of perception. You may also say: **J'entends les enfants qui chantent.**]

espérer + inf. / to hope: **J'espère aller en France** / I hope to go to France.

faire + inf. / to cause, to make, to have something done by someone: **Le professeur fait travailler les élèves dans la salle de classe** / The teacher has the pupils work in the classroom. [This is really the **causative faire**; see §5.]

falloir + inf. / to be necessary: **Il faut être honnête** / One must be honest. See also §19.

laisser + inf. / to let, to allow: **Je vous laisse partir** / I am letting you go.

oser + inf. / to dare: **Ce garçon ose dire n'importe quoi** / This boy dares to say anything.

paraître + inf. / to appear, to seem: **Elle paraît être capable** / She appears to be capable.

penser + inf. / to think, to plan, to intend: **Je pense aller à Paris** / I intend to go to Paris.

pouvoir + inf. / to be able, can: **Je peux marcher mieux maintenant après l'accident** / I can walk better now after the accident.

préférer + inf. / to prefer: **Je préfère manger maintenant** / I prefer to eat now.

regarder + inf. / to look at: **Je regarde voler les oiseaux** / I am looking at the birds flying. [This is a verb of perception. You may also say: **Je regarde les oiseaux qui volent.**]

savoir + inf. / to know, to know how: **Je sais nager** / I know how to swim.

sentir + inf. / to feel: **Je sens s'approcher l'ouragan** / I feel the hurricane approaching. [This is a verb of perception. You can also say: **Je sens l'ouragan qui s'approche.**]

sentir + inf. / to smell: **Je sens venir une odeur agréable du jardin** / I smell a pleasant fragrance coming from the garden. [This is another verb of perception. You may also say: **Je sens une odeur agréable qui vient du jardin.**]

valoir mieux + inf. / to be better: **Il vaut mieux être honnête** / It is better to be honest.

venir + inf. / to come: **Gérard vient voir ma nouvelle voiture** / Gerard is coming to see my new car.

voir + inf. / to see: **Je vois courir les enfants** / I see the children running. [This is another verb of perception. You may also say: **Je vois les enfants qui courent.**]

vouloir + inf. / to want: **Je veux venir chez vous** / I want to come to your house.

§39.50   **Verbs that do not require a preposition, whereas in English a preposition is used**

approuver / to approve of: **J'approuve votre décision** / I approve of your decision.

attendre / to wait for: **J'attends l'autobus depuis vingt minutes** / I have been waiting for the bus for twenty minutes.

chercher / to look for: **Je cherche mon livre** / I'm looking for my book.

demander / to ask for: **Je demande une réponse** / I am asking for a reply.

écouter / to listen to: **J'écoute la musique** / I am listening to the music; **J'écoute le professeur** / I am listening to the teacher.

envoyer chercher / to send for: **J'ai envoyé chercher le docteur** / I sent for the doctor.

essayer / to try on: **Elle a essayé une jolie robe** / She tried on a pretty dress.

habiter / to live in: **J'habite cette maison** / I live in this house.

ignorer / to be unaware of: **J'ignore ce fait** / I am unaware of this fact.

mettre / to put on: **Elle a mis la robe rouge** / She put on the red dress.

payer / to pay for: **J'ai payé le dîner** / I paid for the dinner.

pleurer / to cry about, to cry over: **Elle pleure la perte de son petit chien** / She is crying over the loss of her little dog.

prier / to pray to: **Elle prie le ciel** / She is praying to the heavens; **Elle prie la Vierge** / She is praying to the Holy Mother.

puer / to stink of: **Cet ivrogne pue l'alcool** / This drunkard stinks of alcohol.

regarder / to look at: **Je regarde le ciel** / I am looking at the sky.

sentir / to smell of: **Robert, ta chambre sent la porcherie** / Robert, your room smells like a pigsty (pigpen).

soigner / to take care of: **Cette personne soigne les malades** / This person takes care of (cares for) sick people.

§39.51   **Principal parts of some important verbs—Les temps primitifs de quelques verbes importants**

INFINITIF	PARTICIPE PRÉSENT	PARTICIPE PASSÉ	PRÉSENT DE L'INDICATIF	PASSÉ SIMPLE
aller	allant	allé	je vais	j'allai
avoir	ayant	eu	j'ai	j'eus
battre	battant	battu	je bats	je battis
boire	buvant	bu	je bois	je bus
craindre	craignant	craint	je crains	je craignis
croire	croyant	cru	je crois	je crus
devoir	devant	dû (due)	je dois	je dus
dire	disant	dit	je dis	je dis
écrire	écrivant	écrit	j'écris	j'écrivis
être	étant	été	je suis	je fus
faire	faisant	fait	je fais	je fis
lire	lisant	lu	je lis	je lus
mettre	mettant	mis	je mets	je mis
mourir	mourant	mort	je meurs	je mourus
naître	naissant	né	je nais	je naquis
ouvrir	ouvrant	ouvert	j'ouvre	j'ouvris
porter	portant	porté	je porte	je portai
pouvoir	pouvant	pu	je peux *or* je puis	je pus
prendre	prenant	pris	je prends	je pris

INFINITIF	PARTICIPE PRÉSENT	PARTICIPE PASSÉ	PRÉSENT DE L'INDI-CATIF	PASSÉ SIMPLE
recevoir	recevant	reçu	je reçois	je reçus
savoir	sachant	su	je sais	je sus
venir	venant	venu	je viens	je vins
vivre	vivant	vécu	je vis	je vécus
voir	voyant	vu	je vois	je vis
voler	volant	volé	je vole	je volai

§39.52 The principal parts (**les temps primitifs**) of a verb are very important to know because from them you can easily form all the tenses and moods. See **§39.40** and **§39.41**.

§39.53 **Orthographical changing verbs—verb forms that change in spelling**

§39.54 Verbs that end in —**cer** in the infinitive form change **c** to **ç** when in front of the vowels **a**, **o** or **u** in order to keep the **s** sound in the infinitive form and retain its identity. That little mark under the **c** (**ç**) is called **une cédille**. Actually it is the lower part of the letter **s** which is used in order to tell the reader that the **ç** should be pronounced as an **s**. Without that mark, the letter **c** in front of the vowels **a**, **o** and **u** must be pronounced as a **k** sound. Since the **c** in the ending —**cer** is pronounced like an **s**, that same sound must be retained in all its forms.

§39.55 Some common verbs that end in —**cer** in the infinitive form are:

annoncer / to announce **lancer** / to launch, to hurl
avancer / to advance **menacer** / to threaten
commencer / to begin, to start **placer** / to place, to set
divorcer / to divorce **prononcer** / to pronounce
effacer / to erase, to efface **remplacer** / to replace

§39.56 Examples of when this change occurs:

Present indicative: nous annonçons, nous avançons, nous commençons, nous divorçons, nous effaçons, nous lançons, nous menaçons, nous plaçons, nous prononçons, nous remplaçons.

Imperfect indicative: j'annonçais, tu annonçais, il (elle, on) annonçait; ils (elles) annonçaient [You do the same for the other —**cer** type verbs given above in **§39.55**.]

Passé simple: j'annonçai, tu annonças, il (elle, on) annonça; nous annonçâmes, vous annonçâtes [You do the same for the other —**cer** type verbs given above in **§39.55**.]

Imperfect subjunctive: que j'annonçasse, que tu annonçasses, qu'il (qu'elle, qu'on) annonçât; que nous annonçassions, que vous annonçassiez, qu'ils (qu'elles) annonçassent [Now you do the same for the other —**cer** type verbs given above in **§39.55**.]

§39.57 Verbs that end in —**ger** in the infinitive form change **g** to **ge** in front of the vowels **a**, **o** or **u** in order to keep the soft sound of **g** in the infinitive form and retain its identity; otherwise, **g** in front of **a**, **o** or **u** is normally pronounced hard **g** as in **go**.

§39.58 Some common verbs that end in —**ger** in the infinitive form are:

arranger / to arrange **obliger** / to oblige
changer / to change **partager** / to divide, to share
corriger / to correct **plonger** / to dive, to plunge
déranger / to disturb **ranger** / to arrange by row, put in
manger / to eat order
nager / to swim **songer** / to think, to dream
neiger / to snow **voyager** / to travel

§39.59   Examples of when this change occurs:

Present indicative: nous arrangeons, nous changeons, nous corrigeons, nous dérangeons [Now you do the same for the other —**ger** type verbs given above in **§39.58**]

Imperfect indicative: j'arrangeais, tu arrangeais, il (elle, on) arrangeait; ils (elles) arrangeaient [Now you do the same for the other —**ger** type verbs given above in **§39.58.**]

Passé simple: j'arrangeai, tu arrangeas, il (elle, on) arrangea; nous arrangeâmes, vous arrangeâtes [Now you do the same for the other —**ger** type verbs given above in **§39.58.**]

Imperfect subjunctive: que j'arrangeasse, que tu arrangeasses, qu'il (qu'elle, qu'on) arrangeât; que nous arrangeassions, que vous arrangeassiez, qu'ils (qu'elles) arrangeassent [Just for the fun of it, do the same for the other —**ger** type verbs given above in **§39.58.**]

§39.60   Verbs that end in —**oyer** or —**uyer** in the infinitive form must change **y** to **i** in front of mute **e**.

§39.61   Common verbs that end in —**oyer** or —**uyer** in the infinitive form are:

—OYER   **—UYER**

choyer / to fondle, to coddle   **ennuyer** / to bore, to annoy
employer / to employ, to use   **essuyer** / to wipe
envoyer / to send
nettoyer / to clean

§39.62   Verbs that end in —**AYER** in the infinitive form may change **y** to **i** or may keep **y** in front of mute **e**.

Two common verbs that end in —**ayer** in the infinitive form are: **essayer** / to try, to try on; and **payer** / to pay, to pay for.

§39.63   Examples of when this change occurs:

Present indicative: j'emploie, tu emploies, il (elle, on) emploie; ils (elles) emploient.

Future: j'emploierai, tu emploieras, il (elle, on) emploiera; nous emploierons, vous emploierez, ils (elles) emploieront.

Conditional: j'emploierais, tu emploierais, il (elle, on) emploierait; nous emploierions, vous emploieriez, ils (elles) emploieraient.

Present subjunctive: que j'emploie, que tu emploies, qu'il (qu'elle, qu'on) emploie; qu'ils (qu'elles) emploient.

§39.64   Verbs that contain a mute **e** in the syllable before the infinitive ending —**er**:

ach**e**ter / to buy   l**e**ver / to raise, to lift
ach**e**ver / to complete   se l**e**ver / to get up
am**e**ner / to bring, to lead   m**e**ner / to lead
él**e**ver / to raise   p**e**ser / to weigh
emm**e**ner / to lead away, to take away prom**e**ner / to walk (a person or an animal)
enl**e**ver / to remove, to take off   se prom**e**ner / to take a walk (for yourself)
g**e**ler / to freeze

§39.65   These verbs, given above in **§39.64,** change mute **e** to **è** when, in a verb form, the syllable after it contains another mute **e**.

§39.66   This change occurs because that mute **e** in the stem of the infinitive now becomes pronounced clearly in some verb forms. Examples:

Present indicative: j'achète, tu achètes, il (elle, on) achète; ils (elles) achètent.

Future: j'achèterai, tu achèteras, il (elle, on) achètera; nous achèterons, vous achèterez, ils (elles) achèteront.

Conditional: j'achèterais, tu achèterais, il (elle, on) achèterait; nous achèterions, vous achèteriez, ils (elles) achèteraient.

Present subjunctive: que j'achète, que tu achètes, qu'il (qu'elle, qu'on) achète; qu'ils (qu'elles) achètent.

§39.67   Instead of changing like the verbs above in §39.64—§39.66, the following verbs double the consonant in the syllable that contains the mute **e** in the stem:

app**e**ler / to call   j**e**ter / to throw
rapp**e**ler / to recall   rej**e**ter / to throw again, to throw back
se rapp**e**ler / to remember

Examples of when this spelling change occurs:

Present indicative: je m'appelle, tu t'appelles, il (elle, on) s'appelle; ils (elles) s'appellent.

Future: je m'appellerai, tu t'appelleras, il (elle, on) s'appellera; nous nous appellerons, vous vous appellerez, ils (elles) s'appelleront

Conditional: je m'appellerais, tu t'appellerais, il (elle, on) s'appellerait; nous nous appellerions, vous vous appelleriez, ils (elles) s'appelleraient.

Present subjunctive: que je m'appelle, que tu t'appelles, qu'il (qu'elle, qu'on) s'appelle; qu'ils (qu'elles) s'appellent.

§39.68   Verbs that contain **é** in the syllable before the infinitive ending —**er**:

c**é**der / to cede, to yield, to give up   poss**é**der / to possess, to own
cél**é**brer / to celebrate   préf**é**rer / to prefer
conc**é**der / to concede, to give up   prot**é**ger / to protect
consid**é**rer / to consider   rép**é**ter / to repeat
esp**é**rer / to hope   sugg**é**rer / to suggest

§39.69   These verbs, given above in **§39.68,** change **é** to **è** when, in a verb form, the syllable after it contains mute **e**.

Examples of when this spelling change occurs:

Present indicative: je préfère, tu préfères, il (elle, on) préfère; ils (elles) préfèrent.

Present subjunctive: que je préfère, que tu préfères, qu'il (qu'elle, qu'on) préfère; qu'ils (qu'elles) préfèrent.

§39.70   The names of tenses and moods in French with English equivalents are:

FRENCH

Les Temps simples

1. Présent de l'indicatif
2. Imparfait de l'indicatif
3. Passé simple
4. Futur
5. Conditionnel présent
6. Présent du subjonctif
7. Imparfait du subjonctif

Les Temps composés

8. Passé composé
9. Plus-que-parfait de l'indicatif
10. Passé antérieur
11. Futur antérieur
12. Conditionnel passé
13. Passé du subjonctif
14. Plus-que-parfait du subjonctif

ENGLISH

Simple tenses

1. Present indicative
2. Imperfect indicative
3. Past definite
4. Future
5. Conditional present
6. Present subjunctive
7. Imperfect subjunctive

Compound tenses

8. Past indefinite
9. Pluperfect or Past perfect indicative
10. Past anterior
11. Future perfect or Future anterior
12. Conditional perfect
13. Past subjunctive
14. Pluperfect or Past perfect subjunctive

Impératif   *Imperative or Command*

§39.71   OBSERVATIONS:

§39.72   In French, there are 7 simple tenses and 7 compound tenses. A simple tense means that the verb form consists of one word. A compound tense means that the verb form consists of two words (the auxiliary verb and the past participle). The auxiliary verb is also called a helping verb and in French, as you know, it is any of the 7 simple tenses of **avoir** or **être**.

§39.73   Each compound tense is based on each simple tense. The 14 tenses given above are arranged in the following logical order:

§39.74   Tense number 8 is based on Tense number 1; in other words, you form the Passé composé by using the auxiliary **avoir** or **être** (whichever is appropriate) in the Present indicative plus the past participle of the verb you are using. See **§39.26ff.**

§39.75   Tense number 9 is based on Tense number 2; in other words, you form the Plus–que–parfait de l'indicatif by using the auxiliary **avoir** or **être** (whichever is appropriate) in the Imparfait de l'indicatif plus the past participle of the verb you are using.

§39.76   Tense number 10 is based on Tense number 3; in other words, you form the Passé antérieur by using the auxiliary **avoir** or **être** (whichever is appropriate) in the Passé simple plus the past participle of the verb you are using.

§39.77   Tense number 11 is based on Tense number 4; in other words, you form the Futur antérieur by using the auxiliary **avoir** or **être** (whichever is appropriate) in the Future plus the past participle of the verb you are using.

§39.78   Tense number 12 is based on Tense number 5; in other words, you form the Conditional perfect by using the auxiliary **avoir** or **être** (whichever is appropriate) in the Conditional present plus the past participle of the verb you are using.

§39.79   Tense number 13 is based on Tense number 6; in other words, you form the Past subjunctive by using the auxiliary **avoir** or **être** (whichever is appropriate) in the Present subjunctive plus the past participle of the verb you are using.

§39.80   Tense number 14 is based on Tense number 7; in other words, you form the Pluperfect subjunctive by using the auxiliary **avoir** or **être** (whichever is appropriate) in the Imperfect subjunctive plus the past participle of the verb you are using.

§39.81   What does all the above mean? This: If you ever expect to know or even recognize the meaning of any of the 7 compound tenses, you certainly have to know **avoir** and **être** in the 7 simple tenses. If you do not, you cannot form the 7 compound tenses. This is one perfect example to illustrate that learning French verb forms is a cumulative experience: In order to know the 7 compound tenses, you must first know the forms of **avoir** and **être** in the 7 simple tenses, which are as follows:

AVOIR in the 7 simple tenses

Participe présent	ayant	**Participe passé**	eu	**Infinitif**	avoir
Present participle	having	Past participle	had	Infinitive	to have

1. **Présent indic.**	**j'ai, tu as, il (elle, on) a;** **nous avons, vous avez, ils (elles) ont**	
Present indic.	I have, you have, he (she, it, one) has; we have, you have, they have	

OR:
I do have, you do have, he (she, it, one) does have;
we do have, you do have, they do have
OR:
I am having, you are having, he (she, it, one) is having;
we are having, you are having, they are having

2. Imparf. indic.	**j'avais, tu avais, il (elle, on) avait; nous avions, vous aviez, ils (elles) avaient**	

Imperf. indic.
I had, you had, he (she, it, one) had;
we had, you had, they had
OR:
I used to have, you used to have, he (she, it, one) used to have;
we used to have, you used to have, they used to have
OR:
I was having, you were having, he (she, it, one) was having;
we were having, you were having, they were having

3. Passé simple
J'eus, tu eus, il (elle, on) eut; nous eûmes, vous eûtes, ils (elles) eurent

Past def.
I had, you had, he (she, it, one) had;
we had, you had, they had

4. Futur
j'aurai, tu auras, il (elle, on) aura; nous aurons, vous aurez, ils (elles) auront

Future
I shall have, you will have, he (she, it, one) will have;
we shall have, you will have, they will have

5. Cond. prés.
j'aurais, tu aurais, il (elle, on) aurait; nous aurions, vous auriez, ils (elles) auraient

Cond. pres.
I would have, you would have, he (she, it, one) would have;
we would have, you would have, they would have

6. Prés. subj.
que j'aie, que tu aies, qu'il (qu'elle, qu'on) ait; que nous ayons, que vous ayez, qu'ils (qu'elles) aient

Pres. subj.
that I may have, that you may have, that he (she, it, one) may have;
that we may have, that you may have, that they may have

7. Imparf. subj.
que j'eusse, que tu eusses, qu'il (qu'elle, qu'on) eût; que nous eussions, que vous eussiez, qu'ils (qu'elles) eussent

Imperf. subj.
that I might have, that you might have, that he (she, it, one) might have;
that we might have, that you might have, that they might have

ÊTRE in the 7 simple tenses

Participe présent	étant	**Participe passé**	été	**Infinitif**	être
Present participle	being	Past participle	been	Infinitive	to be

1. Présent indic.
je suis, tu es, il (elle, on) est; nous sommes, vous êtes, ils (elles) sont

Present indic.	I am, you are, he (she, it, one) is; we are, you are, they are **OR:** I am being, you are being, he (she, it, one) is being; we are being, you are being, they are being
2. Imparf. **indic.**	**j'étais, tu étais, il (elle, on) était;** **nous étions, vous étiez, ils (elles) étaient**
Imperf. indic.	I was, you were, he (she, it, one) was; we were, you were, they were **OR:** I used to be, you used to be, he (she, it, one) used to be; we used to be, you used to be, they used to be **OR:** I was being, you were being, he (she, it, one) was being; we were being, you were being, they were being
3. Passé **simple**	**je fus, tu fus, il (elle, on) fut;** **nous fûmes, vous fûtes, ils (elles) furent**
Past def.	I was, you were, he (she, it, one) was; we were, you were, they were
4. Futur	**je serai, tu seras, il (elle, on) sera;** **nous serons, vous serez, ils (elles) seront**
Future	I shall be, you will be, he (she, it, one) will be; we shall be, you will be, they will be
5. Cond. **prés.**	**je serais, tu serais, il (elle, on) serait;** **nous serions, vous seriez, ils (elles) seraient**
Cond. pres.	I would be, you would be, he (she, it, one) would be; we would be, you would be, they would be
6. Prés. **subj.**	**que je sois, que tu sois, qu'il (qu'elle, qu'on) soit;** **que nous soyons, que vous soyez, qu'ils (qu'elles) soient**
Pres. subj.	that I may be, that you may be, that he (she, it, one) may be; that we may be, that you may be, that they may be
7. Imparf. **subj.**	**que je fusse, que tu fusses, qu'il (qu'elle, qu'on) fût;** **que nous fussions, que vous fussiez, qu'ils (qu'elles) fussent**
Imperf. subj.	that I might be, that you might be, that he (she, it, one) might be; that we might be, that you might be, that they might be

§39.82   How do you translate the French verb forms into English? See **§39.81**, **§39.84** and **§39.85**.

§39.83   There are four moods (or modes) in French and English: indicative, subjunctive, conditional, and imperative. For an explanation of this, see **§39.1** and the explanations that begin with **§39.86**.

§39.84   **Sample French verb conjugation using an avoir verb with equivalent English verb forms**

Participe présent parlant   **Participe passé parlé**   **Infinitif parler**
Present participle   talking, speaking   Past participle   talked, spoken   Infinitive   to talk, to speak

1. **Présent**   **je parle, tu parles, il (elle, on) parle;**
   indic.   **nous parlons, vous parlez, ils (elles) parlent**

   Present   I talk, you talk, he (she, it, one) talks;
   indic.   we talk, you talk, they talk
                    OR:
                    I do talk, you do talk, he (she, it, one) does talk;
                    we do talk, you do talk, they do talk
                    OR:
                    I am talking, you are talking, he (she, it, one) is talking;
                    we are talking, you are talking, they are talking

2. **Imparf.**   **je parlais, tu parlais, il (elle, on) parlait;**
   indic.   **nous parlions, vous parliez, ils (elles) parlaient**

   Imperf.   I was talking, you were talking, he (she, it, one) was talking;
   indic.   we were talking, you were talking, they were talking
                    OR:
                    I used to talk, you used to talk, he (she, it, one) used to talk;
                    we used to talk, you used to talk, they used to talk
                    OR:
                    I talked, you talked, he (she, it, one) talked;
                    we talked, you talked, they talked

3. **Passé**   **je parlai, tu parlas, il (elle, on) parla;**
   simple   **nous parlâmes, vous parlâtes, ils (elles) parlèrent**

   Past   I talked, you talked, he (she, it, one) talked;
   def.   we talked, you talked, they talked
                    OR:
                    I did talk, you did talk, he (she, it, one) did talk;
                    we did talk, you did talk, they did talk

4. **Futur**   **je parlerai, tu parleras, il (elle, on) parlera;**
                    nous parlerons, vous parlerez, ils (elles) parleront

   Future   I shall talk, you will talk, he (she, it, one) will talk;
                    we shall talk, you will talk, they will talk

5. **Cond.**   **je parlerais, tu parlerais, il (elle, on) parlerait;**
   prés.   **nous parlerions, vous parleriez, ils (elles) parleraient**

   Cond.   I would talk, you would talk, he (she, it, one) would talk;
   pres.   we would talk, you would talk, they would talk

6. **Prés.**   **que je parle, que tu parles, qu'il (qu'elle, qu'on) parle;**
   subj.   **que nous parlions, que vous parliez, qu'ils (qu'elles) parlent**

   Pres.   that I may talk, that you may talk, that he (she, it, one) may talk;
   subj.   that we may talk, that you may talk, that they may talk

7. **Imparf.**   **que je parlasse, que tu parlasses, qu'il (qu'elle, qu'on) parlât;**
   subj.   **que nous parlassions, que vous parlassiez, qu'ils (qu'elles) parlassent**

Imperf. subj.	that I might talk, that you might talk, that he (she, it, one) might talk; that we might talk, that you might talk, that they might talk	

8. Passé composé
j'ai parlé, tu as parlé, il (elle, on) a parlé;
nous avons parlé, vous avez parlé, ils (elles) ont parlé

Past indef.
I talked, you talked, he (she, it, one) talked;
we talked, you talked, they talked
OR:
I have talked, you have talked, he (she, it, one) has talked;
we have talked, you have talked, they have talked
OR:
I did talk, you did talk, he (she, it, one) did talk;
we did talk, you did talk, they did talk

9. Plus-q-p. indic.
j'avais parlé, tu avais parlé, il (elle, on) avait parlé;
nous avions parlé, vous aviez parlé, ils (elles) avaient parlé

Plup. indic.
I had talked, you had talked, he (she, it, one) had talked;
we had talked, you had talked, they had talked

10. Passé antér.
j'eus parlé, tu eus parlé, il (elle, on) eut parlé;
nous eûmes parlé, vous eûtes parlé, ils (elles) eurent parlé

Past anter.
I had talked, you had talked, he (she, it, one) had talked;
we had talked, you had talked, they had talked

11. Fut. antér.
j'aurai parlé, tu auras parlé, il (elle, on) aura parlé;
nous aurons parlé, vous aurez parlé, ils (elles) auront parlé

Fut. perf.
I shall have talked, you will have talked, he (she, it, one) will have talked;
we shall have talked, you will have talked, they will have talked

12. Cond. passé
j'aurais parlé, tu aurais parlé, il (elle, on) aurait parlé;
nous aurions parlé, vous auriez parlé, ils (elles) auraient parlé

Cond. perf.
I would have talked, you would have talked, he (she, it, one) would have talked;
we would have talked, you would have talked, they would have talked

13. Passé subj.
que j'aie parlé, que tu aies parlé, qu'il (qu'elle, qu'on) ait parlé;
que nous ayons parlé, que vous ayez parlé, qu'ils (qu'elles) aient parlé

Past subj.
that I may have talked, that you may have talked, that he (she, it, one) may have talked;
that we may have talked, that you may have talked, that they may have talked

14. Plus-q-p. subj.
que j'eusse parlé, que tu eusses parlé, qu'il (qu'elle, qu'on) eût parlé;
que nous eussions parlé, que vous eussiez parlé, qu'ils (qu'elles) eussent parlé

Plup. subj.
that I might have talked, that you might have talked, that he (she, it, one) might have talked;
that we might have talked, that you might have talked, that they might have talked

Impér.
Imper.
parle, parlons, parlez
talk, let's talk, talk

NOTE: For an explanation and examples of each of these tenses and moods, with their uses, see §39.86.

§39.85 Sample French verb conjugation using an être verb with equivalent English verb forms

Participe présent	allant	**Participe passé**	allé	**Infinitif**	aller
Present participle	going	Past participle	gone	Infinitive	to go

1. Présent indic.
je vais, tu vas, il (elle, on) va;
nous allons, vous allez, ils (elles) vont

Present indic.
I go, you go, he (she, it, one) goes;
we go, you go, they go
OR:
I do go, you do go, he (she, it, one) does go;
we do go, you do go, they do go
OR:
I am going, you are going, he (she, it, one) is going;
we are going, you are going, they are going

2. Imparf. indic.
j'allais, tu allais, il (elle, on) allait;
nous allions, vous alliez, ils (elles) allaient

Imperf. indic.
I was going, you were going, he (she, it, one) was going;
we were going, you were going, they were going
OR:
I used to go, you used to go, he (she, it, one) used to go;
we used to go, you used to go, they used to go
OR:
I went, you went, he (she, it, one) went;
we went, you went, they went

3. Passé simple
j'allai, tu allas, il (elle, on) alla;
nous allâmes, vous allâtes, ils (elles) allèrent

Past def.
I went, you went, he (she, it, one) went;
we went, you went, they went
OR:
I did go, you did go, he (she, it, one) did go;
we did go, you did go, they did go

4. Futur
j'irai, tu iras, il (elle, on) ira;
nous irons, vous irez, ils (elles) iront

Future
I shall go, you will go, he (she, it, one) will go;
we shall go, you will go, they will go

5. Cond. prés.
j'irais, tu irais, il (elle, on) irait;
nous irions, vous iriez, ils (elles) iraient

Cond. pres.
I would go, you would go, he (she, it, one) would go;
we would go, you would go, they would go

6. Prés. subj.
que j'aille, que tu ailles, qu'il (qu'elle, qu'on) aille;
que nous allions, que vous alliez, qu'ils (qu'elles) aillent

Pres. subj.
that I may go, that you may go, that he (she, it, one) may go;
that we may go, that you may go, that they may go

7. Imparf. subj.
que j'allasse, que tu allasses, qu'il (qu'elle, qu'on) allât;
que nous allassions, que vous allassiez, qu'ils (qu'elles) allassent

| Imperf. | that I might go, that you might go, that he (she, it, one) might go; |
| subj. | that we might go, that you might go, that they might go |

| 8. Passé | **je suis allé(e), tu es allé(e), il (on) est allé, elle est allée;** |
| compose | **nous sommes allé(e)s, vous êtes allé(e)(s), ils sont allés, elles sont allées** |

Past	I went, you went, he (she, it, one) went;
indef.	we went, you went, they went
	OR:
	I have gone, you have gone, he (she, it, one) has gone;
	we have gone, you have gone, they have gone
	OR:
	I did go, you did go, he (she, it, one) did go;
	we did go, you did go, they did go

| 9. Plus-q-p. | **j'étais allé(e), tu étais allé(e), il (on) était allé, elle était allée;** |
| indic. | **nous étions allé(e)s, vous étiez allé(e)(s), ils étaient allés, elles étaient allées** |

| Plup. | I had gone, you had gone, he (she, it, one) had gone; |
| indic. | we had gone, you had gone, they had gone |

| 10. Passé | **je fus allé(e), tu fus allé(e), il (on) fut allé, elle fut allée;** |
| antér. | **nous fûmes allé(e)s, vous fûtes allé(e)(s), ils furent allés, elles furent allées** |

| Past | I had gone, you had gone, he (she, it, one) had gone; |
| anter. | we had gone, you had gone, they had gone |

| 11. Fut. | **je serai allé(e), tu seras allé(e), il (on) sera allé, elle sera allée;** |
| Antér. | **nous serons allé(e)s, vous serez allé(e)(s), ils seront allés, elles seront allées** |

| Fut. | I shall have gone, you will have gone, he (she, it, one) will have gone; |
| perf. | we shall have gone, you will have gone, they will have gone |

| 12. Cond. | **je serais allé(e), tu serais allé(e), il (on) serait allé, elle serait allée;** |
| passé | **nous serions allé(e)s, vous seriez allé(e)(s), ils seraient allés, elles seraient allées** |

| Cond. | I would have gone, you would have gone, he (she, it, one) would have gone; |
| perf. | we would have gone, you would have gone, they would have gone |

| 13. Passé | **que je sois allé(e), que tu sois allé(e), qu'il (qu'on) soit allé, qu'elle soit allée;** |
| subj. | **que nous soyons allé(e)s, que vous soyez allé(e)(s), qu'ils soient allés, qu'elles soient allées** |

| Past | that I may have gone, that you may have gone, that he (she, it, one) may have gone; |
| subj. | that we may have gone, that you may have gone, that they may have gone |

| 14. Plus-q-p. | **que je fusse allé(e), que tu fusses allé(e), qu'il (qu'on) fût allé, qu'elle fût allée;** |
| subj. | **que nous fussions allé(e)s, que vous fussiez allé(e)(s), qu'ils fussent allés, qu'elles fussent allées** |

| Plup. | that I might have gone, that you might have gone, that he (she, it, one) might have gone; |
| subj. | that we might have gone, that you might have gone, that they might have gone |

| **Impér.** | **va, allons, allez** |
| Imper. | go, let's go, go |

NOTE: For an explanation and examples of each of these tenses and moods, with their uses, see **§39.86**.

§39.86 COMPARISON OF MEANINGS AND USES OF FRENCH VERB TENSES AND MOODS AS RELATED TO ENGLISH VERB TENSES AND MOODS

§39.87 The following verb tenses and moods are presented in the same numbered order as in §39.70, §39.84, and §39.85. Please compare those sections with these that follow.

§39.88 **1. Présent de l'indicatif** (Present indicative)

This tense is used most of the time in French and English. It indicates:

(a) An action or a state of being at the present time.

EXAMPLES:
Je **vais** à l'école maintenant. I *am going* to school now.
Je **pense**; donc, je **suis**. I *think;* therefore, I *am*.

(b) Habitual action.

EXAMPLE:
Je **vais** à la bibliothèque tous les jours.
I *go* to the library every day. OR: I *do go* to the library every day.

(c) A general truth, something which is permanently true.

EXAMPLES:
Deux et deux **font** quatre. Two and two *are* four.
Voir c'**est** croire. Seeing *is* believing.

(d) Vividness when talking or writing about past events. This is called the *historical present*.

EXAMPLE:
Marie-Antoinette **est** condamnée à mort. Elle **monte** dans la charrette et **est** en route pour la guillotine.
Marie-Antoinette *is* condemned to die. She *gets* into the cart and *is* on her way to the guillotine.

(e) A near future.

EXAMPLE:
Il **arrive** demain. He *arrives* tomorrow.

(f) An action or state of being that occurred in the past and *continues up to the present*. In English, this tense is the *Present perfect,* which is formed with the Present tense of *to have* (*have* or *has*) plus the past participle of the verb you are using.

EXAMPLES:
Je **suis** ici depuis dix minutes.
I *have been* here for ten minutes. (I am still here at present).
Elle **est** malade depuis trois jours.
She *has been* sick for three days. (She is still sick at present).
J'**attends** l'autobus depuis dix minutes.
I *have been waiting* for the bus for ten minutes.

NOTE: In this last example the formation of the English verb tense is slightly different from the other two examples in English. The present participle (*waiting*) is used instead of the past participle (*waited*). Not so in French: use merely the present tense. This tense is regularly formed as follows:[1]

1st conjugation—**er** verbs: drop the **—er** and add the following endings:
e, es, e; ons, ez, ent

---

[1] Irregular verbs in this tense, and in the other tenses that follow in these pages, are not given because that is not the purpose here. However, I felt the need to give a few common irregular verbs fully conjugated in all the tenses and moods merely as a handy reference. See §40. Irregular verbs must be learned separately in the classroom by constant drill, using them in simple sentences. Consult my book *501 French Verbs fully conjugated in all the tenses in a new easy to learn format,* 2nd ed., which contains them all, also published by Barron's Educational Series, Inc., Woodbury, New York.

2nd conjugation —**ir** verbs: drop the —**ir** and add the following endings:
> **is, is, it; issons, issez, issent**

3rd conjugation —**re** verbs: drop the —**re** and add the following endings:
> **s, s, —; ons, ez, ent**

See also **§39.81** for the present indicative of **avoir** and **être**. For a sample English verb conjugation with equivalent French verb forms in all the tenses, using the verb **avoir** as a helping verb, see **§39.84**. For a sample English verb conjugation with equivalent French verb forms in all the tenses, using the verb **être** as a helping verb, see **§39.85**.

§39.89   **2. Imparfait de l'indicatif** (Imperfect indicative)

This is a past tense. It is used to indicate:

(a) An action that was going on in the past at the same time as another action.

EXAMPLE:
> Il **lisait** pendant que j'**écrivais**. He *was reading* while I *was writing*.

(b) An action that was going on in the past when another action occurred.

EXAMPLE:
> Il **lisait** quand je suis entré. He *was reading* when I came in.

(c) An action that a person did habitually in the past.

EXAMPLE:
> Nous **allions** à la plage tous les jours. We *used to go* to the beach every day.
> **OR:**
> We *would go* to the beach every day.

(d) A description of a mental or physical condition in the past.

EXAMPLES:
> (mental condition)   Il **était** triste quand je l'ai vu. He *was* sad when I saw him.
> (physical condition)   Quand ma mère **était** jeune, elle **était** belle. When my mother *was* young, she *was* beautiful.

(e) An action or state of being that occurred in the past and *lasted for a certain length of time* prior to another past action. In English, it is usually translated as a Pluperfect tense and is formed with *had been* plus the present participle of the verb you are using. It is like the special use of the **Présent de l'Indicatif** described in the above section in paragraph (f), except that the action or state of being no longer exists at present.

EXAMPLE:
> J'**attendais** l'autobus depuis dix minutes quand il est arrivé. I *had been waiting* for the bus for ten minutes when it arrived.

This tense is regularly formed as follows:

For —**er**, —**ir** and —**re** verbs, take the "nous" form in the present indicative tense of the verb you have in mind, drop the ending —**ons** and add the following endings: **ais, ais, ait; ions, iez, aient**.
For the Imperfect indicative of **avoir** and **être**, see **§39.81**.

§39.90   **3. Passé simple** (Past definite or Simple past)

This past tense expresses an action that took place at some definite time. This tense is not ordinarily used in conversational French or in informal writing. It is a literary tense. It is used in formal writing, such as history and literature. You should be able merely to recognize this tense. It should be noted that French writers use the **Passé simple** less and less these days. The **Passé composé** is taking its place in literature, except for **avoir** and **être**, which I give you in **§39.81**, because it is used abundantly in French literature.

This tense is regularly formed as follows:

For all —**er** verbs, drop the —**er** on the infinitive and add the following endings: **ai, as, a; âmes, âtes, èrent.**

For regular —**ir** and —**re** verbs, drop the ending on the infinitive and add the following endings: **is, is, it; îmes, îtes, irent.**

> EXAMPLES:
>
> Il **alla** en Afrique. He *went* to Africa.
>
> Il **voyagea** en Amérique. He *traveled* to America.
>
> Ce château **fut** construit au dix-septième siècle. This castle *was* built in the seventeenth century.
>
> Elle **fut** heureuse. She *was* happy.
>
> Elle **eut** un grand bonheur. She *had* great happiness.
>
> Il **parla** à ses amis et puis il **sortit**. He *spoke* to his friends and then he *went out*.

For the passé simple of **avoir** and **être**, see **§39.81.**

§39.91   **4. Futur** (Future)

In French and English this tense is used to express an action or a state of being which will take place at some time in the future.

> EXAMPLES:
>
> J'**irai** en France l'été prochain. I *shall go* to France next summer.
>
> J'y **penserai**. I *shall think* about it. **OR:** I *will think* about it.
>
> Je **partirai** dès qu'il **arrivera**. I *shall leave* as soon as he arrives.
>
> Je te **dirai** tout quand tu **seras** ici. I *shall tell* you all when you are here.
>
> Je **m'amuserai** au bal ce soir. I *will enjoy myself* at the dance tonight.

If the action of the verb you are using is not past or present and if future time is implied, the future tense is used when the clause begins with the following conjunctions: **aussitôt que** (as soon as), **dès que** (as soon as), **quand** (when), **lorsque** (when), and **tant que** (as long as). Are you consulting the index in the back pages of this book for the location of other topics that interest you?

This tense is regularly formed as follows:

Add the following endings to the whole infinitive, except that for —**re** verbs you must drop the **e** in —**re** before you add the future endings: **ai, as, a; ons, ez, ont.**

For the Future of **avoir** and **être**, see **§39.81.**

§39.92   **5. Conditionnel présent** (Conditional)

The conditional is used in French and English to express:

(a) An action that you would do if something else were possible.

> EXAMPLE:
>
> Je **ferais** le travail si j'avais le temps. I *would do* the work if I had the time. On standardized French tests you can surely expect **Si clauses**. See **§34.—§34.2.**

(b) A conditional desire. This is the conditional of courtesy in French.

> EXAMPLES:
>
> J'**aimerais** du thé. I *would like* some tea. Je **voudrais** du café. I *would like* some coffee.

(c) An obligation or duty.

> EXAMPLE:
>
> Je **devrais** étudier pour l'examen. I *should* study for the examination. **OR:** I *ought to* study for the examination.

NOTE: (1): The French verb **devoir** plus the infinitive is used to express the idea of *should* when you mean *ought to*. See §17.–§17.7.

NOTE: (2): When the Conditional of the verb **pouvoir** is used in French, it is translated into English as *could* or *would be able*. See §28.–§28.3.

EXAMPLE:

Je **pourrais** venir après le dîner. I *could come* after dinner. **OR:** I *would be able* to come after dinner.

This tense is regularly formed as follows:

Add the following endings to the whole infinitive, except that for **—re** verbs you must drop the **e** in **—re** before you add the conditional endings: **ais, ais, ait; ions, iez, aient**. Note that these endings are the same ones you use to form regularly the Imperfect indicative. See §39.89.

For the Conditional of **avoir** and **être**, see §39.81.

§39.93 6. **Présent du subjonctif** (Present subjunctive)

The subjunctive mood is used in French much more than in English. It is disappearing in English, except for the following major uses:

(a) The subjunctive is used in French and English to express a command.

EXAMPLE:

Soyez à l'heure! *Be* on time!

NOTE: In English, the form in the subjunctive applies mainly to the verb *to be*. Also, note that all verbs in French are not in the subjunctive when expressing a command. See **Impératif** in §39.102 farther on.

(b) The subjunctive is commonly used in English to express a condition contrary to fact.

EXAMPLE:

If I *were* you, I would not do it.

NOTE: In French the subjunctive is not used in this instance. Instead, the **Imparfait de l'indicatif** is used if what precedes is *si* (*if*). Same example in French: Si j'**étais** vous, je ne le ferais pas. See §34.–§34.2, **Si clause: a summary**.

(c) The Present subjunctive is used in French and English after a verb that expresses some kind of insistence, preference, or suggestion.

EXAMPLES:

J'insiste que vous **soyez** ici à l'heure. I insist that *you be* here on time.
Je préfère qu'il **fasse** le travail maintenant. I prefer that *he do* the work now.
J'exige qu'il **soit** puni. I demand that *he be* punished.

(d) The subjunctive is used in French after a verb that expresses doubt, fear, joy, sorrow, or some other emotion. Notice in the following examples that the subjunctive is not used in English but it is in French. See §27.–§27.8, **Ne expletive**.

EXAMPLES:

Je doute qu'il **vienne**. I doubt that he *is coming*. **OR:** I doubt that he *will come*.
J'ai peur qu'il ne **soit** malade. I'm afraid he *is* sick.
Je suis heureux qu'il **vienne**. I'm happy that he *is coming*.
Je regrette qu'il **soit** malade. I'm sorry that he *is* sick.

(e) The Present subjunctive is used in French after certain conjunctions. Notice, however, that the subjunctive is not always used in English.

EXAMPLES:

Je partirai **à moins qu'il vienne**. I shall leave unless he *comes*.
Je resterai **jusqu'à ce qu'il vienne**. I shall stay until he *comes*.
Quoiqu'elle soit belle, il ne l'aime pas. Although she *is* beautiful, he does not love her.
Je l'explique **pour qu'elle comprenne**. I'm explaining it *so that she may understand*.

(f) The Present subjunctive is used in French after certain impersonal expressions that show a need, a doubt, a possibility or an impossibility. Notice, however, that the subjunctive is not always used in English in the following examples:

1. Il est urgent qu'il **vienne**. It is urgent that he *come*.
2. Il vaut mieux qu'il **vienne**. It is better that he *come*.
3. Il est possible qu'il **vienne**. It is possible that he *will come*.
4. Il est douteux qu'il **vienne**. It is doubtful that he *will come*.
5. Il est nécessaire qu'il **vienne**. It is necessary that he *come*. **OR:** He *must come*.
6. Il faut qu'il **vienne**. It is necessary that he *come*. **OR:** He *must come*.
7. Il est important que vous **fassiez** le travail. It is important that you *do* the work.
8. Il est indispensable qu'elle **fasse** le travail. It is required that she *do* the work.

The Present subjunctive is regularly formed as follows: Drop the **—ant** ending of the present participle of the verb you are using and add the following endings: **e, es, e; ions, iez, ent**.

For the Present subjunctive of **avoir** and **être**, see **§39.81**. See also **§35.–35.11, Subjunctive.**

§39.94   **7. Imparfait du subjonctif** (Imperfect subjunctive)

L'Imparfait du subjonctif is used for the same reasons as the **Présent du subjonctif**—that is, after certain verbs, conjunctions, and impersonal expressions which were used in examples above in **§39.93, Présent du subjonctif**. The main difference between these two is the time of the action. If present, use the **Présent du subjonctif**. If the action is related to the past, the **Imparfait du subjonctif** is used, provided that the action was *not* completed. If the action was completed, the **Plus-que-parfait du subjonctif** is used. See below under the section, **Plus-que-parfait du subjonctif, §39.101**.

Since the subjunctive mood is troublesome in French and English, you may be pleased to know that this tense is rarely used in English. It is used in French, however, but only in formal writing and in literature. For that reason, you should merely be familiar with it so you can recognize it when you see it on a French test you take. In conversational French and in informal writing, **l'Imparfait du subjonctif** is avoided. Use, instead, the **Présent du subjonctif**.

Notice that the **Imparfait du subjonctif** is used in French in both of the following examples, but is used in English only in the second example:

EXAMPLES:

Je voulais qu'il **vînt**. I wanted him to come. (action not completed; he did not come while I wanted him to come)

NOTE: The subjunctive of **venir** is used because the verb that precedes is one that requires the subjunctive *after* it—in this example it is **vouloir**. In conversational French and informal writing, the **Imparfait du subjonctif** is avoided. Use, instead, the **Présent du subjonctif**: Je voulais qu'il **vienne**.

Je le lui expliquais **pour qu'elle le comprît**. I was explaining it to her *so that she might understand it*. (action not completed; the understanding was not completed at the time of the explaining)

NOTE: The subjunctive of **comprendre** is used because the conjunction that precedes is one that requires the Subjunctive *after* it—in this example it is **pour que**. In conversational French and informal writing, the **Imparfait du subjonctif** is avoided. Use, instead, the **Présent du subjonctif**: Je le lui expliquais pour qu'elle le **comprenne**.

The Imperfect subjunctive is regularly formed as follows: Drop the endings of the Passé simple of the verb you are using and add the following endings:

—er verbs: **asse, asses, ât; assions, assiez, assent**
—ir verbs: **isse, isses, ît; issions, issiez, issent**
—re verbs: **usse, usses, ût; ussions, ussiez, ussent**

For the Imperfect subjunctive of **avoir** and **être**, see **§39.81**. See also **§35.–§35.11, Subjunctive.**

§39.95   **8. Passé composé** (Past indefinite)

This past tense expresses an action that took place at no definite time. It is used in conversational French, correspondence, and other informal writing. The **Passé composé** is used more and more in literature these days and is taking the place of the **Passé simple**. It is a compound tense because it is formed with the **Présent de l'indicatif** of *avoir* or *être* (depending on which of these two auxiliaries is required to form a compound tense) plus the past participle. See **§39.26–§39.29** for the distinction made between verbs conjugated with *avoir* or *être*.

> EXAMPLES:
>
> Il **est allé** à l'école. He *went* to school.
> Il **est allé** à l'école. He *did go* to school.
> Il **est allé** à l'école. He *has gone* to school.
> J'**ai mangé** dans ce restaurant beaucoup de fois. I *have eaten* in this restaurant many times.
>
> NOTE: In examples 3 and 4 in English the verb is formed with the present tense of *to have* (*have* or *has*) plus the past participle of the verb you are using. In English, this form is called the *Present Perfect*.
>
> J'**ai parlé** au garçon. I *spoke* to the boy. **OR:** I *have spoken* to the boy. **OR:** I *did speak* to the boy.

See also **§39.4–§39.25** and **§39.74**. And the present indicative of **avoir** and **être** in **§39.81**. Also, refer frequently to **§39.84** and **§39.85**.

§39.96   **9. Plus-que-parfait de l'indicatif** (Pluperfect or Past perfect indicative)

In French and English this tense is used to express an action which happened in the past *before* another past action. Since it is used in relation to another past action, the other past action is expressed in either the **Passé composé** or the **Imparfait de l'indicatif** in French. This tense is used in formal writing and literature as well as in conversational French and informal writing. The correct use of this tense is strictly observed in French. In English, however, too often we neglect to use it correctly. It is a compound tense because it is formed with the **Imparfait de l'indicatif** of *avoir* or *être* (depending on which of these two auxiliaries is required to form a compound tense) plus the past participle. See **§39.26–§39.29** for the distinction made between verbs conjugated with *avoir* or *être*. In English, this tense is formed with the past tense of *to have* (*had*) plus the past participle of the verb you are using.

> EXAMPLES:
>
> Je me suis rappelé que j'**avais oublié** de le lui dire. I remembered that I *had forgotten* to tell him.
>
> NOTE: It would be incorrect in English to say: I remembered that I *forgot* to tell him. The point here is that *first* I forgot; then, I remembered. Both actions are in the past. The action that occurred in the past *before* the other past action is in the Pluperfect. And in this example it is *I had forgotten* (**j'avais oublié**).
>
> J'**avais étudié** la leçon que le professeur a expliquée. I *had studied* the lesson which the teacher explained.
>
> NOTE: *First* I studied the lesson; then, the teacher explained it. Both actions are in the past. The action that occurred in the past *before* the other past action is in the Pluperfect. And in this example it is *I had studied* (**j'avais étudié**).
>
> J'étais fatigué ce matin parce que je n'**avais** pas **dormi**. I was tired this morning because I *had* not *slept*.

See also **§39.4–§39.25** and **§39.75**. And the Imperfect indicative of **avoir** and **être** in **§39.81**.

§39.97   **10. Passé antérieur** (Past anterior)

This tense is similar to the **Plus-que-parfait de l'indicatif**. The main difference is that in French it is a literary tense; that is, it is used in formal writing, such as history and literature.

More and more French writers today use the **Plus-que-parfait de l'indicatif** instead of this tense. Generally speaking, the **Passé antérieur** is to the **Plus-que-parfait** what the **Passé simple** is to the **Passé composé**. The **Passé antérieur** is a compound tense. In French, it is formed with the **Passé simple** of *avoir* or *être* (depending on which of these two auxiliaries is required to form a compound tense) plus the past participle. In English, it is formed in the same way as the *Pluperfect* or *Past Perfect*. This tense is ordinarily introduced by conjunctions of time: **après que, aussitôt que, dès que, lorsque, quand**.

> EXAMPLE:
> Quand il **eut mangé** tout, il partit. When he *had eaten* everything, he left.
>
> NOTE: In conversational French and informal writing, the **Plus-que-parfait de l'indicatif** is used instead: Quand il **avait mangé** tout, il est parti. The translation into English is the same.

See also the following sections: **§39.4–§39.29** and **§39.76**. And the Passé simple of **avoir** and **être** in **§39.81**.

§39.98   **11. Futur antérieur** (Future perfect or Future anterior)

In French and English this tense is used to express an action which will happen in the future *before* another future action. Since it is used in relation to another future action, the other future action is expressed in the simple Future in French, but not always in the simple Future in English. In French, it is used in conversation and informal writing as well as in formal writing and in literature. It is a compound tense because it is formed with the **Futur** of *avoir* or *être* (depending on which of these two auxiliaries is required to form a compound tense) plus the past participle of the verb you are using. In English, it is formed by using *shall have* or *will have* plus the past participle of the verb you are using.

> EXAMPLES:
> Elle arrivera demain et j'**aurai fini** le travail. She will arrive tomorrow and I *shall have finished* the work.
>
> NOTE: First, I shall finish the work; then, she will arrive. The action that will occur in the future *before* the other future action is in the **Futur antérieur**.
>
> Quand elle arrivera demain, j'**aurai fini** le travail. When she arrives tomorrow, I *shall have finished* the work.
>
> NOTE: The idea of future time here is the same as in the example above. In English, the Present tense is used (*When she arrives . . .*) to express a near future. In French, the **Futur** is used (**Quand elle arrivera . . .**) because **quand** precedes and the action will take place in the future.

See also the following sections: **§39.4–§39.29** and **§39.77**. And the Future of **avoir** and **être** in **§39.81**.

§39.99   **12. Conditionnel passé** (Conditional perfect)

This is used in French and English to express an action that you *would have done* if something else had been possible; that is, you would have done something *on condition* that something else had been possible. It is a compound tense because it is formed with the **Conditionnel présent** of *avoir* or *être* plus the past participle of the verb you are using. In English, it is formed by using *would have* plus the past participle. Observe the difference between the following examples and the one given for the use of the **Conditionnel présent** which was explained and illustrated previously, in **§39.92**.

> EXAMPLES:
> J'**aurais fait** le travail si j'avais étudié. I *would have done* the work if I had studied.
>
> J'**aurais fait** le travail si j'avais eu le temps. I *would have done* the work if I had had the time.

NOTE: Review the **Plus-que-parfait de l'indicatif** which was explained and illustrated previously in order to understand the use of *if I had studied* (**si j'avais étudié**) and *if I had had the time* (**si j'avais eu le temps**). See §34.–§34.2.

NOTE FURTHER: The French verb **devoir** plus the infinitive is used to express the idea of *should* when you mean *ought to*. The past participle of **devoir** is **dû**. It is conjugated with **avoir**. See §17. and §17.6.

EXAMPLE:

J'aurais dû étudier. I *should have* studied. **OR:** I *ought to have* studied.

See also the following sections: §39.4–§39.29 and §39.78. And the conditional of **avoir** and **être** in §39.81. On any standardized test you can surely expect **Si clauses**. See §34.–§34.2.

§39.100   **13. Passé du subjonctif** (Past subjunctive)

This tense is used to express an action which took place in the past in relation to the present time. It is like the **Passé composé**, except that the auxiliary verb (*avoir* or *être*) is in the **Présent du subjonctif**. The subjunctive is used (as was noted in the previous sections of verb tenses in the subjunctive) because what precedes is a certain verb, a certain conjunction, or a certain impersonal expression. The **Passé du subjonctif** is also used in relation to a future time when another action will be completed. This tense is rarely used in English. In French, however, this tense is used in formal writing and in literature as well as in conversational French and informal writing. It is a compound tense because it is formed with the **Présent du subjonctif** of *avoir* or *être* as the auxiliary plus the past participle of the verb you are using.

EXAMPLES:

A past action in relation to the present
Il est possible qu'elle **soit partie**. It is possible that she *may have left*. **OR:** It is possible that she *has left*.
Je doute qu'il **ait fait** cela. I doubt that he *did* that.

An action that will take place in the future
J'insiste que vous **soyez rentré** avant dix heures. I insist that you *be back* before ten o'clock.

See the Present subjunctive of **avoir** and **être** in §39.81. See also §39.4–§39.29 and §39.79.

§39.101   **14. Plus-que-parfait du subjonctif** (Pluperfect or Past perfect subjunctive)

This tense is used for the same reasons as the **Imparfait du subjonctif**—that is, after certain verbs, conjunctions and impersonal expressions which were used in examples previously under **Présent du subjonctif** in §39.93. The main difference between the **Imparfait du subjonctif** and this tense is the time of the action in the past. If the action was *not* completed, the **Imparfait du subjonctif** is used. If the action was completed, this tense is used. It is rarely used in English. In French, it is used only in formal writing and in literature. For that reason, you should merely be familiar with it so you can recognize it in the next standardized French test that you take. In conversational French and in informal writing, this tense is avoided. Use, instead, the **Passé du subjonctif**, explained in §39.100. This is a compound tense. It is formed by using the **Imparfait du subjonctif** of *avoir* or *être* plus the past participle. This tense is like the **Plus-que-parfait de l'indicatif**, except that the auxiliary verb (*avoir* or *être*) is in the **Imparfait du subjonctif**. Review the uses of the subjunctive mood, in §35.–§35.11.

EXAMPLES:

Il était possible qu'elle **fût partie**. It was possible that she *might have left*.

NOTE: Avoid this tense in French. Use, instead, **le Passé du subjonctif**: Il était possible qu'elle *soit partie*.

Je ne croyais pas qu'elle **eût dit** cela. I did not believe that she *had said* that.

NOTE: Avoid this tense in French. Use, instead, **le Passé du subjonctif**: Je ne croyais pas qu'elle **ait dit** cela.

Je n'ai pas cru qu'elle **eût dit** cela. I did not believe that she *had said* that.

NOTE: Avoid this tense in French. Use, instead, **le Passé du subjonctif**: Je n'ai pas cru qu'elle **ait dit** cela.

J'ai craint que vous ne **fussiez tombé**. I was afraid that you *had fallen*.

NOTE: Avoid this tense in French. Use, instead, **le Passé du subjonctif**: J'ai craint que vous ne **soyez tombé**.

For the Imperfect subjunctive of **avoir** and **être**, see §39.81. Also, review §39.4–§39.29 and §39.80. When you take a standardized French test, you ought to be prepared to recognize the following four tenses in the subjunctive mood: Present (§39.93), Imperfect (§39.94), Past subjunctive (§39.100), and Pluperfect subjunctive (§39.101). You will have to recognize these in most reading comprehension passages in French tests.

§39.102   **Impératif** (Imperative or Command)

The Imperative mood is used in French and English to express a command or a request. It is also used to express an indirect request made in the third person, as in the fifth and sixth examples below. In both languages it is formed by dropping the subject and using the present tense. There are a few exceptions in both languages when the **Présent du subjonctif** is used.

    EXAMPLES:

    Sortez! Get out!

    Entrez! Come in!

    Buvons! Let's drink!

    Soyez à l'heure! *Be* on time! (Subjunctive is used)

    Dieu le **veuille**! May God *grant* it! (Subjunctive is used)

    Qu'ils **mangent** du gâteau! Let them eat cake! (Subjunctive is used)

    Asseyez-vous! Sit down!

    Levez-vous! Get up!

There is another exception. You must drop the final **s** in the 2d person singular of an **-er** verb. This is done in the affirmative and negative, as in: **Mange! Ne mange pas!** However, when the pronouns **y** and **en** are linked to it, the **s** is retained in all regular **-er** verbs and in the verb **aller**. Examples: **Donnes-en** (Give some)! **Manges-en** (Eat some)! **Vas-y** (Go there)! The reason for this is that it makes it easier to link the two elements by pronouncing the **s** as a **z**.

Review §35. and §35.5. For the Present subjunctive of **avoir** and **être**, see §39.81. See also my footnote in §39.88.

§40.   **IRREGULAR VERBS COMMONLY USED**

§40.1

Here are fifty commonly used irregular verbs conjugated for you fully in all the tenses and moods. If there are any not given here, but which are of interest to you, consult my book *501 French Verbs fully conjugated in all the tenses in a new easy to learn format*, 2nd ed., which contains them all, also published by Barron's Educational Series, Inc., Woodbury, New York.

The common irregular verb **aller** is conjugated fully for you in all the tenses and moods in §39.85.

In the format of the verbs that follow, the subject pronouns have been omitted in order to emphasize the verb forms. The subject pronouns are, as you know: **je, tu, il (elle, on)** in the singular; **nous, vous, ils (elles)** in the plural.

The numbered sequence of the verb tenses is that used in §39.70, §39.84 and §39.85, which you must consult. A number system is used here in order to conserve space so that you may see, as a picture, all the forms for a particular verb.

aller

Part. pr. **allant**   Part. passé **allé(e)(s)**

to go

The Seven Simple Tenses		The Seven Compound Tenses	
Singular	Plural	Singular	Plural
1 présent de l'indicatif		**8 passé composé**	
vais	allons	suis allé(e)	sommes allé(e)s
vas	allez	es allé(e)	êtes allé(e)(s)
va	vont	est allé(e)	sont allé(e)s
2 imparfait de l'indicatif		**9 plus-que-parfait de l'indicatif**	
allais	allions	étais allé(e)	étions allé(e)s
allais	alliez	étais allé(e)	étiez allé(e)(s)
allait	allaient	était allé(e)	étaient allé(e)s
3 passé simple		**10 passé antérieur**	
allai	allâmes	fus allé(e)	fûmes allé(e)s
allas	allâtes	fus allé(e)	fûtes allé(e)(s)
alla	allèrent	fut allé(e)	furent allé(e)s
4 futur		**11 futur antérieur**	
irai	irons	serai allé(e)	serons allé(e)s
iras	irez	seras allé(e)	serez allé(e)(s)
ira	iront	sera allé(e)	seront allé(e)s
5 conditionnel		**12 conditionnel passé**	
irais	irions	serais allé(e)	serions allé(e)s
irais	iriez	serais all(e)	seriez allé(e)(s)
irait	iraient	serait allé(e)	seraient allé(e)s
6 présent du subjonctif		**13 passé du subjonctif**	
aille	allions	sois allé(e)	soyons allé(e)s
ailles	alliez	sois allé(e)	soyez allé(e)(s)
aille	aillent	soit allé(e)	soient allé(e)s
7 imparfait du subjonctif		**14 plus-que-parfait du subjonctif**	
allasse	allassions	fusse allé(e)	fussions allé(e)s
allasses	allassiez	fusses allé(e)	fussiez allé(e)(s)
allât	allassent	fût allé(e)	fussent allé(e)s

Impératif
va
allons
allez

Common idiomatic expressions using this verb

Comment allez-vous?   **Je vais bien, je vais mal, je vais mieux.**

aller à la pêche   to go fishing
aller à la rencontre de quelqu'un   to go to meet someone
aller à pied   to walk, to go on foot
aller au fond des choses   to get to the bottom of things
Ça va?   Is everything O.K.?   **Oui, ça va!**

Be sure to consult the Appendix for verbs used in idiomatic expressions and §20.–§20.37.

The subject pronouns are found in §40.1.

Part. pr. **s'en allant**   **Part. passé** **en allé(e)(s)**   **s'en aller**

to go away

The Seven Simple Tenses		The Seven Compound Tenses	
Singular	Plural	Singular	Plural
1 présent de l'indicatif		**8 passé composé**	
m'en vais	nous en allons	m'en suis allé(e)	nous en sommes allé(e)s
t'en vas	vous en allez	t'en es allé(e)	vous en êtes allé(e)(s)
s'en va	s'en vont	s'en est allé(e)	s'en sont allé(e)s
2 imparfait de l'indicatif		**9 plus-que-parfait de l'indicatif**	
m'en allais	nous en allions	m'en étais allé(e)	nous en étions allé(e)s
t'en allais	vous en alliez	t'en étais allé(e)	vous en étiez allé(e)(s)
s'en allait	s'en allaient	s'en était allé(e)	s'en étaient allé(e)s
3 passé simple		**10 passé antérieur**	
m'en allai	nous en allâmes	m'en fus allé(e)	nous en fûmes allé(e)s
t'en allas	vous en allâtes	t'en fus allé(e)	vous en fûtes allé(e)(s)
s'en alla	s'en allèrent	s'en fut allé(e)	s'en furent allé(e)s
4 futur		**11 futur antérieur**	
m'en irai	nous en irons	m'en serai allé(e)	nous en serons allé(e)s
t'en iras	vous en irez	t'en seras allé(e)	vous en serez allé(e)(s)
s'en ira	s'en iront	s'en sera allé(e)	s'en seront allé(e)s
5 conditionnel		**12 conditionnel passé**	
m'en irais	nous en irions	m'en serais allé(e)	nous en serions allé(e)s
t'en irais	vous en iriez	t'en serais allé(e)	vous en seriez allé(e)(s)
s'en irait	s'en iraient	s'en serait allé(e)	s'en seraient allé(e)s
6 présent du subjonctif		**13 passé du subjonctif**	
m'en aille	nous en allions	m'en sois allé(e)	nous en soyons allé(e)s
t'en ailles	vous en alliez	t'en sois allé(e)	vous en soyez allé(e)(s)
s'en aille	s'en aillent	s'en soit allé(e)	s'en soient allé(e)s
7 imparfait du subjonctif		**14 plus-que-parfait du subjonctif**	
m'en allasse	nous en allassions	m'en fusse allé(e)	nous en fussions allé(e)s
t'en allasses	vous en allassiez	t'en fusses allé(e)	vous en fussiez allé(e)(s)
s'en allât	s'en allassent	s'en fût allé(e)	s'en fussent allé(e)s

Impératif
va-t'en; ne t'en va pas
allons-nous-en; ne nous en allons pas
allez-vous-en; ne vous en allez pas

Common idiomatic expressions using this verb

This verb also has the following idiomatic meanings: to move away (from one residence to another), to die, to pass away, to steal away.

Monsieur et Madame Moreau n'habitent plus ici. Ils s'en sont allés. Je crois qu'ils sont maintenant à Bordeaux.

Madame Morel est gravement malade; elle s'en va.

Le cambrioleur s'en est allé furtivement avec l'argent et les bijoux.

Be sure to consult the Appendix for verbs used in idiomatic expressions and §20.–§20.37.

apprendre

Part. pr. **apprenant**   Part. passé **appris**

to learn

The Seven Simple Tenses		The Seven Compound Tenses	
Singular	Plural	Singular	Plural
1 présent de l'indicatif		**8 passé composé**	
apprends	apprenons	ai appris	avons appris
apprends	apprenez	as appris	avez appris
apprend	apprennent	a appris	ont appris
2 imparfait de l'indicatif		**9 plus-que-parfait de l'indicatif**	
apprenais	apprenions	avais appris	avions appris
apprenais	appreniez	avais appris	aviez appris
apprenait	apprenaient	avait appris	avaient appris
3 passé simple		**10 passé antérieur**	
appris	apprîmes	eus appris	eûmes appris
appris	apprîtes	eus appris	eûtes appris
apprit	apprirent	eut appris	eurent appris
4 futur		**11 futur antérieur**	
apprendrai	apprendrons	aurai appris	aurons appris
apprendras	apprendrez	auras appris	aurez appris
apprendra	apprendront	aura appris	auront appris
5 conditionnel		**12 conditionnel passé**	
apprendrais	apprendrions	aurais appris	aurions appris
apprendrais	apprendriez	aurais appris	auriez appris
apprendrait	apprendraient	aurait appris	auraient appris
6 présent du subjonctif		**13 passé du subjonctif**	
apprenne	apprenions	aie appris	ayons appris
apprennes	appreniez	aies appris	ayez appris
apprenne	apprennent	ait appris	aient appris
7 imparfait du subjonctif		**14 plus-que-parfait du subjonctif**	
apprisse	apprissions	eusse appris	eussions appris
apprisses	apprissiez	eusses appris	eussiez appris
apprît	apprissent	eût appris	eussent appris

Impératif
apprends
apprenons
apprenez

Common idiomatic expressions using this verb

A l'école j'apprends à lire en français. J'apprends à écrire et à parler. Ce matin mon maître de français m'a dit: —Robert, apprends ce poème par coeur pour demain.

La semaine dernière j'ai appris un poème de Verlaine. Pour demain j'apprendrai la conjugaison du verbe *apprendre*.

apprendre par coeur   to memorize
apprendre à qqn à faire qqch   to teach somebody to do something
apprendre qqch à qqn   to inform someone of something; to teach someone something
apprendre à faire qqch   to learn to do something

The subject pronouns are found in §40.1.

Part. pr. **ayant**   Part. passé **eu**   **avoir**

to have

The Seven Simple Tenses		The Seven Compound Tenses	
Singular	Plural	Singular	Plural
1 présent de l'indicatif		**8 passé composé**	
ai	**avons**	**ai eu**	**avons eu**
as	**avez**	**as eu**	**avez eu**
a	**ont**	**a eu**	**ont eu**
2 imparfait de l'indicatif		**9 plus-que-parfait de l'indicatif**	
avais	**avions**	**avais eu**	**avions eu**
avais	**aviez**	**avais eu**	**aviez eu**
avait	**avaient**	**avait eu**	**avaient eu**
3 passé simple		**10 passé antérieur**	
eus	**eûmes**	**eus eu**	**eûmes eu**
eus	**eûtes**	**eus eu**	**eûtes eu**
eut	**eurent**	**eut eu**	**eurent eu**
4 futur		**11 futur antérieur**	
aurai	**aurons**	**aurai eu**	**aurons eu**
auras	**aurez**	**auras eu**	**aurez eu**
aura	**auront**	**aura eu**	**auront eu**
5 conditionnel		**12 conditionnel passé**	
aurais	**aurions**	**aurais eu**	**aurions eu**
aurais	**auriez**	**aurais eu**	**auriez eu**
aurait	**auraient**	**aurait eu**	**auraient eu**
6 présent du subjonctif		**13 passé du subjonctif**	
aie	**ayons**	**aie eu**	**ayons eu**
aies	**ayez**	**aies eu**	**ayez eu**
ait	**aient**	**ait eu**	**aient eu**
7 imparfait du subjonctif		**14 plus-que-parfait du subjonctif**	
eusse	**eussions**	**eusse eu**	**eussions eu**
eusses	**eussiez**	**eusses eu**	**eussiez eu**
eût	**eussent**	**eût eu**	**eussent eu**

Impératif
aie
ayons
ayez

Common idiomatic expressions using this verb

avoir. . . ans   to be . . . years old
avoir à + inf.   to have to, to be obliged to + inf.
avoir besoin de   to need, to have need of
avoir chaud   to be (feel) warm (persons)
avoir froid   to be (feel) cold (persons)
avoir sommeil   to be (feel) sleepy

avoir qqch à faire   to have
   something to do
avoir de la chance   to be lucky
avoir faim   to be hungry

For more idioms using this verb, consult the Appendix and §20.6.

The subject pronouns are found in §40.1.

boire

Part. pr. **buvant**   Part. passé **bu**

to drink

The Seven Simple Tenses		The Seven Compound Tenses	
Singular	Plural	Singular	Plural
1 présent de l'indicatif		**8 passé composé**	
bois	buvons	ai bu	avons bu
bois	buvez	as bu	avez bu
boit	boivent	a bu	ont bu
2 imparfait de l'indicatif		**9 plus-que-parfait de l'indicatif**	
buvais	buvions	avais bu	avions bu
buvais	buviez	avais bu	aviez bu
buvait	buvaient	avait bu	avaient bu
3 passé simple		**10 passé antérieur**	
bus	bûmes	eus bu	eûmes bu
bus	bûtes	eus bu	eûtes bu
but	burent	eut bu	eurent bu
4 futur		**11 futur antérieur**	
boirai	boirons	aurai bu	aurons bu
boiras	boirez	auras bu	aurez bu
boira	boiront	aura bu	auront bu
5 conditionnel		**12 conditionnel passé**	
boirais	boirions	aurais bu	aurions bu
boirais	boiriez	aurais bu	auriez bu
boirait	boiraient	aurait bu	auraient bu
6 présent du subjonctif		**13 passé du subjonctif**	
boive	buvions	aie bu	ayons bu
boives	buviez	aies bu	ayez bu
boive	boivent	ait bu	aient bu
7 imparfait du subjonctif		**14 plus-que-parfait du subjonctif**	
busse	bussions	eusse bu	eussions bu
busses	bussiez	eusses bu	eussiez bu
bût	bussent	eût bu	eussent bu

Impératif
bois
buvons
buvez

Sentences using this verb and words related to it

—Michel, as-tu bu ton lait?
—Non, maman, je ne l'ai pas bu.
—Bois-le tout de suite, je te dis.
—Tous les jours je bois du lait. N'y a-t-il pas d'autres boissons dans la maison?
— Si, il y a d'autres boissons dans la maison mais les bons garçons comme toi boivent du lait.

boire à la santé de qqn   to drink to someone's health
une boisson   drink; **boisson gazeuse**   carbonated drink
un buveur, une buveuse   drinker; **une buvette**   bar
un buvard   ink blotter; **boire un coup**   to have a drink

Part. pr. **comprenant**   Part. passé **compris**   **comprendre**

to understand

The Seven Simple Tenses		The Seven Compound Tenses	
Singular	Plural	Singular	Plural
1 présent de l'indicatif		**8 passé composé**	
comprends	comprenons	ai compris	avons compris
comprends	comprenez	as compris	avez compris
comprend	comprennent	a compris	ont compris
2 imparfait de l'indicatif		**9 plus-que-parfait de l'indicatif**	
comprenais	comprenions	avais compris	avions compris
comprenais	compreniez	avais compris	aviez compris
comprenait	comprenaient	avait compris	avaient compris
3 passé simple		**10 passé antérieur**	
compris	comprîmes	eus compris	eûmes compris
compris	comprîtes	eus compris	eûtes compris
comprit	comprirent	eut compris	eurent compris
4 futur		**11 futur antérieur**	
comprendrai	comprendrons	aurai compris	aurons compris
comprendras	comprendrez	auras compris	aurez compris
comprendra	comprendront	aura compris	auront compris
5 conditionnel		**12 conditionnel passé**	
comprendrais	comprendrions	aurais compris	aurions compris
comprendrais	comprendriez	aurais compris	auriez compris
comprendrait	comprendraient	aurait compris	auraient compris
6 présent du subjonctif		**13 passé du subjonctif**	
comprenne	comprenions	aie compris	ayons compris
comprennes	compreniez	aies compris	ayez compris
comprenne	comprennent	ait compris	aient compris
7 imparfait du subjonctif		**14 plus-que-parfait du subjonctif**	
comprisse	comprissions	eusse compris	eussions compris
comprisses	comprissiez	eusses compris	eussiez compris
comprît	comprissent	eût compris	eussent compris

Impératif
comprends
comprenons
comprenez

Sentences using this verb and expressions related to it

Je ne comprends jamais la maîtresse de biologie. Je n'ai pas compris la leçon d'hier, je ne comprends pas la leçon d'aujourd'hui, et je ne comprendrai jamais rien.

faire comprendre à qqn que. . .   to make it clear to someone that. . .
la compréhension   comprehension, understanding
Ça se comprend   Of course; That is understood.
y compris   included, including

Consult §33.

Be sure to consult the Appendix for the section on verbs used in idiomatic expressions and §20.–§20.37.

connaître

Part. pr. **connaissant**   Part. passé **connu**

to know, to be acquainted with (persons or places)

The Seven Simple Tenses		The Seven Compound Tenses	
Singular	Plural	Singular	Plural
1 présent de l'indicatif		**8 passé composé**	
connais	connaissons	ai connu	avons connu
connais	connaissez	as connu	avez connu
connaît	connaissent	a connu	ont connu
2 imparfait de l'indicatif		**9 plus-que-parfait de l'indicatif**	
connaissais	connaissions	avais connu	avions connu
connaissais	connaissiez	avais connu	aviez connu
connaissait	connaissaient	avait connu	avaient connu
3 passé simple		**10 passé antérieur**	
connus	connûmes	eus connu	eûmes connu
connus	connûtes	eus connu	eûtes connu
connut	connurent	eut connu	eurent connu
4 futur		**11 futur antérieur**	
connaîtrai	connaîtrons	aurai connu	aurons connu
connaîtras	connaîtrez	auras connu	aurez connu
connaîtra	connaîtront	aura connu	auront connu
5 conditionnel		**12 conditionnel passé**	
connaîtrais	connaîtrions	aurais connu	aurions connu
connaîtrais	connaîtriez	aurais connu	auriez connu
connaîtrait	connaîtraient	aurait connu	auraient connu
6 présent du subjonctif		**13 passé du subjonctif**	
connaisse	connaissions	aie connu	ayons connu
connaisses	connaissiez	aies connu	ayez connu
connaisse	connaissent	ait connu	aient connu
7 imparfait du subjonctif		**14 plus-que-parfait du subjonctif**	
connusse	connussions	eusse connu	eussions connu
connusses	connussiez	eusses connu	eussiez connu
connût	connussent	eût connu	eussent connu

Impératif
connais
connaissons
connaissez

Common idiomatic expressions using this verb and words related to it

—**Connaissez-vous quelqu'un qui puisse m'aider? Je suis touriste et je ne connais pas cette ville.**
—**Non, je ne connais personne. Je suis touriste aussi.**
—**Voulez-vous aller prendre un café? Nous pouvons nous faire connaissance.**

la connaissance   knowledge, understanding, aquaintance
connaisseur, connaisseuse   expert
se connaître   to know each other, to know oneself; **faire connaissance**   to get acquainted

Consult §32.

The subject pronouns are found in §40.1.

Part. pr. **courant**   Part. passé **couru**   **courir**

to run

The Seven Simple Tenses		The Seven Compound Tenses	
Singular	Plural	Singular	Plural
1 présent de l'indicatif		**8 passé composé**	
cours	courons	ai couru	avons couru
cours	courez	as couru	avez couru
court	courent	a couru	ont couru
2 imparfait de l'indicatif		**9 plus-que-parfait de l'indicatif**	
courais	courions	avais couru	avions couru
courais	couriez	avais couru	aviez couru
courait	couraient	avait couru	avaient couru
3 passé simple		**10 passé antérieur**	
courus	courûmes	eus couru	eûmes couru
courus	courûtes	eus couru	eûtes couru
courut	coururent	eut couru	eurent couru
4 futur		**11 futur antérieur**	
courrai	courrons	aurai couru	aurons couru
courras	courrez	auras couru	aurez couru
courra	courront	aura couru	auront couru
5 conditionnel		**12 conditionnel passé**	
courrais	courrions	aurais couru	aurions couru
courrais	courriez	aurais couru	auriez couru
courrait	courraient	aurait couru	auraient couru
6 présent du subjonctif		**13 passé du subjonctif**	
coure	courions	aie couru	ayons couru
coures	couriez	aies couru	ayez couru
coure	courent	ait couru	aient couru
7 imparfait du subjonctif		**14 plus-que-parfait du subjonctif**	
courusse	courussions	eusse couru	eussions couru
courusses	courussiez	eusses couru	eussiez couru
courût	courussent	eût couru	eussent couru

Impératif
cours
courons
courez

Sentences using this verb and words related to it

Les enfants sont toujours prêts à courir. Quand on est jeune on court sans se fatiguer. Michel a couru de la maison jusqu'à l'école. Il a seize ans.

le courrier   courier, messenger, mail
un coureur   runner
faire courir un bruit   to spread a rumor
courir une course   to run a race
courir le monde   to roam all over the world

accourir vers   to come running toward
courir les rues   to run about the streets
par le temps qui court   these days, nowadays
parcourir   to go through, to travel through, to cover (distance)

The subject pronouns are found in §40.1.

couvrir

Part. pr. **couvrant** Part. passé **couvert**

to cover

The Seven Simple Tenses		The Seven Compound Tenses	
Singular	Plural	Singular	Plural

1 présent de l'indicatif

couvre	couvrons
couvres	couvrez
couvre	couvrent

8 passé composé

ai couvert	avons couvert
as couvert	avez couvert
a couvert	ont couvert

2 imparfait de l'indicatif

couvrais	couvrions
couvrais	couvriez
couvrait	couvraient

9 plus-que-parfait de l'indicatif

avais couvert	avions couvert
avais couvert	aviez couvert
avait couvert	avaient couvert

3 passé simple

couvris	couvrîmes
couvris	couvrîtes
couvrit	couvrirent

10 passé antérieur

eus couvert	eûmes couvert
eus couvert	eûtes couvert
eut couvert	eurent couvert

4 futur

couvrirai	couvrirons
couvriras	couvrirez
couvrira	couvriront

11 futur antérieur

aurai couvert	aurons couvert
auras couvert	aurez couvert
aura couvert	auront couvert

5 conditionnel

couvrirais	couvririons
couvrirais	couvririez
couvrirait	couvriraient

12 conditionnel passé

aurais couvert	aurions couvert
aurais couvert	auriez couvert
aurait couvert	auraient couvert

6 présent du subjonctif

couvre	couvrions
couvres	couvriez
couvre	couvrent

13 passé du subjonctif

aie couvert	ayons couvert
aies couvert	ayez couvert
ait couvert	aient couvert

7 imparfait du subjonctif

couvrisse	couvrissions
couvrisses	couvrissiez
couvrît	couvrissent

14 plus-que-parfait du subjonctif

eusse couvert	eussions couvert
eusses couvert	eussiez couvert
eût couvert	eussent couvert

Impératif
couvre
couvrons
couvrez

Sentences using this verb and words related to it

Avant de quitter la maison, Madame Champlain a couvert le lit d'un dessus-de-lit. Puis, elle a couvert son mari de caresses et de baisers.

un couvert place setting (spoon, knife, fork, *etc.)*
acheter des couverts to buy cutlery
mettre le couvert to lay the table
une couverture blanket
Le temps se couvre The sky is overcast.

découvrir to discover, disclose, uncover
se couvrir to cover oneself, to put on one's hat
le couvre-feu curfew

See also **découvrir.**

The subject pronouns are found in §40.1.

Part. pr. **croyant**   Part. passé **cru**

croire

to believe

The Seven Simple Tenses		The Seven Compound Tenses	
Singular	Plural	Singular	Plural
1 présent de l'indicatif		**8 passé composé**	
crois	croyons	ai cru	avons cru
crois	croyez	as cru	avez cru
croit	croient	a cru	ont cru
2 imparfait de l'indicatif		**9 plus-que-parfait de l'indicatif**	
croyais	croyions	avais cru	avions cru
croyais	croyiez	avais cru	aviez cru
croyait	croyaient	avait cru	avaient cru
3 passé simple		**10 passé antérieur**	
crus	crûmes	eus cru	eûmes cru
crus	crûtes	eus cru	eûtes cru
crut	crurent	eut cru	eurent cru
4 futur		**11 futur antérieur**	
croirai	croirons	aurai cru	aurons cru
croiras	croirez	auras cru	aurez cru
croira	croiront	aura cru	auront cru
5 conditionnel		**12 conditionnel passé**	
croirais	croirions	aurais cru	aurions cru
croirais	croiriez	aurais cru	auriez cru
croirait	croiraient	aurait cru	auraient cru
6 présent du subjonctif		**13 passé du subjonctif**	
croie	croyions	aie cru	ayons cru
croies	croyiez	aies cru	ayez cru
croie	croient	ait cru	aient cru
7 imparfait du subjonctif		**14 plus-que-parfait du subjonctif**	
crusse	crussions	eusse cru	eussions cru
crusses	crussiez	eusses cru	eussiez cru
crût	crussent	eût cru	eussent cru

Impératif
crois
croyons
croyez

Sentences using this verb and words related to it

   Est-ce que vous croyez tout ce que vous entendez? Avez-vous cru l'histoire que je vous ai racontée?

Croyez-m'en!   Take my word for it!
se croire   to think oneself, to consider oneself
Paul se croit beau   Paul thinks himself handsome.
croyable   believable
incroyable   unbelievable

croire à qqch   to believe in something
croire en qqn   to believe in someone

Consult the Appendix for the section on verbs used in idiomatic expressions and §20.–§20.37.

The subject pronouns are found in §40.1.

découvrir

Part. pr. **découvrant**   Part. passé **découvert**

to discover, to uncover

The Seven Simple Tenses		The Seven Compound Tenses	
Singular	Plural	Singular	Plural
1 présent de l'indicatif		**8 passé composé**	
découvre	découvrons	ai découvert	avons découvert
découvres	découvrez	as découvert	avez découvert
découvre	découvrent	a découvert	ont découvert
2 imparfait de l'indicatif		**9 plus-que-parfait de l'indicatif**	
découvrais	découvrions	avais découvert	avions découvert
découvrais	découvriez	avais découvert	aviez découvert
découvrait	découvraient	avait découvert	avaient découvert
3 passé simple		**10 passé antérieur**	
découvris	découvrîmes	eus découvert	eûmes découvert
découvris	découvrîtes	eus découvert	eûtes découvert
découvrit	découvrirent	eut découvert	eurent découvert
4 futur		**11 futur antérieur**	
découvrirai	découvrirons	aurai découvert	aurons découvert
découvriras	découvrirez	auras découvert	aurez découvert
découvrira	découvriront	aura découvert	auront découvert
5 conditionnel		**12 conditionnel passé**	
découvrirais	découvririons	aurais découvert	aurions découvert
découvrirais	découvririez	aurais découvert	auriez découvert
découvrirait	découvriraient	aurait découvert	auraient découvert
6 présent du subjonctif		**13 passé du subjonctif**	
découvre	découvrions	aie découvert	ayons découvert
découvres	découvriez	aies découvert	ayez découvert
découvre	découvrent	ait découvert	aient découvert
7 imparfait du subjonctif		**14 plus-que-parfait du subjonctif**	
découvrisse	découvrissions	eusse découvert	eussions découvert
découvrisses	découvrissiez	eusses découvert	eussiez découvert
découvrît	découvrissent	eût découvert	eussent découvert

Impératif
découvre
découvrons
découvrez

Sentences using this verb and words related to it

Ce matin j'ai couvert ce panier de fruits et maintenant il est découvert. Qui l'a découvert?

un découvreur   discoverer
une découverte   a discovery, invention
se découvrir   to take off one's clothes; to take off one's hat
aller à la découverte   to explore
Découvrir saint Pierre pour couvrir saint Paul   to rob Peter to pay Paul.

See also **couvrir.**

The subject pronouns are found in §40.1.

Part. pr. devenant   **Part. passé devenu(e)(s)**   **devenir**

to become

The Seven Simple Tenses		The Seven Compound Tenses	
Singular	Plural	Singular	Plural
1 présent de l'indicatif		**8 passé composé**	
deviens	devenons	suis devenu(e)	sommes devenu(e)s
deviens	devenez	es devenu(e)	êtes devenu(e)(s)
devient	deviennent	est devenu(e)	sont devenu(e)s
2 imparfait de l'indicatif		**9 plus-que-parfait de l'indicatif**	
devenais	devenions	étais devenu(e)	étions devenu(e)s
devenais	deveniez	étais devenu(e)	étiez devenu(e)(s)
devenait	devenaient	était devenu(e)	étaient devenu(e)s
3 passé simple		**10 passé antérieur**	
devins	devînmes	fus devenu(e)	fûmes devenu(e)s
devins	devîntes	fus devenu(e)	fûtes devenu(e)(s)
devint	devinrent	fut devenu(e)	furent devenu(e)s
4 futur		**11 futur antérieur**	
deviendrai	deviendrons	serai devenu(e)	serons devenu(e)s
deviendras	deviendrez	seras devenu(e)	serez devenu(e)(s)
deviendra	deviendront	sera devenu(e)	seront devenu(e)s
5 conditionnel		**12 conditionnel passé**	
deviendrais	deviendrions	serais devenu(e)	serions devenu(e)s
deviendrais	deviendriez	serais devenu(e)	seriez devenu(e)(s)
deviendrait	deviendraient	serait devenu(e)	seraient devenu(e)s
6 présent du subjonctif		**13 passé du subjonctif**	
devienne	devenions	sois devenu(e)	soyons devenu(e)s
deviennes	deveniez	sois devenu(e)	soyez devenu(e)(s)
devienne	deviennent	soit devenu(e)	soient devenu(e)s
7 imparfait du subjonctif		**14 plus-que-parfait du subjonctif**	
devinsse	devinssions	fusse devenu(e)	fussions devenu(e)s
devinsses	devinssiez	fusses devenu(e)	fussiez devenu(e)(s)
devînt	devinssent	fût devenu(e)	fussent devenu(e)s

Impératif
deviens
devenons
devenez

Common idiomatic expressions using this verb

   J'entends dire que Claudette est devenue docteur. Et vous, qu'est-ce que vous voulez devenir?

devenir fou, devenir folle   to go mad, crazy
Qu'est devenue votre soeur?   What has become of your sister?

devoir

Part. pr. **devant**   Part. passé **dû (due)**

to have to, must, ought, owe, should

The Seven Simple Tenses		The Seven Compound Tenses	
Singular	Plural	Singular	Plural
1 présent de l'indicatif		**8 passé composé**	
dois	devons	ai dû	avons dû
dois	devez	as dû	avez dû
doit	doivent	a dû	ont dû
2 imparfait de l'indicatif		**9 plus-que-parfait de l'indicatif**	
devais	devions	avais dû	avions dû
devais	deviez	avais dû	aviez dû
devait	devaient	avait dû	avaient dû
3 passé simple		**10 passé antérieur**	
dus	dûmes	eus dû	eûmes dû
dus	dûtes	eus dû	eûtes dû
dut	durent	eut dû	eurent dû
4 futur		**11 futur antérieur**	
devrai	devrons	aurai dû	aurons dû
devras	devrez	auras dû	aurez dû
devra	devront	aura dû	auront dû
5 conditionnel		**12 conditionnel passé**	
devrais	devrions	aurais dû	aurions dû
devrais	devriez	aurais dû	auriez dû
devrait	devraient	aurait dû	auraient dû
6 présent du subjonctif		**13 passé du subjonctif**	
doive	devions	aie dû	ayons dû
doives	deviez	aies dû	ayez dû
doive	doivent	ait dû	aient dû
7 imparfait du subjonctif		**14 plus-que-parfait du subjonctif**	
dusse	dussions	eusse dû	eussions dû
dusses	dussiez	eusses dû	eussiez dû
dût	dussent	eût dû	eussent dû

Impératif
dois
devons
devez

Common idiomatic expressions using this verb

   Hier soir je suis allé au cinéma avec mes amis. **Vous auriez dû venir avec nous. Le film était excellent.**

Vous auriez dû venir / You should have come.
le devoir   duty, obligation
les devoirs   homework
Cette grosse somme d'argent est due lundi.

Consult §17. – §17.7.

The subject pronouns are found in §40.1.

Part. pr. **disant** Part. passé **dit** **dire**

to say, to tell

The Seven Simple Tenses		The Seven Compound Tenses	
Singular	Plural	Singular	Plural
1 présent de l'indicatif		**8 passé composé**	
dis	disons	ai dit	avons dit
dis	dites	as dit	avez dit
dit	disent	a dit	ont dit
2 imparfait de l'indicatif		**9 plus-que-parfait de l'indicatif**	
disais	disions	avais dit	avions dit
disais	disiez	avais dit	aviez dit
disait	disaient	avait dit	avaient dit
3 passé simple		**10 passé antérieur**	
dis	dîmes	eus dit	eûmes dit
dis	dîtes	eus dit	eûtes dit
dit	dirent	eut dit	eurent dit
4 futur		**11 futur antérieur**	
dirai	dirons	aurai dit	aurons dit
diras	direz	auras dit	aurez dit
dira	diront	aura dit	auront dit
5 conditionnel		**12 conditionnel passé**	
dirais	dirions	aurais dit	aurions dit
dirais	diriez	aurais dit	auriez dit
dirait	diraient	aurait dit	auraient dit
6 présent du subjonctif		**13 passé du subjonctif**	
dise	disions	aie dit	ayons dit
dises	disiez	aies dit	ayez dit
dise	disent	ait dit	aient dit
7 imparfait du subjonctif		**14 plus-que-parfait du subjonctif**	
disse	dissions	eusse dit	eussions dit
disses	dissiez	eusses dit	eussiez dit
dît	dissent	eût dit	eussent dit

Impératif
dis
disons
dites

Common idiomatic expressions using this verb

—**Qu'est-ce que vous avez dit? Je n'ai pas entendu.**
—**J'ai dit que je ne vous ai pas entendu. Parlez plus fort.**

c'est-à-dire that is, that is to say
entendre dire que to hear it said that
vouloir dire to mean
dire du bien de to speak well of

For more idioms using this verb, see the Appendix for the section on verbs used in idiomatic expressions.

écrire

Part. pr. **écrivant**   Part. passé **écrit**

to write

The Seven Simple Tenses		The Seven Compound Tenses	
Singular	Plural	Singular	Plural
1 présent de l'indicatif		**8 passé composé**	
écris	écrivons	ai écrit	avons écrit
écris	écrivez	as écrit	avez écrit
écrit	écrivent	a écrit	ont écrit
2 imparfait de l'indicatif		**9 plus-que-parfait de l'indicatif**	
écrivais	écrivions	avais écrit	avions écrit
écrivais	écriviez	avais écrit	aviez écrit
écrivait	écrivaient	avait écrit	avaient écrit
3 passé simple		**10 passé antérieur**	
écrivis	écrivîmes	eus écrit	eûmes écrit
écrivis	écrivîtes	eus écrit	eûtes écrit
écrivit	écrivirent	eut écrit	eurent écrit
4 futur		**11 futur antérieur**	
écrirai	écrirons	aurai écrit	aurons écrit
écriras	écrirez	auras écrit	aurez écrit
écrira	écriront	aura écrit	auront écrit
5 conditionnel		**12 conditionnel passé**	
écrirais	écririons	aurais écrit	aurions écrit
écrirais	écririez	aurais écrit	auriez écrit
écrirait	écriraient	aurait écrit	auraient écrit
6 présent du subjonctif		**13 passé du subjonctif**	
écrive	écrivions	aie écrit	ayons écrit
écrives	écriviez	aies écrit	ayez écrit
écrive	écrivent	ait écrit	aient écrit
7 imparfait du subjonctif		**14 plus-que-parfait du subjonctif**	
écrivisse	écrivissions	eusse écrit	eussions écrit
écrivisses	écrivissiez	eusses écrit	eussiez écrit
écrivît	écrivissent	eût écrit	eussent écrit

Impératif
écris
écrivons
écrivez

Sentences using this verb and words related to it

  Jean: **As-tu écrit ta composition pour la classe de français?**
Jacques: **Non, je ne l'ai pas écrite.**
  Jean: **Écrivons-la ensemble.**

un écrivain   writer;   **une femme écrivain**   woman writer
écriture *(f.)*   handwriting, writing
écrire un petit mot à qqn   to write a note to someone

Consult the Appendix for verbs used in idiomatic expressions.

The subject pronouns are found in §40.1.

Part. pr. étant   Part. passé été

être

to be

The Seven Simple Tenses		The Seven Compound Tenses	
Singular	Plural	Singular	Plural
1 présent de l'indicatif		**8 passé composé**	
suis	sommes	ai été	avons été
es	êtes	as été	avez été
est	sont	a été	ont été
2 imparfait de l'indicatif		**9 plus-que-parfait de l'indicatif**	
étais	étions	avais été	avions été
étais	étiez	avais été	aviez été
était	étaient	avait été	avaient été
3 passé simple		**10 passé antérieur**	
fus	fûmes	eus été	eûmes été
fus	fûtes	eus été	eûtes été
fut	furent	eut été	eurent été
4 futur		**11 futur antérieur**	
serai	serons	aurai été	aurons été
seras	serez	auras été	aurez été
sera	seront	aura été	auront été
5 conditionnel		**12 conditionnel passé**	
serais	serions	aurais été	aurions été
serais	seriez	aurais été	auriez été
serait	seraient	aurait été	auraient été
6 présent du subjonctif		**13 passé du subjonctif**	
sois	soyons	aie été	ayons été
sois	soyez	aies été	ayez été
soit	soient	ait été	aient été
7 imparfait du subjonctif		**14 plus-que-parfait du subjonctif**	
fusse	fussions	eusse été	eussions été
fusses	fussiez	eusses été	eussiez été
fût	fussent	eût été	eussent été

Impératif
sois
soyons
soyez

Common idiomatic expressions using this verb

être en train de + inf.   to be in the act of + pres. part., to be in the process of, to be
busy + pres. part.;
Mon père est en train d'écrire une lettre à mes grands parents.

être à l'heure   to be on time   **Je suis à vous**   I am at your service.
être à temps   to be in time   **Je suis d'avis que. . .**   I am of the opinion that. . .
être pressé(e)   to be in a hurry

For more idiomatic expressions using this verb, consult the Appendix and §20.17.

faire

Part. pr. **faisant**   Part. passé **fait**

to do, to make

The Seven Simple Tenses		The Seven Compound Tenses	
Singular	Plural	Singular	Plural
1 présent de l'indicatif		**8 passé composé**	
fais	faisons	ai fait	avons fait
fais	faites	as fait	avez fait
fait	font	a fait	ont fait
2 imparfait de l'indicatif		**9 plus-que-parfait de l'indicatif**	
faisais	faisions	avais fait	avions fait
faisais	faisiez	avais fait	aviez fait
faisait	faisaient	avait fait	avaient fait
3 passé simple		**10 passé antérieur**	
fis	fîmes	eus fait	eûmes fait
fis	fîtes	eus fait	eûtes fait
fit	firent	eut fait	eurent fait
4 futur		**11 futur antérieur**	
ferai	ferons	aurai fait	aurons fait
feras	ferez	auras fait	aurez fait
fera	feront	aura fait	auront fait
5 conditionnel		**12 conditionnel passé**	
ferais	ferions	aurais fait	aurions fait
ferais	feriez	aurais fait	auriez fait
ferait	feraient	aurait fait	auraient fait
6 présent du subjonctif		**13 passé du subjonctif**	
fasse	fassions	aie fait	ayons fait
fasses	fassiez	aies fait	ayez fait
fasse	fassent	ait fait	aient fait
7 imparfait du subjonctif		**14 plus-que-parfait du subjonctif**	
fisse	fissions	eusse fait	eussions fait
fisses	fissiez	eusses fait	eussiez fait
fît	fissent	eût fait	eussent fait

Impératif
fais
faisons
faites

Common idiomatic expressions using this verb

faire beau   to be beautiful weather
faire chaud   to be warm weather
faire froid   to be cold weather
faire de l'autostop   to hitchhike
faire attention à qqn ou à qqch   to pay attention to someone or to something

For more idioms using this verb, see §5.ff, §20.18, and the Appendix.

Part. pr. (inusité)   Part. passé fallu   **falloir**

to be necessary, must, to be lacking to (à), to need

The Seven Simple Tenses	The Seven Compound Tenses
Singular	Singular
1 présent de l'indicatif **il faut**	8 passé composé **il a fallu**
2 imparfait de l'indicatif **il fallait**	9 plus-que-parfait de l'indicatif **il avait fallu**
3 passé simple **il fallut**	10 passé antérieur **il eut fallu**
4 futur **il faudra**	11 futur antérieur **il aura fallu**
5 conditionnel **il faudrait**	12 conditionnel passé **il aurait fallu**
6 présent du subjonctif **qu'il faille**	13 passé du subjonctif **qu'il ait fallu**
7 imparfait du subjonctif **qu'il fallût**	14 plus-que-parfait du subjonctif **qu'il eût fallu**

Impératif
(inusité)

Common idiomatic expressions using this verb

Il faut que je fasse mes leçons avant de regarder la télé. Il faut me coucher tôt parce qu'il faut me lever tôt. Il faut faire attention en classe, et il faut être sage. Si je fais toutes ces choses, je serai récompensé.

comme il faut as is proper
agir comme il faut to behave properly
Il me faut de l'argent I need some money.

Il faut manger pour vivre It is necessary to eat in order to live.
Il ne faut pas parler sans politesse One must not talk impolitely.

This is an impersonal verb and is used in the tenses given above with the subject *il*.

Consult §19. ff and the Appendix for idiomatic expressions.

The subject pronouns are found in §40.1.

lire

Part. pr. **lisant**   Part. passé **lu**

to read

The Seven Simple Tenses		The Seven Compound Tenses	
Singular	Plural	Singular	Plural
1 présent de l'indicatif		**8 passé composé**	
lis	lisons	ai lu	avons lu
lis	lisez	as lu	avez lu
lit	lisent	a lu	ont lu
2 imparfait de l'indicatif		**9 plus-que-parfait de l'indicatif**	
lisais	lisions	avais lu	avions lu
lisais	lisiez	avais lu	aviez lu
lisait	lisaient	avait lu	avaient lu
3 passé simple		**10 passé antérieur**	
lus	lûmes	eus lu	eûmes lu
lus	lûtes	eus lu	eûtes lu
lut	lurent	eut lu	eurent lu
4 futur		**11 futur antérieur**	
lirai	lirons	aurai lu	aurons lu
liras	lirez	auras lu	aurez lu
lira	liront	aura lu	auront lu
5 conditionnel		**12 conditionnel passé**	
lirais	lirions	aurais lu	aurions lu
lirais	liriez	aurais lu	auriez lu
lirait	liraient	aurait lu	auraient lu
6 présent du subjonctif		**13 passé du subjonctif**	
lise	lisions	aie lu	ayons lu
lises	lisiez	aies lu	ayez lu
lise	lisent	ait lu	aient lu
7 imparfait du subjonctif		**14 plus-que-parfait du subjonctif**	
lusse	lussions	eusse lu	eussions lu
lusses	lussiez	eusses lu	eussiez lu
lût	lussent	eût lu	eussent lu

Impératif
lis
lisons
lisez

Words and expressions related to this verb

C'est un livre à lire   It's a book worth reading.
lisible   legible, readable
lisiblement   legibly
lecteur, lectrice   reader (a person who reads)
un lecteur d'épreuves, une lectrice d'épreuves   proof reader
la lecture   reading
lectures pour la jeunesse   juvenile reading
Dans l'espoir de vous lire. . .
    I hope to receive a letter from you soon.

lire à haute voix   to read aloud
lire à voix basse   to read in a low voice
lire tout bas   to read to oneself
relire   to reread

The subject pronouns are found in §40.1.

Part. pr. **mettant**   Part. passé **mis**   **mettre**

to put, to place

The Seven Simple Tenses		The Seven Compound Tenses	
Singular	Plural	Singular	Plural
1 présent de l'indicatif		8 passé composé	
mets	mettons	ai mis	avons mis
mets	mettez	as mis	avez mis
met	mettent	a mis	ont mis
2 imparfait de l'indicatif		9 plus-que-parfait de l'indicatif	
mettais	mettions	avais mis	avions mis
mettais	mettiez	avais mis	aviez mis
mettait	mettaient	avait mis	avaient mis
3 passé simple		10 passé antérieur	
mis	mîmes	eus mis	eûmes mis
mis	mîtes	eus mis	eûtes mis
mit	mirent	eut mis	eurent mis
4 futur		11 futur antérieur	
mettrai	mettrons	aurai mis	aurons mis
mettras	mettrez	auras mis	aurez mis
mettra	mettront	aura mis	auront mis
5 conditionnel		12 conditionnel passé	
mettrais	mettrions	aurais mis	aurions mis
mettrais	mettriez	aurais mis	auriez mis
mettrait	mettraient	aurait mis	auraient mis
6 présent du subjonctif		13 passé du subjonctif	
mette	mettions	aie mis	ayons mis
mettes	mettiez	aies mis	ayez mis
mette	mettent	ait mis	aient mis
7 imparfait du subjonctif		14 plus-que-parfait du subjonctif	
misse	missions	eusse mis	eussions mis
misses	missiez	eusses mis	eussiez mis
mît	missent	eût mis	eussent mis

Impératif
mets
mettons
mettez

Words and expressions related to this verb

mettre la table   to set the table
mettre de côté   to lay aside, to save
mettre en cause   to question
mettre qqn à la porte   to kick somebody
   out the door
mettre au courant   to inform
See also **se mettre**.

mettre le couvert   to set the table
mettre au point   to make clear
mettre la télé   to turn on the TV
mettre la radio   to turn on the radio
mettre fin à qqch   to put an end to
   something

Try reading aloud as fast as you can this play on the sound **mi**:
Mimi a mis ses amis à Miami.   Mimi dropped off her friends in Miami.

Consult the Appendix for idiomatic expressions.

se mettre

Part. pr. **se mettant**   Part. passé **mis(e)(es)**

to begin, to start, to place oneself

The Seven Simple Tenses		The Seven Compound Tenses	
Singular	Plural	Singular	Plural
1 présent de l'indicatif		**8 passé composé**	
me mets	nous mettons	me suis mis(e)	nous sommes mis(es)
te mets	vous mettez	t'es mis(e)	vous êtes mis(e)(es)
se met	se mettent	s'est mis(e)	se sont mis(es)
2 imparfait de l'indicatif		**9 plus-que-parfait de l'indicatif**	
me mettais	nous mettions	m'étais mis(e)	nous étions mis(es)
te mettais	vous mettiez	t'étais mis(e)	vous étiez mis(e)(es)
se mettait	se mettaient	s'était mis(e)	s'étaient mis(es)
3 passé simple		**10 passé antérieur**	
me mis	nous mîmes	me fus mis(e)	nous fûmes mis(es)
te mis	vous mîtes	te fus mis(e)	vous fûtes mis(e)(es)
se mit	se mirent	se fut mis(e)	se furent mis(es)
4 futur		**11 futur antérieur**	
me mettrai	nous mettrons	me serai mis(e)	nous serons mis(es)
te mettras	vous mettrez	te seras mis(e)	vous serez mis(e)(es)
se mettra	se mettront	se sera mis(e)	se seront mis(es)
5 conditionnel		**12 conditionnel passé**	
me mettrais	nous mettrions	me serais mis(es)	nous serions mis(es)
te mettrais	vous mettriez	te serais mis(e)	vous seriez mis(e)(es)
se mettrait	se mettraient	se serait mis(e)	se seraient mis(es)
6 présent du subjonctif		**13 passé du subjonctif**	
me mette	nous mettions	me sois mis(e)	nous soyons mis(es)
te mettes	vous mettiez	te sois mis(e)	vous soyez mis(e)(es)
se mette	se mettent	se soit mis(e)	se soient mis(es)
7 imparfait du subjonctif		**14 plus-que-parfait du subjonctif**	
me misse	nous missions	me fusse mis(e)	nous fussions mis(es)
te misses	vous missiez	te fusses mis(e)	vous fussiez mis(e)(es)
se mît	se missent	se fût mis(e)	se fussent mis(es)

Impératif
mets-toi; ne te mets pas
mettons-vous; ne nous mettons pas
mettez-vous; ne vous mettez pas

Words and expressions related to this verb

se mettre à + inf.   to begin, to start + inf.
se mettre à table   to go sit at the table
se mettre en colère   to get angry
mettable   wearable; **se mettre en grande toilette**   to dress for an occasion;
   se mettre en smoking   to put on a dinner jacket
mettre en scène   to stage; **un metteur en scène**   director of a play, film
See also **mettre**.

Consult the Appendix for idiomatic expressions.

The subject pronouns are found in §40.1.

Part. pr. **mourant**   Part. passé **mort(e)(s)**

mourir

to die

The Seven Simple Tenses		The Seven Compound Tenses	
Singular	Plural	Singular	Plural

1 présent de l'indicatif

meurs	mourons
meurs	mourez
meurt	meurent

8 passé composé

suis mort(e)	sommes mort(e)s
es mort(e)	êtes mort(e)(s)
est mort(e)	sont mort(e)s

2 imparfait de l'indicatif

mourais	mourions
mourais	mouriez
mourait	mouraient

9 plus-que-parfait de l'indicatif

étais mort(e)	étions mort(e)s
étais mort(e)	étiez mort(e)(s)
était mort(e)	étaient mort(e)s

3 passé simple

mourus	mourûmes
mourus	mourûtes
mourut	moururent

10 passé antérieur

fus mort(e)	fûmes mort(e)s
fus mort(e)	fûtes mort(e)(s)
fut mort(e)	furent mort(e)s

4 futur

mourrai	mourrons
mourras	mourrez
mourra	mourront

11 futur antérieur

serai mort(e)	serons mort(e)s
seras mort(e)	serez mort(e)(s)
sera mort(e)	seront mort(e)s

5 conditionnel

mourrais	mourrions
mourrais	mourriez
mourrait	mourraient

12 conditionnel passé

serais mort(e)	serions mort(e)s
serais mort(e)	seriez mort(e)(s)
serait mort(e)	seraient mort(e)s

6 présent du subjonctif

meure	mourions
meures	mouriez
meure	meurent

13 passé du subjonctif

sois mort(e)	soyons mort(e)s
sois mort(e)	soyez mort(e)(s)
soit mort(e)	soient mort(e)s

7 imparfait du subjonctif

mourusse	mourussions
mourusses	mourussiez
mourût	mourussent

14 plus-que-parfait du subjonctif

fusse mort(e)	fussions mort(e)s
fusses mort(e)	fussiez mort(e)(s)
fût mort(e)	fussent mort(e)s

Impératif
meurs
mourons
mourez

Words and expressions related to this verb

mourir de faim   to starve to death
la mort   death
Elle est mourante   She is dying; **Elle se meure**   She is dying.
mourir d'ennui   to be bored to tears
mourir de chagrin   to die of a broken heart
mourir de soif   to die of thirst
mourir de rire   to die laughing
mourir d'envie de faire qqch   to be very eager to do something

naître

Part. pr. **naissant** Part. passé **né(e)(s)**

to be born

The Seven Simple Tenses		The Seven Compound Tenses	
Singular	Plural	Singular	Plural
1 présent de l'indicatif		**8 passé composé**	
nais	naissons	suis né(e)	sommes né(e)s
nais	naissez	es né(e)	êtes né(e)(s)
naît	naissent	est né(e)	sont né(e)s
2 imparfait de l'indicatif		**9 plus-que-parfait de l'indicatif**	
naissais	naissions	étais né(e)	étions né(e)s
naissais	naissiez	étais né(e)	étiez né(e)(s)
naissait	naissaient	était né(e)	étaient né(e)s
3 passé simple		**10 passé antérieur**	
naquis	naquîmes	fus né(e)	fûmes né(e)s
naquis	naquîtes	fus né(e)	fûtes né(e)(s)
naquit	naquirent	fut né(e)	furent né(e)s
4 futur		**11 futur antérieur**	
naîtrai	naîtrons	serai né(e)	serons né(e)s
naîtras	naîtrez	seras né(e)	serez né(e)(s)
naîtra	naîtront	sera né(e)	seront né(e)s
5 conditionnel		**12 conditionnel passé**	
naîtrais	naîtrions	serais né(e)	serions né(e)s
naîtrais	naîtriez	serais né(e)	seriez né(e)(s)
naîtrait	naîtraient	serait né(e)	seraient né(e)s
6 présent du subjonctif		**13 passé du subjonctif**	
naisse	naissions	sois né(e)	soyons né(e)s
naisses	naissiez	sois né(e)	soyez né(e)(s)
naisse	naissent	soit né(e)	soient né(e)s
7 imparfait du subjonctif		**14 plus-que-parfait du subjonctif**	
naquisse	naquissions	fusse né(e)	fussions né(e)s
naquisses	naquissiez	fusses né(e)	fussiez né(e)(s)
naquît	naquissent	fût né(e)	fussent né(e)s

Impératif
nais
naissons
naissez

Words and expressions related to this verb

la naissance birth
un anniversaire de naissance a birthday anniversary
donner naissance à to give birth to; **la naissance du monde** beginning of the world
Anne est Française de naissance Anne was born French.
renaître to be born again
faire naître to cause, to give rise to
Je ne suis pas né(e) d'hier! I wasn't born yesterday!

The subject pronouns are found in §40.1.

Part. pr. **obtenant**   Part. passé **obtenu**   **obtenir**

to obtain, to get

The Seven Simple Tenses		The Seven Compound Tenses	
Singular	Plural	Singular	Plural
1 présent de l'indicatif		**8 passé composé**	
obtiens	obtenons	ai obtenu	avons obtenu
obtiens	obtenez	as obtenu	avez obtenu
obtient	obtiennent	a obtenu	ont obtenu
2 imparfait de l'indicatif		**9 plus-que-parfait de l'indicatif**	
obtenais	obtenions	avais obtenu	avions obtenu
obtenais	obteniez	avais obtenu	aviez obtenu
obtenait	obtenaient	avait obtenu	avaient obtenu
3 passé simple		**10 passé antérieur**	
obtins	obtînmes	eus obtenu	eûmes obtenu
obtins	obtîntes	eus obtenu	eûtes obtenu
obtint	obtinrent	eut obtenu	eurent obtenu
4 futur		**11 futur antérieur**	
obtiendrai	obtiendrons	aurai obtenu	aurons obtenu
obtiendras	obtiendrez	auras obtenu	aurez obtenu
obtiendra	obtiendront	aura obtenu	auront obtenu
5 conditionnel		**12 conditionnel passé**	
obtiendrais	obtiendrions	aurais obtenu	aurions obtenu
obtiendrais	obtiendriez	aurais obtenu	auriez obtenu
obtiendrait	obtiendraient	aurait obtenu	auraient obtenu
6 présent du subjonctif		**13 passé du subjonctif**	
obtienne	obtenions	aie obtenu	ayons obtenu
obtiennes	obteniez	aies obtenu	ayez obtenu
obtienne	obtiennent	ait obtenu	aient obtenu
7 imparfait du subjonctif		**14 plus-que-parfait du subjonctif**	
obtinsse	obtinssions	eusse obtenu	eussions obtenu
obtinsses	obtinssiez	eusses obtenu	eussiez obtenu
obtînt	obtinssent	eût obtenu	eussent obtenu

Impératif
obtiens
obtenons
obtenez

Words and expressions related to this verb

l'obtention   obtainment
obtenir de qqn qqch de force   to get something out of someone by force
s'obtenir de   to be obtained from

See also **tenir.**

Consult §37.—§37.5 for verbs used in weather expressions.

offrir
Part. pr. **offrant**   Part. passé **offert**

to offer

The Seven Simple Tenses		The Seven Compound Tenses	
Singular	Plural	Singular	Plural
1 présent de l'indicatif		**8 passé composé**	
offre	offrons	ai offert	avons offert
offres	offrez	as offert	avez offert
offre	offrent	a offert	ont offert
2 imparfait de l'indicatif		**9 plus-que-parfait de l'indicatif**	
offrais	offrions	avais offert	avions offert
offrais	offriez	avais offert	aviez offert
offrait	offraient	avait offert	avaient offert
3 passé simple		**10 passé antérieur**	
offris	offrîmes	eus offert	eûmes offert
offris	offrîtes	eus offert	eûtes offert
offrit	offrirent	eut offert	eurent offert
4 futur		**11 futur antérieur**	
offrirai	offrirons	aurai offert	aurons offert
offriras	offrirez	auras offert	aurez offert
offrira	offriront	aura offert	auront offert
5 conditionnel		**12 conditionnel passé**	
offrirais	offririons	aurais offert	aurions offert
offrirais	offririez	aurais offert	auriez offert
offrirait	offriraient	aurait offert	auraient offert
6 présent du subjonctif		**13 passé du subjonctif**	
offre	offrions	aie offert	ayons offert
offres	offriez	aies offert	ayez offert
offre	offrent	ait offert	aient offert
7 imparfait du subjonctif		**14 plus-que-parfait du subjonctif**	
offrisse	offrissions	eusse offert	eussions offert
offrisses	offrissiez	eusses offert	eussiez offert
offrît	offrissent	eût offert	eussent offert

Impératif
offre
offrons
offrez

Words and expressions related to this verb

offrir qqch à qqn   to offer (to present) something to someone
une offre   an offer, a proposal
une offrande   gift, offering
l'offre et la demande   supply and demand

Consult §39.42 — §39.50 for verbs that require certain prepositions.

The subject pronouns are found in §40.1.

Part. pr. **ouvrant**   Part. passé **ouvert**   **ouvrir**

to open

The Seven Simple Tenses		The Seven Compound Tenses	
Singular	Plural	Singular	Plural
1 présent de l'indicatif		**8 passé composé**	
ouvre	ouvrons	ai ouvert	avons ouvert
ouvres	ouvrez	as ouvert	avez ouvert
ouvre	ouvrent	a ouvert	ont ouvert
2 imparfait de l'indicatif		**9 plus-que-parfait de l'indicatif**	
ouvrais	ouvrions	avais ouvert	avions ouvert
ouvrais	ouvriez	avais ouvert	aviez ouvert
ouvrait	ouvraient	avait ouvert	avaient ouvert
3 passé simple		**10 passé antérieur**	
ouvris	ouvrîmes	eus ouvert	eûmes ouvert
ouvris	ouvrîtes	eus ouvert	eûtes ouvert
ouvrit	ouvrirent	eut ouvert	eurent ouvert
4 futur		**11 futur antérieur**	
ouvrirai	ouvrirons	aurai ouvert	aurons ouvert
ouvriras	ouvrirez	auras ouvert	aurez ouvert
ouvrira	ouvriront	aura ouvert	auront ouvert
5 conditionnel		**12 conditionnel passé**	
ouvrirais	ouvririons	aurais ouvert	aurions ouvert
ouvrirais	ouvririez	aurais ouvert	auriez ouvert
ouvrirait	ouvriraient	aurait ouvert	auraient ouvert
6 présent du subjonctif		**13 passé du subjonctif**	
ouvre	ouvrions	aie ouvert	ayons ouvert
ouvres	ouvriez	aies ouvert	ayez ouvert
ouvre	ouvrent	ait ouvert	aient ouvert
7 imparfait du subjonctif		**14 plus-que-parfait du subjonctif**	
ouvrisse	ouvrissions	eusse ouvert	eussions ouvert
ouvrisses	ouvrissiez	eusses ouvert	eussiez ouvert
ouvrît	ouvrissent	eût ouvert	eussent ouvert

Impératif
ouvre
ouvrons
ouvrez

Words and expressions related to this verb

ouvert, ouverte   open
ouverture *(f.)*   opening
ouvrir le gaz   to turn on the gas
ouvrir de force   to force open

rouvrir   to reopen, to open again
entrouvrir   to open just a bit
s'ouvrir à   to confide in

The subject pronouns are found in §40.1.

partir

Part. pr. **partant**   Part. passé **parti(e)(s)**

to leave, to depart

The Seven Simple Tenses		The Seven Compound Tenses	
Singular	Plural	Singular	Plural
1 présent de l'indicatif		**8 passé composé**	
pars	partons	suis parti(e)	sommes parti(e)s
pars	partez	es parti(e)	êtes parti(e)(s)
part	partent	est parti(e)	sont parti(e)s
2 imparfait de l'indicatif		**9 plus-que-parfait de l'indicatif**	
partais	partions	étais parti(e)	étions parti(e)s
partais	partiez	étais parti(e)	étiez parti(e)(s)
partait	partaient	était parti(e)	étaient parti(e)s
3 passé simple		**10 passé antérieur**	
partis	partîmes	fus parti(e)	fûmes parti(e)s
partis	partîtes	fus parti(e)	fûtes parti(e)(s)
partit	partirent	fut parti(e)	furent parti(e)s
4 futur		**11 futur antérieur**	
partirai	partirons	serai parti(e)s	serons parti(e)s
partiras	partirez	seras parti(e)	serez parti(e)(s)
partira	partiront	sera parti(e)	seront parti(e)s
5 conditionnel		**12 conditionnel passé**	
partirais	partirions	serais parti(e)	serions parti(e)s
partirais	partiriez	serais parti(e)	seriez parti(e)(s)
partirait	partiraient	serait parti(e)	seraient parti(e)s
6 présent du subjonctif		**13 passé du subjonctif**	
parte	partions	sois parti(e)	soyons parti(e)s
partes	partiez	sois parti(e)	soyez parti(e)(s)
parte	partent	soit parti(e)	soient parti(e)s
7 imparfait du subjonctif		**14 plus-que-parfait du subjonctif**	
partisse	partissions	fusse parti(e)	fussions parti(e)s
partisses	partissiez	fusses parti(e)	fussiez parti(e)(s)
partît	partissent	fût parti(e)	fussent parti(e)s

Impératif
pars
partons
partez

Words and expressions related to this verb

A quelle heure part le train pour Paris?   At what time does the train for Paris leave?
à partir de maintenant   from now on; **à partir d'aujourd'hui**   from today on
le départ   departure
partir en voyage   to go on a trip
partir en vacances   to leave for a vacation
repartir   to leave again, to set out again
Consult the Appendix for verbs used in idiomatic expressions.

The subject pronouns are found in §40.1.

Part. pr. **permettant**   Part. passé **permis**   **permettre**

to permit, to allow, to let

The Seven Simple Tenses		The Seven Compound Tenses	
Singular	Plural	Singular	Plural
1 présent de l'indicatif		**8 passé composé**	
permets	permettons	ai permis	avons permis
permets	permettez	as permis	avez permis
permet	permettent	a permis	ont permis
2 imparfait de l'indicatif		**9 plus-que-parfait de l'indicatif**	
permettais	permettions	avais permis	avions permis
permettais	permettiez	avais permis	aviez permis
permettait	permettaient	avait permis	avaient permis
3 passé simple		**10 passé antérieur**	
permis	permîmes	eus permis	eûmes permis
permis	permîtes	eus permis	eûtes permis
permit	permirent	eut permis	eurent permis
4 futur		**11 futur antérieur**	
permettrai	permettrons	aurai permis	aurons permis
permettras	permettrez	auras permis	aurez permis
permettra	permettront	aura permis	auront permis
5 conditionnel		**12 conditionnel passé**	
permettrais	permettrions	aurais permis	aurions permis
permettrais	permettriez	aurais permis	auriez permis
permettrait	permettraient	aurait permis	auraient permis
6 présent du subjonctif		**13 passé du subjonctif**	
permette	permettions	aie permis	ayons permis
permettes	permettiez	aies permis	ayez permis
permette	permettent	ait permis	aient permis
7 imparfait du subjonctif		**14 plus-que-parfait du subjonctif**	
permisse	permissions	eusse permis	eussions permis
permisses	permissiez	eusses permis	eussiez permis
permît	permissent	eût permis	eussent permis

Impératif
permets
permettons
permettez

Common idiomatic expressions using this verb and words related to it

La maîtresse de français a permis à l'élève de quitter la salle de classe quelques minutes avant la fin de la leçon.

permettre à qqn de faire qqch   to permit (to allow) someone to do something
Vous permettez?   May I? Do you mind?   **se permettre de faire qqch**   to take the
s'il est permis   if it is allowed, permitted   liberty to do something; to venture to
un permis   permit   do something
un permis de conduire   driving license
la permission   permission

plaire

Part. pr. **plaisant**   Part. passé **plu**

to please

The Seven Simple Tenses		The Seven Compound Tenses	
Singular	Plural	Singular	Plural
1 présent de l'indicatif		**8 passé composé**	
plais	plaisons	ai plu	avons plu
plais	plaisez	as plu	avez plu
plaît	plaisent	a plu	ont plu
2 imparfait de l'indicatif		**9 plus-que-parfait de l'indicatif**	
plaisais	plaisions	avais plu	avions plu
plaisais	plaisiez	avais plu	aviez plu
plaisait	plaisaient	avait plu	avaient plu
3 passé simple		**10 passé antérieur**	
plus	plûmes	eus plu	eûmes plu
plus	plûtes	eus plu	eûtes plu
plut	plurent	eut plu	eurent plu
4 futur		**11 futur antérieur**	
plairai	plairons	aurai plu	aurons plu
plairas	plairez	auras plu	aurez plu
plaira	plairont	aura plu	auront plu
5 conditionnel		**12 conditionnel passé**	
plairais	plairions	aurais plu	aurions plu
plairais	plairiez	aurais plu	auriez plu
plairait	plairaient	aurait plu	auraient plu
6 présent du subjonctif		**13 passé du subjonctif**	
plaise	plaisions	aie plu	ayons plu
plaises	plaisiez	aies plu	ayez plu
plaise	plaisent	ait plu	aient plu
7 imparfait du subjonctif		**14 plus-que-parfait du subjonctif**	
plusse	plussions	eusse plu	eussions plu
plusses	plussiez	eusses plu	eussiez plu
plût	plussent	eût plu	eussent plu

Impératif
plais
plaisons
plaisez

Common idiomatic expressions using this verb

plaire à qqn   to please, to be pleasing to someone;   **Son mariage a plu à sa famille**
Her (his) marriage pleased her (his) family. **Est-ce que ce cadeau lui plaira?**   Will
this present please her (him)? Will this gift be pleasing to her (to him)?
se plaire à   to take pleasure in;   **Robert se plaît à ennuyer son petit frère**   Robert
takes pleasure in bothering his little brother.
le plaisir   delight, pleasure;   **complaire à**   to please;   **déplaire à**   to displease
s'il vous plaît; s'il te plaît   please (if it is pleasing to you)
Il a beaucoup plu hier et cela m'a beaucoup plu.   It rained a lot yesterday and that pleased
me a great deal. (See **pleuvoir**)

Part. pr. **pleuvant**   Part. passé **plu**   **pleuvoir**

to rain

The Seven Simple Tenses	The Seven Compound Tenses
Singular	Singular
1 présent de l'indicatif **il pleut**	8 passé composé **il a plu**
2 imparfait de l'indicatif **il pleuvait**	9 plus-que-parfait de l'indicatif **il avait plu**
3 passé simple **il plut**	10 passé antérieur **il eut plu**
4 futur **il pleuvra**	11 futur antérieur **il aura plu**
5 conditionnel **il pleuvrait**	12 conditionnel passé **il aurait plu**
6 présent du subjonctif **qu'il pleuve**	13 passé du subjonctif **qu'il ait plu**
7 imparfait du subjonctif **qu'il plût**	14 plus-que-parfait du subjonctif **qu'il eût plu**

Impératif
Qu'il pleuve!   (Let it rain!)

Sentences using this verb and words related to it

Hier il a plu, il pleut maintenant, et je suis certain qu'il pleuvra demain.

la pluie	the rain	**bruiner**	to drizzle
pluvieux, pluvieuse	rainy	**Il pleut à seaux**	It's raining in buckets.
pleuvoter	to drizzle	**Il pleut à verse**	It's raining hard.

Il a beaucoup plu hier et cela m'a beaucoup plu.   It rained a lot yesterday and that pleased me a great deal. (See **plaire**)

Do not confuse the past part. of this verb with the past part. of **plaire,** which are identical.

Consult §37.–§37.5 for the section on weather expressions using verbs.

The subject pronouns are found in §40.1.

pouvoir

Part. pr. **pouvant**   Part. passé **pu**

to be able, can

The Seven Simple Tenses		The Seven Compound Tenses	
Singular	Plural	Singular	Plural
1 présent de l'indicatif		**8 passé composé**	
peux *or* **puis**	**pouvons**	**ai pu**	**avons pu**
peux	**pouvez**	**as pu**	**avez pu**
peut	**peuvent**	**a pu**	**ont pu**
2 imparfait de l'indicatif		**9 plus-que-parfait de l'indicatif**	
pouvais	**pouvions**	**avais pu**	**avions pu**
pouvais	**pouviez**	**avais pu**	**aviez pu**
pouvait	**pouvaient**	**avait pu**	**avaient pu**
3 passé simple		**10 passé antérieur**	
pus	**pûmes**	**eus pu**	**eûmes pu**
pus	**pûtes**	**eus pu**	**eûtes pu**
put	**purent**	**eut pu**	**eurent pu**
4 futur		**11 futur antérieur**	
pourrai	**pourrons**	**aurai pu**	**aurons pu**
pourras	**pourrez**	**auras pu**	**aurez pu**
pourra	**pourront**	**aura pu**	**auront pu**
5 conditionnel		**12 conditionnel passé**	
pourrais	**pourrions**	**aurais pu**	**aurions pu**
pourrais	**pourriez**	**aurais pu**	**auriez pu**
pourrait	**pourraient**	**aurait pu**	**auraient pu**
6 présent du subjonctif		**13 passé du subjonctif**	
puisse	**puissions**	**aie pu**	**ayons pu**
puisses	**puissiez**	**aies pu**	**ayez pu**
puisse	**puissent**	**ait pu**	**aient pu**
7 imparfait du subjonctif		**14 plus-que-parfait du subjonctif**	
pusse	**pussions**	**eusse pu**	**eussions pu**
pusses	**pussiez**	**eusses pu**	**eussiez pu**
pût	**pussent**	**eût pu**	**eussent pu**

Impératif
(inusité)

Common idiomatic expressions using this verb and words related to it

si l'on peut dire   if one may say so
se pouvoir: Cela se peut   That may be.
le pouvoir   power
avoir du pouvoir sur soi-même   to have self control
n'y pouvoir rien   not to be able to do anything about it;   **Que me voulez-vous?**   What
do you want from me?   **Je n'y peux rien.**   I can't help it; I can't do anything
about it.
Puis-je entrer? Est-ce que je peux entrer?   May I come in?

Consult §28.–§28.3 and the Appendix for idiomatic expressions.

The subject pronouns are found in §40.1.

Part. pr. **prenant**   Part. passé **pris**   **prendre**

to take

The Seven Simple Tenses		The Seven Compound Tenses	
Singular	Plural	Singular	Plural
1 présent de l'indicatif		**8 passé composé**	
prends	prenons	ai pris	avons pris
prends	prenez	as pris	avez pris
prend	prennent	a pris	ont pris
2 imparfait de l'indicatif		**9 plus-que-parfait de l'indicatif**	
prenais	prenions	avais pris	avions pris
prenais	preniez	avais pris	aviez pris
prenait	prenaient	avait pris	avaient pris
3 passé simple		**10 passé antérieur**	
pris	prîmes	eus pris	eûmes pris
pris	prîtes	eus pris	eûtes pris
prit	prirent	eut pris	eurent pris
4 futur		**11 futur antérieur**	
prendrai	prendrons	aurai pris	aurons pris
prendras	prendrez	auras pris	aurez pris
prendra	prendront	aura pris	auront pris
5 conditionnel		**12 conditionnel passé**	
prendrais	prendrions	aurais pris	aurions pris
prendrais	prendriez	aurais pris	auriez pris
prendrait	prendraient	aurait pris	auraient pris
6 présent du subjonctif		**13 passé du subjonctif**	
prenne	prenions	aie pris	ayons pris
prennes	preniez	aies pris	ayez pris
prenne	prennent	ait pris	aient pris
7 imparfait du subjonctif		**14 plus-que-parfait du subjonctif**	
prisse	prissions	eusse pris	eussions pris
prisses	prissiez	eusses pris	eussiez pris
prît	prissent	eût pris	eussent pris

Impératif
prends
prenons
prenez

Sentences using this verb and words related to it

—**Qui a pris les fleurs qui étaient sur la table?**
—**C'est moi qui les ai prises.**

à tout prendre   on the whole, all in all
un preneur, une preneuse   taker, purchaser
s'y prendre   to go about it, to handle it, to set about it
Je ne sais comment m'y prendre   I don't know how to go about it.
C'est à prendre ou à laisser   Take it or leave it.
prendre à témoin   to call to witness

For more idiomatic expressions using this verb, see §20.26 and the Appendix.

promettre

Part. pr. **promettant** Part. passé **promis**

to promise

The Seven Simple Tenses		The Seven Compound Tenses	
Singular	Plural	Singular	Plural
1 présent de l'indicatif		**8 passé composé**	
promets	promettons	ai promis	avons promis
promets	promettez	as promis	avez promis
promet	promettent	a promis	ont promis
2 imparfait de l'indicatif		**9 plus-que-parfait de l'indicatif**	
promettais	promettions	avais promis	avions promis
promettais	promettiez	avais promis	aviez promis
promettait	promettaient	avait promis	avaient promis
3 passé simple		**10 passé antérieur**	
promis	promîmes	eus promis	eûmes promis
promis	promîtes	eus promis	eûtes promis
promit	promirent	eut promis	eurent promis
4 futur		**11 futur antérieur**	
promettrai	promettrons	aurai promis	aurons promis
promettras	promettrez	auras promis	aurez promis
promettra	promettront	aura promis	auront promis
5 conditionnel		**12 conditionnel passé**	
promettrais	promettrions	aurais promis	aurions promis
promettrais	promettriez	aurais promis	auriez promis
promettrait	promettraient	aurait promis	auraient promis
6 présent du subjonctif		**13 passé du subjonctif**	
promette	promettions	aie promis	ayons promis
promettes	promettiez	aies promis	ayez promis
promette	promettent	ait promis	aient promis
7 imparfait du subjonctif		**14 plus-que-parfait du subjonctif**	
promisse	promissions	eusse promis	eussions promis
promisses	promissiez	eusses promis	eussiez promis
promît	promissent	eût promis	eussent promis

Impératif
promets
promettons
promettez

Common idiomatic expressions using this verb

promettre de faire qqch   to promise to do something
une promesse   promise
tenir sa promesse   to keep one's promise
promettre à qqn de faire qqch   to promise someone to do something
Ça promet!   It looks promising!
se promettre   to promise oneself

See also **mettre** and compounds of **mettre**, e.g., **permettre**.

Part. pr. recevant   **Part. passé reçu**

recevoir

to receive, to get

The Seven Simple Tenses		The Seven Compound Tenses	
Singular	Plural	Singular	Plural
1 présent de l'indicatif		**8 passé composé**	
reçois	recevons	ai reçu	avons reçu
reçois	recevez	as reçu	avez reçu
reçoit	reçoivent	a reçu	ont reçu
2 imparfait de l'indicatif		**9 plus-que-parfait de l'indicatif**	
recevais	recevions	avais reçu	avions reçu
recevais	receviez	avais reçu	aviez reçu
recevait	recevaient	avait reçu	avaient reçu
3 passé simple		**10 passé antérieur**	
reçus	reçûmes	eus reçu	eûmes reçu
reçus	reçûtes	eus reçu	eûtes reçu
reçut	reçurent	eut reçu	eurent reçu
4 futur		**11 futur antérieur**	
recevrai	recevrons	aurai reçu	aurons reçu
recevras	recevrez	auras reçu	aurez reçu
recevra	recevront	aura reçu	auront reçu
5 conditionnel		**12 conditionnel passé**	
recevrais	recevrions	aurais reçu	aurions reçu
recevrais	recevriez	aurais reçu	auriez reçu
recevrait	recevraient	aurait reçu	auraient reçu
6 présent du subjonctif		**13 passé du subjonctif**	
reçoive	recevions	aie reçu	ayons reçu
reçoives	receviez	aies reçu	ayez reçu
reçoive	reçoivent	ait reçu	aient reçu
7 imparfait du subjonctif		**14 plus-que-parfait du subjonctif**	
reçusse	reçussions	eusse reçu	eussions reçu
reçusses	reçussiez	eusses reçu	eussiez reçu
reçût	reçussent	eût reçu	eussent reçu

Impératif
reçois
recevons
recevez

Words and expressions related to this verb

réceptif, réceptive receptive
une réception reception, welcome
un, une réceptionniste receptionist
un reçu a receipt
au reçu de on receipt of

recevable receivable
un receveur, une receveuse receiver
être reçu à un examen to pass an exam

revenir

Part. pr. revenant   **Part. passé revenu(e)(s)**

to come back

The Seven Simple Tenses		The Seven Compound Tenses	
Singular	Plural	Singular	Plural
1 présent de l'indicatif		**8 passé composé**	
reviens	revenons	suis revenu(e)	sommes revenu(e)s
reviens	revenez	es revenu(e)	êtes revenu(e)(s)
revient	reviennent	est revenu(e)	sont revenu(e)s
2 imparfait de l'indicatif		**9 plus-que-parfait de l'indicatif**	
revenais	revenions	étais revenu(e)	étions revenu(e)s
revenais	reveniez	étais revenu(e)	étiez revenu(e)(s)
revenait	revenaient	était revenu(e)	étaient revenu(e)s
3 passé simple		**10 passé antérieur**	
revins	revînmes	fus revenu(e)	fûmes revenu(e)s
revins	revîntes	fus revenu(e)	fûtes revenu(e)(s)
revint	revinrent	fut revenu(e)	furent revenu(e)s
4 futur		**11 futur antérieur**	
reviendrai	reviendrons	serai revenu(e)	serons revenu(e)s
reviendras	reviendrez	seras revenu(e)	serez revenu(e)(s)
reviendra	reviendront	sera revenu(e)	seront revenu(e)s
5 conditionnel		**12 conditionnel passé**	
reviendrais	reviendrions	serais revenu(e)	serions revenu(e)s
reviendrais	reviendriez	serais revenu(e)	seriez revenu(e)(s)
reviendrait	reviendraient	serait revenu(e)	seraient revenu(e)s
6 présent du subjonctif		**13 passé du subjonctif**	
revienne	revenions	sois revenu(e)	soyons revenu(e)s
reviennes	reveniez	sois revenu(e)	soyez revenu(e)(s)
revienne	reviennent	soit revenu(e)	soient revenu(e)s
7 imparfait du subjonctif		**14 plus-que-parfait du subjonctif**	
revinsse	revinssions	fusse revenu(e)	fussions revenu(e)s
revinsses	revinssiez	fusses revenu(e)	fussiez revenu(e)(s)
revînt	revinssent	fût revenu(e)	fussent revenu(e)s

Impératif
reviens
revenons
revenez

Words and expressions related to this verb

le revenu   revenue, income
à revenu fixe   fixed interest
revenir d'une erreur   to realize one's mistake
revenir au même   to amount to the same thing
revenir sur ses pas   to retrace one's steps
revenir sur le sujet   to get back to the subject
revenir sur sa parole   to go back on one's word
Tout revient à ceci. . .   It all boils down to this. . .

Part. pr. revoyant   **Part. passé revu**   **revoir**

to see again, to see once more

The Seven Simple Tenses		The Seven Compound Tenses	
Singular	Plural	Singular	Plural
1 présent de l'indicatif		**8 passé composé**	
revois	revoyons	ai revu	avons revu
revois	revoyez	as revu	avez revu
revoit	revoient	a revu	ont revu
2 imparfait de l'indicatif		**9 plus-que-parfait de l'indicatif**	
revoyais	revoyions	avais revu	avions revu
revoyais	revoyiez	avais revu	aviez revu
revoyait	revoyaient	avait revu	avaient revu
3 passé simple		**10 passé antérieur**	
revis	revîmes	eus revu	eûmes revu
revis	revîtes	eus revu	eûtes revu
revit	revirent	eut revu	eurent revu
4 futur		**11 futur antérieur**	
reverrai	reverrons	aurai revu	aurons revu
reverras	reverrez	auras revu	aurez revu
reverra	reverront	aura revu	auront revu
5 conditionnel		**12 conditionnel passé**	
reverrais	reverrions	aurais revu	aurions revu
reverais	reverriez	aurais revu	auriez revu
reverrait	reverraient	aurait revu	auraient revu
6 présent du subjonctif		**13 passé du subjonctif**	
revoie	revoyions	aie revu	ayons revu
revoies	revoyiez	aies revu	ayez revu
revoie	revoient	ait revu	aient revu
7 imparfait du subjonctif		**14 plus-que-parfait du subjonctif**	
revisse	revissions	eusse revu	eussions revu
revisses	revissiez	eusses revu	eussiez revu
revît	revissent	eût revu	eussent revu

Impératif
revois
revoyons
revoyez

Words and expressions related to this verb

au revoir   good-bye, see you again, until we meet again
se revoir   to see each other again
une revue   review, magazine
un, une revuiste   a writer of reviews
une révision   revision; **à revoir**   to be revised

rire

Part. pr. **riant**   Part. passé **ri**

to laugh

The Seven Simple Tenses		The Seven Compound Tenses	
Singular	Plural	Singular	Plural
1 présent de l'indicatif		**8 passé composé**	
ris	rions	ai ri	avons ri
ris	riez	as ri	avez ri
rit	rient	a ri	ont ri
2 imparfait de l'indicatif		**9 plus-que-parfait de l'indicatif**	
riais	riions	avais ri	avions ri
riais	riiez	avais ri ·	aviez ri
riait	riaient	avait ri	avaient ri
3 passé simple		**10 passé antérieur**	
ris	rîmes	eus ri	eûmes ri
ris	rîtes	eus ri	eûtes ri
rit	rirent	eut ri	eurent ri
4 futur		**11 futur antérieur**	
rirai	rirons	aurai ri	aurons ri
riras	rirez	auras ri	aurez ri
rira	riront	aura ri	auront ri
5 conditionnel		**12 conditionnel passé**	
rirais	ririons	aurais ri	aurions ri
rirais	ririez	aurais ri	auriez ri
rirait	riraient	aurait ri	auraient ri
6 présent du subjonctif		**13 passé du subjonctif**	
rie	riions	aie ri	ayons ri
ries	riiez	aies ri	ayez ri
rie	rient	ait ri	aient ri
7 imparfait du subjonctif		**14 plus-que-parfait du subjonctif**	
risse	rissions	eusse ri	eussions ri
risses	rissiez	eusses ri	eussiez ri
rît	rissent	eût ri	eussent ri

Impératif
ris
rions
riez

Words and expressions related to this verb

éclater de rire   to burst out laughing
dire qqch pour rire   to say something just for a laugh
rire au nez de qqn   to laugh in someone's face
rire de bon coeur   to laugh heartily
le rire   laughter;   **un sourire**   smile;   **risible**   laughable

Consult the Appendix for verbs used in idiomatic expressions.

The subject pronouns are found in §40.1.

Part. pr. **sachant**   Part. passé **su**   **savoir**

to know (how)

The Seven Simple Tenses		The Seven Compound Tenses	
Singular	Plural	Singular	Plural
1 présent de l'indicatif		**8 passé composé**	
sais	savons	ai su	avons su
sais	savez	as su	avez su
sait	savent	a su	ont su
2 imparfait de l'indicatif		**9 plus-que-parfait de l'indicatif**	
savais	savions	avais su	avions su
savais	saviez	avais su	aviez su
savait	savaient	avait su	avaient su
3 passé simple		**10 passé antérieur**	
sus	sûmes	eus su	eûmes su
sus	sûtes	eus su	eûtes su
sut	surent	eut su	eurent su
4 futur		**11 futur antérieur**	
saurai	saurons	aurai su	aurons su
sauras	saurez	auras su	aurez su
saura	sauront	aura su	auront su
5 conditionnel		**12 conditionnel passé**	
saurais	saurions	aurais su	aurions su
saurais	sauriez	aurais su	auriez su
saurait	sauraient	aurait su	auraient su
6 présent du subjonctif		**13 passé du subjonctif**	
sache	sachions	aie su	ayons su
saches	sachiez	aies su	ayez su
sache	sachent	ait su	aient su
7 imparfait du subjonctif		**14 plus-que-parfait du subjonctif**	
susse	sussions	eusse su	eussions su
susses	sussiez	eusses su	eussiez su
sût	sussent	eût su	eussent su

Impératif
sache
sachons
sachez

Words and expressions related to this verb

le savoir   knowledge
le savoir-faire   know-how, tact, ability
le savoir-vivre   to be well-mannered, well-bred
faire savoir   to inform
Pas que je sache   Not to my knowledge

savoir faire qqch   to know how to do something; **Savez-vous jouer du piano?**
Autant que je sache. . .   As far as I know. . .
C'est à savoir   That remains to be seen.

Consult §31.–§32. and the Appendix for the section on verbs used in idiomatic expressions.

The subject pronouns are found in §40.1.

servir

Part. pr. **servant**   Part. passé **servi**

to serve

The Seven Simple Tenses		The Seven Compound Tenses	
Singular	Plural	Singular	Plural
1 présent de l'indicatif		**8 passé composé**	
sers	servons	ai servi	avons servi
sers	servez	as servi	avez servi
sert	servent	a servi	ont servi
2 imparfait de l'indicatif		**9 plus-que-parfait de l'indicatif**	
servais	servions	avais servi	avions servi
servais	serviez	avais servi	aviez servi
servait	servaient	avait servi	avaient servi
3 passé simple		**10 passé antérieur**	
servis	servîmes	eus servi	eûmes servi
servis	servîtes	eus servi	eûtes servi
servit	servirent	eut servi	eurent servi
4 futur		**11 futur antérieur**	
servirai	servirons	aurai servi	aurons servi
serviras	servirez	auras servi	aurez servi
servira	serviront	aura servi	auront servi
5 conditionnel		**12 conditionnel passé**	
servirais	servirions	aurais servi	aurions servi
servirais	serviriez	aurais servi	auriez servi
servirait	serviraient	aurait servi	auraient servi
6 présent du subjonctif		**13 passé du subjonctif**	
serve	servions	aie servi	ayons servi
serves	serviez	aies servi	ayez servi
serve	servent	ait servi	aient servi
7 imparfait du subjonctif		**14 plus-que-parfait du subjonctif**	
servisse	servissions	eusse servi	eussions servi
servisses	servissiez	eusses servi	eussiez servi
servît	servissent	eût servi	eussent servi

Impératif
sers
servons
servez

Words and expressions related to this verb

le serveur   waiter
la serveuse   waitress
le service   service
une serviette   napkin
un serviteur   servant
la servitude   servitude
desservir   to clear off the
   table

se servir   to serve oneself, to help oneself
se servir de qqch   to use something, to avail oneself
   of something, to make use of something
servir à qqch   to be of some use
servir à rien   to be of no use
   Cela ne sert à rien   That serves no purpose

Consult the Appendix for idiomatic expressions.

The subject pronouns are found in §40.1.

Part. pr. se servant   Part. passé servi(e)(s)   se servir

to serve oneself, to help oneself (to food and drink)

The Seven Simple Tenses		The Seven Compound Tenses	
Singular	Plural	Singular	Plural
1 présent de l'indicatif		**8 passé composé**	
me sers	nous servons	me suis servi(e)	nous sommes servi(e)s
te sers	vous servez	t'es servi(e)	vous êtes servi(e)(s)
se sert	se servent	s'est servi(e)	se sont servi(e)s
2 imparfait de l'indicatif		**9 plus-que-parfait de l'indicatif**	
me servais	nous servions	m'étais servi(e)	nous étions servi(e)s
te servais	vous serviez	t'étais servi(e)	vous étiez servi(e)(s)
se servait	se servaient	s'était servi(e)	s'étaient servi(e)s
3 passé simple		**10 passé antérieur**	
me servis	nous servîmes	me fus servi(e)	nous fûmes servi(e)s
te servis	vous servîtes	te fus servi(e)	vous fûtes servi(e)(s)
se servit	se servirent	se fut servi(e)	se furent servi(e)s
4 futur		**11 futur antérieur**	
me servirai	nous servirons	me serai servi(e)	nous serons servi(e)s
te serviras	vous servirez	te seras servi(e)	vous serez servi(e)(s)
se servira	se serviront	se sera servi(e)	se seront servi(e)s
5 conditionnel		**12 conditionnel passé**	
me servirais	nous servirions	me serais servi(e)	nous serions servi(e)s
te servirais	vous serviriez	te serais servi(e)	vous seriez servi(e)(s)
se servirait	se serviraient	se serait servi(e)	se seraient servi(e)s
6 présent du subjonctif		**13 passé du subjonctif**	
me serve	nous servions	me sois servi(e)	nous soyons servi(e)s
te serves	vous serviez	te sois servi(e)	vous soyez servi(e)(s)
se serve	se servent	se soit servi(e)	se soient servi(e)s
7 imparfait du subjonctif		**14 plus-que-parfait du subjonctif**	
me servisse	nous servissions	me fusse servi(e)	nous fussions servi(e)s
te servisses	vous servissiez	te fusses servi(e)	vous fussiez servi(e)(s)
se servît	se servissent	se fût servi(e)	se fussent servi(e)s

Impératif
sers-toi; ne te sers pas
servons-nous; ne nous servons pas
servez-vous; ne vous servez pas

Words and expressions related to this verb

un serviteur servant
la servitude servitude
le serveur waiter
la serveuse waitress
le service service
une serviette napkin

se servir de qqch to use something, to make use of something
se servir to serve oneself, to help oneself;
Servez-vous, je vous en prie! Help yourself, please!

Consult the Appendix for idiomatic expressions.

sortir

Part. pr. **sortant**   Part. passé **sorti(e)(s)**

to go out, to leave

The Seven Simple Tenses		The Seven Compound Tenses	
Singular	Plural	Singular	Plural
1 présent de l'indicatif		**8 passé composé**	
sors	sortons	suis sorti(e)	sommes sorti(e)s
sors	sortez	es sorti(e)	êtes sorti(e)(s)
sort	sortent	est sorti(e)	sont sorti(e)s
2 imparfait de l'indicatif		**9 plus-que-parfait de l'indicatif**	
sortais	sortions	étais sorti(e)	étions sorti(e)s
sortais	sortiez	étais sorti(e)	étiez sorti(e)(s)
sortait	sortaient	était sorti(e)	étaient sorti(e)s
3 passé simple		**10 passé antérieur**	
sortis	sortîmes	fus sorti(e)	fûmes sorti(e)s
sortis	sortîtes	fus sorti(e)	fûtes sorti(e)(s)
sortit	sortirent	fut sorti(e)	furent sorti(e)s
4 futur		**11 futur antérieur**	
sortirai	sortirons	serai sorti(e)	serons sorti(e)s
sortiras	sortirez	seras sorti(e)	serez sorti(e)(s)
sortira	sortiront	sera sorti(e)	seront sorti(e)s
5 conditionnel		**12 conditionnel passé**	
sortirais	sortirions	serais sorti(e)	serions sorti(e)s
sortirais	sortiriez	serais sorti(e)	seriez sorti(e)(s)
sortirait	sortiraient	serait sorti(e)	seraient sorti(e)s
6 présent du subjonctif		**13 passé du subjonctif**	
sorte	sortions	sois sorti(e)	soyons sorti(e)s
sortes	sortiez	sois sorti(e)	soyez sorti(e)(s)
sorte	sortent	soit sorti(e)	soient sorti(e)s
7 imparfait du subjonctif		**14 plus-que-parfait du subjonctif**	
sortisse	sortissions	fusse sorti(e)	fussions sorti(e)s
sortisses	sortissiez	fusses sorti(e)	fussiez sorti(e)(s)
sortît	sortissent	fût sorti(e)	fussent sorti(e)s

Impératif
sors
sortons
sortez

This verb is conjugated with **avoir** when it has a direct object.

Example: **Elle a sorti son mouchoir.**   She took out her handkerchief.

BUT: **Elle est sortie hier soir.**   She went out last night.

Words and expressions related to this verb

ressortir   to go out again
une sortie   exit;
  une sortie de secours
  emergency exit

sortir du lit   to get out of bed
se sortir d'une situation   to get oneself out
  of a situation

Part. pr. **se souvenant**	Part. passé **souvenu(e)(s)**	**se souvenir**
		to remember, to recall

The Seven Simple Tenses		The Seven Compound Tenses	
Singular	Plural	Singular	Plural
1 présent de l'indicatif		**8 passé composé**	
me souviens	nous souvenons	me suis souvenu(e)	nous sommes souvenu(e)s
te souviens	vous souvenez	t'es souvenu(e)	vous êtes souvenu(e)(s)
se souvient	se souviennent	s'est souvenu(e)	se sont souvenu(e)s
2 imparfait de l'indicatif		**9 plus-que-parfait de l'indicatif**	
me souvenais	nous souvenions	m'étais souvenu(e)	nous étions souvenu(e)s
te souvenais	vous souveniez	t'étais souvenu(e)	vous étiez souvenu(e)(s)
se souvenait	se souvenaient	s'était souvenu(e)	s'étaient souvenu(e)s
3 passé simple		**10 passé antérieur**	
me souvins	nous souvînmes	me fus souvenu(e)	nous fûmes souvenu(e)s
te souvins	vous souvîntes	te fus souvenu(e)	vous fûtes souvenu(e)(s)
se souvint	se souvinrent	se fut souvenu(e)	se furent souvenu(e)s
4 futur		**11 futur antérieur**	
me souviendrai	nous souviendrons	me serai souvenu(e)	nous serons souvenu(e)s
te souviendras	vous souviendrez	te seras souvenu(e)	vous serez souvenu(e)(s)
se souviendra	se souviendront	se sera souvenu(e)	se seront souvenu(e)s
5 conditionnel		**12 conditionnel passé**	
me souviendrais	nous souviendrions	me serais souvenu(e)	nous serions souvenu(e)s
te souviendrais	vous souviendriez	te serais souvenu(e)	vous seriez souvenu(e)(s)
se souviendrait	se souviendraient	se serait souvenu(e)	se seraient souvenu(e)s
6 présent du subjonctif		**13 passé du subjonctif**	
me souvienne	nous souvenions	me sois souvenu(e)	nous soyons souvenu(e)s
te souviennes	vous souveniez	te sois souvenu(e)	vous soyez souvenu(e)(s)
se souvienne	se souviennent	se soit souvenu(e)	se soient souvenu(e)s
7 imparfait du subjonctif		**14 plus-que-parfait du subjonctif**	
me souvinsse	nous souvinssions	me fusse souvenu(e)	nous fussions souvenu(e)s
te souvinsses	vous souvinssiez	te fusses souvenu(e)	vous fussiez souvenu(e)(s)
se souvînt	se souvinssent	se fût souvenu(e)	se fussent souvenu(e)s

Impératif
souviens-toi; ne te souviens pas
souvenons-nous; ne nous souvenons pas
souvenez-vous; ne vous souvenez pas

Words and expressions related to this verb

un souvenir   souvenir, remembrance
Je m'en souviendrai!   I'll remember that! I won't forget that!
se souvenir de qqn ou de qqch   to remember someone or something

Consult §39.42–§39.50 for the section on verbs with prepositions.

The subject pronouns are found in §40.1.

suivre

Part. pr. **suivant**   Part. passé **suivi**

to follow

The Seven Simple Tenses		The Seven Compound Tenses	
Singular	Plural	Singular	Plural
1 présent de l'indicatif		**8 passé composé**	
suis	suivons	ai suivi	avons suivi
suis	suivez	as suivi	avez suivi
suit	suivent	a suivi	ont suivi
2 imparfait de l'indicatif		**9 plus-que-parfait de l'indicatif**	
suivais	suivions	avais suivi	avions suivi
suivais	suiviez	avais suivi	aviez suivi
suivait	suivaient	avait suivi	avaient suivi
3 passé simple		**10 passé antérieur**	
suivis	suivîmes	eus suivi	eûmes suivi
suivis	suivîtes	eus suivi	eûtes suivi
suivit	suivirent	eut suivi	eurent suivi
4 futur		**11 futur antérieur**	
suivrai	suivrons	aurai suivi	aurons suivi
suivras	suivrez	auras suivi	aurez suivi
suivra	suivront	aura suivi	auront suivi
5 conditionnel		**12 conditionnel passé**	
suivrais	suivrions	aurais suivi	aurions suivi
suivrais	suivriez	aurais suivi	auriez suivi
suivrait	suivraient	aurait suivi	auraient suivi
6 présent du subjonctif		**13 passé du subjonctif**	
suive	suivions	aie suivi	ayons suivi
suives	suiviez	aies suivi	ayez suivi
suive	suivent	ait suivi	aient suivi
7 imparfait du subjonctif		**14 plus-que-parfait du subjonctif**	
suivisse	suivissions	eusse suivi	eussions suivi
suivisses	suivissiez	eusses suivi	eussiez suivi
suivît	suivissent	eût suivi	eussent suivi

Impératif
suis
suivons
suivez

Words and expressions related to this verb

suivant according to
suivant que. . . according as . . .
la suite continuation
à la suite de coming after
de suite in succession
à suivre to be continued

le jour suivant on the following day
les questions suivantes the following questions
tout de suite immediately
suivre un cours to take a course

Part. pr. **se taisant**   Part. passé **tu(e)(s)**   **se taire**

to be silent, to be quiet, not to speak

The Seven Simple Tenses		The Seven Compound Tenses	
Singular	Plural	Singular	Plural
1 présent de l'indicatif		**8 passé composé**	
me tais	nous taisons	me suis tu(e)	nous sommes tu(e)s
te tais	vous taisez	t'es tu(e)	vous êtes tu(e)(s)
se tait	se taisent	s'est tu(e)	se sont tu(e)s
2 imparfait de l'indicatif		**9 plus-que-parfait de l'indicatif**	
me taisais	nous taisions	m'étais tu(e)	nous étions tu(e)s
te taisais	vous taisiez	t'étais tu(e)	vous étiez tu(e)(s)
se taisait	se taisaient	s'était tu(e)	s'étaient tu(e)s
3 passé simple		**10 passé antérieur**	
me tus	nous tûmes	me fus tu(e)	nous fûmes tu(e)s
te tus	vous tûtes	te fus tu(e)	vous fûtes tu(e)(s)
se tut	se turent	se fut tu(e)	se furent tu(e)s
4 futur		**11 futur antérieur**	
me tairai	nous tairons	me serai tu(e)	nous serons tu(e)s
te tairas	vous tairez	te seras tu(e)	vous serez tu(e)(s)
se taira	se tairont	se sera tu(e)	se seront tu(e)s
5 conditionnel		**12 conditionnel passé**	
me tairais	nous tairions	me serais tu(e)	nous serions tu(e)s
te tairais	vous tairiez	te serais tu(e)	vous seriez tu(e)(s)
se tairait	se tairaient	se serait tu(e)	se seraient tu(e)s
6 présent du subjonctif		**13 passé du subjonctif**	
me taise	nous taisions	me sois tu(e)	nous soyons tu(e)s
te taise	vous taisiez	te sois tu(e)	vous soyez tu(e)(s)
se taise	se taisent	se soit tu(e)	se soient tu(e)s
7 imparfait du subjonctif		**14 plus-que-parfait du subjonctif**	
me tusse	nous tussions	me fusse tu(e)	nous fussions tu(e)s
te tusses	vous tussiez	te fusses tu(e)	vous fussiez tu(e)(s)
se tût	se tussent	se fût tu(e)	se fussent tu(e)s

Impératif
tais-toi; ne te tais pas
taisons-nous; ne nous taisons pas
taisez-vous; ne vous taisez pas

—Marie, veux-tu te taire! Tu es trop bavarde. Et toi, Hélène, tais-toi aussi.
Les deux élèves ne se taisent pas. La maîtresse de chimie continue:
—Taisez-vous, je vous dis, toutes les deux; autrement, vous resterez dans cette salle après la classe.
Les deux jeunes filles se sont tues.

tenir

Part. pr. **tenant**   Part. passé **tenu**

to hold, to grasp

The Seven Simple Tenses		The Seven Compound Tenses	
Singular	Plural	Singular	Plural
1 présent de l'indicatif		8 passé composé	
tiens	tenons	ai tenu	avons tenu
tiens	tenez	as tenu	avez tenu
tient	tiennent	a tenu	ont tenu
2 imparfait de l'indicatif		9 plus-que-parfait de l'indicatif	
tenais	tenions	avais tenu	avions tenu
tenais	teniez	avais tenu	aviez tenu
tenait	tenaient	avait tenu	avaient tenu
3 passé simple		10 passé antérieur	
tins	tînmes	eus tenu	eûmes tenu
tins	tîntes	eus tenu	eûtes tenu
tint	tinrent	eut tenu	eurent tenu
4 futur		11 futur antérieur	
tiendrai	tiendrons	aurai tenu	aurons tenu
tiendras	tiendrez	auras tenu	aurez tenu
tiendra	tiendront	aura tenu	auront tenu
5 conditionnel		12 conditionnel passé	
tiendrais	tiendrions	aurais tenu	aurions tenu
tiendrais	tiendriez	aurais tenu	auriez tenu
tiendrait	tiendraient	aurait tenu	auraient tenu
6 présent du subjonctif		13 passé du subjonctif	
tienne	tenions	aie tenu	ayons tenu
tiennes	teniez	aies tenu	ayez tenu
tienne	tiennent	ait tenu	aient tenu
7 imparfait du subjonctif		14 plus-que-parfait du subjonctif	
tinsse	tinssions	eusse tenu	eussions tenu
tinsses	tinssiez	eusses tenu	eussiez tenu
tînt	tinssent	eût tenu	eussent tenu

Impératif
tiens
tenons
tenez

Words and expressions related to this verb

tenir de qqn   to take after (to favor) someone;
   Robert tient de son père   Robert takes after his father.
tenir de bonne source   to have on good authority
tenir à qqch   to cherish something

Part. pr. **valant**   Part. passé **valu**   **valoir**

to be worth, to be as good as, to deserve, to merit

The Seven Simple Tenses		The Seven Compound Tenses	
Singular	Plural	Singular	Plural
1 présent de l'indicatif		**8 passé composé**	
vaux	valons	ai valu	avons valu
vaux	valez	as valu	avez valu
vaut	valent	a valu	ont valu
2 imparfait de l'indicatif		**9 plus-que-parfait de l'indicatif**	
valais	valions	avais valu	avions valu
valais	valiez	avais valu	aviez valu
valait	valaient	avait valu	avaient valu
3 passé simple		**10 passé antérieur**	
valus	valûmes	eus valu	eûmes valu
valus	valûtes	eus valu	eûtes valu
valut	valurent	eut valu	eurent valu
4 futur		**11 futur antérieur**	
vaudrai	vaudrons	aurai valu	aurons valu
vaudras	vaudrez	auras valu	aurez valu
vaudra	vaudront	aura valu	auront valu
5 conditionnel		**12 conditionnel passé**	
vaudrais	vaudrions	aurais valu	aurions valu
vaudrais	vaudriez	aurais valu	auriez valu
vaudrait	vaudraient	aurait valu	auraient valu
6 présent du subjonctif		**13 passé du subjonctif**	
vaille	valions	aie valu	ayons valu
vailles	valiez	aies valu	ayez valu
vaille	vaillent	ait valu	aient valu
7 imparfait du subjonctif		**14 plus-que-parfait du subjonctif**	
valusse	valussions	eusse valu	eussions valu
valusses	valussiez	eusses valu	eussiez valu
valût	valussent	eût valu	eussent valu

Impératif
vaux
valons
valez

Words and expresions related to this verb

la valeur value
valeureusement valorously
valeureux, valeureuse valorous
Cela vaut la peine It's worth the trouble.
faire valoir to make the most of, to invest one's money

la validation validation
valide valid
Mieux vaut tard que jamais. Better late than never.

Consult the Appendix for verbs used in idiomatic expressions.

The subject pronouns are found in §40.1.

venir

Part. pr. **venant**   Part. passé **venu(e)(s)**

to come

The Seven Simple Tenses		The Seven Compound Tenses	
Singular	Plural	Singular	Plural

1   présent de l'indicatif

		8 passé composé	
viens	venons	suis venu(e)	sommes venu(e)s
viens	venez	es venu(e)	êtes venu(e)(s)
vient	viennent	est venu(e)	sont venu(e)s

2   imparfait de l'indicatif

		9 plus-que-parfait de l'indicatif	
venais	venions	étais venu(e)	étions venu(e)s
venais	veniez	étais venu(e)	étiez venu(e)(s)
venait	venaient	était venu(e)	étaient venu(e)s

3   passé simple

		10 passé antérieur	
vins	vînmes	fus venu(e)	fûmes venu(e)s
vins	vîntes	fus venu(e)	fûtes venu(e)(s)
vint	vinrent	fut venu(e)	furent venu(e)s

4   futur

		11 futur antérieur	
viendrai	viendrons	serai venu(e)	serons venu(e)s
viendras	viendrez	seras venu(e)	serez venu(e)(s)
viendra	viendront	sera venu(e)	seront venu(e)s

5   conditionnel

		12 conditionnel passé	
viendrais	viendrions	serais venu(e)	serions venu(e)s
viendrais	viendriez	serais venu(e)	seriez venu(e)(s)
viendrait	viendraient	serait venu(e)	seraient venu(e)s

6   présent du subjonctif

		13 passé du subjonctif	
vienne	venions	sois venu(e)	soyons venu(e)s
viennes	veniez	sois venu(e)	soyez venu(e)(s)
vienne	viennent	soit venu(e)	soient venu(e)s

7   imparfait du subjonctif

		14 plus-que-parfait du subjonctif	
vinsse	vinssions	fusse venu(e)	fussions venu(e)s
vinsses	vinssiez	fusses venu(e)	fussiez venu(e)(s)
vînt	vinssent	fût venu(e)	fussent venu(e)s

Impératif
viens
venons
venez

Words and expressions related to this verb

venir de faire qqch   to have just done something
Je viens de manger   I have just eaten
venir à + inf.   to happen to; **Si je viens à devenir
  riche. . .**   If I happen to become rich. . .

faire venir   to send for
venir chercher   call for, to
  come to get
D'où vient cela?   Where does
  that come from?

Consult the Appendix for verbs used in idiomatic expressions.

Part. pr. **vivant**   Part. passé **vécu**

vivre

to live

The Seven Simple Tenses		The Seven Compound Tenses	
Singular	Plural	Singular	Plural
1 présent de l'indicatif		**8 passé composé**	
vis	vivons	ai vécu	avons vécu
vis	vivez	as vécu	avez vécu
vit	vivent	a vécu	ont vécu
2 imparfait de l'indicatif		**9 plus-que-parfait de l'indicatif**	
vivais	vivions	avais vécu	avions vécu
vivais	viviez	avais vécu	aviez vécu
vivait	vivaient	avait vécu	avaient vécu
3 passé simple		**10 passé antérieur**	
vécus	vécûmes	eus vécu	eûmes vécu
vécus	vécûtes	eus vécu	eûtes vécu
vécut	vécurent	eut vécu	eurent vécu
4 futur		**11 futur antérieur**	
vivrai	vivrons	aurai vécu	aurons vécu
vivras	vivrez	auras vécu	aurez vécu
vivra	vivront	aura vécu	auront vécu
5 conditionnel		**12 conditionnel passé**	
vivrais	vivrions	aurais vécu	aurions vécu
vivrais	vivriez	aurais vécu	auriez vécu
vivrait	vivraient	aurait vécu	auraient vécu
6 présent du subjonctif		**13 passé du subjonctif**	
vive	vivions	aie vécu	ayons vécu
vives	viviez	aies vécu	ayez vécu
vive	vivent	ait vécu	aient vécu
7 imparfait du subjonctif		**14 plus-que-parfait du subjonctif**	
vécusse	vécussions	eusse vécu	eussions vécu
vécusses	vécussiez	eusses vécu	eussiez vécu
vécût	vécussent	eût vécu	eussent vécu

Impératif
vis
vivons
vivez

Words and expressions related to this verb

revivre   to relive, to revive
survivre à   to survive
Vive la France!   Long live France!
avoir de quoi vivre   to have enough
   to live on
vivre de   to subsist on

savoir-vivre   to be well-mannered
Vivent les Etats-Unis!   Long live the
   United States!
le vivre et le couvert   board and room

Consult the Appendix for idiomatic expressions.

The subject pronouns are found in §40.1.

voir
Part. pr. **voyant**   Part. passé **vu**

to see

The Seven Simple Tenses		The Seven Compound Tenses	
Singular	Plural	Singular	Plural
1 présent de l'indicatif		**8 passé composé**	
vois	voyons	ai vu	avons vu
vois	voyez	as vu	avez vu
voit	voient	a vu	ont vu
2 imparfait de l'indicatif		**9 plus-que-parfait de l'indicatif**	
voyais	voyions	avais vu	avions vu
voyais	voyiez	avais vu	aviez vu
voyait	voyaient	avait vu	avaient vu
3 passé simple		**10 passé antérieur**	
vis	vîmes	eus vu	eûmes vu
vis	vîtes	eus vu	eûtes vu
vit	virent	eut vu	eurent vu
4 futur		**11 futur antérieur**	
verrai	verrons	aurai vu	aurons vu
verras	verrez	auras vu	aurez vu
verra	verront	aura vu	auront vu
5 conditionnel		**12 conditionnel passé**	
verrais	verrions	aurais vu	aurions vu
verrais	verriez	aurais vu	auriez vu
verrait	verraient	aurait vu	auraient vu
6 présent du subjonctif		**13 passé du subjonctif**	
voie	voyions	aie vu	ayons vu
voies	voyiez	aies vu	ayez vu
voie	voient	ait vu	aient vu
7 imparfait du subjonctif		**14 plus-que-parfait du subjonctif**	
visse	vissions	eusse vu	eussions vu
visses	vissiez	eusses vu	eussiez vu
vît	vissent	eût vu	eussent vu

Impératif
vois
voyons
voyez

Words and expressions related to this verb

revoir   to see again
faire voir   to show
voir la vie en rose   to see the bright side of life
Voyez vous-même!   See for yourself!

entrevoir   to catch a glimpse, to glimpse
C'est à voir   It remains to be seen.
Cela se voit   That's obvious.
Voyons!   See here now!

See also **revoir.**

Consult the Appendix for verbs used in idiomatic expressions.

Part. pr. **voulant**   Part. passé **voulu**   **vouloir**

to want, to wish

The Seven Simple Tenses		The Seven Compound Tenses	
Singular	Plural	Singular	Plural
1 présent de l'indicatif		**8 passé composé**	
veux	voulons	ai voulu	avons voulu
veux	voulez	as voulu	avez voulu
veut	veulent	a voulu	ont voulu
2 imparfait de l'indicatif		**9 plus-que-parfait de l'indicatif**	
voulais	voulions	avais voulu	avions voulu
voulais	vouliez	avais voulu	aviez voulu
voulait	voulaient	avait voulu	avaient voulu
3 passé simple		**10 passé antérieur**	
voulus	voulûmes	eus voulu	eûmes voulu
voulus	voulûtes	eus voulu	eûtes voulu
voulut	voulurent	eut voulu	eurent voulu
4 futur		**11 futur antérieur**	
voudrai	voudrons	aurai voulu	aurons voulu
voudras	voudrez	auras voulu	aurez voulu
voudra	voudront	aura voulu	auront voulu
5 conditionnel		**12 conditionnel passé**	
voudrais	voudrions	aurais voulu	aurions voulu
voudrais	voudriez	aurais voulu	auriez voulu
voudrait	voudraient	aurait voulu	auraient voulu
6 présent du subjonctif		**13 passé du subjonctif**	
veuille	voulions	aie voulu	ayons voulu
veuilles	vouliez	aies voulu	ayez voulu
veuille	veuillent	ait voulu	aient voulu
7 imparfait du subjonctif		**14 plus-que-parfait du subjonctif**	
voulusse	voulussions	eusse voulu	eussions voulu
voulusses	voulussiez	eusses voulu	eussiez voulu
voulût	voulussent	eût voulu	eussent voulu

Impératif
veuille
veuillons
veuillez

Words and expressions related to this verb

un voeu   a wish
meilleurs voeux   best wishes
Vouloir c'est pouvoir   Where there's a will there's a way.
vouloir dire   to mean;   **Qu'est-ce que cela veut dire?**   What does that mean?
vouloir bien faire qqch   to be willing to do something
sans le vouloir   without meaning to, unintentionally
en temps voulu   in due time
en vouloir à qqn   to bear a grudge against someone
Que voulez-vous dire par là?   What do you mean by that remark?

Consult the Appendix for verbs used in idiomatic expressions.

§41. Common irregular French verb forms and uncommon French verb forms identified by infinitive

A

a **avoir**
ai **avoir**
aie **avoir**
aient **avoir**
aies **avoir**
aille **aller**
ait **avoir**
as **avoir**
aurai, *etc.* **avoir**
avaient **avoir**
avais **avoir**
avait **avoir**
avez **avoir**
aviez **avoir**
avions **avoir**
avons **avoir**
ayant **avoir**
ayons, *etc.* **avoir**

B

bu **boire**
bûmes **boire**
burent **boire**
bus **boire**
bussent **boire**
but **boire**
bûtes **boire**
buvant **boire**

C

crois **croire**
croîs **croître**
croit **croire**
croît **croître**
croyais, *etc.* **croire**
cru **croire**
crû, crue **croître**
crûmes **croire, croître**
crurent **croire**
crûrent **croître**
crus **croire**
crûs **croître**
crûsse, *etc.* **croître**
crût **croire, croître**

D

dîmes **dire**
disais, *etc.* **dire**
disse, *etc.* **dire**
dit, dît **dire**
dois **devoir**
doive, *etc.* **devoir**
dors **dormir**
dû, due **devoir**
dûmes **devoir**

dus, dussent **devoir**
dut, dût **devoir**

E

es **être**
est **être**
étais, *etc.* **être**
été **être**
êtes **être**
étiez **être**
eu **avoir**
eûmes **avoir**
eurent **avoir**
eus **avoir**
eusse, *etc.* **avoir**
eut, eût **avoir**
eûtes **avoir**

F

faille **faillir, falloir**
fais, *etc.* **faire**
fasse, *etc.* **faire**
faudra **faillir, falloir**
faudrait **faillir, falloir**
faut **faillir, falloir**
faux **faillir**
ferai, *etc.* **faire**
fîmes **faire**
firent **faire**
fis, *etc.* **faire**
font **faire**
fûmes **être**
furent **être**
fus, *etc.* **être**
fut, fût **être**
fuyais, *etc.* **fuir**

G

gisons, *etc.* **gésir**
gît **gésir**

I

ira, irai, iras, *etc.* **aller**

L

lis, *etc.* **lire**
lu **lire**
lus, *etc.* **lire**

M

meure, *etc.* **mourir**
meus, *etc.* **mouvoir**

mîmes **mettre**
mirent **mettre**
mis **mettre**
misses, *etc.* **mettre**
mit **mettre**
mort **mourir**
moulons, *etc.* **moudre**
moulu **moudre**
mû, mue **mouvoir**
mussent **mouvoir**
mut **mouvoir**

N

naquîmes, *etc.* **naître**
né **naître**

O

omis **omettre**
ont **avoir**

P

pars **partir**
paru **paraître**
peignis, *etc.* **peindre**
peuvent **pouvoir**
peux, *etc.* **pouvoir**
plu **plaire, pleuvoir**
plurent **plaire**
plut, plût **plaire, pleuvoir**
plûtes **plaire**
pourrai, *etc.* **pouvoir**
prîmes **prendre**
prirent **prendre**
pris **prendre**
prisse, *etc.* **prendre**
pu **pouvoir**
puis **pouvoir**
puisse, *etc.* **pouvoir**
pûmes, *etc.* **pouvoir**
purent **pouvoir**
pus **pouvoir**
pusse **pouvoir**
put, pût **pouvoir**

R

reçois, *etc.* **recevoir**
reçûmes, *etc.* **recevoir**
relu **relire**
reviens, *etc.* **revenir**
revins, *etc.* **revenir**
riiez **rire**
ris, *etc.* **rire**

S

sache, *etc.* **savoir**
sais, *etc.* **savoir**
saurai, *etc.* **savoir**
séant **seoir**
serai, *etc.* **être**
sers, *etc.* **servir**
seyant **seoir**
sied **seoir**
siéent **seoir**
siéra, *etc.* **seoir**
sois, *etc.* **être**
sommes **être**
sont **être**
sors, *etc.* **sortir**
soyez **être**
soyons **être**
su **savoir**
suis **être, suivre**
suit **suivre**
sûmes **savoir**
surent **savoir**
survécu **survivre**

susse, *etc.* **savoir**
sut, sût **savoir**

T

tiendrai, *etc.* **tenir**
tienne, *etc.* **tenir**
tînmes **tenir**
tins, *etc.* **tenir**
trayant **traire**
tu **taire**
tûmes **taire**
turent **taire**
tus **taire**
tusse, *etc.* **taire**
tut, tût **taire**

V

va **aller**
vaille **valoir**
vais **aller**
vas **aller**
vaudrai, *etc.* **valoir**

vaux, *etc.* **valoir**
vécu **vivre**
vécûmes, *etc.* **vivre**
verrai, *etc.* **voir**
veuille, *etc.* **vouloir**
veulent **vouloir**
veux, *etc.* **vouloir**
viendrai, *etc.* **venir**
vienne, *etc.* **venir**
viens, *etc.* **venir**
vîmes **voir**
vînmes **venir**
vinrent **venir**
vins, *etc.* **venir**
virent **voir**
vis **vivre, voir**
visse, *etc.* **voir**
vit **vivre, voir**
vît **voir**
vîtes **voir**
vont **aller**
voudrai, *etc.* **vouloir**
voyais, *etc.* **voir**
vu **voir**

§42. SUMMARIES OF WORD ORDER OF ELEMENTS IN A FRENCH SENTENCE

§42.1 Summary of word order of elements in a French declarative sentence with a verb in a simple tense (*e.g.*, present)

SUBJECT	ne	me	le	lui	y	en	VERB	pas
	n'	m'	la	leur				
		te	l'					
		t'	les					
		se						
		s'						
		nous						
		vous						

EXAMPLES:

Il ne me les donne pas / He is not giving them to me.

Je ne le leur donne pas / I am not giving it to them.

Il n'y en a pas / There aren't any of them.

Je ne m'en souviens pas / I don't remember it.

Je n'y en mets pas / I am not putting any of them there.

§42.2   **Summary of word order of elements in a French declarative sentence with a verb in a compound tense** (*e.g.*, passé composé)

SUBJECT	ne	me	le	lui	y	en	VERB	pas	past
	n'	m'	la	leur			(Auxiliary verb		participle
		te	l'				**avoir** or **être** in		
		t'	les				a simple tense)		
		se							
		s'							
		nous							
		vous							

EXAMPLES:

Yvonne ne s'est pas lavée / Yvonne did not wash herself.

Il ne m'en a pas envoyé / He did not send any of them to me.

Je ne le lui ai pas donné / I did not give it to him (to her).

Nous ne vous les avons pas données / We have not given them to you.

Ils ne s'en sont pas allés / They did not go away.

Je ne t'en ai pas envoyé / I have not sent any of them to you.

Je n'y ai pas répondu / I have not replied to it.

Je ne m'en suis pas souvenu / I did not remember it.

Vous ne vous en êtes pas allé / You did not go away.

Robert ne les lui a pas envoyés / Robert did not send them to him (to her).

§42.3   **Summary of word order of elements in a French affirmative imperative sentence**

VERB	le	moi	lui	y	en
	la	m'	leur		
	l'	toi			
	les	t'			
		nous			
		vous			

EXAMPLES:

Mettez-l'y / Put it in it (on it) **OR:** Put it there.

Donnez-les-leur / Give them to them.

Assieds-toi / Sit down.

Allez-vous-en! / Go away!

Asseyez-vous / Sit down.

Mettez-y-en! / Put some in it (on it, there)!

Apportez-le-moi / Bring it to me.

Donnez-m'en / Give me some.

Allez-y! / Go to it! **OR:** Go there!

Mangez-en! / Eat some (of it)!

§42.4   **Summary of word order of elements in a French negative imperative sentence**

Ne	me	le	lui		y	en	**VERB**	pas
N'	m'	la	leur					
	te	l'						
	t'	les						
	nous							
	vous							

EXAMPLES:

Ne l'y mettez pas / Do not put it in it **OR:** Do not put it there.

Ne les leur donnez pas / Do not give them to them.

Ne t'assieds pas! / Don't sit down!

Ne vous en allez pas! / Don't go away!

Ne vous asseyez pas! / Don't sit down!

Ne me les donnez pas / Don't give them to me.

Ne m'en envoyez pas / Don't send me any (of them).

Ne nous en écrivez pas / Do not write about it to us.

N'y allez pas! / Don't go there!

Ne nous y asseyons pas / Let's not sit there (in it, on it, *etc.*)

Note that the order of the following object pronouns is always the same, whether in front of a verb form or after a verb form or in front of an infinitive: **le lui, la lui, les lui; le leur, la leur, les leur.** For practice, pronounce them out loud. To help you understand that **le, la** or **les** always come in front of **lui** or **leur**, think of certain words in English expressions that are customarily grouped together: for example, we say *ham and eggs* (not *eggs and ham*), *peanut butter and jelly* (not *jelly and peanut butter*), *bread and butter* (not *butter and bread*). So it is with these direct and indirect object pronouns in French: **le lui/la lui/les lui; le leur/la leur/les leur.**

§43.   VINGT PROVERBES (Twenty Proverbs)

1. **Le chat parti, les souris dansent.**   (When the cat is away, the mice will play.)

2. **L'appétit vient en mangeant.**   (The more you have, the more you want.)   (*i.e.,* Appetite comes while eating.)

3. **A bon chat, bon rat.**   (Tit for tat).   (*i.e.,* A good cat is entitled to a good rat.)

4. **Loin des yeux, loin du coeur.**   (Out of sight, out of mind.)

5. **Bien faire et laisser dire.**   (Do your work well and never mind the critics.)

6. **Tel père, tel fils.**   (Like father, like son.)

7. **Telle mère, telle fille.**   (Like mother, like daughter.)

8. **Il n'y a pas de fumée sans feu.**   (Where there's smoke, there's fire.)

9. **Mains froides, coeur chaud.**   (Cold hands, warm heart.)

10. **Mieux vaut tard que jamais.**   (Better late than never.)

11. **Les murs ont des oreilles.**   (Walls have ears.)

12. **Chacun son goût.**   (To each his own.)   (*i.e.,* Each person has his/her own tastes.)

13. **Tout est bien qui finit bien.**   (All's well that ends well.)

14. **Qui se ressemble s'assemble.**   (Birds of a feather flock together.)

15. **Qui ne risque rien n'a rien.**   (Nothing ventured, nothing gained.)

16. **Vouloir, c'est pouvoir.**   (Where there's a will, there's a way.)

17. **Beaucoup de bruit pour rien.**   (Much ado about nothing.)

18. **Qui vivra verra.**   (Time will tell.)

19. **L'habit ne fait pas le moine.**   (Clothes don't make the person.)

20. **Rira bien qui rira le dernier.**   (She/He who laughs last laughs best.)

Vocabulaire

l'appétit *n.,* the appetite
assembler *v.,* to assemble; **s'assembler** *refl. v.,* to gather, to meet
le bruit *n.,* the noise
le feu *n.,* the fire
la fumée *n.,* the smoke
l'habit *n. m.,* attire, costume, dress
loin *adv.,* far

mangeant *pres. part. of* **manger; en mangeant** while eating
le moine *n.,* the monk
le mur *n.,* the wall
l'oeil *n. m.,* the eye; **les yeux** the eyes
l'oreille *n. f.,* the ear
pouvoir *v.,* to be able
qui *pron.,* who (sometimes: he/she who)

se ressembler *refl. v.,* to resemble each other
rira *v. form of* **rire** (to laugh)
risquer *v.,* to risk
la souris *n.,* the mouse
tel *m.,* **telle** *f., adj.,* such
vaut *v. form of* **valoir** (to be worth)
verra *v. form of* **voir** (to see)
vivra *v. form of* **vivre** (to live)
vouloir *v.,* to want

Le chat parti, les souris dansent.

L'appétit vient en mangeant.

§44.   UNE FABLE (A Fable)

La cigale et la fourmi

— adapté de la fable de Jean de La Fontaine

La cigale a chanté tout l'été.
Elle n'a pas travaillé.

L'hiver arrive et
Elle n'a rien à manger.

Elle n'a pas un seul petit morceau
De mouche ou de vermisseau.

Elle va chez la fourmi, sa voisine,
Et elle lui dit:

— Ma chère amie, je n'ai rien à
manger et j'ai faim. Pouvez-vous
me prêter un grain de quelque chose
jusqu'au printemps?

Mais la fourmi ne donne jamais
Rien à ses voisins.

Elle a travaillé pendant l'été
Pour avoir quelque chose à manger
Pendant l'hiver.

La fourmi demande à la cigale:

— Qu'est-ce que vous avez fait
pendant l'été? Avez-vous travaillé?

La cigale répond à la fourmi:

— Je n'ai pas travaillé.
J'ai chanté.

Et la fourmi lui dit:

— Ah! Vous avez chanté! Dansez maintenant!

Vocabulaire

la cigale *n.,* the cicada (an insect; the male cicada makes a prolonged shrill, droning sound on hot days in the summer)

l'été *n. m.,* the summer
la fourmi *n.,* the ant
l'hiver *n. m.,* the winter
jusque *prep.,* as far as, up to; **jusqu'au printemps** until

spring
le printemps *n.,* the spr
travailler *v.,* to work
le vermisseau *n.,* the s
worm

La fourmi répond à la cigale: "Ah! Vous avez chanté! Dansez maintenant!"

§45.   REVIEW OF BASIC VOCABULARY BY TOPICS

§45.1   L'école (School)

le banc *n.*, the seat, the bench

la bibliothèque *n.*, the library

le bureau *n.*, the desk, the office

le cahier *n.*, the notebook

le calendrier *n.*, the calendar

le carnet *n.*, the small notebook

la carte *n.*, the map

la classe *n.*, the class; **la classe de français** French class

le congé *n.*, leave, permission; **jour de congé** day off (from school or work)

la cour *n.*, the playground, the courtyard

la craie *n.*, the chalk

le crayon *n.*, the pencil; **le crayon feutre** the crayon

les devoirs *n. m.*, homework assignments

la dictée *n.*, the dictation

le drapeau *n.*, the flag

l'école *n. f.*, the school

écrire *v.*, to write

l'élève *n. m. f.*, the pupil

l'encre *n. f.*, the ink

étudier *v.*, to study; **les études** *n. f. pl.*, the studies

l'étudiant *m.*, **l'étudiante** *f.*, *n.*, the student

l'examen *n. m.*, the examination

l'exercice *n. m.*, the exercise

expliquer *v.*, to explain

la faute *n.*, the mistake

la leçon *n.*, the lesson; **leçon de français** French lesson

le livre *n.*, the book

le livret d'exercices *n.*, the workbook

le lycée *n.*, the high school

le maître *m.*, **la maîtresse** *f.*, *n.*, the teacher

le papier *n.*, the paper; **une feuille de papier** a sheet of paper

passer *v.*, to pass; **passer un examen** to take an exam

poser *v.*, to pose; **poser une question** to ask a question

le professeur *m.*, **la professeur-dame, une femme professeur** *f.*, *n.*, the professor

le pupitre *n.*, the desk (student's)

la règle *n.*, the rule, the ruler

répondre *v.*, to respond, to answer, to reply

la réponse *n.*, the answer

réussir *v.*, to succeed; **réussir à un examen** to pass an exam

la salle *n.*, the room; **la salle de classe** the classroom

le stylo *n.*, the pen

le tableau noir *n.*, the blackboard, the chalkboard

l'université *n. f.*, the university

le vocabulaire *n.*, the vocabulary

§45.2 **Les jours de la semaine, les mois de l'année, les saisons, et les jours de fête** (Days of the Week, Months of the Year, Seasons, and Holidays)

Les jours de la semaine

le dimanche, Sunday
le lundi, Monday
le mardi, Tuesday
le mercredi, Wednesday
le jeudi, Thursday
le vendredi, Friday
le samedi, Saturday

Les saisons

le printemps, spring
l'été *(m.)*, summer
l'automne *(m.)*, autumn, fall
l'hiver *(m.)*, winter

Les mois de l'année

janvier, January
février, February
mars, March
avril, April
mai, May
juin, June
juillet, July
août, August
septembre, September
octobre, October
novembre, November
décembre, December

Les jours de fête

fêter *v.*, to celebrate a holiday; **bonne fête!** happy holiday!
l'anniversaire *m.*, anniversary, birthday; **bon anniversaire!** happy anniversary! *or* happy birthday!
le Jour de l'An, New Year's Day
Bonne année! Happy New Year!
les Pâques, Easter; **Joyeuses Pâques,** Happy Easter
la Pâque, Passover
le quatorze juillet (Bastille Day), July 14, French "Independence Day"
les grandes vacances, summer vacation
la Toussaint, All Saints' Day (le premier novembre)
le Noël, Christmas; **Joyeux Noël!** Merry Christmas!
à vous de même! the same to you!

§45.3   **Les légumes, les poissons, les viandes, les produits laitiers, les desserts, les fromages et les boissons** (Vegetables, Fish, Meats, Dairy Products, Desserts, Cheeses, and Beverages)

Les légumes

l'aubergine *f.*, the eggplant
la carotte, the carrot
le champignon, the mushroom
les épinards *m.*, the spinach
les haricots verts *m.*, the string beans
le maïs, the corn
l'oignon *m.*, the onion
les petits pois *m.*, the peas
la pomme de terre, the potato

Les viandes

l'agneau *m.*, the lamb; **la côte d'agneau,** the lamb chop
le biftek, the steak
le jambon, the ham
le porc, the pork
le poulet, the chicken
le rosbif, the roast beef
le veau, the veal; **la côte de veau,** the veal chop

Les poissons

le maquereau, the mackerel
la morue, the cod
le saumon, the salmon
la sole, the sole
la truite, the trout

Les produits laitiers

le beurre, the butter
la crème, the cream
le fromage, the cheese
le lait, the milk
l'oeuf *m.*, the egg

Les desserts

le fruit, the fruit
le gâteau, the cake; **le gâteau sec,** the cookie
la glace, the ice cream
la pâtisserie, the pastry

Les fromages

le brie
le camembert
le gruyère
le petit suisse
le port-salut
le roquefort

Les boissons

la bière, the beer
le cacao, the cocoa
le café, the coffee
le chocolat chaud, the hot chocolate
le cidre, the cider
l'eau minérale *f.*, the mineral water
le jus, the juice; **le jus de tomate,** the tomato juice
le thé, the tea
le vin, the wine

§45.4 **Les animaux, les fleurs, les couleurs, les arbres et les fruits** (Animals, Flowers, Colors, Trees, and Fruits)

Les animaux

l'âne *m.*, the donkey
le chat *m.*, **la chatte** *f.*, the cat
le cheval, the horse
le chien *m.*, **la chienne** *f.*, the dog
le cochon, the pig
le coq, the rooster
l'éléphant *m.*, the elephant
le lapin, the rabbit
le lion, the lion
l'oiseau *m.*, the bird
la poule, the hen
le poulet, the chicken
le renard, the fox
la souris, the mouse
le tigre, the tiger
la vache, the cow

Les fleurs

l'iris *m.*, the iris
le lilas, the lilac
le lis, the lily
la marguerite, the daisy
l'oeillet *m.*, the carnation
la rose, the rose
la tulipe, the tulip
la violette, the violet

Les couleurs

blanc, white
bleu, blue
brun, brown
gris, gray
jaune, yellow
noir, black
rouge, red
vert, green

Les arbres

le bananier, the banana tree
le cerisier, the cherry tree
le citronnier, the lemon tree
l'oranger *m.*, the orange tree
le palmier, the palm tree
le pêcher, the peach tree
le poirier, the pear tree
le pommier, the apple tree

Les fruits

la banane, the banana
la cerise, the cherry
le citron, the lemon; **citron vert,** lime
la fraise, the strawberry
la framboise, the raspberry
l'orange *f.*, the orange
le pamplemousse, the grapefruit
la pêche, the peach
la poire, the pear
la pomme, the apple
le raisin, the grape
la tomate, the tomato

§45.5   **Le corps humain, les vêtements, la toilette** (The Human Body, Clothing, Washing and Dressing)

Le corps humain

la bouche, mouth
le bras, arm
les cheveux *m.,* hair
le cou, neck
les dents *f.,* teeth
le doigt, finger; **doigt de pied,** toe
l'épaule *f.,* shoulder
l'estomac *m.,* stomach
le genou, knee
la jambe, leg
la langue, tongue
les lèvres *f.,* lips
la main, hand
le menton, chin
le nez, nose
l'oeil *m.,* eye; **les yeux,** eyes
l'oreille *f.,* ear
la peau, skin
le pied, foot
la poitrine, chest
la tête, head
le visage, face

La toilette

se baigner *v.,* to bathe oneself
la baignoire *n.,* the bathtub
le bain *n.,* the bath
la brosse *n.,* the brush; **brosse à dents,** toothbrush
brosser *v.,* to brush; **se brosser les dents,** to brush one's teeth
la cuvette *n.,* the toilet bowl
le dentifrice *n.,* the toothpaste
le déodorant *n.,* deodorant
déshabiller *v.,* to undress; **se déshabiller,** to undress oneself
la douche *n.,* the shower; **prendre une douche,** to take a shower
enlever *v.,* to remove, to take off
le gant de toilette *n.,* the washcloth
la glace *n.,* the hand mirror
s'habiller *v.,* to dress oneself
le lavabo *n.,* the washroom, washstand
laver *v.,* to wash; **se laver,** to wash oneself
mettre *v.,* to put on
le miroir *n.,* the mirror
ôter *v.,* to take off, to remove
le peigne *n.,* the comb; **se peigner les cheveux,** to comb one's hair
porter *v.,* to wear
la salle de bains *n.,* the bathroom
le savon *n.,* the soap
la serviette *n.,* the towel
le shampooing *n.,* the shampoo

Les vêtements

le bas, stocking
le béret, beret
la blouse, blouse, smock
le blouson, jacket (often with zipper)
le chandail, sweater
le chapeau, hat
la chaussette, sock
la chaussure, shoe
la chemise, shirt
le complet, suit
le costume, suit
la cravate, necktie
l'écharpe *f.,* scarf
le gant, glove
la jupe, skirt
le maillot de bain, swim suit
le manteau, coat
le pantalon, trousers, pants
la pantoufle, slipper
le pardessus, overcoat
la poche, pocket
le pullover, pullover or long-sleeved sweater
la robe, dress
le soulier, shoe
le veston, (suit) coat

§45.6   **La famille, la maison, les meubles** (Family, Home, Furniture)

La famille

le cousin, la cousine,
   cousin
l'enfant *m. f.,* child
l'époux *m.,* **l'épouse** *f.,*
   spouse (husband/wife)
la femme, wife
la fille, daughter
le fils, son
le frère, brother; **le**
   beau-frère, brother-in-law
la grand-mère, grandmother
le grand-père, grandfather
les grands-parents,
   grandparents
le mari, husband
la mère, la maman, mother;
   la belle-mère,
   mother-in-law
le neveu, nephew
la nièce, niece
l'oncle *m.,* uncle
le père, le papa, father; **le**
   beau-père, father-in-law
le petit-fils, grandson
la petite-fille,
   granddaughter
les petits-enfants,
   grandchildren
la soeur, sister; **la**
   belle-soeur, sister-in-law
la tante, aunt

La maison

la cave, the cellar
la chambre, the room;
   chambre à coucher,
   bedroom
la cheminée, the fireplace,
   chimney
la cuisine, the kitchen
l'escalier *m.,* the stairs,
   staircase
la fenêtre, the window
le mur, the wall
la pièce, the room
le plafond, the ceiling
le plancher, the floor
la porte, the door
la salle, the room; **la salle à**
   manger, the dining room;
   la salle de bains,
   bathroom
le salon, the living room
le toit, the roof

Les meubles

l'armoire *f.,* the wardrobe
   closet
le bureau, the desk
le canapé, the sofa, couch
la chaise, the chair
la commode, the dresser,
   chest of drawers
la couchette, the bunk
l'évier *m.,* the kitchen sink
le fauteuil, the armchair
le four, the oven
la fournaise, the furnace
le fourneau, the kitchen
   stove, range
la lampe, the lamp
le lit, the bed
le phonographe, the
   phonograph
le piano, the piano
la radio stéréophonique,
   the stereophonic radio
la table, the table
le tapis, the carpet
le téléphone, the telephone
le téléviseur, the television
   (set)

§45.7   La ville, les bâtiments, les magasins, les divers modes de transport (The City, Buildings, Stores, Various Means of Transportation)

La ville

l'avenue *f.,* the avenue
la boîte aux lettres, the mailbox
la bouche de métro, the subway entrance
le boulevard, the boulevard
le bruit, the noise
la chaussée, the road
défense d'afficher, post no bills
les feux *m.,* the traffic lights
le parc, the park
la pollution, the pollution
la rue, the street
le trottoir, the sidewalk
la voiture de police, the police car

Les bâtiments

la banque, the bank
la bibliothèque, the library
le bureau de poste, the post office
la cathédrale, the cathedral
la chapelle, the chapel
le château, the castle
le cinéma, the movie theatre
l'école *f.,* the school
l'église *f.,* the church
la gare, the railroad station
la grange, the barn

le gratte-ciel, the skyscraper
l'hôpital *m.,* the hospital
l'hôtel *m.,* the hotel
l'hôtel de ville, the city hall
la hutte *f.,* the hut, cabin
l'immeuble d'habitation, the apartment building
le musée, the museum
le palais, the palace
la synagogue, the synagogue
le temple, the temple
le théâtre, the theatre
l'usine *f.,* the factory

Les divers modes de transport

l'autobus *m.,* the city bus
l'autocar *m.,* the interurban bus
l'automobile *f.,* the car
l'avion *m.,* the plane
le bateau, the boat
la bicyclette, the bicycle
le camion, the truck
le chemin de fer, the railroad
le métro, the subway
la moto, the motorcycle
le train, the train
le transatlantique, the ocean liner
le vélo, the bike
la voiture, the car

Les magasins

la bijouterie, the jewelry shop
la blanchisserie, the laundry
la boucherie, the butcher shop
la boulangerie, the bakery (mostly for bread)
la boutique, the (small) shop
le bureau de tabac, the tobacco shop
le café, the café
la charcuterie, the pork store, delicatessen
la crémerie, the dairy store
l'épicerie *f.,* the grocery store
le grand magasin, the department store
la librairie, the bookstore
le magasin, the store
la pâtisserie, the pastry shop
la pharmacie, the drugstore
le supermarché, the supermarket

§45.8 **Les métiers et les professions, les langues, les pays et les continents** (Trades and Professions, Languages, Countries, and Continents)

Les métiers et les professions

l'acteur *m.,* **l'actrice** *f.,* actor, actress

l'agent de police *m.,* police officer

l'auteur, author (of a book) *or* composer (of a song) *or* painter (of a picture)

l'avocat *m.,* **la femme-avocat** *f.,* lawyer

le bijoutier, la bijoutière, jeweler

le blanchisseur, la blanchisseuse, launderer

le boucher, la bouchère, butcher

le boulanger, la boulangère, baker

le charcutier, la charcutière, pork butcher

le chauffeur, driver, chauffeur

le coiffeur, la coiffeuse, hairdresser, barber

le, la dentiste, dentist

l'épicier, l'épicière, grocer

le facteur, letter carrier

le fermier, la fermière, farmer

le, la libraire, bookseller

le maître, la maîtresse, teacher

le marchand, la marchande, merchant

le médecin, la femme-médecin, doctor

le pâtissier, la pâtissière, pastry chef

le pharmacien, la pharmacienne, pharmacist

le professeur, la femme-professeur, professor

le sénateur, senator

le serveur, la serveuse, waiter, waitress

le tailleur, la tailleuse, tailor

le vendeur, la vendeuse, salesperson

Les langues
(all are masculine)

allemand, German
anglais, English
chinois, Chinese
danois, Danish
espagnol, Spanish;
  castillan, Castilian (Spanish)
français, French
grec ancien, Ancient Greek
grec moderne, Modern Greek
hébreu, Hebrew
italien, Italian
japonais, Japanese
latin, Latin
norvégien, Norwegian
portugais, Portuguese
russe, Russian
suédois, Swedish

Les pays, les continents

l'Allemagne *f.,* Germany; **l'Allemagne de l'Ouest,** West Germany; **l'Allemagne de l'Est,** East Germany

l'Angleterre *f.,* England
l'Australie *f.,* Australia
la Belgique, Belgium
le Canada, Canada
la Chine, China
le Danemark, Denmark
l'Espagne *f.,* Spain
les États-Unis *m.,* United States
l'Europe *f.,* Europe
la France, France
la Grande-Bretagne, Great Britain
la Grèce, Greece
la Hollande, Holland
l'Irlande *f.,* Ireland
l'Israël *m.,* Israel
l'Italie *f.,* Italy
le Japon, Japan
le Luxembourg, Luxembourg
le Mexique, Mexico
la Norvège, Norway
la Pologne, Poland
le Porto Rico, Puerto Rico
le Portugal, Portugal
la Russie, Russia; **U.R.S.S.,** Union des républiques socialistes soviétiques (U.S.S.R)
la Suède, Sweden
la Suisse, Switzerland

§45.9 Poids, mesures, valeurs (Weights, Measures, Values★)

un gramme = 0.035274 ounce (1 gram)

28.3 grammes = 1 ounce

100 grammes = 3.52 ounces

453.6 grammes = 1 pound

500 grammes = 17.63 ounces
(about 1.1 pounds)

1000 grammes = 1 kilogram

un kilogramme = 2.2 pounds
(1 kilogram)

une livre = 17.63 ounces
(about 1.1 pounds)

un litre = 1.0567 quarts
(0.26417 gallon)

---

un franc = 20 cents
(There are **100 centimes** in one franc.)

5 francs = $1.00

25 francs = $5.00

50 francs = $10.00

---

un kilomètre = 0.62137 mile
(about ⅝ mile or 1000 meters)

1.61 kilomètres = 1 mile

10 kilomètres = 6.21 miles

---

un centimètre = 0.39 inch
(1 centimeter)

2.54 centimètres = 1 inch

30.5 centimètres = 1 foot

91.4 centimètres = 1 yard

un mètre = 39.37 inches
(100 centimeters)

0.9144 mètre = 1 yard

---

1. To convert Fahrenheit degrees into Celsius (Centigrade): subtract 32, multiply by 5, and divide by 9.

2. To convert Celsius (Centigrade) into Fahrenheit: multiply by 9, divide by 5, and add 32.

3. A Fahrenheit degree is smaller than a Celsius degree. One F degree is ⅝ of a C degree.

4. France uses the Celsius scale.

★ All the equivalents given are approximate. To obtain the current rate of exchange of American dollars for French francs, inquire at a commercial bank.

PART II

FIVE
PRACTICE TESTS

USE THE SPECIAL ANSWER SHEET ON PAGE 202
THE TIME LIMIT FOR EACH TEST IS ONE HOUR.

Choose the word or words that **can be substituted** for the italized word or words in each sentence so that they fit grammatically and sensibly in the sentence given. Blacken the space under the letter of your choice on the special answer sheet.

1. *Marguerite et Joseph* sont partis tôt.
   A. Henri et moi
   B. Guy et Paul
   C. Elles
   D. Lui et moi

2. De *quoi* parlez-vous?
   A. qui
   B. quel
   C. lequel
   D. lesquelles

3. Ce matin Elizabeth est *arrivée* à l'école à huit heures.
   A. venue
   B. marché
   C. partie
   D. quitté

4. *Qui* a fait ce gâteau?
   A. Que
   B. Qui est-ce qu'
   C. Qui est-ce qui
   D. Quelle

5. Cette maison est à *nous*.
   A. il
   B. ils
   C. eux
   D. me

6. *Qui* voyez-vous?
   A. Que
   B. Qui est-ce qui
   C. Lui
   D. Qu'est-ce qui

7. Joséphine n'a pas encore *répondu*.
   A. accepté
   B. acceptée
   C. accepter
   D. accepte

8. Voyez-vous cet *homme* là-bas?
   A. femme
   B. arbre
   C. garçon
   D. personne

162

9. J'ai un ami qui va au *cinéma* tous les jours.
   A. musée
   B. bibliothèque
   C. gare
   D. école

10. M'aimes-tu, Michel? . . . –moi.
   A. Embrasse
   B. Embrassez
   C. Embrasser
   D. Embrasses

11. François est grand, blond, beau, et il a . . . yeux bleus.
   A. ses
   B. les
   C. quelques
   D. nothing needed

12. Brigitte est . . . et elle s'est fait mal au genou.
   A. tombé
   B. tombée
   C. tombant
   D. tombante

13. A qui est ce livre? Il est à
   A. me.
   B. le.
   C. lui.
   D. leur.

14. *Rien n*'arrive.
   A. Quelque chose n'
   B. Tout le monde n'
   C. Personne n'
   D. Quelqu'un n'

15. *Lequel de* ces livres préférez-vous?
   A. Combien de
   B. Lesquelles de
   C. Quels
   D. De laquelle

16. La semaine prochaine ce groupe ira au *Canada*.
   A. Etats-Unis.
   B. France.
   C. Portugal.
   D. Amérique du Sud.

17. *Auquel* de vos amis écrivez-vous tous les jours?
   A. Auxquels
   B. Duquel
   C. Laquelle
   D. Quel

18. *Qui* cherchez-vous?
   A. Qu'est-ce que
   B. Que
   C. Qui est-ce qui
   D. Quoi

19. Que voulez-vous que je vous *dise?*
  A. réponde
  B. fais
  C. dites
  D. faites

In each of the following sentences, choose the word or words that will complete each sentence and fit grammatically and sensibly.

20. Je doute fort que Madame Dulac . . . malade.
  A. a
  B. ait
  C. soit
  D. devient

21. Si vous . . . , vous sauriez la leçon.
  A. étudiez
  B. étudiiez
  C. étudierez
  D. avez étudié

22. Avez-vous mis l'argent dans le tiroir? Oui, je . . . ai mis.
  A. l'y
  B. lui en
  C. le leur
  D. l'en

23. Que faites-vous ici? J'attends l'autobus . . . vingt minutes.
  A. pour
  B. dès
  C. par
  D. depuis

24. J'espère qu'il . . . demain.
  A. viendra
  B. vienne
  C. soit venu
  D. sera venu

25. Si je vous dis que j'agis à la légère, cela veut dire que
  A. je ne suis pas sérieux dans mes actions.
  B. je suis bien certain de ce que je fais.
  C. je me rends compte de ce que je fais.
  D. je refuse d'agir.

26. Quand je suis entré dans la cuisine ma mère
  A. a préparé le dîner.
  B. prépara le repas.
  C. est en train de préparer la soupe.
  D. était en train de faire la cuisine.

27. Je suis tellement fâché que
  A. je suis hors de moi.
  B. je l'ai échappé belle.
  C. je connais à fond.
  D. j'ai une faim de loup.

28. Quand nous avons fait du camping, nous avons
   A. fait autant.
   B. dormi à la belle étoile.
   C. eu la langue bien pendue.
   D. regardé de plus près.

29. Quand une personne me dit "merci", je réponds:
   A. Je suis à tue-tête.
   B. Je vous en prie.
   C. J'ai de quoi vivre.
   D. Ne dites pas de mal.

30. Madame Duval a acheté un nouveau chapeau mais
   A. il ne lui va pas bien.
   B. elle reprend la parole.
   C. elle lui en veut.
   D. elle parvient à tout ce qu'elle fait.

31. Ma soeur a refusé de garder les enfants des voisins parce qu'elle
   A. ne veut pas s'en charger.
   B. n'aime pas faire la grasse matinée.
   C. s'en est servi.
   D. pense ne pas avoir inventé la poudre.

32. Samedi prochain nous . . . chez nos voisins.
   A. dînerons
   B. dînerions
   C. ayons dîné
   D. aurions dîné

33. Mon père s'est fait mal en . . . la viande.
   A. couper
   B. coupant
   C. coupé
   D. ayant coupé

34. Henri est le plus grand garçon . . . la classe.
   A. dans
   B. en
   C. de
   D. à

35. Aimez-vous les fleurs que je viens . . . acheter?
   A. à
   B. de
   C. en
   D. d'

36. Je n'aime pas la blouse que vous avez
   A. acheter.
   B. acheté.
   C. achètes.
   D. achetée.

37. Je veux voir votre père parce que j'ai besoin . . . parler.
   A. de lui
   B. lui
   C. de le
   D. à lui

38. Maman va nous dire tout de suite que le déjeuner . . . prêt.
   A. soit
   B. est
   C. a
   D. ait

39. Voilà une heure que . . . l'ouverture du guichet.
   A. j'ai attendu
   B. j'attends
   C. j'attende
   D. j'attendrai

40. Les deux jeunes filles ont souri
   A. en se quittant.
   B. ayant quitté.
   C. avoir quitté.
   D. s'être quittées.

41. Je vais me promener dans le parc bien qu'il
   A. pleuve.
   B. pleut.
   C. pleure.
   D. fait froid.

42. Sans doute tous les étudiants . . . reçus.
   A. sera
   B. seront
   C. soient
   D. aient été

43. Avez-vous oublié votre carte d'identité? J'ai
   A. le mien.
   B. la mienne.
   C. les miennes.
   D. mien.

44. Ce matin, . . . d'entrer dans mon bureau quand le téléphone a sonné.
   A. je viens
   B. je venais
   C. je suis venu
   D. je vins

45. Je vois des gouttes d'eau sur les fleurs dans le jardin et la terre est mouillée. Est-ce qu'il . . . cette nuit?
   A. a fait froid
   B. a plu
   C. a neigé
   D. y avait une lune visible

46. Paul, as-tu les billets?—Oui, je les ai . . . ce matin.
   A. acheté
   B. achetée
   C. achetés
   D. achetées

47. Savez-vous . . . est ce chapeau?
   A. à quoi
   B. à qui
   C. dont
   D. laquelle

48. Si elle m'avait parlé, je lui . . . répondu.
   A. avais
   B. eus
   C. aurai
   D. aurais

49. Dis-moi, Pierre, à . . . penses-tu?
   A. lequel
   B. lesquels
   C. qui
   D. quel

50. Monsieur et Madame Arland . . . allés au théâtre s'ils avaient eu le temps d'y aller.
   A. sont
   B. seront
   C. étaient
   D. seraient

Read each passage and select the best answer to each question by blackening the space under the letter of your choice on the special answer sheet.

Dans le Val de Loire, en Normandie, en Bretagne ou en Touraine, on rencontre partout des centaines de splendides châteaux qui s'acheminent, lentement mais sûrement, vers la ruine et l'abandon. Les châtelains d'autrefois ne peuvent plus faire face aux frais d'entretien et aux taxes considérables que leur vaut une telle propriété déclarée. Le prix de vente de ces magnifiques demeures rend la vie de château accessible à tous ceux qui en rêvent et qui sont assurés, voilà l'important, d'un excellent revenu.

Le château d'Avray, près d'Orléans, vient d'être vendu à une société qui a entrepris la remise en état et la transformation des lieux en quarante petits appartements qui seront vendus en co-propriété. Pour un prix d'environ quinze mille dollars, vous aurez le bonheur d'être propriétaire d'un petit appartement dans le château d'Avray, mais trente-neuf autres propriétaires partageront ce bonheur avec vous.

51. Selon l'article précédent, on peut voir dans plusieurs provinces de France
   A. des palais non achevés.
   B. beaucoup de châteaux sans cheminée.
   C. des châteaux détériorés mais encore habitables.
   D. des ruines sur des routes abandonnées.

52. Cet état de choses existe parce que
  A. les châtelains ne s'intéressent pas à leurs affaires.
  B. les dépenses sont trop élevées.
  C. les prix de ces immeubles sont exorbitants.
  D. ces propriétés sont mal construites.

53. Pour devenir propriétaire d'un château il est nécessaire
  A. d'avoir eu des ancêtres nobles.
  B. d'avoir beaucoup d'influence.
  C. d'avoir suffisamment d'argent.
  D. d'être d'origine française.

54. Le but de la société mentionnée dans l'article est de
  A. remplacer les châteaux par des bâtiments modernes.
  B. changer la façade des châteaux.
  C. restaurer les châteaux pour les faire habiter.
  D. vendre ces châteaux tels qu'ils sont.

55. Quel sera peut-être le plus grand désavantage de la propriété en commun?
  A. On aura trop peu de solitude.
  B. Les châteaux seront mal entretenus.
  C. Les logements seront trop petits.
  D. La conversion sera trop lente.

Un mot de Madame de Montespan fut cause de la guerre de Hollande. Les Hollandais offraient toutes sortes de satisfactions sur les plaintes du Roi, et Monsieur de Colbert dit: "Sire, vous ne pourriez en exiger davantage, si vous les aviez battus."

Le Roi avait promis de voir leur ambassadeur. Le Roi revenant de chasse, dit à Mme de Montespan qu'il avait fait une belle chasse.

"Ne vous lasserez-vous point, dit-elle, de suivre des bêtes, pendant que les autres gagnent des batailles?"
Le Roi, là-dessus, résolut la guerre.

56. Qu'est-ce qui força le Roi à prendre une décision?
  A. les observations d'une personne influente
  B. les offres peu avantageuses de la Hollande
  C. le mécontentement des Hollandais
  D. le besoin de bêtes à chasser

57. Colbert pensait que les offres des Hollandais étaient
  A. absurdes.
  B. intéressantes.
  C. provocatrices.
  D. inacceptables.

58. De quoi le Roi était-il si content ce jour-là?
  A. de la décision de ses courtisans
  B. de la beauté de sa dame préférée
  C. des promesses de son représentant aux étrangers
  D. d'avoir tué plusieurs animaux

59. Mme de Montespan dit au Roi qu'il
  A. devrait retourner à ses plaisirs sportifs.
  B. devrait se reposer.
  C. employait mal son temps.
  D. était très sage.

60. Qu'est-ce que le Roi décida de faire?
  A. de laisser faire les Hollandais
  B. de rester tranquille
  C. de garder le silence
  D. d'essayer de remporter des victoires

END OF TEST NO. 1

TEST 2

USE THE SPECIAL ANSWER SHEET ON PAGE 203.
THE TIME LIMIT FOR EACH TEST IS ONE HOUR.

Each of the incomplete statements or questions below is followed by four suggested answers. Select the most appropriate completion and blacken the space under the letter of your choice on the special answer sheet.

1. J'ai mes grands défauts et ma soeur a
   A. les siennes.
   B. les siens.
   C. ses.
   D. son.

2. Je t'ai prêté mon stylo. Maintenant . . . tu veux?
   A. quoi
   B. qui est-ce qui
   C. qu'est-ce qui
   D. qu'est-ce que

3. Je vous attendrai pourvu que vous . . . avant cinq heures.
   A. revenez
   B. reveniez
   C. reviendrez
   D. reviendriez

4. Mon meilleur ami habite
   A. à la France.
   B. la France.
   C. France.
   D. dans la France.

5. Je doute que Robert . . . le faire.
   A. puisse
   B. pourra
   C. peut
   D. pourrait

6. Je voudrais boire encore
   A. café.
   B. le café.
   C. du café.
   D. de café.

7. Si nous l'avions su, nous . . . voir ce film.
   A. irions
   B. irons
   C. serions allés
   D. étions allés

169

8. Ils se parlent
   A. l'un l'autre.
   B. l'un à l'autre.
   C. les uns les autres.
   D. les unes les autres.

9. Nouse commencerons à manger dès qu'il
   A. arrive.
   B. arrivera.
   C. soit arrivé.
   D. est arrivé.

10. Montrez-moi les gants qu'elle a
   A. choisis.
   B. choisies.
   C. choisi.
   D. choisie.

11. J'irai au cinéma après . . . mes devoirs.
   A. avoir fini
   B. ayant fini
   C. finir
   D. finissant

12. Michel a passé ses vacances . . . Italie.
   A. dans l'
   B. en
   C. à
   D. au

13. Il faut que vous . . . me voir demain.
   A. venez
   B. viendrez
   C. veniez
   D. viendriez

14. Mon oncle achètera ces bonbons uniquement
   A. faire plaisir aux enfants.
   B. pour faire plaisir aux enfants.
   C. à faire plaisir aux enfants.
   D. de faire plaisir aux enfants.

15. Monsieur Maillet s'en est allé sans . . . ses adieux.
   A. faire
   B. faisant
   C. fait
   D. que faire

Read the statements given below and select the best answer which is related to the situation described. Blacken the space under the letter of your choice on the special answer sheet.

16. Un voyageur, qui veut aller à Marseille le lendemain, va au bureau de la garde de la Société des Chemins de Fer Français pour obtenir des renseignements.

   Il demande à l'employé au guichet:
   A. Vous désirez des renseignements, Monsieur?
   B. Dites-moi s'il y avait un train hier pour Marseille vers trois heures de l'après-midi, s'il vous plaît.
   C. Dites-moi s'il y a un train pour Marseille cet après-midi vers deux heures.
   D. Je voudrais savoir s'il y a un train qui part pour Marseille demain matin vers neuf heures.

17. Votre ami Paul et vous constatez que ce dimanche en huit c'est l'anniversaire de naissance de Pierre, un autre ami. Vous proposez une petite fête. Puis, vous discutez du cadeau à lui acheter, de l'endroit, des invités, et des distractions.

Paul dit: Nous ne pouvons pas avoir la fête chez moi parce que mes parents reçoivent des amis ce soir-là.

Vous répondez:
A. Nous inviterons seulement les meilleurs amis.
B. Nous servirons des sandwichs, du café et de la glace.
C. Achetons-lui un disque.
D. Nous pouvons nous réunir tous chez moi, si tu veux.

18. Monsieur Potin téléphone au restaurant Normandie pour retenir une table. Il donne au maître d'hôtel tous les renseignements nécessaires et promet enfin de l'avertir s'il y a un changement dans ses projets.

Monsieur Potin dit: Je voudrais retenir une table pour demain soir.

Le maître d'hôtel répond:
A. Ce sera pour combien de personnes?
B. Je compte sur vous.
C. Je crois qu'il va pleuvoir demain soir.
D. Savez-vous quel temps il fait en ce moment?

19. Votre mère et vous, vous êtes pressés de sortir pour acheter quelques provisions à l'épicerie et à la dernière minute votre mère ne peut pas trouver la liste.

Votre mère s'exclame: Malheur! Où ai-je mis la liste?

Vous répondez:
A. Tu as dit que nous avions besoin de quelques provisions pour la cuisine.
B. Il nous faut partir tout de suite!
C. Tu les a dans ta bourse.
D. Elle est là, sur la table.

20. Madame Arland entre dans une pharmacie pour acheter quelques aspirines parce qu'elle a mal à la tête. Puis, elle veut savoir s'il y a un docteur dans le quartier. Le pharmacien lui donne les aspirines et il lui demande: Y a-t-il autre chose, madame?

Elle répond:
A. Si ça ne va pas mieux demain, que faudra-t-il que je fasse?
B. Voici l'argent pour les aspirines. Maintenant, pouvez-vous me donner le nom et l'adresse d'un bon médecin qui a son bureau près d'ici?
C. Combien d'aspirines dois-je prendre?
D. J'ai passé plus de deux heures à étudier hier soir. C'est bien, n'est-ce pas?

21. Mademoiselle Piquot entre dans un magasin pour s'acheter des chaussures. Le vendeur a le modèle qu'elle aime et elle achète les souliers.

Le vendeur lui demande: Avez-vous besoin d'autre chose, mademoiselle?

Elle répond:
A. Je voudrais acheter des souliers.
B. Je prends d'ordinaire du 8 et je préfère le brun.
C. Elles me vont très bien, n'est-ce pas?
D. Non, c'est tout pour aujourd'hui.

22. C'est la veille de Noël. Monsieur Milot rencontre Monsieur Bleau dans la rue et celui-là lui dit: Je vous souhaite Joyeux Noël et bonne année!

Monsieur Bleau répond:
A. Merci! Et à vous de même!
B. Nous avons beaucoup de neige cet hiver, n'est-ce pas?
C. Il fait bien froid aujourd'hui!
D. Est-ce que le Père Noël est venu chez vous?

23. Votre grand'mère vous a donné une somme d'argent pour votre anniversaire de naissance. Vous discutez avec votre mère comment utiliser cet argent.

Votre mère vous dit: Tu auras besoin de cet argent pour t'acheter des vêtements pour l'école.

Vous êtes d'accord avec ce qu'elle dit et vous répondez:
A. Mais elle a tout ce qu'il lui faut!
B. Non, je ne veux pas faire cela.
C. Oui, tu as raison; je vais acheter une nouvelle bicyclette.
D. Oui, c'est une bonne idée; j'ai besoin d'un pullover.

24. Debby vient d'arriver en France par avion et elle rencontre son amie française, Suzanne, à l'aéroport.

Suzanne lui demande: Est-ce que tu as eu des difficultés en passant par la douane?

Debby répond:
A. Mais non, pas du tout, tout était parfait dans l'avion.
B. Oui, je n'ai pas aimé les repas dans l'avion.
C. Non, le voyage a été bien fatigant.
D. Oui, on m'a fait ouvrir toutes mes valises.

25. Louise et Brigitte parlent au téléphone de leurs emplettes. Brigitte dit qu'elle a acheté une jolie robe rouge et elle veut savoir ce que Louise a acheté.

Louise répond:
A. Je suis allée faire des emplettes.
B. Je suis rentrée à quatre heures.
C. Je me suis acheté une jolie blouse blanche.
D. La prochaine fois je vais acheter un joli chapeau jaune.

*Choose the word or words that can be **substituted** for the underlined word or words in each sentence so that they fit grammatically in the sentence given. There is only one correct answer that fits in each given sentence from the four choices. Blacken the space under the letter of your choice on the special answer sheet.*

Example: Janine aime sa mère.

     A. parle

     B. téléphone

     C. écrit

     D. écoute

(The correct answer is **D, écoute;** choices A, B, and C cannot fit grammatically because each verb requires the preposition à after it, but choice **D** does fit grammatically because it does not require à after it.)

26. Vous pensez toujours à tout.
A. tout le temps
B. jamais
C. que
D. pas

27. Qu'est-ce qui arrive?
A. Qu'est-ce que
B. Qui
C. Que
D. Quoi

28. Vous allez rester chez <u>moi</u> ce soir, n'est-ce pas?
   A. eux
   B. ils
   C. votre
   D. tu

29. Monique répond <u>à la lettre</u>.
   A. le professeur.
   B. à l'employé.
   C. le vendeur.
   D. sa mère.

30. Dites-moi ce que vous <u>avez l'intention</u> de faire en France.
   A. allez essayer
   B. pensez
   C. penser
   D. voulez

31. Je suis très heureux de <u>vous</u> voir!
   A. lui
   B. toi
   C. la
   D. leur

32. Alors, Suzanne, <u>votre</u> voyage n'a pas été trop fatigant, j'espère.
   A. ta
   B. sa
   C. ton
   D. leurs

33. Georges a rencontré <u>son</u> amie Pauline.
   A. ta
   B. ton
   C. ma
   D. sa

34. Savez-vous jouer <u>du piano</u>?
   A. de la guitare?
   B. le violon?
   C. à cartes?
   D. tennis?

35. Monsieur Godard <u>a décidé</u> tout à coup de prendre un café au lait.
   A. a voulu
   B. a désiré
   C. a essayé
   D. a pensé

Read the following statements and choose the correct missing word or words that would fit grammatically and sensibly in each statement. Blacken the space under the letter of your choice on the special answer sheet.

Janine a été très . . . quand son père . . . a donné la permission

   36. A. heureux   **37.** A. lui
        B. heureuses   B. l'
        C. content   C. la
        D. contente   D. les

d'aller en France avec . . . et . . . amis. Le départ . . . lieu

38. A. moi	**39.** A. notre	**40.** A. aura
B. soi	B. nos	B. a eu
C. les	C. votre	C. avait
D. nos	D. son	D. auraient

lundi prochain.

Nous allons prendre un avion . . . compagnie Air France. Trois professeurs

41. A. de la
B. de
C. du
D. avec

vont . . . le voyage avec nous. Nous . . . de Kennedy pour arriver à

42. A. prendre	**43.** A. partirons
B. font	B. sommes partis
C. faire	C. partions
D. faisant	D. partiront

Orly le lendemain matin. Là-bas, j'aimerais rencontrer beaucoup . . . Français

44. A. des
B. du
C. de
D. très

et parler avec . . .

45. A. ils.
B. les.
C. elle.
D. eux.

Hier, j'ai . . . une promenade en voiture avec . . . meilleur ami.

46. A. eu	**47.** A. ma
B. été	B. mes
C. pris	C. sa
D. fait	D. mon

Comme ma mère était . . . , la voiture était . . . . Il . . .

48. A. présent	**49.** A. libre	**50.** A. faisait
B. absent	B. libres	B. fera
C. absente	C. occupé	C. ferait
D. absents	D. pris	D. font

un temps splendide et nous nous sommes bien amusés.

Read each passage and select the best answer to each question by blackening the space under the letter of your choice on the special answer sheet.

Les arbres plantés au bord des routes sont utiles pour plusieurs raisons mais peuvent causer des accidents. Certaines routes américaines sont bordées de rangées d'arbres qui forment un véritable rideau. On propose de faire couper ces arbres afin de réduire le nombre des accidents de la route ou pour en rendre les effets moins graves.

51. Pourquoi veut-on enlever les arbres qui bordent les routes?
   A. pour diminuer le danger
   B. pour en faire du bois de construction
   C. pour les remplacer par des chaînes
   D. pour construire des voies plus larges

Sur le port de Marseille, au Café du Marché, les clients ont l'habitude de discuter les prochaines élections avec le patron en prenant leurs rafraîchissements.
   —Cette année, dit un jeune homme, la bataille n'a pas encore commencé.
   —Sois tranquille, dit le patron, ça va venir. Avec les taxes qu'on a eu à payer, on n'a pas de raisons d'être content.

52. De quoi parle-t-on généralement au Café du Marché?
   A. de la guerre
   B. de la navigation
   C. de la politique
   D. du prix des repas

Une dame riche, mais avare, monte dans un train en route pour Toulouse. Elle est accompagnée de son petit chien. Comme le contrôleur passe pour vérifier les billets, la dame en profite pour lui présenter une objection.
   —C'est une honte de faire payer un billet pour cette pauvre petite bête! Rendez-moi l'argent de son billet!

53. Pourquoi la dame est-elle de mauvaise humeur?
   A. Elle a perdu son billet.
   B. Elle a dû payer une somme supplémentaire parce que son petit chien l'accompagne.
   C. Elle ne peut pas garder son chien avec elle.
   D. Elle déteste le transport en commun.

Dimanche dernier, Paris ressemblait à une ville transformée: toutes les rues de la capitale, en effet, étaient recouvertes d'une couche de glace où les enfants s'amusaient à patiner; et par une température de zéro degré centigrade chacun a préféré rester chez soi.

54. Qu'est-ce qui a forcé les Parisiens à rester chez eux?
   A. la réparation des routes publiques
   B. un désastre national
   C. un froid glacial
   D. les ordres de la police

A New York, on a organisé une réception pour des marchands de vin et pour des membres de la presse américaine. A cette occasion, les tables étaient couvertes de plats typiques des Etats-Unis et de bouteilles de vin français. Ainsi on a pu apprécier le célèbre steak grillé au feu de bois du Texas, en même temps qu'un bon vin rouge venant de France. Les organisateurs de cette présentation ont réussi à prouver que les vins français vont très bien avec la cuisine américaine.

55. Qu'est-ce qu'on a découvert à cette réception franco-américaine?
   A. Les vins français accompagnent bien les plats américains.
   B. Les Américains n'aiment pas boire le vin français.
   C. Les vins américains sont meilleurs que ceux de France.
   D. Les Français détestent la cuisine américaine.

François Truffaut, metteur en scène d'importants films français, tourne des films qui sont vivants et extrêmement divertissants. Il déclare avoir vu deux mille films avant l'âge de vingt ans. C'est peut-être pourquoi son premier film, "Les quatre cents Coups," est principalement autobiographique. C'est une étude des jeunes de son époque. Il s'agit d'un adolescent abandonné et incompris qui se laisse aller à la délinquance.

56. Quel est le sujet du premier film de Truffaut?
   A. C'est un grand roman d'amour.
   B. C'est une comédie musicale.
   C. C'est l'histoire d'un jeune homme abandonné et incompris.
   D. C'est un film de gangsters.

En juillet, cent vingt jeunes Français garçons et filles de plus de dix-huit ans vont s'embarquer à Deauville pour faire le tour du monde sur douze bateaux à voile. Dans chaque pays visité, des produits français seront présentés, des conférences et des jeux seront organisés. Le but du voyage est de créer une atmosphère d'amitié entre les Français et les étrangers dans les domaines du commerce et de l'industrie.

57. Dans quelle intention a-t-on organisé ce voyage?
   A. pour battre un record de vitesse
   B. pour préparer des échanges scolaires
   C. pour former une marine internationale
   D. pour établir de bonnes relations

Nous avons débarqué ce matin vers onze heures après une traversée assez mouvementée. On avait plusieurs heures de retard. D'abord, le moteur ne marchait pas bien. Ensuite, il y a eu du brouillard, puis du vent, enfin, il a plu. La mer était très agitée et beaucoup de voyageurs étaient malades. Moi aussi, naturellement. Je t'assure que le mal de mer, ça n'est pas agréable du tout!

58. Comment cette personne a-t-elle fait le voyage?
   A. en bateau
   B. en avion
   C. en train
   D. en voiture

Le premier Festival International du Film pour l'Enfance et la Jeunesse a eu lieu à la Bourboule sous le haut patronage de Madame Giscard d'Estaing, en présence de nombreuses personnalités étrangères. Pour donner le prix au meilleur film, il y avait un jury de sept enfants âgés de 8 à 13 ans.

59. Qui a choisi le meilleur film de ce festival?
   A. la femme du Président de la République
   B. des actrices étrangères
   C. un groupe de jeunes gens
   D. le directeur du festival

Les Parisiens ont besoin de cinq paires de chaussures par an. Les autres Français en ont besoin de trois seulement. C'est peut-être parce que, dans la capitale, on est toujours pressé et on court tout le temps.

60. Pourquoi les Parisiens ont-ils peut-être besoin de plus de chaussures que les autres Français?
   A. Ils se dépêchent trop.
   B. Ils sont plus riches.
   C. Ils ont des chaussures de qualité inférieure.
   D. Ils en prennent beaucoup soin.

END OF TEST NO. 2

**USE THE SPECIAL ANSWER SHEET ON PAGE 204.
THE TIME LIMIT FOR EACH TEST IS ONE HOUR.**

Each of the incomplete statements or questions below is followed by four suggested answers. Select the most appropriate completion and blacken the space under the letter of your choice on the special answer sheet.

1. Mon cher ami, vous êtes très maigre! N'avez-vous . . . envie de manger?
   A. aucune
   B. aucun
   C. lequel
   D. laquelle

2. Et vous, monsieur? . . . est votre métier?
   A. Quel
   B. Quelle
   C. Quoi
   D. Auquel

3. Je ne reçois jamais . . . j'ai besoin.
   A. dont
   B. ce dont
   C. que
   D. ce que

4. Tu peux venir chez moi cet après-midi, ce soir, ou demain; en bref, n'importe
   A. quand.
   B. où.
   C. quoi.
   D. qui.

5. Cette femme irait à Paris, à New York, à Chicago ou n'importe . . . pour trouver un mari!
   A. quand
   B. où
   C. comment
   D. qui

6. Ce matin j'ai entendu Monique . . . un air joli.
   A. chantant
   B. chantante
   C. chante
   D. chantée

7. Si vous voulez le faire, alors faites-le! Cela dépend . . . vous voulez faire.
   A. de ce que
   B. ce que
   C. de
   D. que

177

8. Après . . . bu son café, il s'en est allé.
  A. ayant
  B. être
  C. avoir
  D. été

9. Après . . . sortie, elle est allée voir son fiancé.
  A. ayant
  B. être
  C. avoir
  D. été

10. Monsieur Paré a lu son journal avant . . . dîner.
  A. de
  B. d'avoir
  C. que
  D. à

11. Dans la classe de français, Paul lève toujours . . . bras gauche quand il veut poser une question.
  A. son
  B. le
  C. leur
  D. les

12. Les deux jeunes filles se sont . . . les cheveux.
  A. lavé
  B. lavée
  C. lavés
  D. lavées

13. Henriette est la plus intelligente . . . la classe.
  A. dans
  B. de
  C. à
  D. en

14. Mon père est obligé . . . aller au travail tous les jours.
  A. à
  B. de
  C. d'
  D. pour

15. Après . . . couchée, elle s'endormit.
  A. s'être
  B. avoir
  C. s'étant
  D. ayant

Read the statements given below and select the best answer which is related to the situation described. Blacken the space under the letter of your choice on the special answer sheet.

16. Les élèves dans la classe de français aimeraient aller dîner dans un restaurant français. Il s'agit du prix du dîner qui devrait être raisonnable. Vous n'avez pas beaucoup d'argent et vous dites:
  A. De toute façon, il faut choisir un restaurant où tout est cher.
  B. Quant à moi, mes ressources financières sont bien limitées.
  C. Nous pouvons dîner n'importe où pour n'importe quel prix.
  D. Pourquoi voulez-vous aller toujours à cet endroit-là?

17. Vous êtes dans un bureau de poste à Paris. Vous voulez envoyer des cartes postales à des amis.

    Vous parlez à l'employé du bureau de poste et vous lui demandez:
    A. Dites-moi, s'il vous plaît, ai-je mis assez de timbres sur ces cartes postales?
    B. Je vous prie de me dire si j'ai assez de monnaie sur moi.
    C. Ces cartes postales sont jolies, n'est-ce pas?
    D. J'aimerais expédier ce paquet aux Etats-Unis.

18. Vous êtes à Paris et un monsieur qui est assis à côté de vous dans un autobus vous demande si la Cathédrale Notre-Dame de Paris est loin de l'arrêt de l'autobus où vous vous trouvez. Le monsieur veut savoir s'il doit descendre ou continuer son chemin.

    Vous lui répondez:
    A. Vous devriez descendre tout de suite. Ne voyez-vous pas la Cathédrale là-bas de l'autre côte de la rue?
    B. Oui, il y a beaucoup d'églises à visiter.
    C. La Cathédrale Notre-Dame de Paris est la plus belle.
    D. Il faut continuer votre chemin si vous voulez voir ce musée.

19. Un soir, au théâtre, vous rencontrez un ami que vous n'avez pas vu depuis longtemps. Il ne vous reconnaît pas mais vous le reconnaissez tout de suite.

    Vous lui dites:
    A. Est-ce que vous aimez le spectacle?
    B. J'ai fait la connaissance de plusieurs personnes ce soir au théâtre. Et vous?
    C. Jacques! C'est bien toi?!
    D. Pourquoi me regardez-vous? Je ne vous connais point!

20. Madame Gervais se trouve dans un magasin où elle essaye de nombreux chapeaux. Après vingt minutes, elle fait un choix et elle dit à la vendeuse:
    A. Tous vos chapeaux sont beaux.
    B. Je ne suis pas venue pour acheter mais pour essayer.
    C. J'ai laissé mon chapeau et mon parapluie dans l'autobus ce matin.
    D. Je prends celui-ci. Combien coûte-t-il?

21. Madame Béry attend son amie à l'arrêt de l'autobus depuis trente minutes. Elle devient impatiente et elle est sur le point de partir quand elle voit son amie qui descend de l'autobus. Elle lui dit:
    A. Tu sais, tu es toujours à l'heure.
    B. Il ne faut pas être impatiente, ma chère amie!
    C. Pourquoi es-tu toujours en retard quand nous avons rendez-vous à une heure précise?
    D. Je sais qu'il pleut à verse et j'ai oublié mon imperméable et mon parapluie à la maison!

22. Vous travaillez comme réceptionniste dans un hôtel pour l'été. Le téléphone sonne, vous décrochez et vous dites:
    A. Allô! J'écoute!
    B. Allô! Ma foi! Je ne sais pas ce que je dois faire!
    C. Allô! Je vais décrocher maintenant!
    D. Allô! Je vais raccrocher maintenant!

23. Sally, une jeune fille américaine qui étudie le français dans une école, est à Paris avec une camarade anglaise, Priscilla. Les deux demoiselles sont assises sur la terrasse d'un café en train de manger leur glace au chocolat.

    Priscilla demande à sa camarade: Dis-moi, comment s'appelait Paris autrefois?

    Sally répond:
    A. La Gaule.
    B. Parisii.
    C. Lutèce.
    D. L'île de la Cité.

24. Votre amie Colette est malade depuis quelques jours à cause d'un mal aux dents. Vous allez la voir et vous lui apportez un cadeau. C'est une boîte de chocolats.

En ouvrant la boîte, Colette s'exclame:
A. Bravo! Comment puis-je manger du chocolat puisque tu vois que j'ai mal aux dents!
B. Je ne savais pas que tu avais mal aux dents!
C. Tu sais, il y a un proverbe français qui dit: Qui se ressemble s'assemble!
D. La prochaine fois tu m'apporteras une boîte de chocolats! Merci pour le miel!

25. La petite Hélène ne peut pas s'endormir et elle demande à sa mère de lui dire un conte de fées. Sa mère commence à lire:
A. Il était une fois une jeune princesse, belle et gaie . . .
B. Je vais compter à dix et si tu ne dors pas, je te donne une belle gifle . . .
C. Il était une fois une petite fille nommée Hélène. Elle ne pouvait pas s'endormir et elle a demandé à sa mère une bonne tape . . .
D. Je te dis une fois que si tu ne t'endors pas, tu vas passer une nuit blanche . . .

*Choose the word or words that **cannot be substituted** for the underlined word or words in each of the following statements or questions. The correct answer is the one that does **not** fit grammatically or sensibly. Blacken the space under the letter of your choice on the special answer sheet.*

Example: Qui parle?
    A. Qui est-ce qui
    B. Est-ce que l'enfant
    C. Est-ce que c'est le professeur qui
    D. Que

(The correct answer is **D. Que;** choices A, B, and C can fit grammatically and sensibly, but choice D does NOT fit because que cannot be used as the subject of a verb.)

26. Lequel de ces deux garçons est plus intelligent?
A. hommes
B. messieurs
C. camionneurs
D. jeunes filles

27. Que cherchez-vous?
A. faites-vous?
B. chantez-vous?
C. cherche-t-il?
D. écoutez-vous?

28. Ecoute! Ne dis rien!
A. bouge
B. parlez
C. fais
D. chante

29. Je parle à Paul.
A. cherche
B. réponds
C. demande
D. pense

30. Ses vêtements coûtent moins cher que les vôtres.
A. miens.
B. nôtres.
C. leur.
D. tiens.

*Choose the word or words that can be **substituted** for the underlined word or words in each sentence so that they fit grammatically in the sentence given. There is only one correct answer that fits in each given sentence of the four choices. Blacken the space under the letter of your choice on the special answer sheet.*

Example: Janine <u>aime</u> sa mère.
   A. parle
   B. téléphone
   C. écrit
   D. écoute

(The correct answer is **D. écoute;** choices A, B, and C cannot fit grammatically because each verb requires the preposition à after it, but choice D does fit grammatically because it does not require à after it.)

31. <u>Les hommes</u> auxquels vous avez parlé sont mes cousins.
   A. Les garçons
   B. Les dames
   C. Les étudiantes
   D. Les jeunes filles

32. Dans la <u>valise</u> de qui a-t-on trouvé un revolver?
   A. paquet
   B. colis
   C. malle
   D. pantalon

33. La maison que nous avons <u>trouvée</u> est très moderne.
   A. vendu
   B. acheté
   C. vue
   D. visité

34. Nous vous verrons à la fin du <u>déjeuner</u>.
   A. la semaine.
   B. la journée.
   C. l'été.
   D. cours.

35. Qu'est-ce <u>qui</u> arrive?
   A. Que
   B. Quoi
   C. Qui
   D. Qu'est-ce que

Read the following statements and choose the correct missing word or words that would fit grammatically and sensibly in each statement. Blacken the space under the letter of your choice on the special answer sheet.

J'aime la campagne parce que . . . amuse bien. Pendant les mois

   36. A. je m'
       B. j'amuse
       C. je me suis
       D. je m'y

de l'année je suis . . . ville, mais . . . mois de juillet et août

   37. A. à   38. A. au
       B. dans   B. à la
       C. en   C. à les
       D. au   D. aux

je passe . . . vacances à la campagne. Mon plus grand plaisir consiste à

39. A. la
B. mon
C. ma
D. mes

. . une promenade le long d'un chemin tortueux à la nuit . . .

40. A. prendre
B. exécuter
C. remplir
D. faire

41. A. tombée.
B. tombant.
C. tombante.
D. tombé.

J'ai passé . . . premier jour à l'école d'une manière très agréable.

42. A. ma
B. mes
C. mon
D. leurs

. . . arrivé avec mon ami Henri à huit heures . . . .

43. A. J'ai
B. Je suis
C. J'y suis
D. Nous sommes

44. A. précise
B. précis
C. exacte
D. précises

Nous sommes . . . dans l'édifice et nous avons vu nos professeurs.

45. A. entré
B. entrés
C. entrant
D. entrer

Read each passage and select the best answer to each question by blackening the space under the letter of your choice on the special answer sheet.

—A ce compte, dit la marquise, la philosophie en est arrivée au point de suivre les lois qui règlent les machines?

—A tel point, répondis-je, que je crains qu'on n'en ait bientôt honte. On veut que l'univers ne soit en grand que ce qu'une montre est en petit, et que tout s'y conduise par des mouvements réglés qui dépendent de l'arrangement des parties.

—Et moi, répliqua-t-elle, j'estime l'univers beaucoup plus depuis que vous me dites tout cela. Il est surprenant que l'ordre de la nature ne roule que sur des choses si simples.

—Je ne sais pas, lui répondis-je, qui vous a donné des idées si saines; mais en vérité, il n'est pas trop commun de les avoir. Assez de gens ont toujours dans la tête un faux merveilleux, enveloppé d'une obscurité qu'ils respectent. Ils n'admirent la nature que parce qu'ils la croient une espèce de magie où l'on n'entend rien.

46. La philosophie de nos jours
A. est très mécanique.
B. donne lieu à la honte.
C. règle les lois de l'univers.
D. est peu mécanique.

47. Certaines gens disent que l'univers
A. est petit comme une montre.
B. ne ressemble aucunement à une montre.
C. donne peu d'indications d'ordre.
D. est réglé comme une montre.

48. La marquise est surprise
  A. que tout soit si incompréhensible.
  B. qu'il n'y ait que confusion dans le monde.
  C. que le principe de l'univers soit tellement facile à comprendre.
  D. que l'ordre des choses soit si compliqué.

49. Les idées saines sont
  A. peu communes.
  B. forcément claires.
  C. obscures.
  D. très communes.

50. Certaines personnes admirent
  A. ce qui fait du bruit.
  B. ce qu'ils ne comprennent pas.
  C. ce qui est silencieux.
  D. ce qui est clair.

"Pour Dieu, dit le maréchal, que cette bataille nous apporte honneur! Celui qui se conduirait mal serait banni de la gloire de Notre-Seigneur. Souvenez-vous de nos ancêtres très courageux dont les noms sont encore rappelés dans les histoires. Sachez bien que celui qui mourra pour Dieu dans cette bataille, son âme s'en ira toute fleurie en paradis. Le champ de bataille est à nous, pourvu que nous ayons pleine foi en Dieu. Si les ennemis sont plus nombreux que nous, que nous importe? Ils sont arrogants aujourd'hui parce qu'ils nous ont trouvés ces jours-ci un peu las; mais nous voilà reposés et prêts à les étonner. Pour Dieu, n'attendons pas qu'ils nous attaquent les premiers. J'ai assez l'expérience de la guerre pour savoir que si on attaque ses ennemis du premier coup avec promptitude, on a moins de peine à les mettre en déroute. Allons! celui qui s'épargnera dans ce combat, que le Dieu de gloire ne lui donne jamais honneur!"

51. Nous savons que nos ancêtres
  A. n'ont pas oublié leurs noms.
  B. sont restés dans l'oubli.
  C. se racontaient des histoires.
  D. vivent dans les livres d'histoire.

52. Celui qui mourra dans cette bataille
  A. sera banni de la gloire de Notre-Seigneur.
  B. ira au ciel.
  C. sera vite oublié.
  D. recevra le blâme de la postérité.

53. Pour gagner la bataille, il faut
  A. croire en Dieu.
  B. être arrogant.
  C. être plus nombreux que l'ennemi.
  D. mourir.

54. Aujourd'hui l'ennemi va nous trouver
  A. disposés à fuir.
  B. sur le point de dormir.
  C. désireux de combattre.
  D. résignés devant la mort.

55. Dans la bataille, il vaut mieux
  A. prendre ses aises.
  B. attendre l'attaque de l'adversaire.
  C. éviter le combat.
  D. attaquer d'abord l'adversaire.

In the following passage there are five blank spaces numbered 56 through 60. Each blank space represents a missing word or expression. For each blank space, four possible completions are provided. Only one of them makes sense in the context of the passage.

First, read the passage in its entirety to determine its general meaning. Then read it a second time. For each blank space, choose the completion that makes the best sense and write its letter in the space provided on the special answer sheet.

Quand vous faites du camping, rappelez-vous qu'il est possible que vous rencontriez un ours. Ceci ne signifie pas qu'il vous attaquera. Les ours noirs sont moins agressifs que les grizzlis; toutefois, même les réactions des ours noirs sont imprévisibles. Si un ours est pris au dépourvu, si une mère est séparée de ses petits, ou si vous vous approchez trop de sa proie, l'ours peut vous __(56)__ .

Voici quelques conseils qui pourraient être utiles si vous êtes attaqué par un ours:

La fuite n'est pas une __(57)__ car la plupart des ours peuvent courir aussi vite qu'un cheval de course. De plus, en courant, vos mouvements peuvent provoquer une attaque.

Un ours qui se met debout n'est pas toujours prêt à attaquer. S'il tourne la tête d'un côté à l'autre, c'est parce qu'il essaie de vous apercevoir ou plus exactement de vous sentir car sa vue est très __(58)__ . Restez tranquille et ne parlez qu'à voix basse. Ceci peut lui montrer que vous ne constituez pas un danger.

Si vous rencontrez un grizzli dans un endroit boisé, parlez-lui à voix basse et reculez lentement. Déposez lentement votre sac afin de distraire l'ours et montez le plus __(59)__ possible dans un arbre. En général, les grizzlis adultes ne peuvent pas grimper, mais ils peuvent facilement étendre une patte jusqu'à une hauteur de dix pieds.

Cette stratégie est moins efficace si vous faites face à un ours noir qui, lui, est un excellent grimpeur. Dans ce cas, ou en dernier recours, votre meilleure protection est de "faire le mort". Allongez-vous par terre et, quoi qu'il arrive, ne bougez pas. Ceci demande beaucoup de __(60)__ , mais la résistance serait inutile.

56. A. embrasser
    B. amuser
    C. attaquer
    D. suivre

57. A. compétition
    B. solution
    C. stratégie
    D. distraction

58. A. perçante
    B. dangereuse
    C. développée
    D. faible

59. A. tard
    B. loin
    C. haut
    D. près

60. A. temps
    B. force
    C. vitesse
    D. courage

END OF TEST NO. 3

USE THE SPECIAL ANSWER SHEET ON PAGE 205.
THE TIME LIMIT FOR EACH TEST IS ONE HOUR.

Each of the incomplete statements or questions below is followed by four suggested answers. Select the most appropriate completion and blacken the space under the letter of your choice on the special answer sheet.

1. Je ne peux pas écrire une composition parce que je n'ai ni papier . . . stylo.
   A. ne
   B. ni
   C. plus
   D. pas

2. J'ai l'habitude de boire mon café dans
   A. une jupe.
   B. une tasse.
   C. un soulier.
   D. une chaussure.

3. Aimes-tu mon nouveau chapeau?—Oui, j'aime beaucoup le tien, mais je n'aime pas . . . de Marguerite.
   A. le sien
   B. la sienne
   C. celle
   D. celui

4. Après avoir . . . la lettre, il sortit.
   A. lu
   B. lire
   C. lisant
   D. lit

5. C'est dommage que Paul . . . rarement nous voir.
   A. viens
   B. vient
   C. vienne
   D. est venu

6. Dans . . . mettez-vous vos vêtements pour voyager?
   A. que
   B. quel
   C. l'un
   D. quoi

7. Oui, je . . . l'été que nous avons passé ensemble au bord de la mer.
   A. me souviens de
   B. se souvient
   C. me souviens
   D. me souvènir

8. Je regrette, monsieur, mais la directrice est très . . . en ce moment.
- A. occupé
- B. occupée
- C. occupés
- D. occupées

9. Veuillez accepter, chère madame, l'expression de mes . . . sentiments.
- A. meilleurs
- B. meilleures
- C. meilleur
- D. meilleure

10. Il y a un proverbe français qui dit: Qui ne risque rien . . . rien.
- A. a
- B. n'a
- C. ni a
- D. n'a pas

11. Je demeure . . . une grande maison avec ma famille.
- A. en
- B. à
- C. dans
- D. à la

12. Où se trouve la bibliothèque municipale, s'il vous plaît?—Elle se trouve . . . ici.
- A. près
- B. auprès
- C. près à
- D. près d'

13. Aimez-vous notre jardin?—Oui, il y a beaucoup . . . fleurs dans votre jardin.
- A. de
- B. des
- C. du
- D. Nothing needed

14. Votre maison est plus jolie que
- A. le mien.
- B. la mienne.
- C. les siens.
- D. le sien.

15. Je m'intéresse plus à mes devoirs qu'
- A. les siens.
- B. les siennes.
- C. les tiens.
- D. aux vôtres.

Read the statements given below and select the best answer which is related to the situation described. Blacken the space under the letter of your choice on the special answer sheet.

16. Monsieur et Madame Auclair sont à table pour dîner, mais leur fille Simone n'est pas encore là.

Monsieur Auclair demande à sa femme: Où donc est Simone? Elle sait très bien que nous dînons toujours à huit heures.

Madame répond:
A. Mais, tu vois, la soupe est excellente.
B. Je suis certaine qu'il est déjà huit heures!
C. Je ne peux pas m'occuper de toutes ces histoires maintenant!
D. Je n'ai aucune idée. Tant pis pour elle! Mangeons sans elle!

17. Robert entre chez un fleuriste pour acheter un cadeau pour sa mère; il n'a pas beaucoup d'argent et il dit au fleuriste:
A. J'aimerais bien acheter ce joli bracelet pour ma mère mais je n'ai pas beaucoup d'argent sur moi.
B. Je voudrais acheter une jolie rose pour ma mère.
C. Ma mère a besoin d'une jolie robe. Est-ce que je peux vous payer demain?
D. Est-ce que je peux vous aider?

18. Miss Jones, une jeune dame américaine, est à Paris et un jour elle entre dans une banque. Elle veut échanger quelques dollars.

Le caissier lui demande: Vous voulez échanger combien d'argent?

Miss Jones répond:
A. Je n'ai pas beaucoup d'argent sur moi.
B. Le dollar est plus bas que la semaine dernière.
C. Vous désirez?
D. Cent dollars.

19. Robert et Marc parlent de l'équipe de basket-ball de leur école. Marc dit: Richard est notre meilleur joueur, n'est-ce pas?

Robert répond:
A. Oui, c'est lui qui marque toujours le plus de points.
B. Oui, nous avons une bonne équipe.
C. Non, je doute fort que nous soyons les champions cette saison.
D. Oui, nous jouons notre dernier match la semaine prochaine.

20. Charles et Jacques parlent de leurs projets pour les grandes vacances. Jacques dit à Charles qu'il a trouvé du travail pour l'été.

Charles dit:
A. Il faut faire des projets pour les grandes vacances.
B. Tu crois que mon père pourrait trouver du travail?
C. Ah, bon! Tu as trouvé du travail pour l'été! Où est-ce que tu vas travailler?
D. Oui, j'ai trouvé du travail pour l'été!

21. Guillaume téléphone à Denise pour l'inviter à aller au cinéma avec lui. Guillaume dit: J'ai entendu dire qu'il y a un bon film au cinéma ce soir. Tu veux y aller?

Denise lui répond:
A. Oui, avec plaisir.
B. Pourquoi Jacques ne peut-il pas aller au cinéma avec toi?
C. Pourquoi veux-tu y aller sans moi?
D. J'irai seule au cinéma si tu ne veux pas y aller avec moi!

22. Monsieur Perrault conduit sa voiture. Tout à coup, un agent de police arrête sa voiture et il lui dit: Pourquoi est-ce que vous ne vous êtes pas arrêté au feu rouge?

Monsieur Perrault lui répond:
A. Vous avez l'air pressé!
B. Il y a longtemps que j'ai mon permis de conduire.
C. Voyez-vous, c'est une voiture toute neuve!
D. Je ne l'ai pas vu, Monsieur!

23. Vous venez d'arriver à Paris et un représentant des services de la compagnie aérienne vous pose quelques questions.

D'abord, il vous demande: Est-ce que vous connaissez déjà la France?

Vous répondez:
A. Non, c'est ma première visite.
B. Oui, les questions que vous me posez sont bonnes.
C. Oui, les repas français dans l'avion étaient excellents.
D. Non, je ne connais personne.

24. Dick Smith passe un an dans un lycée français à Paris. Son ami Pierre lui téléphone pour lui demander de l'aider à faire un devoir d'anglais très difficile.

Pierre lui demande: Tu peux m'aider à faire mon devoir d'anglais? Je n'y comprends rien.

Dick répond:
A. C'est une très longue traduction, n'est-ce pas? Tu ne peux pas faire ce devoir?
B. Bien sûr, je veux bien assister au cours d'anglais avec toi.
C. Je vais assister à une conférence au lycée aujourd'hui; veux-tu venir avec moi?
D. Très volontiers.

25. Les Cartier comptent faire un voyage à Québec. Monsieur Cartier en parle avec vous parce que vous y êtes allé l'année dernière. Monsieur vous demande des renseignements; il veut savoir si vous connaissez un bon endroit où lui et sa famille peuvent trouver du logement.

Vous lui répondez:
A. J'ai l'adresse d'un hôtel qui n'est pas trop cher.
B. J'ai l'adresse d'un musée où vous et votre famille pouvez voir des objets d'art.
C. Vous avez de la chance. La ville de Québec est très belle.
D. Quand partirez-vous? J'aimerais y aller avec vous.

Choose the word or words that **cannot be substituted** *for the underlined word or words in each of the following statements or questions. The correct answer is the one that does* **not** *fit grammatically or sensibly. Blacken the space under the letter of your choice on the special answer sheet.*

Example: Qui parle?
    A. Qui est-ce qui
    B. Est-ce que le bébé
    C. Est-ce que c'est la dame qui
    D. Que

(The correct answer is **D. Que;** choices A, B, and C can fit grammatically and sensibly, but choice D does not fit because que cannot be used as the subject of a verb.)

26. Où étiez-vous exactement quand l'accident est arrivé?
A. l'homme
B. le monsieur
C. la dame
D. le garçon

27. Qui a téléphoné à la police?
A. gare
B. bibliothèque
C. maison
D. magasin

28. Quelle voiture avez-vous d'abord remarquée?
A. dame
B. femme
C. homme
D. étudiante

29. Dites-moi <u>comment</u> l'accident est arrivé.
   A. quand
   B. où
   C. combien
   D. pourquoi

30. Attendez! Ne <u>parlez</u> pas si vite!
   A. marchez
   B. marche
   C. courez
   D. finissez

*Choose the word or words that can be **substituted** for the underlined word or words in each sentence so that they fit grammatically in the sentence given. There is only one correct answer that fits in each given sentence from the four choices. Blacken the space under the letter of your choice on the special answer sheet.*

Example: Janine <u>aime</u> sa mère.
   A. parle
   B. téléphone
   C. écrit
   D. écoute

(The correct answer is **D, écoute**; choices A, B, and C cannot fit grammatically because each verb requires the preposition **à** after it, but choice D does fit grammatically because it does not require **à** after it.)

31. Ce parc est vraiment <u>immense</u>.
   A. énorme.
   B. grande.
   C. petite.
   D. jolie.

32. J'ai mal aux <u>pieds</u>.
   A. cou.
   B. tête.
   C. genou.
   D. mains.

33. Nous sommes près du <u>lac</u>.
   A. école.
   B. église.
   C. jeune fille.
   D. magasin.

34. Nous allons maintenant louer un <u>appartement</u>.
   A. maison.
   B. chambre.
   C. bateau.
   D. cabane.

35. Je ne sais pas s'il me reste assez <u>d'argent</u>.
   A. de temps.
   B. monnaie.
   C. gâteau.
   D. glace.

Read the following statements and choose the correct missing word or words that would fit grammatically and sensibly in each statement. Blacken the space under the letter of your choice on the special answer sheet.

Anne s'est . . . à neuf heures . . . matin. Pour le petit

36. A. levé   **37.** A. ce
    B. lever   B. cet
    C. levait   C. la
    D. levée   D. cette

déjeuner elle . . . pris un petit pain, . . . croissants, . . .

38. A. est   **39.** A. de   **40.** A. de la
    B. a   B. des   B. du
    C. allait   C. du   C. des
    D. veut   D. un   D. de

confiture, . . . beurre, et . . . café . . . lait.

41. A. du   **42.** A. de   **43.** A. à
    B. de la   B. du   B. en
    C. des   C. une   C. au
    D. une   D. de la   D. à la

Elle n'a pas . . . la maison. Pendant . . . la matinée

44. A. laissé   **45.** A. tout
    B. laissée   B. tous
    C. quitté   C. toute
    D. quittée   D. toutes

elle . . . étudié les mathématiques. A midi et quart elle . . . dans

46. A. est   **47.** A. était
    B. a   B. serais
    C. allait   C. serait
    D. voulait   D. eut été

l'autobus . . . route pour le lycée. Après . . . rentrée, elle

48. A. en   **49.** A. avoir
    B. à   B. être
    C. pour   C. été
    D. la   D. eu

a fait une partie de tennis avec . . . amis.

50. A. son
    B. sa
    C. ses
    D. quelque

Read each passage and select the best answer to each question by blackening the space under the letter of your choice on the special answer sheet.

Vos animaux favoris s'attendent à ce que vous les aidiez à supporter les chaleurs de l'été. Quant à votre oiseau en cage, sortir dehors ne l'intéresse pas. Il est même possible que cela lui fasse peur; que des chiens, des chats, ou des oiseaux plus gros l'attaquent; ou que le soleil soit trop chaud ou trop brillant pour lui. Gardez-le plutôt dans une pièce ni trop chaude ni trop froide, sans courants d'air. Suspendez un os pour lui. Ajoutez un peu de laitue et des jaunes d'oeufs durs à sa portion de graines afin de soigner son alimentation. Nettoyez ses perchoirs tous les jours et plongez-les dans l'eau bouillante au moins deux fois la semaine. Essuyez-les bien avant de les remettre en place. Changez chaque jour le papier qui couvre le fond de sa cage et recouvrez de sable propre.

51. Si vous avez un oiseau en cage, il faut
   A. jouer avec lui chaque matin.
   B. le mettre au soleil.
   C. le laisser voler à l'extérieur.
   D. lui donner très peu de liberté.

52. Pour le confort de l'oiseau, il faudrait le
   A. laisser dans une salle où la température est modérée.
   B. mettre près d'une fenêtre ouverte.
   C. faire sortir souvent de sa cage.
   D. garder avec d'autres animaux.

53. Il faut donner des jaunes d'oeufs à l'oiseau pour
   A. le tenir occupé.
   B. lui conserver sa couleur.
   C. lui donner de l'intelligence.
   D. le nourrir mieux.

54. Il faut nettoyer les perchoirs en les
   A. frottant avec du sable.
   B. mettant dans un courant d'air.
   C. lavant avec du lait.
   D. stérilisant fréquemment.

55. Quant au papier qui sert de tapis, il importe
   A. de le remplacer tous les jours.
   B. d'en couvrir la cage.
   C. d'employer une couleur qui plaise.
   D. de le plier en forme d'accordéon.

Il y a quelques années nous avons salué à Paris l'arrivée d'un pianiste inconnu en France, mais que nous trouvions grand. Après un travail continu, Cziffra est devenu aujourd'hui un virtuose qui a autant d'admirateurs qu'une grande étoile de music-hall et c'est bien rassurant pour la musique classique et pour le piano.

Il est agréable de fêter la même année l'anniversaire du premier concert à Paris de Cziffra et le cent cinquantenaire de Liszt dont il est le plus célèbre interprète. En cinq ans Cziffra est devenu pour le monde entier l'interprète romantique pour qui Liszt semble avoir écrit ses plus brillantes compositions musicales.

Généreux et tourmenté, ce pianiste impétueux et violent vit paisiblement dans une grande maison près de Paris, entouré de sa femme, de ses enfants, de ses six chiens et d'autant de pianos. Là, ce grand travailleur voudrait oublier le charme de l'ancienne ville de Budapest qu'il a quittée il y a moins de dix ans.

56. Au moment de son arrivée à Paris, le pianiste était
   A. célèbre dans tous les pays.
   B. peu connu dans sa nouvelle patrie.
   C. entouré d'amis.
   D. révolté contre le sort.

57. Pendant ses premières années à Paris, Cziffra a
   A. fait du cinéma.
   B. abandonné la musique.
   C. chanté à l'Opéra.
   D. fait du piano.

58. Le succès de Cziffra prouve que le public moderne
   A. apprécie la musique des grands compositeurs.
   B. aime seulement la musique de danse.
   C. préfère le concert de musique populaire.
   D. s'intéresse peu aux instruments à cordes.

59. Cziffra est de nos jours l'interprète de Liszt qui
   A. chante le mieux.
   B. est le plus connu.
   C. est le plus âgé.
   D. reste le plus ignoré.

60. La vie de ce musicien est
   A. très solitaire.
   B. une chose qu'il essaie d'oublier.
   C. marquée par beaucoup de travail.
   D. continuellement troublée par des considérations politiques.

END OF TEST NO. 4

USE THE SPECIAL ANSWER SHEET ON PAGE 206.
THE TIME LIMIT FOR EACH TEST IS ONE HOUR.

Each of the incomplete statements or questions below is followed by four suggested answers. Select the most appropriate completion and blacken the space under the letter of your choice on the special answer sheet.

1. Je viens d'acheter un livre . . . j'ai besoin.
   A. dont
   B. laquelle
   C. lequel
   D. que

2. Paul n'a pas . . . soeurs.
   A. des
   B. de
   C. d'
   D. de la

3. Cet homme-là est riche; . . . est pauvre.
   A. celui-ci
   B. celle-ci
   C. ceux-ci
   D. celles-là

4. Robert veut . . . présenter.
   A. me les
   B. les me
   C. moi les
   D. les moi

5. Je vais partir maintenant parce qu'il faut que je . . . à l'heure.
   A. suis
   B. sois
   C. viens
   D. arrive

6. J'exige que vous . . . au lit parce que vous avez de la fièvre.
   A. restez
   B. vous reposez
   C. ayez
   D. restiez

7. Ma mère . . . descendu la valise.
   A. est
   B. a
   C. soit
   D. ait

193

8. Voulez-vous . . . fromage, monsieur?
   A. du
   B. de
   C. des
   D. de la

9. Y a-t-il du café sur la table?—Oui, il . . . a.
   A. en y
   B. y en
   C. y
   D. y a-t-il

10. Ma soeur . . . descendue vite ce matin pour aller à l'école.
   A. a
   B. est
   C. va
   D. ait

11. Ma soeur . . . descendu une chaise de sa chambre.
   A. a
   B. est
   C. va
   D. ait

12. Aimes-tu le cadeau que je t'ai . . . ?
   A. donné
   B. donnée
   C. donner
   D. donnes

13. Aimes-tu la rose que je t'ai . . . ?
   A. donné
   B. donnée
   C. donner
   D. donnes

14. A qui as-tu . . . la rose?
   A. donné
   B. donnée
   C. donner
   D. donnes

15. Aimes-tu les chocolats . . . je t'ai donnés?
   A. que
   B. qui
   C. quels
   D. quelles

16. La semaine prochaine je . . . dans un restaurant français.
   A. dînerais
   B. dînerai
   C. dîne
   D. dînais

17. Il vaut toujours mieux que vous . . . vos devoirs tous les jours.
   A. faites
   B. avez fait
   C. aurez fait
   D. fassiez

18. Aimez-vous les belles fleurs que j'ai . . . ?
   A. acheté
   B. achetée
   C. achetées
   D. achetés

19. Madame Poulin se maquille toujours . . . figure avant de sortir.
   A. la
   B. de la
   C. à la
   D. sa

20. Monsieur et Madame Paré . . . à Paris depuis une semaine.
   A. ont été
   B. seront
   C. sont
   D. soient

21. Janine . . . descendue vite quand sa mère a appelé.
   A. est
   B. a
   C. soit
   D. sera

22. Voilà bien vingt minutes . . . j'attends l'autobus.
   A. qui
   B. que
   C. ce que
   D. qu'est-ce que

Read the following statements and choose the correct missing word or words that would fit grammatically and sensibly in each statement.

Une dame . . . de soixante ans, Mme Lucille Belair, s'est . . .

23. A. âgé
   B. âgée
   C. avoir
   D. ayant

24. A. défendue
   B. défendu
   C. défendait
   D. défenderait

comme une lionne . . . un bandit masque l'a surprise un jour dans . . . boutique.

25. A. puisqu'
   B. lorsqu'
   C. de sorte qu'
   D. pourvu qu'

26. A. sa
   B. son
   C. ses
   D. leurs

En Belgique, on parlait recemment d'une jeune . . . qui etait . . .

27. A. Français
   B. Américaine
   C. Espagnol
   D. Italien

28. A. tombé
   B. tomber
   C. tombée
   D. tombant

dans une rivière glacée. Elle . . . est restée dix jours, et a été retirée

29. A. y
    B. en
    C. y en
    D. en y

presque . . . de froid.

30. A. mort
    B. morte
    C. mourant
    D. mourante

A minuit Pierre . . . réveille et dit à son frère: Lève- . . . ! J'entends

31. A. me
    B. se
    C. te
    D. nous

32. A. moi
    B. toi
    C. nous
    D. vous

marcher quelqu'un . . . bas dans la salle . . . manger!

33. A. à
    B. en
    C. au
    D. de

34. A. de
    B. pour
    C. à
    D. en

---

*Choose the word or words that **cannot be substituted** for the underlined word or words in each of the following statements or questions. The correct answer is the one that does **not** fit grammatically or sensibly. Blacken the space under the letter of your choice on the special answer sheet.*

Example: Qu'est-ce que vous <u>dites</u>?
    A. racontez
    B. préférez
    C. suit
    D. cherchez

(The correct answer is **C. suit**; choices A, B, and D can fit grammatically and sensibly, but choice **C** does not fit because it is not the correct form of the verb "suivre" with the subject "vous.")

35. Qu'est-ce que vous <u>voulez</u>, monsieur?
    A. cherchez
    B. faites
    C. avez
    D. obéissez

36. Je <u>lui</u> ai dit de venir tôt.
    A. les
    B. vous
    C. leur
    D. t'

37. J'ai attrapé <u>un rhume</u>.
    A. une balle.
    B. l'autobus.
    C. le train.
    D. le ciel.

38. Paul est Français.
    A. Américain.
    B. Anglais.
    C. Espagnole.
    D. Belge.

39. Madame Piquot est une belle femme.
    A. petite
    B. grand
    C. jolie
    D. bonne

40. Suzanne obéit à sa mère.
    A. parle
    B. écoute
    C. écrit
    D. désobéit

41. Ce monsieur a acheté une belle voiture.
    A. a vendu
    B. a obtenu
    C. a reçu
    D. est descendu

42. Anne n'a pas fait les devoirs pour aujourd'hui.
    A. leçons
    B. composition
    C. exercices
    D. gâteaux

43. Avez-vous téléphoné à vos amis?
    A. ses
    B. leurs
    C. leur
    D. mes

44. Nos voisins sont partis en vacances.
    A. Mes
    B. Ses
    C. Vos
    D. Notre

45. L'été passé nous sommes allés dans les montagnes.
    A. avons passé une semaine
    B. avons été
    C. irons
    D. nous sommes bien amusés

46. Le professeur me souhaite bonne chance dans les examens.
    A. vous
    B. nous
    C. te
    D. eux

47. Est-ce que vous vous intéressez à la musique <u>française</u>?
    A. italienne?
    B. anglaise?
    C. américaine?
    D. allemand?

48. C'est pour <u>moi</u> seulement
    A. toi
    B. vous
    C. elle
    D. il

49. Ce matin, Janine <u>s'est habillée</u> vite avant de quitter la maison.
    A. s'est lavée
    B. s'est levée
    C. a déjeuné
    D. est parti

50. As-tu <u>envoyé</u> la lettre à tes parents?
    A. écrit
    B. composé
    C. fini
    D. reçue

51. Ma dernière <u>classe</u> finit à trois heures et demie.
    A. cours
    B. leçon
    C. heure de pratique
    D. récitation

Read each passage and select the best answer to each question by blackening the space under the letter of your choice on the special answer sheet.

En 1795, deux jeunes hommes qui habitaient un village des environs de la baie Mahone eurent l'idée d'aller chasser le canard dans les îles; on leur avait dit que les animaux qu'on prend à la chasse étaient très abondants dans l'Ile-au-Chêne et ils se dirigèrent de ce côté-là.

Ils venaient de débarquer et inspectaient les lieux quand ils découvrirent un endroit de la forêt où les arbres étaient moins nombreux et qui présentait une légère dépression vers le centre. Un chêne solitaire étendait une forte branche au-dessus de cette dépression et son tronc portait une inscription rendue illisible par les années.

La curiosité des hommes fut éveillée. Examinant le sol à l'endroit de la dépression, ils constatèrent qu'on avait visiblement creusé un trou en ce lieu. Les légendes concernant les trésors cachés dans la région leur revinrent à la mémoire: ils avaient la certitude d'avoir fait une découverte beaucoup plus intéressante que toute chasse au canard.

Gardant pour eux-mêmes leur précieux secret, ils retournèrent en hâte au village pour revenir bientôt armés de pelles et d'instruments. Une excavation de dix pieds de profondeur révéla une plate-forme de pièces de bois très épaisses; tremblant d'émotion, les hommes continuèrent à creuser. A vingt pieds, une seconde plate-forme fut déterrée; puis une troisième à trente pieds. A chaque fois ils croyaient découvrir le trésor, mais chaque fois, ils étaient déçus.

La tâche était trop rude pour deux hommes seulement et ils durent renoncer à leur projet. Tentant d'obtenir de l'aide, ils eurent à faire face à la crainte superstitieuse des villageois de Chester, car la rumeur courait qu'on voyait d'étranges lumières dans l'île la nuit.

52. Les deux hommes allèrent à l'Ile-au-Chêne parce qu'ils
   A. y avaient caché un tresor.
   B. voulaient abattre un arbre.
   C. espéraient y faire une bonne chasse.
   D. voulaient y planter des arbres.

53. En débarquant ils trouvèrent un
   A. terrain singulier.
   B. livre très vieux.
   C. magnifique bijou.
   D. dépôt de munitions.

54. Ils retournèrent au village pour
   A. annoncer leur découverte.
   B. chercher des outils.
   C. vendre des canards.
   D. écrire leurs mémoires.

55. Les hommes abandonnèrent leur travail
   A. parce qu'il était trop difficile.
   B. parce qu'on se moquait d'eux.
   C. parce qu'ils avaient découvert ce qu'ils cherchaient.
   D. parce qu'ils avaient été expulsés de l'île.

In the following passage there are five blank spaces numbered 56 through 60. Each blank space represents a missing word or expression. For each blank space, four possible completions are provided. Only one of them makes sense in the context of the passage.

First, read the passage in its entirety to determine its general meaning. Then read it a second time. For each blank space, choose the completion that makes the best sense and write its letter in the space provided on the special answer sheet.

L'orchestre de l'Ecole César-Franck interprète un morceau intitulé "les Indiens". Le plus jeune élève a trois ans. Dans ses mains, il tient un violon à sa taille. C'est probablement le plus __(56)__ violon qui existe en France. C'est une copie miniature mais exacte de l'instrument classique. Dans l'orchestre, ils sont une vingtaine __(57)__ de trois à huit ans, et tous tiennent un miniviolon. Les plus jeunes ne savent pas __(58)__ les notes, mais ils les chantent.

Devant chaque élève, il y a une vraie feuille de musique et chacun joue avec attention. Dans la salle, des __(59)__ leur donnent des conseils et corrigent leur posture. Tous sont attentifs et heureux.

C'est grâce à l'un de ses anciens élèves que l'Ecole de Musique César-Franck a maintenant cet orchestre remarquable. C'est lui qui a envoyé une trentaine de violons miniatures à l'école, et c'est lui aussi qui est venu à Paris pour __(60)__ l'orchestre selon une nouvelle méthode.

56.
   A. beau
   B. petit
   C. solide
   D. difficile

57.
   A. d'étrangers
   B. de professeurs
   C. d'enfants
   D. d'acteurs

58.
   A. lire
   B. compter
   C. écrire
   D. trouver

59.
   A. chanteurs
   B. interprètes
   C. professeurs
   D. chauffeurs

60.
   A. organiser
   B. peindre
   C. critiquer
   D. acheter

END OF TEST NO. 5

ANSWER SHEETS FOR TESTS 1 TO 5

ANSWER SHEET • TEST 1

Use a soft lead pencil to blacken the space under the letter which you choose as your answer. If you finish the test before the time limit has expired, go over the questions and your answers again and, if necessary, be sure that you erase completely before you blacken another space. The time limit is one hour.

	A B C D		A B C D		A B C D
1	‖ ‖ ‖ ‖	21	‖ ‖ ‖ ‖	41	‖ ‖ ‖ ‖
2	‖ ‖ ‖ ‖	22	‖ ‖ ‖ ‖	42	‖ ‖ ‖ ‖
3	‖ ‖ ‖ ‖	23	‖ ‖ ‖ ‖	43	‖ ‖ ‖ ‖
4	‖ ‖ ‖ ‖	24	‖ ‖ ‖ ‖	44	‖ ‖ ‖ ‖
5	‖ ‖ ‖ ‖	25	‖ ‖ ‖ ‖	45	‖ ‖ ‖ ‖
6	‖ ‖ ‖ ‖	26	‖ ‖ ‖ ‖	46	‖ ‖ ‖ ‖
7	‖ ‖ ‖ ‖	27	‖ ‖ ‖ ‖	47	‖ ‖ ‖ ‖
8	‖ ‖ ‖ ‖	28	‖ ‖ ‖ ‖	48	‖ ‖ ‖ ‖
9	‖ ‖ ‖ ‖	29	‖ ‖ ‖ ‖	49	‖ ‖ ‖ ‖
10	‖ ‖ ‖ ‖	30	‖ ‖ ‖ ‖	50	‖ ‖ ‖ ‖
11	‖ ‖ ‖ ‖	31	‖ ‖ ‖ ‖	51	‖ ‖ ‖ ‖
12	‖ ‖ ‖ ‖	32	‖ ‖ ‖ ‖	52	‖ ‖ ‖ ‖
13	‖ ‖ ‖ ‖	33	‖ ‖ ‖ ‖	53	‖ ‖ ‖ ‖
14	‖ ‖ ‖ ‖	34	‖ ‖ ‖ ‖	54	‖ ‖ ‖ ‖
15	‖ ‖ ‖ ‖	35	‖ ‖ ‖ ‖	55	‖ ‖ ‖ ‖
16	‖ ‖ ‖ ‖	36	‖ ‖ ‖ ‖	56	‖ ‖ ‖ ‖
17	‖ ‖ ‖ ‖	37	‖ ‖ ‖ ‖	57	‖ ‖ ‖ ‖
18	‖ ‖ ‖ ‖	38	‖ ‖ ‖ ‖	58	‖ ‖ ‖ ‖
19	‖ ‖ ‖ ‖	39	‖ ‖ ‖ ‖	59	‖ ‖ ‖ ‖
20	‖ ‖ ‖ ‖	40	‖ ‖ ‖ ‖	60	‖ ‖ ‖ ‖

ANSWER SHEET ▪ TEST 2

Use a soft lead pencil to blacken the space under the letter which you choose as your answer. If you finish the test before the time limit has expired, go over the questions and your answers again and, if necessary, be sure that you erase completely before you blacken another space. The time limit is one hour.

	A B C D		A B C D		A B C D
1	‖ ‖ ‖ ‖	21	‖ ‖ ‖ ‖	41	‖ ‖ ‖ ‖
2	‖ ‖ ‖ ‖	22	‖ ‖ ‖ ‖	42	‖ ‖ ‖ ‖
3	‖ ‖ ‖ ‖	23	‖ ‖ ‖ ‖	43	‖ ‖ ‖ ‖
4	‖ ‖ ‖ ‖	24	‖ ‖ ‖ ‖	44	‖ ‖ ‖ ‖
5	‖ ‖ ‖ ‖	25	‖ ‖ ‖ ‖	45	‖ ‖ ‖ ‖
6	‖ ‖ ‖ ‖	26	‖ ‖ ‖ ‖	46	‖ ‖ ‖ ‖
7	‖ ‖ ‖ ‖	27	‖ ‖ ‖ ‖	47	‖ ‖ ‖ ‖
8	‖ ‖ ‖ ‖	28	‖ ‖ ‖ ‖	48	‖ ‖ ‖ ‖
9	‖ ‖ ‖ ‖	29	‖ ‖ ‖ ‖	49	‖ ‖ ‖ ‖
10	‖ ‖ ‖ ‖	30	‖ ‖ ‖ ‖	50	‖ ‖ ‖ ‖
11	‖ ‖ ‖ ‖	31	‖ ‖ ‖ ‖	51	‖ ‖ ‖ ‖
12	‖ ‖ ‖ ‖	32	‖ ‖ ‖ ‖	52	‖ ‖ ‖ ‖
13	‖ ‖ ‖ ‖	33	‖ ‖ ‖ ‖	53	‖ ‖ ‖ ‖
14	‖ ‖ ‖ ‖	34	‖ ‖ ‖ ‖	54	‖ ‖ ‖ ‖
15	‖ ‖ ‖ ‖	35	‖ ‖ ‖ ‖	55	‖ ‖ ‖ ‖
16	‖ ‖ ‖ ‖	36	‖ ‖ ‖ ‖	56	‖ ‖ ‖ ‖
17	‖ ‖ ‖ ‖	37	‖ ‖ ‖ ‖	57	‖ ‖ ‖ ‖
18	‖ ‖ ‖ ‖	38	‖ ‖ ‖ ‖	58	‖ ‖ ‖ ‖
19	‖ ‖ ‖ ‖	39	‖ ‖ ‖ ‖	59	‖ ‖ ‖ ‖
20	‖ ‖ ‖ ‖	40	‖ ‖ ‖ ‖	60	‖ ‖ ‖ ‖

ANSWER SHEET ▪ TEST 3

Use a soft lead pencil to blacken the space under the letter which you choose as your answer. If you finish the test before the time limit has expired, go over the questions and your answers again and, if necessary, be sure that you erase completely before you blacken another space. The time limit is one hour.

	A B C D		A B C D		A B C D
1	‖ ‖ ‖ ‖	21	‖ ‖ ‖ ‖	41	‖ ‖ ‖ ‖
2	‖ ‖ ‖ ‖	22	‖ ‖ ‖ ‖	42	‖ ‖ ‖ ‖
3	‖ ‖ ‖ ‖	23	‖ ‖ ‖ ‖	43	‖ ‖ ‖ ‖
4	‖ ‖ ‖ ‖	24	‖ ‖ ‖ ‖	44	‖ ‖ ‖ ‖
5	‖ ‖ ‖ ‖	25	‖ ‖ ‖ ‖	45	‖ ‖ ‖ ‖
6	‖ ‖ ‖ ‖	26	‖ ‖ ‖ ‖	46	‖ ‖ ‖ ‖
7	‖ ‖ ‖ ‖	27	‖ ‖ ‖ ‖	47	‖ ‖ ‖ ‖
8	‖ ‖ ‖ ‖	28	‖ ‖ ‖ ‖	48	‖ ‖ ‖ ‖
9	‖ ‖ ‖ ‖	29	‖ ‖ ‖ ‖	49	‖ ‖ ‖ ‖
10	‖ ‖ ‖ ‖	30	‖ ‖ ‖ ‖	50	‖ ‖ ‖ ‖
11	‖ ‖ ‖ ‖	31	‖ ‖ ‖ ‖	51	‖ ‖ ‖ ‖
12	‖ ‖ ‖ ‖	32	‖ ‖ ‖ ‖	52	‖ ‖ ‖ ‖
13	‖ ‖ ‖ ‖	33	‖ ‖ ‖ ‖	53	‖ ‖ ‖ ‖
14	‖ ‖ ‖ ‖	34	‖ ‖ ‖ ‖	54	‖ ‖ ‖ ‖
15	‖ ‖ ‖ ‖	35	‖ ‖ ‖ ‖	55	‖ ‖ ‖ ‖
16	‖ ‖ ‖ ‖	36	‖ ‖ ‖ ‖	56	‖ ‖ ‖ ‖
17	‖ ‖ ‖ ‖	37	‖ ‖ ‖ ‖	57	‖ ‖ ‖ ‖
18	‖ ‖ ‖ ‖	38	‖ ‖ ‖ ‖	58	‖ ‖ ‖ ‖
19	‖ ‖ ‖ ‖	39	‖ ‖ ‖ ‖	59	‖ ‖ ‖ ‖
20	‖ ‖ ‖ ‖	40	‖ ‖ ‖ ‖	60	‖ ‖ ‖ ‖

ANSWER SHEET ▪ TEST 4

Use a soft lead pencil to blacken the space under the letter which you choose as your answer. If you finish the test before the time limit has expired, go over the questions and your answers again and, if necessary, be sure that you erase completely before you blacken another space. The time limit is one hour.

	A	B	C	D			A	B	C	D			A	B	C	D
1	‖	‖	‖	‖		21	‖	‖	‖	‖		41	‖	‖	‖	‖
2	‖	‖	‖	‖		22	‖	‖	‖	‖		42	‖	‖	‖	‖
3	‖	‖	‖	‖		23	‖	‖	‖	‖		43	‖	‖	‖	‖
4	‖	‖	‖	‖		24	‖	‖	‖	‖		44	‖	‖	‖	‖
5	‖	‖	‖	‖		25	‖	‖	‖	‖		45	‖	‖	‖	‖
6	‖	‖	‖	‖		26	‖	‖	‖	‖		46	‖	‖	‖	‖
7	‖	‖	‖	‖		27	‖	‖	‖	‖		47	‖	‖	‖	‖
8	‖	‖	‖	‖		28	‖	‖	‖	‖		48	‖	‖	‖	‖
9	‖	‖	‖	‖		29	‖	‖	‖	‖		49	‖	‖	‖	‖
10	‖	‖	‖	‖		30	‖	‖	‖	‖		50	‖	‖	‖	‖
11	‖	‖	‖	‖		31	‖	‖	‖	‖		51	‖	‖	‖	‖
12	‖	‖	‖	‖		32	‖	‖	‖	‖		52	‖	‖	‖	‖
13	‖	‖	‖	‖		33	‖	‖	‖	‖		53	‖	‖	‖	‖
14	‖	‖	‖	‖		34	‖	‖	‖	‖		54	‖	‖	‖	‖
15	‖	‖	‖	‖		35	‖	‖	‖	‖		55	‖	‖	‖	‖
16	‖	‖	‖	‖		36	‖	‖	‖	‖		56	‖	‖	‖	‖
17	‖	‖	‖	‖		37	‖	‖	‖	‖		57	‖	‖	‖	‖
18	‖	‖	‖	‖		38	‖	‖	‖	‖		58	‖	‖	‖	‖
19	‖	‖	‖	‖		39	‖	‖	‖	‖		59	‖	‖	‖	‖
20	‖	‖	‖	‖		40	‖	‖	‖	‖		60	‖	‖	‖	‖

ANSWER SHEET ▪ TEST 5

Use a soft lead pencil to blacken the space under the letter which you choose as your answer. If you finish the test before the time limit has expired, go over the questions and your answers again and, if necessary, be sure that you erase completely before you blacken another space. The time limit is one hour.

	A B C D		A B C D		A B C D
1	‖ ‖ ‖ ‖	21	‖ ‖ ‖ ‖	41	‖ ‖ ‖ ‖
2	‖ ‖ ‖ ‖	22	‖ ‖ ‖ ‖	42	‖ ‖ ‖ ‖
3	‖ ‖ ‖ ‖	23	‖ ‖ ‖ ‖	43	‖ ‖ ‖ ‖
4	‖ ‖ ‖ ‖	24	‖ ‖ ‖ ‖	44	‖ ‖ ‖ ‖
5	‖ ‖ ‖ ‖	25	‖ ‖ ‖ ‖	45	‖ ‖ ‖ ‖
6	‖ ‖ ‖ ‖	26	‖ ‖ ‖ ‖	46	‖ ‖ ‖ ‖
7	‖ ‖ ‖ ‖	27	‖ ‖ ‖ ‖	47	‖ ‖ ‖ ‖
8	‖ ‖ ‖ ‖	28	‖ ‖ ‖ ‖	48	‖ ‖ ‖ ‖
9	‖ ‖ ‖ ‖	29	‖ ‖ ‖ ‖	49	‖ ‖ ‖ ‖
10	‖ ‖ ‖ ‖	30	‖ ‖ ‖ ‖	50	‖ ‖ ‖ ‖
11	‖ ‖ ‖ ‖	31	‖ ‖ ‖ ‖	51	‖ ‖ ‖ ‖
12	‖ ‖ ‖ ‖	32	‖ ‖ ‖ ‖	52	‖ ‖ ‖ ‖
13	‖ ‖ ‖ ‖	33	‖ ‖ ‖ ‖	53	‖ ‖ ‖ ‖
14	‖ ‖ ‖ ‖	34	‖ ‖ ‖ ‖	54	‖ ‖ ‖ ‖
15	‖ ‖ ‖ ‖	35	‖ ‖ ‖ ‖	55	‖ ‖ ‖ ‖
16	‖ ‖ ‖ ‖	36	‖ ‖ ‖ ‖	56	‖ ‖ ‖ ‖
17	‖ ‖ ‖ ‖	37	‖ ‖ ‖ ‖	57	‖ ‖ ‖ ‖
18	‖ ‖ ‖ ‖	38	‖ ‖ ‖ ‖	58	‖ ‖ ‖ ‖
19	‖ ‖ ‖ ‖	39	‖ ‖ ‖ ‖	59	‖ ‖ ‖ ‖
20	‖ ‖ ‖ ‖	40	‖ ‖ ‖ ‖	60	‖ ‖ ‖ ‖

ANSWER KEYS TO TESTS 1 TO 5

#	A	B	C	D		#	A	B	C	D		#	A	B	C	D
1		●				21		●				41	●			
2	●					22	●					42		●		
3	●					23				●		43	●			
4			●			24	●					44		●		
5			●			25		●				45	●			
6	●					26				●		46			●	
7	●					27	●					47		●		
8	●					28		●				48				●
9	●					29		●				49			●	
10	●					30	●					50				●
11		●				31	●					51			●	
12		●				32	●					52		●		
13			●			33		●				53			●	
14			●			34			●			54			●	
15	●					35				●		55	●			
16			●			36				●		56	●			
17	●					37	●					57	●			
18		●				38		●				58				●
19	●					39		●				59			●	
20			●			40	●					60				●

#	Answer	#	Answer	#	Answer
1	B	21	D	41	A
2	D	22	A	42	C
3	B	23	C	43	A
4	B	24	D	44	C
5	A	25	C	45	D
6	C	26	A	46	D
7	C	27	B	47	B
8	B	28	A	48	C
9	B	29	B	49	A
10	A	30	A	50	A
11	A	31	C	51	A
12	B	32	C	52	C
13	C	33	B	53	A
14	B	34	A	54	C
15	A	35	C	55	A
16	D	36	D	56	C
17	D	37	D	57	D
18	A	38	A	58	A
19	D	39	A	59	C
20	B	40	A	60	A

ANSWER KEY ▪ TEST 3

#	Ans	#	Ans	#	Ans
1	A	21	C	41	C
2	A	22	A	42	C
3	B	23	C	43	D
4	A	24	A	44	D
5	B	25	A	45	C
6	A	26	D	46	A
7	A	27	D	47	C
8	C	28	B	48	C
9	B	29	A	49	A
10	A	30	C	50	B
11	B	31	A	51	D
12	A	32	A	52	B
13	B	33	B	53	A
14	C	34	D	54	C
15	A	35	C	55	D
16	B	36	D	56	C
17	A	37	B	57	A
18	A	38	D	58	D
19	C	39	D	59	C
20	D	40	D	60	D

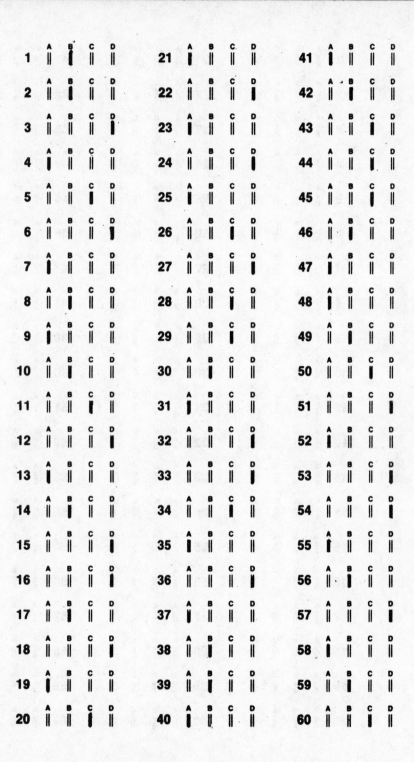

#	A	B	C	D		#	A	B	C	D		#	A	B	C	D
1	▮					21	▮					41				▮
2		▮				22	▮					42		▮		
3	▮					23		▮				43			▮	
4	▮					24	▮					44				▮
5		▮				25						45			▮	
6				▮		26	▮					46				▮
7	▮					27	▮					47		▮		
8	▮					28	▮					48	▮			
9		▮				29	▮					49				▮
10		▮				30		▮				50				▮
11	▮					31		▮				51	▮			
12	▮					32	▮					52			▮	
13	▮					33	▮					53	▮			
14	▮					34			▮			54		▮		
15	▮					35			▮			55	▮			
16		▮				36	▮					56		▮		
17				▮		37				▮		57			▮	
18			▮			38				▮		58	▮			
19	▮					39	▮					59	▮			
20			▮			40		▮				60	▮			

212

ANSWERS EXPLAINED TO TESTS 1 TO 5

ANSWERS EXPLAINED ▪ TEST 1

Students, please note: Throughout the *Answers Explained* section, question numbers that are omitted are those that do not require grammatical explanations because they test a knowledge of French vocabulary, idioms, and skill in general reading comprehension. If you had an incorrect answer because you did not recognize the meaning of a French word or idiom, look it up in the French-English vocabulary at the end of this book, in the Comprehensive Index, in §20.ff and §45.ff. If it is not there, consult a standard French-English dictionary.

1. See §39.2.

2. See §29.24, §29.28, §29.29, §29.32.

3. See §39.2, §39.4, §39.26–§39.29.

4. See §29.24–§29.26 (1) & (2), §29.27ff, §29.53.

5. See §29.22 (a) & (d).

6. See §29.24, §29.26 (2), §29.27 (1), §29.30 (1), §29.31 (1).

7. See §39.–§39.23, §39.26ff.

8. See §1.9.

9. See §4.3 (r).

10. See §39.102.

11. See §1.19.

12. See §39.4, §39.25–§39.29 (16).

13. See §29.22 (a) & (d).

14. See §30., §30.1.

15. See **combien de** listed alphabetically in §20.14.

16. See §4.—§4.8, in particular §4.3(m), §4.3(n).

17. See §29.28.

18. See §29.27 and §29.31.

19. See §35., §35.8 (where **vouloir que** is listed alphabetically), and §39.93.

20. See §35., §35.8 (where **douter que** is listed alphabetically), and §39.93.

21. See §34.—§34.2, in particular §34.2(d), §39.89, §39.92.

22. See §29.9, §29.19, and §42.—§42.4.

23. See §10.1 and §39.88(f).

24. The verb **espérer** in the affirmative does not require the subjunctive of the verb in the following clause; the indicative is used. The future is used if future time is implied. For certain verbs that require the subjunctive in the clause that follows, see §35.8 and, in particular, §35.10.

25. See note to students above.

26. See §39.89 (b).

27 to 31. See note to students above.

32. You need the future tense here because the key words in the statement are **samedi prochain**. See §39.91.

33. See §39.38.

34. See §1.17(c).

35. See **venir de + inf.** listed alphabetically in §20.38.

36. See §39.12—§39.22, in particular, §39.17.

37. See **avoir besoin de** listed alphabetically in §20.6. See also §29.20 to review the indirect object pronouns. Direct and indirect object pronouns are normally placed in front of an infinitive.

38. There is no need for the subjunctive here because nothing special precedes the **que** clause. Review the forms of **être** in §40.1.

39. See §11.—§11.3.

40. See §39.38.

41. See §35. and §35.1 where **bien que** is listed alphabetically.

42. There is no need for the subjunctive here because nothing special precedes the verb form you need to choose. That eliminates choices C and D. You are left with choices A and B which are both in the future. Review §39.2 and the future of **être** in §39.81 and in §40.1.

43. See §29.35ff.

44. See §39.46 where **venir de** is listed. See also §39.89.

45. See the irregular past part. **plu** in §39.24. Also consult §41. as needed.

46. See §39.12 and §39.13.

47. See **être à qqn** in §20.38. See also §29.22(d) and §29.28.

48. See §34.—§34.2(e) and §39.99(b). See also §39.84(9).

49. See **penser à qqn ou à qqch** in §39.43. See also §29.28(2) and the note given there. Also consult §1.12 for an explanation of incorrect choice D.

50. See §34.—§34.2(e), §39.4, §39.29, and **aller** in the conditional perfect in §39.85(12).

ANSWERS EXPLAINED ■ TEST **2**

1. See §29.35 (a) and (b); **défauts** is masc. pl. and you can tell because of the masc. pl. adjective **grands** in front of it in the sentence.

2. See §29.24, §29.29, §29.31 (4).

3. See §35., §35.1 (where **pourvu que** is listed), §39.93 (e), and §40.1 for the forms of the present subjunctive of **venir** (**revenir** is conjugated in the same way).

4. The verb **habiter** may be transitive or intransitive. Note the following: **habiter la campagne** or **habiter à la campagne**. Normally, we say **habiter la France**. Regarding transitive and intransitive verbs, see §39.30—§39.34.

5. See §35., §35.8 (where **douter que** is listed), §39.70 (6), §39.93, §39.93 (d) (1), §40.1 where **pouvoir** is conjugated in all the tenses.

6. See §25., §25.1 (a) and (b).

7. See §34.—§34.2 (e), §39.51 (where the principal parts of **savoir** are given), §39.70 (9), §39.75, §39.85 (where **aller** is conjugated in all the tenses), §39.96, and §39.99.

8. See §39.8—§39.11, in particular §39.9.

9. See §7.—§7.3 (a) where **dès que** is listed, §39.41 where **arriver** is conjugated in all the tenses, and §39.91.

10. See §39., §39.1, §39.12, §39.17, §39.95.

11. See §21.8.

12. See §4.4 (f).

13. See §35., §35.6 where **il faut que** is listed, §39.70 (6), §39.93, §40.1 where **venir** is conjugated fully in all the tenses.

14. To express *in order + inf.*, use **pour + inf.** See §20.18 where **faire plaisir à** is listed. As for the form **achètera** in this sentence, see §39.53, §39.65, §39.66.

15. See §21., §21.1, §21.6. As for the form **s'en est allé**, it is the passé composé of **s'en aller** (*to leave, to go away*).

27. For the underlined words (**qu'est-ce qui**) see §29.24, §29.29, §29.30 (1). For the use of **qui**, see §29.25 and §29.26 (1)—§29.28. For the use of **que** and **qu'est-ce que**, see §29.29 and §29.31. For the use of **quoi**, see §29.29 and §29.32.

28. See §29.22 and §29.22 (a)ff.

29. See §39.42 and §39.43 where **répondre à qqn ou à qqch** is listed.

30. See §39.42 and §39.46 where **essayer de + inf.** is listed.

31. See §29.19—§29.22.

32. See §1., §1.16, §1.16 (a)ff.

33. See §1., §1.16 (a), (d) and (e).

34. See §39.42, §39.45 where **jouer de** is listed.

35. See §39.42, §39.46 where **essayer de** is listed.

36. See §1.1; as for **a été**, it is the passé composé of **être**. See §40.1.

37. See §29.19—§29.20, §42.2.

38. See §29.22 and §29.22 (a).

39. See §1., §1.16, §1.16 (a) and (c).

40. See §20., §20.1, §20.6 where **avoir lieu** is listed, §39.70 (4), §39.91, and §40.1 where **avoir** is conjugated in all the tenses.

41. See §4.—§4.3 (r).

42. See §20., §20.1, §20.18.

43. See §39.70 (4) and §39.91.

44. See §2.14, §25.1 (i), §29.7.

45. See §29.22 and §29.22 (a).

46. See §20., §20.1, §20.18, §39.51 (**faire**), §39.70 (8), §39.71—§39.74, §39.95, and §40.1 (**faire**).

47. See §1., §1.16 (a) and (d).

48 and 49. See §1. and §1.1.

50. See §37.ff.

ANSWERS EXPLAINED ▪ TEST 3

1. See §1.1, §30.–§30.1.

2. See §1., §1.1, §1.12, §20.27, §20.28.

3. See §29.43, §29.44, §29.47.

4. See §29.23; **n'importe quand** means *anytime*.

5. See §29.23; **n'importe où** means *anywhere*.

6. See §39.35—§39.37.

7. See §29.48 and §39.45 where **dépendre de** is listed.

8 and 9. See §21., §21.1, §21.8.

10. See §21., §21.1, §21.6.

11. See §1.19 (c).

12. See §1.19 (b), §39., §39.1, §39.3, §39.5, §39.6, §39.26, §39.28.

13. See §1.17 (c).

14. Generally speaking, **être + adj.** takes **de** when an inf. follows, *e.g.*, **Nous sommes heureux de vous voir; Je suis obligé de faire mes devoirs**. See also §39.42—§39.50.

15. See §21.8.

26. See §29.24—§29.26 (3) and (4).

27. See §29.24, §29.29, §29.31.

28. Here, you are dealing with the imperative of the **tu** form. Choice B is the imperative of the **vous** form. See §39.102 and the imperative of **dire** in §40.1.

29. Choices B, C and D take the prep. **à** but choice A requires no prep. See §39.49 and §39.50 (**chercher**).

30. See §29. and §29.35.

31. When you take the French CBAT, make absolutely certain that you read the directions carefully. There are different types of questions. In the block of questions 26 through 30 the directions state to choose the word or words that **cannot be** substituted. Here, in questions 31 through 35, you are to choose the word or words that **can be** substituted. See §29.24, §29.25, §29.28.

32. See §4.—§4.2.

33. See §39., §39.1, §39.17, §39.23, §41. (**vu**).

34. See §4.—§4.3 (r).

35. See §29.24—§29.26, §29.29, §29.30.

36. See §29.9, §29.10; the **y** in **je m'y amuse** refers to the place **à la campagne**.

37. See §20., §20.1, §20.16.

38. See §4.—§4.3 (r), §8.3.

39. See §1., §1.16 (c).

40. See §20., §20.1, §20.18.

41. See §39.35—§39.39.

42. See §1., §1.16 (a) and (d).

43. See §29.9, §29.10; the **y** in **J'y suis arrivé** refers to the place **à l'école**; always keep in mind §39.26—§39.29. See also §39.41.

44. See §1.1, §9.—§9.3, in particular §9.1 (m).

45. See §39., §39.1, §39.4, §39.25, §39.26, §39.29 (c) (5), §39.70 (8), §39.74, §39.95.

ANSWERS EXPLAINED ▪ TEST 4

1. See §4.4 (l), §30.—§30.1.

3. See §29., §29.13—§29.16.

4. See §21.8.

5. See §35. and §35.6.

6. See §29.24, §29.29, §29.32.

7. See §39.42, §39.45 (**se souvenir de**), and §40.1 (**venir**).

8. See §1.1. There is no need for the subjunctive here because you are not dealing with **Je regrette que** . . . ; the statement contains **Je regrette mais** . . . .

9. See §1.1. As for the form **veuillez**, see the imperative of **vouloir** in §40.1 and §36.3.

10. See §30. and §30.1.

11. See §38.—§38.2 (**habiter/demeurer**).

12. See §20., §20.1, §20.14 (**près de**).

13. See §2.14, §4.4 (m), §25.1 (i), §29.7.

14. See §29. and §29.35.

15. See §29., §29.35 (c). See also §39.42, §39.43 (**s'intéresser à qqn ou à qqch**).

26. See §39.—§39.1, §39.4, §39.26—§39.29 (c) and (2), §39.30—§39.34, §39.41, §39.70 (8), §39.74, §39.95.

27. See §4.—§4.3 (r).

28. See §1.1, §1.12, §39., §39.1, §39.18.

30. The imperative **parlez** is in the **vous** form and choice B is the imperative of **marcher** in the **tu** form. You cannot switch from **vous** to **tu**. See §39.84 (15).

31. See §1.1. The adjective must be masc. sing. because **ce parc** is masc. sing. Choices B, C and D are fem. sing. Choice A can be masc. or fem. See also §1.11 (b).

32. See §4.—§4.3(r), §20., §20.1, §20.6 (**avoir mal à**).

33. See §4.—§4.3 (r), §20., §20.1, §20.14 (**près de**).

34. See §4.5—§4.8. This question tests specifically your observation of gender.

35. See §4.1—§4.3, §4.4 (m).

36. See §39., §39.1, §39.3, §39.5, §39.26, §39.28, §39.70 (8), §39.74, §39.86, §39.87, §39.95.

37. See §1.1, §1.7—§1.9.

38. See §39.24 (**prendre**), §39.25, §39.26, §39.27ff, §39.51 (**prendre**), §39.95, §40.1 (**prendre**).

39 to 42. See §4.—§4.3 (r), §25.—§25.1.

43. See §20., §20.1, §20.3 (**café au lait**).

44. See explanation to question no. 29 in Test 1. See also §39.16 and §39.26—§39.34.

45. See §1.1 and §20.36.

46. See §39.—§39.2, §39.16, §39.27, §39.95.

47. See §39.—§39.2, §39.89, §40.1 (**être**).

48. See §4.4 (c); **en route** means *on the way*.

49. See §21., §21.1, §21.8, §39.23, §39.26, §39.29 (11).

50. See §1.1, §1.16 (c).

ANSWERS EXPLAINED ▪ TEST 5

1. See §29.46.

2. See §25. (2.Simple Negative), §25.1 (g).

3. See §29.13—§29.16.

4. See §29.19—§29.21.

5. See §35., §35.6 where **il faut que** is listed, §39.93, §40.1 where the present subjunctive of **être** is given.

6. See §35., §35.8 where **exiger que** is listed, §39.93.

7. See §39.29 (c) (3). See also §39.14.

8. See §25. (1.Simple Affirmative), §25.1 (b).

9. See §29.—§29.2 and §42.1.

10. See §39.2, §39.4, §39.29 (c) (3).

11. See §39.29 (c) (3). See also §39.14.

12. See §39.17.

13. See §39.17.

14. See §39.16.

15. See §29.43, §29.44, §29.52.

16. The key words in this sentence are **la semaine prochaine**, which means that you need the future tense of the missing verb. See §39.91.

17. See §35., §35.6 where **il vaut mieux que** is listed, §39.93, §40.1 where **faire** is conjugated in all the tenses.

18. See §39.17.

19. See §1.19 (b).

20. See §10., §10.1, §39.88 (f).

21. See §39.29 (c) (3).

22. See §11.—§11.3.

23. See §1.1.

24. See §39.2, §39.3, §39.5.

25. This question tests your knowledge of French conjunctions. See §7.—§7.4.

26. See §1.1, §1.16.

27. The fem. sing. form is needed here because the statement contains **"une jeune"**.

28. See §39.4, §39.29 (c) (16), §39.70 (9), §39.75, §39.96.

29. See §29.9, §29.10, §29.10 (d).

30. See §1.1, §41.

31. See §39.3.

32. See §29.22, §39.102, §42.3.

33. See §20.16 where **en bas** is listed.

35. See §39.43 where **obéir à qqn** is listed. Choice D cannot be substituted for the underlined word because there is no prep. **à** (or a form of **à**) in the given statement.

36. The underlined word to be substituted is an indirect obj. pronoun. Choice A is not an indirect obj. pronoun. Review the direct and indirect obj. pronouns in §29.19—§29.21.

38. The underlined word to be substituted is masc. sing. Keep §1.1 in mind.

39. See §1.1.

40. The verb in choice B does not take the prep. **à**, whereas the remaining choices do. See §39.50.

41. The underlined verb form is a transitive verb and it has a direct object, whereas the verb form in choice D is intransitive and does not take a direct object. See §39.29 (c) (3) and (6). See also §39.26—§39.34.

42. See §4.2.

43. The underlined word to be substituted is a possessive adjective in the plural, whereas the word in choice C is singular. See §1.16. Also review §29.20.

44. The underlined word to be substituted is a possessive adjective in the plural, whereas the word in choice D is singular. See §1.16.

45. The key words in the given sentence are **l'été passé** and this suggests that the verb form must be a past tense. Choice C is a form of **aller** in the future. See §39.85 (4).

46. The underlined word is an indirect object pronoun (as are the choices in A, B and C), whereas the word in choice D is a disjunctive pronoun. See §29.20 and §29.22.

47. See §1.1.

48. The underlined word is a disjunctive pronoun (as are the choices in A, B and C), whereas the word in choice D is a subject pronoun. See §29.12 and §29.22.

49. See §39.4 and §39.29 (c) (9). Besides, choice D is not sensible if you think about its meaning.

50. See §39.14. Besides, choice D is not sensible if you think about its meaning.

51. See §1.1.

END OF ANSWERS EXPLAINED TO TESTS 1 TO 5

FRENCH-ENGLISH VOCABULARY

If you look up a French word and it is not listed in the pages that follow, consult the vocabulary given in Part I: Grammar and Vocabulary, beginning with §1. In particular, see Antonyms in §3.ff, Conjunctions and Conjunctive Locutions in §7.ff, idioms and idiomatic expressions in §20., Synonyms in §38.ff, and Review of Basic Vocabulary by Topics in §45.ff. There are other § numbers in this book that contain many French words with English equivalents. The abbreviation ff means *and the following*. See the list of abbreviations on p. ix.

To find certain categories and types of words, especially needed for a mastery of grammatical control, you must consult the Comprehensive Index. For other French words of interest to you that are not given here, consult your French-English dictionary.

A

à *prep.* at, to; see idioms & idiomatic expressions with **à**, §20.2.

à moins que *conj.* unless; *see* conjunctions & conjunctive locutions, §7.ff, §27.7, §29.52, §35.1ff

abaisser *v.* to lower

abattre *v.* to knock down, to fell, to cut down

abeille *n.f.* bee

abîmer *v.* to spoil, to ruin

aboie *v. form of* **aboyer**

abondamment *adv.* abundantly

aborder qqn/to approach someone

aboutir *v.* to lead to, to come to an end

aboyer *v.* to bark

abréger *v.* to abridge, to shorten

abri *n.m.* shelter; **abriter**/to shelter

absolument *adv.* absolutely

accablant, accablante *adj.* overwhelming; **accabler**/to overwhelm

accepter *v.* to accept

accompagner *v.* to accompany

accord *n.m.* agreement; **d'accord**/O.K., in agreement

accorder *v.* to grant, to accord

accourir *v.* to run up to, to rush forward, to hasten to

accoutumé, accoutumée *adj.* accustomed

accrocher *v.* to hang (up)

accueillir *v.* to welcome

achat *n.m.* purchase

s'acheminer *v.* to proceed to lead to (road), to be on the way

acheter *v.* to buy, to purchase

achever *v.* to achieve, to end, to terminate, to finish; **achevé, achevée** *adj.* completed, achieved, finished

acier *n.m.* steel

acquérir *v.* to acquire; *past part.* **acquis**

actuel, actuelle *adj.* present, of the present time

actuellement *adv.* at present, now

addition *n.f.* check, bill (to pay in a restaurant)

adieu *n.m., adv.* farewell, good-bye

admettre *v.* to admit

admirateur *n.m.* admirer

adoucir *v.* to make sweet, to sweeten, to make soft, to soften

adroit, adroite *adj.* skilled, skillful, clever

affaire *n.f.* affair, business; **un homme d'affaires**/businessman; **Occupez-vous de vos affaires**/Mind your own business

affamé, affamée *adj.* famished, starving

affranchi, affranchie *adj.* liberated

affreux, affreuse *adj.* frightful

afin de + inf. in order (to)

agacer *v.* to annoy, to bother, to irritate; **agaçant, agaçante** *adj.* annoying, irritating

s'agenouiller *refl. v.* to kneel

agile *adj.* nimble, agile

agir *v.* to act, to behave; **s'agir de** *refl. v.* to be a question of, to be a matter of

agiter *v.* to move, to shake, to stir

agoniser *v.* to be in agony

agrandir *v.* to grow tall, big

agréable *adj.* pleasant, agreeable

aide See §23.1ff

aient *v. form of* **avoir;** *see* §40.1 and §41.

aigle *n.m.* eagle

aigu, aiguë *adj.* acute, sharp

aiguille *n.f.* needle

aile *n.f.* wing

ailleurs *adv.* elsewhere, somewhere else; **d'ailleurs**/besides, moreover

aimable *adj.* pleasant, kind, amiable

aimer *v.* to love; **Michel, je t'aime**/Michael, I love you.

ainsi *adv.* thus; **et ainsi de suite**/and so forth; *see* idioms with **de**, §20.14

ainsi que *conj.* as well as; *see* §7.ff

aise *n.f.* ease; **à l'aise**/at ease

ajouter *v.* to add

alimentaire *adj.* alimentary; **produit alimentaire**/food product

alimentation *n.f.* food

aliter *v.* to keep in bed

alla *v. form of* **aller;** *see* §39.85

Allemagne *n.f.* Germany

allemand *n.m.* German (language); **Allemand, Allemande** *n.* German (person)

aller *v.* to go; **s'en aller**/to go away; *see* idioms with **aller,** §20.5; *see also* §39.85

allèrent *v. form of* **aller;** *see* §39.85

allonger *v.* to lengthen, to extend

allons/let's go; *see* §39.85

allumer *v.* to light

alors *adv.* so, well, then

alouette *n.f.* lark, skylark

alpinisme *n.m.* mountain climbing

amateur *n.m.* amateur, lover (of)

âme *n.f.* soul

améliorer *v.* to improve, to ameliorate

amener *v.* to lead, to bring along, to take (someone somewhere)

amer, amère *adj.* bitter

ami, amie *n.* friend

amical, amicale *adj.* friendly

amitié *n.f.* friendship

amour *n.m.* love

amusant, amusante *adj.* funny, amusing

amuser *v.* to amuse; **s'amuser**/to amuse oneself, to have fun, to have a good time

an *n.m.* year

ancêtre *n.m.* ancestor

ancien, ancienne *adj.* old, ancient, former

Angleterre *n.f.* England

animé, animée *adj.* animated, lively

année *n.f.* year (long)

anniversaire *n.m.* anniversary; **anniversaire de naissance**/birthday

annonce *n.f.* announcement

apaiser *v.* to appease

apercevoir *v.* to notice, to perceive

apparaître *v.* to appear

appareil *n.m.* apparatus

appartenir à *v.* to belong to, to pertain to

appel *n.m.* appeal, call

appeler *v.* to call; **s'appeler**/to be named, to call oneself

appellation *n.f.* name

appétissant, appétissante *adj.* appetizing

appétit *n.m.* appetite; **do bon appétit; *see* idioms with de, §20.14**

applaudir *v.* to applaud

appliquer *v.* to apply

apporter *v.* to bring, to carry away

apprendre *v.* to learn, to teach; *see* §40.ff

approcher *v.* to bring near; **s'approcher de**/to approach, to draw near

appuyer *v.* to lean, to press

après *prep., adv.* after; **après-midi**/afternoon

arbre *n.m.* tree

arbuste *n.m.* bush, shrub

ardoise *n.f.* slate

argent *n.m.* money

argile *n.f.* clay

arme *n.f.* weapon, arm

armée *n.f.* army

arracher *v.* to pull out, to pull off, to tear away

arrêt *n.m.* stop; **arrêter, s'arrêter**/to

stop; **s'arrêter net**/to stop short

arrière *n.m.* rear, back; **en arrière**/backwards

arrivée *n.f.* arrival

arriver *v.* to arrive, to happen, to succeed

ascenseur *n.m.* elevator

s'assembler *v.* to assemble; **Qui se ressemble s'assemble**/Birds of a feather flock together

asseoir *v.* to seat; **s'asseoir**/to sit down, to seat oneself; **asseyez-vous**/sit down

assez *adv.* enough, rather, somewhat

assis, assise *adj.* seated

assister à *v.* to be present at, to attend

atelier *n.m.* studio, workroom, atelier

attaquer *v.* to attack

atteindre *v.* to attain, to reach

attendre *v.* to wait for; *see* §39.50; **s'attendre à**/to expect

attente *n.f.* waiting; **la salle d'attente**/waiting room

attestation *n.f.* proof

attirer *v.* to attract

attitude *n.f.* position, attitude

attraper *v.* to catch

au *See* idioms with **au**, §20.3.

aubaine *n.f.* luck, windfall, Godsend, stroke of good luck

auberge *n.f.* inn

aucun, aucune *See* negations, §30.ff

aucunement *adv.* in no way, not at all

au-dessous *adv.* below, underneath

au-dessus *adv.* above, over

augmenter *v.* to increase, to augment

auguste *adj.* majestic, august

aumône *n.f.* alms, charity

auprès de/next to, near

aussi *adv.* also, too

aussi . . . que/as . . . as; *see* §1.2ff

aussitôt *adv.* at once, immediately

aussitôt dit aussitôt fait/no sooner said than done

aussitôt que *conj.* as soon as; *see* conjunctions, §7.ff

autant *adv.* as much, as many

autant que *conj.* as much as, as far as; *see* §7.ff

autel *n.m.* altar (church)

auteur *n.m.* author; **une femme auteur**/woman author

autour de/around

autrefois *adv.* formerly; *see* Adverbs, §2.ff

autrement/otherwise

Autriche *n.f.* Austria

Autrichien, Autrichienne *n.* Aus-

trian (person)

aux *See* idioms and idiomatic expressions with **aux**, §20.4.

avaler *v.* to swallow; **avaler des yeux**/to eye greedily, to be fascinated by

avancer, s'avancer *v.* to advance, to come forward; **d'avance**/in advance; *see* idioms with **d'**, §20.13

avant que *conj.* before; *see* §7.ff

avantage *n.m.* advantage; **d'avantage**/more

avare *adj.* miserly, stingy

avenir *n.m.* future; **à l'avenir**/in the future, henceforth; **d'avenir**/with a future

avertir *v.* to warn, to inform

avertissement *n.m.* warning

aveugle *adj.* blind

avide *adj.* eager (for), keen (on)

avis *n.m.* opinion

aviser *v.* to notice, to consider, to advise

avocat *n.m.* lawyer; **une femme avocat**/woman lawyer

avoir *v.* to have; *see* §40.ff and idioms and idiomatic expressions with **avoir**, §20.6

avouer *v.* to admit, to confess

B

bac *abbrev.* of **baccalauréat** *n.m.* scholastic degree

bachelier, bachelière *n.* a student who has taken the **baccalauréat**

bague *n.f.* ring (on finger)

baie *n.f.* bay

se baigner *refl. v.* to bathe oneself

bain *n.m.* bath; **la salle de bains**/bathroom

baisser *v.* to lower

bal *n.m.* dance

balai *n.m.* broom

balance *n.f.* scale (weighing)

balayer *v.* to sweep

balle *n.f.* ball

banc *n.m.* bench

bande *n.f.* recording tape, group, band

banlieue *n.f.* suburbs, outskirts (of a city)

bannir *v.* to banish, to exile

banque *n.f.* bank

barbe *n.f.* beard; **pousser une barbe**/to grow a beard

bas *n.m.* stocking

bas *adv.* low; **en bas**/down, downstairs; **bas, basse** *adj.* low; *see* idioms & idiomatic expressions with **bas**, §20.7 and with **au**, §20.3

bataille *n.f.* battle; **livrer bataille**/to give battle

bateau *n.m.* boat; **bateau à voile**/ sailboat; **bateau-mouche**/small passenger boat

bâti, bâtie *adj.* built

bâtiment *n.m.* building

bâtir *v.* to build

bâton *n.m.* stick

battre *v.* to beat; **battre des mains**/ to clap hands, to applaud

bavard, bavarde *adj.* talkative

bavardage *n.m.* chattering, talkativeness

bavarder *v.* to chat, to chatter, to prattle

beau, bel, belle, beaux, belles *adj.* beautiful, fine, handsome; *see* Adjectives, §1.ff; *see also* idioms & idiomatic expressions with **avoir**, §20.6

beaucoup (de) *adv.* much, many; *see* Antonyms, §3.ff

beaux-arts *n.m.* fine arts

bec *n.m.* beak

bée; bouche bée/open-mouthed

Belge *n.* Belgian (person)

Belgique *n.f.* Belgium

bénir *v.* to bless

berceau *n.m.* cradle

berger, bergère *n.* shepherd, shepherdess

besogne *n.f.* work, toil

besoin *n.m.* need; **avoir besoin de**/ to need, to have need of; *see* idioms & idiomatic expressions with **avoir**, §20.6

bête *n.f.* animal, beast; *adj.* foolish, stupid, silly

bêtise *n.f.* nonsense, stupidity

beurre *n.m.* butter

bibliothèque *n.f.* library

bien *adv.* well; **bien des**/many; *see* idioms & idiomatic expressions with **bien**, §20.8

bien que *conj.* although; *see* Conjunctions & conjunctive locutions, §7.ff; also, §35.1ff.

bienfaiteur *n.m.* benefactor

bientôt *adv.* soon

bijou *n.m.* jewel

bilingue *adj.* bilingual

billet *n.m.* ticket, note

bistro(t) *n.m.* café, pub

bizarre *adj.* strange, bizarre

blanc, blanche *adj.* white

blesser *v.* to injure, to wound

blessure *n.f.* wound, injury

boire *v.* to drink; *see* §40.ff

bois *n.m.* wood, woods

boisé *adj.* woody, wooded

boîte *n.f.* box

bon, bonne *adj.* good; *see* idioms & idiomatic expressions with **bon**, §20.9

bonbons *n.m.* candies

bonheur *n.m.* happiness

bonhomme de neige/snowman; **un bonhomme de paille**/scarecrow

bonté *n.f.* goodness, kindness

bord *n.m.* edge

bordé, bordée *adj.* bordered

borne *n.f.* boundary, limit

borner *v.* to bound

bouche *n.f.* mouth; **bouche bée**/ open-mouthed

boucle *n.f.* buckle, lock of hair

bouffée *n.f.* puff

bouger *v.* to budge, to move

bouillant, bouillante *adj.* boiling

bouillir *v.* to boil

boulanger, boulangère *n.* baker

boulangerie *n.f.* bakery

bouleverser *v.* to dumbfound, to overwhelm, to bowl over

bourgeois, bourgeoise *n.* middle-class person

bourse *n.f.* purse

bousculer *v.* to push, to shove

bout *n.m.* end, tip; *see* idioms & idiomatic expressions with **au**, §20.3

bouteille *n.f.* bottle

boutique *n.f.* shop, small store

boutiquier, boutiquière *n.* shopkeeper

bouton *n.m.* button, pimple

Brahmane *n.m.* Brahman, Brahmin

bras *n.m.* arm; **bras dessus, bras dessous**/arm in arm

briller *v.* to shine, to glitter

briser *v.* to break, to shatter

brosse *n.f.* brush; **brosser**/to brush

brouillard *n.m.* fog

bruit *n.m.* noise

brûlé, brûlée *adj.* burned

brûler *v.* to burn

brume *n.f.* mist, fog

brumeux, brumeuse *adj.* misty, foggy

brunir *v.* to tan, to brown

brusquement *adv.* abruptly

bruyant, bruyante *adj.* noisy

bubonique *adj.* bubonic

bûche *n.f.* log

bureau *n.m.* desk, office; **bureau de poste**/post office

but *n.m.* goal, aim, purpose

buveur, buveuse *n.* drinker

C

ça *See* idiomatic expressions with **ça**, §20.10

cabane *n.f.* hut

cabinet *n.m.* closet, office

cacher, se cacher *v.* to hide, to hide oneself

cadeau *n.m.* gift

cadre *n.m.* frame

cahier *n.m.* notebook

caisse *n.f.* cash register

caissier, caissière *n.* cashier

cambrioleur *n.m.* burglar

camion *n.m.* truck

camionneur *n.m.* truck driver

campagne *n.f.* country(side)

canard *n.m.* duck

canne *n.f.* cane, walking stick

car *conj.* for; *see* Conjunctions and conjunctive locutions, §7.ff

carré *n.m.* square

carrière *n.f.* career

carte *n.f.* card, map

cas *n.m.* case

casser *v.* to break; **casser la croûte**/ to have a bite, to have a snack

cause *n.f.* cause; **à cause de**/on account of; *see* idioms and idiomatic expressions with **à**, §20.2

causer *v.* to chat, to talk

cave *n.f.* cellar

caverne *n.f.* cave

ce *See* dem. adj., §1.ff; *see also* idioms & idiomatic expressions with **ce**, §20.12

ceci *See* pronouns, §29.ff

céder *v.* to cede, to yield

ceinture *n.f.* belt

cela *See* pronouns, §29.ff; *see also* idioms & idiomatic expressions with **cela**, §20.11

célèbre *adj.* famous, celebrated

célibataire *adj.* unmarried, single

celle, celle-ci, celle-là, celui, celui-ci, celui-là; *see* dem. pronouns, §29.13ff

cellule *n.f.* cell

centaine *n.f.* about a hundred; **centaines**/hundreds

cependant *conj.* however; *see also* other conjunctions you ought to know in §7.–§7.4

cercle *n.m.* circle, club

cerise *n.f.* cherry

certitude *n.f.* certitude, certainty

cerveau *n.m.* brain

cesser *v.* to stop, to cease

c'est, c'est-à-dire; *see* idioms and idiomatic expressions with **ce, c'est, est-ce**, §20.12

ceux, ceux-ci, ceux-là; *see* dem. pronouns, §29.13ff

chacun, chacune *pron.* each one

chagrin *n.m.* sorrow, grief

chaîne *n.f.* chain

chaleur *n.f.* heat, warmth

chaleureusement *adv.* warmly

champ *n.m.* field; **le champ de bataille**/battle field

chance *n.f.* chance, luck

chandelle *n.f.* candle

changement *n.m.* change

chanson *n.f.* song

chanter *v.* to sing

chanteur, chanteuse *n.* singer

chapitre *n.m.* chapter

chaque *adj.* each

charbon *n.m.* coal

charcuterie *n.f.* pork shop

charcutier, charcutière *n.* pork butcher

charger *v.* to load, to charge; **chargé de**/filled with, jammed with; **se charger de** *v.* to take charge of; **s'en charger**/to take charge of

chasse *n.f.* chase, hunt, hunting

chasser *v.* to hunt

chasseur *n.m.* hunter

château *n.m.* castle, manor; **faire des châteaux en Espagne**/to build castles in the air (in Spain)

châtelain, châtelaine *n.* lord, lady of a manor, a castle

chatouiller *v.* to tickle

chaud, chaude *adj.* warm

chaudement *adv.* warmly

chauffage *n.m.* heat

chauffeur *n.m.* driver

chaussette *n.f.* sock

chaussure *n.f.* shoe

chemin *n.m.* road, way; **chemin de fer**/railroad; **chemin faisant**/on the way

chêne *n.m.* oak

cher, chère *adj.* dear, expensive; **chéri, chérie**/dear, honey, darling

chercher *v.* to get, to look for, to try

cheval *n.m.* horse; **cheval de course**/race horse; **chevaux-vapeur**/horse-power

cheveu, cheveux *n.m.* hair

chez *prep.* at the place of, at the home of, at the shop of; **chez soi**/in (at) one's house (home)

choix *n.m.* choice

chose *n.f.* thing

chrétien, chrétienne *adj.* Christian

christianisme *n.m.* Christianity

chuchoter *v.* to whisper

ciel *n.m.* sky, heaven

circulation *n.f.* circulation, traffic

cirer *v.* to wax, to polish

cireur *n.m.* shoe shiner, shoe polisher (person)

cité *n.f.* city (usually, the oldest section of a city; *e.g.,* **l'île de la Cité** is the oldest section of Paris)

citoyen, citoyenne *n.* citizen

citoyenneté *n.f.* citizenship

citron *n.m.* lemon; **citronnier** *n.m.* lemon tree

clair, claire *adj.* clear

clé, clef *n.f.* key

client, cliente *n.* customer, client

cligner *v.* to blink, to wink; **un clin d'oeil**/a wink

cloche *n.f.* bell

clou *n.m.* nail

clouer *v.* to nail

coeur *n.m.* heart; *see* idioms & idiomatic expressions with **avoir**, §20.6; with **bon**, §20.9; and with **de**, §20.14

coffre, coffret *n.m.* case, box, small chest

coiffeur *n.m.* barber, hair stylist

coiffeuse *n.f.* hairdresser, hair stylist

coiffure *n.f.* hairdressing, hair style, headdress

coin *n.m.* corner

colère *n.f.* anger

coller *v.* to glue, to paste, to stick

collier *n.m.* necklace, collar

colline *n.f.* hill

combattre *v.* to fight, to combat

combler *v.* to fill in, fill up, fill with (de)

comédien, comédienne *n.* actor, actress

commandement *n.m.* command

commander *v.* to order

comme *adv.* how; *conj.* as; **comme d'habitude**/as usual

commentaire *n.m.* comment, commentary

commerçant, commerçante *n.* merchant, business person

commun, commune *adj.* common; **peu commun, peu commune**/uncommon

complet *n.* suit

complet, complète *adj.* complete; **au complet**/filled up

se comporter *refl. v.* to behave

comprendre *v.* to understand, to include

compris *past part.* of **comprendre**; *see* §20.37, **y compris**/including

compte *n.m.* account

compter *v.* to count, to rank, to include

compter + inf. *v.* to intend + inf.

compter sur *v.* to count on

comte, comtesse *n.* count, countess

conclure *v.* to conclude

concours *n.m.* contest

concurrent *n.m.* contestant

condamner *v.* to condemn

conduire *v.* to drive, to conduct, to lead, to take (someone somewhere)

se conduire *refl. v.* to behave oneself, to conduct oneself

conduite *n.f.* conduct, behavior

conférence *n.f.* meeting, lecture

conférencier, conférencière *n.* lecturer

confiance *n.f.* confidence

confiserie *n.f.* candy store

confiseur, confiseuse *n.* confectioner, candy maker, candy seller

confort *n.m.* comfort

congé *n.m.* holiday, day off from work

connaissance *n.f.* acquiantance

connaître *v.* to know; *see* §40.ff; **connu** *past part.*

se consacrer *refl. v.* to devote oneself

conseil *n.m.* advice

conseiller *v.* to advise, to counsel

consentir *v.* to consent

consommer *v.* to consume

consonne *n.f.* consonant

constamment *adv.* constantly; *see* §2.ff

constater *v.* to figure out, to ascertain, to notice, to observe

constation *n.f.* finding, opinion

constituer *v.* to constitute

construit, construite *adj.* built

conte *n.m.* story

content, contente *adj.* content, happy; *see* Antonyms, §3.ff and Synonyms, §38.ff

se contenter *refl. v.* to content oneself

contenu *n.m.* content, contents

contrôleur *n.m.* ticket taker

convaincre *v.* to convince

convenir à *v.* to be convenient, to be suitable

coque *n.f.* shell; **un oeuf à la coque**/boiled egg

coquille *n.f.* shell

corbeau *n.m.* crow, raven

corbeille *n.f.* basket

corde *n.f.* cord, string; **un instrument à corde**/string instrument

corps *n.m.* body

corriger *v.* to correct

costume *n.m.* suit

côté *n.m.* side; **de mon côté**/for my part; *see* idioms & idiomatic expressions with **de**, §20.14

cou *n.m.* neck; **prendre ses jambes à son cou**/to run fast

couche *n.f.* layer

coucher *v.* to lay, to lay down

se coucher *refl. v.* to lie down, to go to bed

coude *n.m.* elbow

coudre *v.* to sew

couloir *n.m.* hallway

coup *n.m.* hit, knock, blow; **un coup de main**/a helping hand

coupable *adj.* guilty

couper *v.* to cut; **se couper**/to cut oneself

cour *n.f.* court, courtyard, yard

courant *n.m.* current; **un courrant d'air**/draft, air current

courier *n.m.* mail

courir *v.* to run

cours *n.m.* course; **au cours de**/in the course of, during the course of; *see also* idioms with **au**, §20.3

course *n.f.* race; **cheval de course**/race horse

court *v. form of* **courir**/to run

court, courte *adj.* short; *see* Antonyms, §3.ff

courtoisie *n.f.* courtesy

coussin *n.m.* cushion

couteau *n.m.* knife

coûter *v.* to cost

coutume *n.f.* custom

couturier *n.m.* fashion designer

couturière *n.f.* seamstress, dressmaker, fashion designer

couvert, couverte *adj.* covered

craignaient, craignant *forms of* **craindre** *v.* to fear

crainte *n.f.* fear

craintif, craintive *adj.* fearful

crâne *n.m.* skull

cravate *n.f.* necktie

crayon *n.m.* pencil

créer *v.* to create

crêpe *See* §23.1ff

creuser *v.* to dig

cri *n.m.* cry, shout

crier *v.* to cry out, to shout

crise *n.f.* crisis; **crise cardiaque**/heart attack

critique *See* §23.1ff

critiquer *v.* to criticize

croire *v.* to believe; *see* §40.ff

croiser *v.* to cross

croûte *n.f.* crust; **casser la croûte**/to have a bite, snack

cueillir *v.* to gather, to pick

cuiller, cuillère *n.f.* spoon

cuisine *n.f.* cooking, kitchen; **faire la cuisine**/to do the cooking, to cook; *see also* other idioms & idiomatic expressions with **faire** §20.18

cuisinier, cuisinière *n.* cook

cuisson *n.f.* cooking time

culinaire *adj.* culinary

culotte *n.f.* shorts (clothing), knickers, breeches

D

d' *prep.* of, from; **d'abord**/at first. *See* idioms with **d'**, §20.13; *see also* Prepositions

dater (de) *v.* to date (from)

davantage *adv.* enough, more

de *prep.* of, from; **de fait**/as a matter of fact; **de nos jours**/these days, in our time; **de nouveau**/again; **de parti pris**/on purpose, deliberately; **de plus**/besides; **de plus en plus**/more and more; **de sorte que**/*conj.* so that. *See* idioms and idiomatic expressions with **de**, §20.14; *see also* Prepositions

débarquer *v.* to disembark

se débarrasser de *refl. v.* to get rid of, to do away with

debout *adv.* standing (up), on one's feet

début *n.m.* beginning

décevoir *v.* to deceive, to disappoint

décourager *v.* to discourage

découverte *n.f.* discovery

découvrir *v.* to discover

décrire *v.* to describe

décrit, décrite *adj.* described

décrocher *v.* to unhook, to pick up the receiver of a telephone

déçu, déçue *adj.* deceived, disappointed

déesse *n.f.* goddess

défaire *v.* to undo, to unpack

défaite *n.f.* failure

défaut *n.m.* fault, defect

défendre *v.* to forbid, to prohibit, to defend; **se défendre**/to defend oneself

dégoût *n.m.* disgust

dégoûter *v.* to disgust

dehors *adv.* outside. *See* Antonyms, §3.ff

déjà *adv.* already

délice *n.m.* delight

délinquance *n.f.* delinquency

demander *v.* to ask, to request; **se demander**/to wonder

demeure *n.f.* dwelling, residence

demeurer *v.* to remain, to dwell, to live (in a place)

demi, demie *adj.* half

démontrer *v.* to demonstrate

denrée *n.f.* commodity, produce

dent *n.f.* tooth

départ *n.m.* departure

dépasser *v.* to surpass, to go beyond

se dépêcher *refl. v.* to hurry; **dépêchons-nous!**/let's hurry!

dépenser *v.* to spend (money)

dépenses *n.f.* expenses

déplacer, se déplacer *v.* to move, to displace, to budge

dépouiller *v.* to skin

dépourvu *adj.* destitute, unprovided; **au dépourvu**/by surprise

dépression *n.f.* depression, recess, flattening

déprimer *v.* to depress, to weaken

depuis *adv.* since; **depuis longtemps**/for a long time; **depuis lors**/since then, since that time. *See* §10–§10.5

déranger *v.* to disturb

dernier, dernière *adj.* last

dès *prep.* from, since; **dès aujourd'hui**/from today; **dès que** *conj.* as soon as. *See* Conjunctions & conjunctive locutions, §7.ff and §35.1

désagréable *adj.* unpleasant

descendre *v.* to go down, to come down, to descend; *see* §39.29; **faire descendre**/to make or to have someone or something come down. *See* causative **faire** in §5.ff

désert *n.m.* desert

désespéré, désespérée *adj.* in despair

déshonorer *v.* to dishonor

désormais *adv.* from now on

dessein *n.m.* project, plan, design

dessert *n.m.* dessert

dessin *n.m.* drawing, sketch

dessous *prep., adv.* under; **par-dessous**/below

dessus *prep., adv.* above; **par-dessus**/above

déterrer *v.* to unearth

détruire *v.* to destroy

dette *n.f.* debt

deuil *n.m.* mourning

devant *prep.* before, in front of

devenir *v.* to become; *see* §40.ff

deviner *v.* to guess

devinrent, devint *v. forms of* **devenir**; *see* §40.ff

devoir *n.m.* duty, obligation, homework

devoir *v.* to owe, to have to, must, ought, should; *see* §17., §39.92, §40.

devrais *v. form of* **devoir**

diminuer *v.* to diminish, to lessen

dire *v.* to say, to tell; **dire du mal de**/to speak ill of; **vouloir dire**/to mean; see §20.12 and §40.

diriger *v.* to direct; **se diriger** *refl. v.* to go toward, to head for

discours *n.m.* speech
disparaître *v.* to disappear
disparition *n.f.* disappearance
disputer, se disputer *v.* to quarrel, to dispute
distraire *v.* to distract
distrait, distraite *adj.* distracted
divertissant, divertissante *adj.* entertaining; **divertissement** *n.m.* amusement
dizaine *n.f.* about ten
doigt *n.m.* finger
dois, doit *v. forms of* **devoir**; *see* §17., §40.1, and §41.
domaine *n.m.* domain, realm
domestique *n.* servant
donc *conj.* therefore; when not used as a conj., **donc** is used as a locution to emphasize (usually the verb) what is being said, *e.g.:* **Où donc allez-vous?**/Where *are* you going? **Où donc est Simone?**/Where *is* Simone?
donner *v.* to give; **donner sur**/to face, to overlook, to look out upon; **donner un coup de main**/to give a helping hand; *see* idioms with **sur**, §20.32
dont *pron.* of which, whose, *etc.; see* §29.15 and §29.43ff; for the many uses of **dont**, see this entry in the General Index.
doré, dorée *adj.* decorated
dorénavant *adv.* from now on, henceforth
dormir *v.* to sleep; **dormir à la belle étoile**/to sleep outdoors, under the stars; **dormir sur les deux oreilles**/to sleep soundly
dortoir *n.m.* dormitory
dos *n.m.* back (of a person); **en avoir plein le dos**/to have it up to here, to be sick and tired of something; *see* idioms with **avoir**, §20.6
douane *n.f.* customs (entering or leaving a country)
douanier *n.m.* customs official
doucement *adv.* softly, quietly, sweetly
douceur *n.f.* sweetness, pleasantness
douche *n.f.* shower
douter *v.* to doubt; **se douter**/to suspect
doux, douce *adj.* sweet, pleasant
drapeau *n.m.* flag
drôle *adj.* funny, droll
du *See* idioms with **du**, §20.15
dû *past part. of* **devoir**; *see* §17., §17.6, §39.51, §40.1. You must know the various uses of the verb **devoir** and its different meanings.

dur, dure *adj.* hard
durable *adj.* lasting, durable
durée *n.f.* duration, length
durent, dut *v. forms of* **devoir**; *see* **devoir** and references to this important verb

E

échanger *v.* to exchange
échapper, s'échapper *v.* to escape; **l'échapper belle**/to have a narrow escape
échelle *n.f.* ladder
échouer *v.* to fail
éclair *n.m.* lightning
éclaircir *v.* to brighten up, to clear up
éclairer *v.* to light, to light up
éclatant, éclatante *adj.* striking, dazzling
éclater *v.* to burst (out)
écolier, écolière *n.* schoolboy, school girl
économe *adj.* thrifty
écouler *v.* to flow, to flow by, to slip away
écouter *v.* to listen to
écrin *n.m.* case, jewel case
écrire *v.* to write; *see* §40.ff
écriture *n.f.* handwriting
écrivain *n.m.* writer; **une femme écrivain**/woman writer
écume *n.f.* foam, froth
écureuil *n.m.* squirrel
écurie *n.f.* stable (for animals)
édicter *v.* to issue an edict, to promulgate
édifice *n.m.* building, edifice
effacer *v.* to erase, to efface
efficace *adj.* effective
effrayer *v.* to frighten
effroi *n.m.* fright
égal, égale *adj.* equal
s'égarer *refl. v.* to go astray
égoïste *n.* egoist
égorger *v.* to cut the throat of, to slaughter, to butcher
élève *n.m.f.* pupil
éloigner, s'éloigner *v.* to move away from, to keep distant
embarquer, s'embarquer *v.* to embark
embrasser *v.* to embrace, to kiss
émettre *v.* to emit, to issue
émouvoir *v.* to move, to stir, to affect
empêcher *v.* to prevent

emplette *n.f.* purchase; **faire des emplettes;** *see* idioms with **faire**, §20.18
emploi *n.m.* employment
employé, employée *n.* employee
employer *v.* to use, to employ
emporter *v.* to carry off, to carry away, to sweep away
emprisonné, emprisonnée *adj.* enclosed, imprisoned
emprunter *v.* to borrow
en *See* idioms with **en**, §20.16
encore *adv.* still, again, more, yet
encre *n.f.* ink
endormi, endormie *adj.* asleep; **s'endormir**/to fall asleep
endroit *n.m.* place
enfance *n.f.* infancy, childhood
enfant *n.m.f.* child
enfer *n.m.* Hades, Hell
enflé, enflée *adj.* swollen
enfoncer *v.* to push in, to stick in, to drive in
s'enfuir *refl. v.* to flee, to run away
enlever *v.* to remove, to take off; *see* §39.64
s'ennuyer *refl. v.* to be bored
enquête *n.f.* inquiry
enregistrer *v.* to record (on a tape, record)
s'enrhumer *refl. v.* to catch a cold
enseigne *See* §23.1ff
enseigner *v.* to teach
enseignement *v.* teaching
ensoleillé, ensoleillée *adj.* sunny
ensuite *adv.* then, next
entendre *v.* to hear, to understand; *see* §33.; **entendre dire que**/to hear it said that; **entendre parler de**/to hear about; **s'entendre avec qqn**/to get along with someone
entêté, entêtée *adj.* stubborn
entier, entière *adj.* entire
entouré de/surrounded by
entracte *n.m.* intermission
entraînement *n.m.* training
entraîner *v.* to bring about, to carry along
entre *prep.* among, between
entre chien et loup/at dusk
entrée *n.f.* entrance
entreprendre *v.* to undertake; *past part.,* **entrepris**
entreprise *n.f.* industry
entretenir *v.* to maintain
entretien *n.m.* upkeep
envers *prep.* toward; *see* §18.
envie *n.f.* envy, longing, desire; **avoir envie de**/to feel like; *see* idioms with **avoir**, §20.6
environ *adv.* nearly, about

environs *n.m.* suburbs, outskirts (of a city)

s'envoler *refl. v.* to fly away

envoyer *v.* to send; **envoyer chercher**/to send for

épais, épaisse *adj.* thick

épargner *v.* to save (money), to spare; **s'épargner**/to spare oneself, to save oneself

épaule *n.f.* shoulder

éperdu, éperdue *adj.* distracted, frantic, dumbfounded

épices *n.f.* spices

épicier, épicière *n.* grocer

épingle *n.f.* pin

éponge *n.f.* sponge

époque *n.f.* epoch, time, period

épouse *n.f.* wife; *see* Synonyms, §38.ff

époux *n.m.* husband; *see* Synonyms, §38.ff

éprouver *v.* to feel, to experience

équilibre *n.m.* balance, equilibrium

équipe *n.f.* team

ère *n.f.* era

escadrille *n.f.* flight

espace *n.m.* space

Espagne *n.f.* Spain

espèce *n.f.* type, species, kind

espérance *n.f.* hope

espérer *v.* to hope

esprit *n.m.* spirit, mind

essayer *v.* to try on; **essayer de**/to try (to)

essence *n.f.* gasoline, essence; **poste d'essence**/gas station

essuyer *v.* to wipe; *see* §39.61

est-ce *See* idioms and idiomatic expressions with **est-ce**, §20.12

estimer *v.* to value, to consider

établir *v.* to establish

étage *n.m.* floor (of a building)

étain *n.m.* tin

été *n.m.* summer; also *past part.* of **être**; *see* §39.81

éteindre *v.* to extinguish

éteint, éteinte *adj.* extinguished

étendre *v.* to extend

étendue *n.f.* extent, expanse

étoile *n.f.* star; **à la belle étoile**/under the stars; *see* §20.2

étonnement *n.m.* astonishment

étonner *v.* to astonish, to surprise

étourdi, étourdie *adj.* giddy, dizzy, light-headed

étranger *n.m.* overseas, abroad

étranger, étrangère *n.* foreigner

être *v.* to be; *see* §39.81 and §40.ff; *see also* idioms and idiomatic expressions with **être**, §20.17

étroit, étroite *adj.* narrow; *see* Synonyms, §3.ff

étude *n.f.* study

eu, eus, eut, eurent *v. forms of* avoir; *see* §39.81, §40.1, and §41. You must know all the forms of avoir.

éveiller *v.* to awaken

éviter *v.* to avoid

évoquer *v.* to evoke

examen *n.m.* examination, exam

s'exclamer *refl. v.* to exclaim

s'exercer *refl. v.* to exert oneself, to try hard

exiger *v.* to demand, to insist, to require

expédier *v.* to expedite

exprès/on purpose, deliberately

exprimer *v.* to express

expulser *v.* to drive out, to expel

extérieur *n.m.* exterior, outside

extrait *n.m.* extract

F

fable *n.f.* story, fable

fabrique *n.f.* manufacture

fabriquer *v.* to manufacture, to fabricate

face/en face de *See* idioms with **en**, §20.16 and with **faire**, §20.18

fâché, fâchée *adj.* angry, upset

fâcher *v.* to anger; **se fâcher**/to get angry, to become upset

facile *adj.* easy; **facilement** *adv.* easily

façon *n.f.* way, manner; **de toute façon**/any way, in any case

fade *adj.* tasteless

faible *adj.* weak; *see* Antonyms, §3.ff

faillir + *inf.* to almost (do something); **J'ai failli tomber**/I almost fell.

faim *n.f.* hunger

faire *v.* to do, to make; *see* §40.ff and idioms with **faire**, §20.18

faire *v.* to do, to make; *see* §40.ff and idioms with **faire**, §20.18. You must know those idioms to recognize them on the CBAT.

faire + *inf. See* **Causative faire**, §5.

se faire *v.* to be done; **Cela ne se fait pas ici**/That isn't done here.

se faire mal *v.* fo hurt oneself

fait *n.m.* fact; **au fait**/as a matter of fact; **de fait**/as a matter of fact; *see* idioms with **au**, §20.3; **Comment se fait-il?**/How come?

faites comme chez vous/make yourself at home; *see* §20.18

falloir *v.* to be necessary; *see* §19.

familial, familiale *adj.* family

fatigant, fatigante *adj.* tiring

fatigué, fatiguée *adj.* tired

faute *n.f.* lack, error, mistake

fauteuil *n.m.* arm chair, seat (in a theater)

faux *n.m.* falsehood

faux, fausse *adj.* false

fée *n.f.* fairy; **un conte de fées**/fairy tale

féliciter *v.* to congratulate

femme *n.f.* woman; **femme de chambre**/chamber maid; wife; *see* Synonyms, §38.

fer *n.m.* iron; **le chemin de fer**/railroad

ferme *n.f.* farm

ferme *adj.* firm

fermer *v.* to close; **fermer à clef**/to lock

fermier, fermière *n.* farmer

fête *n.f.* holiday, feast, party

fêter *v.* to celebrate

feu *n.m.* fire; **le feu rouge**/red light (traffic)

feuille *n.f.* leaf, sheet of paper

se fiancer *refl. v.* to become engaged

ficelle *n.f.* string

fier, fière *adj.* proud

fierté *n.f.* pride

fièvre *n.f.* fever

figure *n.f.* face

figurer *v.* to figure in, to be included in

fil *n.m.* thread, string, wire; **la télégraphie sans fil (T.S.F.)**/wireless (radio)

fille *n.f.* daughter; **une jeune fille**/girl

fils *n.m.* son; **fils unique**/only son

fin *n.f.* end; **fin de semaine**/weekend

fis, fit, fîmes, fîtes, firent, fisse, fît, fissions *v. forms of* faire; *see* §40.1 and §41.

fixer *v.* to fix, to attach

flamme *n.f.* flame

Flandre *n.f.* Flanders

fleur *n.f.* flower

fleuri, fleurie *adj.* flowered, in bloom; **fleuriste** *n.m.f.*/florist

fleuve *n.m.* river

florin *n.m.* florin (coin, money)

foi *n.f.* faith; **ma foi!**/my word!

fois *n.f.* time; **la première fois**/the first time; **à la fois**/at the same time; **Il était une fois**/Once upon a time there was . . . *See* idioms and idiomatic expressions with **fois**, §20.19 and with **à**, §20.2

fol, folle *adj.* crazy

fonctionnaire *n.m.* official; civil servant

fond *n.m.* bottom; **à fond**/thoroughly
fonder *v.* to found, to establish
force *n.f.* force; **à force de**/by dint of
forcément *adv.* naturally, forcefully
forêt *n.f.* forest
formidable *adj.* amazing, wonderful
fossé *n.m.* ditch
fou, fol, folle *adj.* crazy
foudre *n.f.* lightning
foule *n.f.* crowd
four *n.m.* oven
fourchette *n.f.* fork
fournir *v.* to furnish
fourrure *n.f.* fur
foyer *n.m.* lobby, home, hearth
frais *n.m.pl.* expenses
frais, fraîche *adj.* cool, healthy
fraise *n.f.* strawberry
framboise *n.f.* raspberry
franc, franche *adj.* frank
franchement *adv.* frankly
frapper *v.* to hit, to knock, to strike
frémir *v.* to shudder, to shiver
fréquemment *adv.* frequently
fromage *n.m.* cheese
front *n.m.* forehead
frotter *v.* to rub
fuir *v.* to flee, to run away
fuite *n.f.* flight, escape
furent, fussent, fut, fût *v. forms of* être; *see* §39.81, §40.1, *and* §41.ff. You must know all those forms of être, at least to recognize them and their meaning when you see them.
fuyait *v. form of* **fuir**; *see* §41.ff

G

gagner *v.* to earn, to gain, to win
gai, gaie *adj.* gay
gant *n.m.* glove
garde *n.f.* watch, surveillance
garder *v.* to keep, to guard; **garder le lit**/to stay in bed
gare *n.f.* station
gare!/look out! beware!
garni, garnie *adj.* garnished, decorated
gaspiller *v.* to waste
gastronomique *adj.* gastronomical (having to do with cooking and eating food)
gâteau *n.m.* cake
gâter *v.* to spoil
geler *v.* to freeze; *see* §37.ff
gémir *v.* to groan, to moan
gendre *n.m.* son-in-law
généreux, généreuse *adj.* generous

genou *n.m.* knee
genre *n.m.* type, kind
gens *n.f.m.* people; **jeunes gens**/young people
gentil, gentille *adj.* nice, pleasant
geste *n.m.* gesture
gibier *n.m.* game (hunting)
gifle *n.f.* slap
gigantesque *adj.* gigantic
gilet *n.m.* vest
glace *n.f.* hand mirror, ice cream
glacé, glacée *adj.* frozen, icy cold
glacial, glaciale *adj.* freezing
glacière *n.f.* refrigerator
gloire *n.f.* glory
gomme *n.f.* eraser
gorge *n.f.* throat
gourmand, gourmande *adj.* gluttonous
gourmandise *n.f.* gluttony, greediness, love of good food
goût *n.m.* taste
goûter *v.* to taste
goutte *n.f.* drop (liquid)
grâce à/thanks to
grand, grande *adj.* great, big, large
Grande Bretagne *n.f.* Great Britain
grandir *v.* to grow, to grow big, to become large
grange *n.f.* barn
gras, grasse *adj.* fat; **faire la grasse matinée**/to sleep late in the morning; *see* idioms with **faire**, §20.18
gratification *n.f.* gratification, tip (money)
gratte-ciel *n.m.* skyscraper
gratter *v.* to scratch
gratuit, gratuite *adj.* free, gratis
gratuitement *adv.* free of charge
grave *adj.* serious, grave; **gravement**/seriously
gré *n.m.* will, pleasure; *see* idioms with **à**, §20.2 *and* with **bon**, §20.9
grec, grecque *adj.* Greek; **à la grecque**/Greek style
Grèce *n.f.* Greece
grimper *v.* to climb
grimpeur *n.m.* climber
gris, grise *adj.* gray
gronder *v.* to scold
gros, grosse *adj.* big, fat, large; **avoir le coeur gros**/to be heartbroken
grosseur *n.f.* size, thickness
guérir *v.* to cure
guerre *n.f.* war
gueule *n.f.* mouth (of an animal)
guichet *n.m.* box office, teller's window
guide *See* §23.1ff

H

habile *adj.* skilled, skillful
habiller *v.* to dress (someone); **s'habiller**/to dress oneself
habit *n.m.* clothes, clothing
habitant *n.m.* inhabitant
habitation *n.f.* house
habitude *n.f.* habit, custom; **d'habitude**/usually, ordinarily; **comme d'habitude**/as usual
haleine *n.f.* breath; **reprendre haleine**/to catch one's breath
hasard *n.m.* chance, risk, danger; **par hasard**/by chance; *see* idioms with **par**, §20.22
hâte *n.f.* haste; **à la hâte**/hastily
hausser les épaules/to shrug one's shoulders
haut, haute *adj.* high, tall; **en haut**/up, above, upstairs; *see* idioms with **en**, §20.16
hauteur *n.f.* height
hectare *n.m.* hectare (about 2.47 acres)
herbe *n.f.* grass
héritier, héritière *n.* heir, heiress
heureusement *adv.* fortunately, happily
heureux, heureuse *adj.* happy; *see* Antonyms, §3.ff *and* Synonyms, §38.ff
hibou *n.m.* owl
hideux, hideuse *adj.* hideous
Hollandais, Hollandaise *n.* Dutch (person)
homme *n.m.* man; **homme d'état**/statesman
honte *n.f.* shame
horaire *n.m.* time schedule, time table
horloge *n.f.* clock
hors *adv.* outside
huile *n.f.* oil
humeur *n.f.* humor, mood, disposition

I

île *n.f.* island
illisible *adj.* illegible
illustre *adj.* famous, illustrious
image *n.f.* picture, image
immeuble *n.m.* building
imperméable *n.m.* raincoat
impétueux, impétueuse *adj.* impetuous
importe; il importe/it is important
imprévisible *adj.* unforeseeable
imprimer *v.* to print

inattention *n.f.* inattention, absent-mindedness; **par inattention**/carelessly

incendie *n.m.* fire

inclinaison *n.f.* bow

incompris, incomprise *adj.* misunderstood

inconnu, inconnue *adj.* unknown

indice *n.m.* indication, sign, mark

inférieur, inférieure *adj.* lower

innombrable *adj.* innumerable

inondation *n.f.* flood, inundation

inquiet, inquiète *adj.* restless

inquiétant, inquiétante *adj.* upsetting, disturbing, disquieting

inquiétude *n.f.* restlessness, anxiety

inscrire *v.* to inscribe; **inscrit, inscrite** *adj.* inscribed

insensé, insensée *adj.* insane

instant *n.m.* instant; **à l'instant**/instantly; *see* idioms with **à**, §20.2

s'instruire *refl. v.* to inform oneself

interdire *v.* to prohibit, to forbid, to interdict

interdit, interdite *adj.* forbidden, prohibited

interprète *n.m.f.* interpreter

interrompre *v.* to interrupt

intitulé entitled

inutile *adj.* useless; *see* Antonyms, §3.ff

inutilement *adv.* uselessly

invité, invitée *n.* guest

irai, iras, ira, *etc. v. forms of* **aller;** *see* §39.85

irriter *v.* to irritate

issue *n.f.* result, outcome

Italie *n.f.* Italy

Italien, Italienne *n.* Italian (person)

italien *n.m.* Italian (language)

ivre *adj.* drunk

J

jadis *adv.* formerly, in days gone by

jamais *adv.* never; **à jamais**/forever

jambe *n.f.* leg; **prendre ses jambes à son cou**/to run fast

jambon *n.m.* ham

Japon *n.m.* Japan

Japonais, Japonaise *n.* Japanese (person)

jardinier, jardinière *n.* gardener; **jardinière des neiges**/babysitter at a ski resort

jeter *v.* to throw; **jeter un coup d'oeil**/to glance

jeu *n.m.* game

jeunes, jeunes gens *n.m.f.* young people, youth

jeunesse *n.f.* youth

jeux *n.m.pl.* games

joindre *v.* to join; **joindre les deux bouts**/to make ends meet

joue *n.f.* cheek

jouer *v.* to play; **jouer gros jeux**/to take chances

jouet *n.m.* toy

joueur, joueuse *n.* player

jouir (de) *v.* to enjoy

jour *n.m.* day; **de nos jours**/in our day

journal *n.m.* newspaper

journée *n.f.* day

joyeux, joyeuse *adj.* joyous, happy, merry; *see* Antonyms, §3.ff and Synonyms, §38.ff

jupe *n.f.* skirt

jusqu'à up to, until

K

kilo, kilogramme *n.m.* kilogram (1 kilogram equals about 2.2 pounds)

kilomètre *n.m.* kilometer (1 kilometer equals about 0.62137 mile or about ⅝ mile, or 1,000 meters)

L

là *adv.* there; **là-dessus**/there on, thereupon, on that

lac *n.m.* lake

laid, laide *adj.* ugly; *see* Antonyms, §3.ff

laisser *v.* to leave (something); **laisser tomber** *v.* to let fall, to drop

laitier, laitière *adj.* dairy

laitue *n.f.* lettuce

lame *n.f.* blade

langue *n.f.* tongue, language; **avoir la langue bien pendue;** *see* idioms & idiomatic expressions with **avoir**, §20.6

laquelle, lesquelles; *see* §29.26ff

large *adj.* wide; *see* Antonyms, §3.ff

larme *n.f.* tear (from eyes)

las, lasse *adj.* tired, weary

lasser *v.* to tire, to weary; **se lasser**/to become tired, to become weary

laver *v.* to wash (someone or something); **se laver**/to wash oneself

lecteur, lectrice *n.* reader (person who reads)

lecture *n.f.* reading

léger, légère *adj.* light (in weight); **à la légère;** *see* idioms & idiomatic expressions with **à**, §20., §20.1, §20.2ff

légèrement *adv.* lightly

légume *n.m.* vegetable

lendemain *n.m.* the following day, the following morning

lent, lente *adj.* slow

lentement *adv.* slowly; *see* Adverbs, §2.ff

lequel, lesquels, lesquelles; *see* §29.26

lever *n.m.* the raising; **le lever du soleil**/sun rise; **le lever du rideau**/curtain rise (theater)

lever *v.* to raise; *see* §39.53ff; **se lever** *refl. v.* to get up

lèvre *n.f.* lip

libraire *n.* bookseller

librairie *n.f.* book shop

licencié, licenciée *n.* person with a scholastic degree

lien *n.m.* tie, bond

lier *v.* to tie, to link, to bind; **lier connaissance**/to become acquainted

lieu *n.m.* place; **avoir lieu**/to take place; **au lieu de**/instead of, in place of; *see* idioms & idiomatic expressions with **au**, §20.3 and with **avoir**, §20.6

linge *n.m.* linen, laundry

lion, lionne *n.* lion, lioness

lire *v.* to read; *see* §40.ff

livre *n.m.* book

livrer *v.* to deliver; **livrer bataille**/to wage a battle, to give battle; **se livrer à**/to devote oneself to

logement *n.m.* lodging, housing

loger *v.* to lodge, to dwell

logis *n.m.* lodging, dwelling

loi *n.f.* law

loin *adv.* far; **au loin**/in the distance; *see* idioms with **au**, §20.3

Londres *n.m.* London

long, longue *adj.* long; **à la longue**/in the long run, in the end; **le long de**/along

longtemps *adv.* for a long time

lors *adv.* then, at the time

lorsque *adv.* when; *see* Adverbs, §2.ff

louer *v.* to rent, to praise

loup *n.m.* wolf; **à pas de loup**/softly, quietly; *see* idioms and idiomatic expressions with **à**, §20.2

lourd, lourde *adj.* heavy

lumière *n.f.* light

lune *n.f.* moon

lutter *v.* to fight, to combat, to struggle

lycée *n.m.* lyceum; French secondary school

lycéen, lycéenne *n.* high school student

Consult the Comprehensive Index for additional § references.

M

maigre *adj.* thin; *see* Antonyms, §3.ff and Synonyms, §38.ff

main *n.f.* hand; **un coup de main**/helping hand; **main-d'oeuvre** *n.f.* manpower, labor

maintenir *v.* to maintain

maintien *n.m.* maintenance

maire *n.m.* mayor

maïs *n.m.* corn

maître, maîtresse *n.* teacher, master, mistress

majestueux, majestueuse *adj* majestic

mal *n.m.* evil, harm; **se faire mal**/to hurt (harm) oneself; **le mal de mer**/seasickness; **mal à l'aise**/ill at ease; *as an adv.* badly, poorly

malade *n.m.f.* sick person

malade *adj.* sick, ill

maladie *n.f.* illness, sickness, malady

maladroit, maladroite *adj.* clumsy

malcontent, malcontente *adj.* unhappy; *see* Antonyms, §3.ff

malgré *prep.* in spite of

malheur *n.m.* unhappiness, misfortune; **Malheur!**/What a bad fix!

malhonnête *adj.* dishonest

malle *n.f.* trunk (luggage)

manche *n.f.* sleeve; *see* §23.1

mannequin *n.m.* mannequin, fashion model

manque *n.m.* lack

manquer *v.* to miss; **manquer (de)**/to lack, to fail to

manteau *n.m.* coat, overcoat

manucure *n.f.* manicure

se maquiller *refl. v.* to put make-up on one's face

marchand, marchande *n.* merchant

marche *n.f.* step (of stairs)

marché *n.m.* market; **bon marché**; *see* idioms and idiomatic expressions with **bon**, §20.9

marcher *v.* to walk, to march, to run (of a machine)

maréchal *n.m.* marshal

marguerite *n.f.* daisy

mari *n.m.* husband; *see* Synonyms, §38.

marier *v.* to marry someone to someone; **se marier**/to get married

marin *n.m.* sailor

marine *n.f.* navy

marquer *v.* to mark, to hit (a score)

marron *n.m.* brown, chestnut brown

marteau *n.m.* hammer

matelas *n.m.* mattress

matelot *n.m.* sailor, seaman

matinée *n.f.* morning; **faire la grasse matinée**; *see* idioms & idiomatic expressions with **faire**, §20.18

mauvais, mauvaise *adj.* bad

méchant, méchante *adj.* mean, nasty

mécontent, mécontente *adj.* unhappy

mécontentement *n.m.* dissatisfaction

médaille *n.f.* medal

médecin *n.m.* doctor; **une femme médecin**/woman doctor

médecine *n.f.* medicine (profession)

médicament *n.m.* medicine (that you take)

se méfier (de) *refl. v.* to distrust, to watch out for

meilleur, meilleure *adj.* better; *see* §22.; **meilleur marché**/at a better price, at a lower price

mêler *v.* to mix, to mingle; **se mêler de ses affaires**/to mind one's own business; **Mêlez-vous de vos affaires!**/Mind your own business!

même *adj., adv.* same, even; **le même jour**/the same day; **le jour même**/the very day

ménage *n.m.* household, home, married couple; **ménagère** *n.f.* housewife

mener *v.* to lead

mensonge *n.m.* lie, falsehood

menton *n.m.* chin

mer *n.f.* sea; **mal de mer**/seasickness

messager, *n.m.* messenger

métier *n.m.* trade, occupation

metteur en scène/director (theater, film)

mettre *v.* to put, to place; *see* §40.; **mettre à la porte**/to send out of the room, to put out, to dismiss, to discharge; **mettre au courant**/to inform; **mettre du temps**/to spend some time; **mettre fin à**/to put an end to; **mettre une lettre à la poste**/to mail (post) a letter; **se mettre en colère**/to become angry, upset; **se mettre à** + *inf.*/to begin (to); **se mettre debout**/to stand up

meuble *n.m.* piece of furniture; **meubles** *n.m.pl.* furniture

meurt *v. form of* **mourir**; *see* §41.

midi *n.m.* noon

miel *n.m.* honey

mieux *adv.* better; *see* §22.; *see also* idioms & idiomatic expressions with **mieux**, §20.20 and with **tant**, §20.33

milieu *n.m.* middle

millier *n.m.* thousand

mineur *n.m.* miner

mineur, mineure *adj.* minor

ministre *n.m.* minister

minuit *n.m.* midnight

se mirer *refl. v.* to look at oneself, to be reflected

mis *past part. of* **mettre**; *see* §39.51 and §40.1, §41.

mis, mise *adj.* placed, put; **mise au point**/perfected

misérable *adj.* miserable, wretch

misère *n.f.* misery; **un chien de misère**/a stray dog

mit *form of* **mettre**; *see* §40.1 and §41.

mobilier *n.m.* furniture, furnishings

mode *See* §23.1; *see also* idioms and idiomatic expressions with **à**, §20.2

modéré, modérée *adj.* moderated

moindre *adj.* least

mois *n.m.* month

monde *n.m.* world, people; **beaucoup de monde**/many people

mondial, mondiale *adj.* world

monnaie *n.f.* change (money)

montagne *n.f.* mountain; **montagnard, montagnarde**/mountain person

monter *v.* to go up, to come up, to get on; *see* §39.29; **monter à cheval**/to go horseback riding; **monter dans**/to get into (a vehicle); **monter la garde**/to place a watch (surveillance)

montre *n.f.* watch

montrer *v.* to show; **montrer de doigt**/to point out, to indicate by pointing

se moquer *v.* to make fun of

morceau *n.m.* piece, morsel

morne *adj.* sad, cheerless

mort *n.f.* death; *also past part. of* **mourir**; **faire le mort** to play dead

mot *n.m.* word (written); **parole** *n.f.* word (spoken)

mouche *n.f.* fly (insect)

se moucher *refl. v.* to wipe one's nose with a handkerchief

mouchoir *n.m.* handkerchief

mouillé, mouillée *adj.* wet, damp

mourir *v.* to die

mourut *passé simple of* **mourir**

mouton *n.m.* sheep

mouvementé, mouvementée *adj.* eventful, lively, choppy (travel on water)

moyen *n.m.* means, way; **au moyen de**/by means of; **Moyen Age**/Middle Ages

moyen, moyenne *n. adj.* average

moyennant *prep.* thanks to, by means of

mur *n.m.* wall
mûr, mûre *adj.* ripe
musée *n.m.* museum

N

nage *n.f.* swimming
naissaient *v. form of* **naître**
naître *v.* to be born
naquis, naquit, naquîmes, *etc. passé simple of* **naître;** *see* §41.
natal, natale *adj.* native
natation *n.f.* swimming
navire *n.m.* boat
ne . . . plus; *see* Negations, §30.
négligé, négligée *adj.* careless, neglectful
neige *n.f.* snow; **un bonhomme de neige**/snowman
nettoyer *v.* to clean; *see* §39.61
neuf, neuve *adj.* (brand) new
neveu *n.m.* nephew
nez *n.m.* nose
n'importe quel, quoi, où, quand, *etc.; see* Indefinite pronouns, §29.23
Noël *n.m.* Christmas; **Joyeux Noël!**/ Merry Christmas! **le Père Noël**/ Santa Claus
nombreux, nombreuse *adj.* numerous
non *See* idioms and idiomatic expressions with **non,** §20.21
nord *n.m.* north
note *n.f.* grade, mark, note
nouer *v.* to tie; **nouer les deux bouts**/to make both ends meet
nouilles *n.f.pl.* noodles
nourri, nourrie *adj.* nourished, fed
nourrir *v.* to nourish, to feed; **se nourrir**/to feed oneself
nourriture *n.f.* nourishment, food
nouveau, nouvelle *adj.* new; **de nouveau**/again; *see* idioms and idiomatic expressions with **de,** §20.14
nouvelles *n.f.pl.* news
nuit *n.f.* night; **passer une nuit blanche**/to spend a sleepless night
nul, nulle/no one, not any one, *etc.; see* §30.

O

obéissant, obéissante *adj.* obedient
obstinément *adv.* obstinately; **s'obstiner** *refl. v.* to be obstinate
occasion *n.f.* opportunity, occasion
occupé, occupée *adj.* busy, occupied; **s'occuper de** *refl. v.* to be busy with, to take care of, to mind;

occupez-vous de vos affaires/ mind your own business
oeil *n.m.* eye; **les yeux**/the eyes
oeillet *n.m.* carnation
oeuf *n.m.* egg; **un oeuf à la coque**/ boiled egg, *i.e.,* in the shell (coque)
oeuvre *n.f.* work (of art)
offrir *v.* to offer; **s'offrir**/to offer to each other
oiseau *n.m.* bird
ongle *n.m.* fingernail
opprimer *v.* to oppress
or *n.m.* gold; *as a conj.* now, well
orage *n.m.* storm
oranger *n.m.* orange tree
ordinaire *adj.* ordinary; **d'ordinaire**/ ordinarily
ordonner *v.* to order
oreille *n.f.* ear; **dormir sur les deux oreilles**/to sleep soundly
organisateur *n.m.* organizer
orgueil *n.m.* pride; **orgueilleux, orgueilleuse** *adj.* proud
orné, ornée *adj.* decorated
orteil *n.m.* toe
orthographe *n.f.* spelling
os *n.m.* bone
oubli *n.m.* oblivion; **oublier**/to forget
ouïr *v.* to hear
ours *n.m.* bear (animal)
outil *n.m.* tool
outre *prep.* in addition to; **en outre**/ besides
ouverture *n.f.* opening
ouvrage *n.m.* work
ouvreur, ouvreuse *n.* usher
ouvrier, ouvrière *n.* worker, laborer
ouvrir *v.* to open; *see* §40.

P

pacifier *v.* to pacify
page *See* §23.1
paille *n.f.* straw; **un bonhomme de paille**/scarecrow
pain *n.m.* bread
paisiblement *adv.* peacefully; *see* Adverbs, §2.
paix *n.f.* peace
palais *n.m.* palace
pantoufle *n.f.* slipper
papeterie *n.f.* stationery store
papillon *n.m.* butterfly
paquebot *n.m.* boat, steamship liner
Pâques *n.f.pl.* Easter
paquet *n.m.* package, parcel
par *prep.* by, on; **par contre**/on the other hand; **par terre**/on the

ground, on the floor; for other idioms & idiomatic expressions with **par,** *see* §20.22
paradis *n.m.* paradise
paraître *v.* to seem, to appear
parapluie *n.m.* umbrella
parce que *conj.* because; *see* §7.ff
parcimonieux, parcimonieuse *adj.* sparing, parsimonious, frugal
parcourir *v.* to pass by, through, over, to cover distance
pardessus *n.m.* overcoat
pareil, pareille *adj.* such, similar; **sans pareil**/unparalleled
paresseux, paresseuse *adj.* lazy; *see* Antonyms, §3.
parfois *adv.* at times
parloir *n.m.* parlor (the word is based on the *v.* **parler,** to talk, so that a **parloir** is a room where people talk.)
parmi *prep.* among
parole *n.f.* word (spoken); **le mot** (written word); *see* idioms & idiomatic expressions with **parole,** §20.23
part *n.f.* part, share; **quelque part**/somewhere
partager *v.* to share
parti *n.m.* political party, side; **de parti pris**/on purpose, deliberately, foregone conclusion; *see* idioms & idiomatic expressions with **de,** §20.14
partie *n.f.* part, game; **faire partie de**/to take part in
partir *v.* to leave, to depart; *see* §40.; **à partir de**/beginning with; *see* idioms & idiomatic expressions with **à,** §20.2
partout *adv.* everywhere
parvenir (à) *v.* to reach, to attain, to succeed in
pas *n.m.* step (foot)
pas du tout/not at all
passer *v.* to spend (time); to go by, to pass by, to pass; *see* §39.29; **passer une nuit blanche**/to spend a sleepless night; **se passer** *v.* to happen; **se passer de**/to do without
pâte *n.f.* paste, pasta
patiner *v.* to skate
pâtisserie *n.f.* pastry shop
pâtissier, pâtissière *n.* pastry cook
patrie *n.f.* country
patron, patronne *n.* owner, proprietor
patte *n.f.* paw
pauvre *adj.* poor; **pauvrement** *adv.* poorly (*see* §2.ff); **pauvreté** *n.f.* poverty

---

payer *v.* to pay (for); *see* §39.50, §39.53ff

Pays-Bas *n.m.pl.* Low Countries, Netherlands

paysan, paysanne *n., adj.* farmer, country

peau *n.f.* skin

pêche *n.f.* peach

pêche *n.f.* fishing; **aller à la pêche**/to go fishing; **faire la pêche**/to fish, to go fishing; *see also* idioms & idiomatic expressions with **aller**, §20.5 and with **faire**, §20.18

pêcher *v.* to fish

péché *n.m.* sin

pécher *v.* to sin

peigne *n.m.* comb

peigné, peignée *adj.* combed

peindre *v.* to paint; **peint**, *past part.*

peine *n.f.* pain, hardship; **à peine**/hardly, scarcely; *see* idioms & idiomatic expressions with **à**, §20.2

peint *past. part. of* **peindre**

peinture *n.f.* painting

pelle *n.f.* shovel

pendant *prep.* during; **pendant que** *conj.* while, during; *see* Conjunctions, §7.ff

pénible *adj.* painful

péniblement *adv.* painfully

pensée *n.f.* thought

penser *v.* to think

penser à *See* §39.43 and §39.49

perçant *adj.* piercing

perchoir *n.m.* perch

perdre *v.* to lose, to waste

Père Noël *n.m.* Santa Claus

permis *n.m.* permit

perruque *n.f.* wig

personnage *n.m.* character, personage

personne *n.f.* person; with **ne . . .**/no one, nobody; *see* §30.ff

perte *n.f.* loss

peser *v.* to weigh; *see* §39.64

petit *adj.* small

petit-fils *n.m.* grandson

peu *adv.* little; **peu à peu**/little by little; *see* idioms with **à**, §20.2

peur *n.f.* fear; **avoir peur**/to be afraid; *see* idioms with **avoir**, §20.6; **faire peur**/to frighten; *see* idioms with **faire**, §20.18

peuvent *v. form of* **pouvoir**

pharmacie *n.f.* pharmacy, drug store; **pharmacien, pharmacienne** *n.* pharmacist, druggist

pièce *n.f.* play (theater); room (of an apartment, a house)

pied *n.m.* foot; **à pied**/on foot; **aller**

à pied/to walk

pierre *n.f.* stone; **faire d'une pierre deux coups**/to kill two birds with one stone, to hit two with one blow

pin *n.m.* pine wood

pis; tant pis; *see* idioms & idiomatic expressions with **tant**, §20.33

piscine *n.f.* swimming pool

pitoyable *adj.* pitiful

pittoresque *adj.* picturesque

place *n.f.* seat

plafond *n.m.* ceiling

plage *n.f.* seashore, beach

plaignit *v. form of* **plaindre**

plaindre, se plaindre *v.* to complain

plainte *n.f.* complaint

plaintif, plaintive *adj.* complaining, plaintive

plaire *v.* to please; *see* idioms and idiomatic expressions with **plaire**, §20.24

plaisir *n.m.* pleasure

plancher *n.m.* floor

plein, pleine *adj.* full; *see* Antonyms, §3.; **plein de**/full of; **en plein air**/outdoors, in the open air; *see* idioms & idiomatic expressions with **en**, §20.16

pleurer *v.* to cry, to weep

pleuvoir *v.* to rain; *past part.*, **plu**

pli *n.m.* crease, fold, pleat

plier *v.* to fold

plonger *v.* to dive, to plunge

plu *past part. of* **pleuvoir** and **plaire**

pluie *n.f.* rain

plupart *n.f.* most

plus *adv.* more; **de plus en plus**/more and more; **plus de**/more than; *see* idioms with **plus**, §20.25, and with **en**, §20.16

plusieurs *adv.* several

plut *passé simple of* **plaire** and **pleuvoir**

plutôt *adv.* rather, instead

poche *n.f.* pocket

podomètre *n.m.* pedometer

poêle *See* §23.2

poids *n.m.* weight

poignet *n.m.* wrist

poil *n.m.* hair (on one's body, *e.g.*, face, arms, legs)

point *n.m.* period, point; **à point**/well done; **mise au point**/perfected

poison *n.m.* poison

poisson *n.m.* fish

poivre *n.m.* pepper

poli, polie *adj.* polite

politesse *n.f.* courtesy, politeness

pomme *n.f.* apple; **pommier** *n.m.* apple tree; **une pomme de terre**/potato; **pommes frites**/French fries

pompier *n.m.* fireman

porc *n.m.* pork

portée *n.f.* reach; **à la portée**/within reach

porter *v.* to bear, to carry, to wear

porteur *n.m.* bearer, porter

poser *v.* to put, to pose, to place; **poser une question**/to ask a question; **se poser**/to place oneself

posséder *v.* to possess

poste *n.m.* job, position, post; *n.f.* post, mail; **un bureau de poste**/post office; *see* §23.1

potage *n.m.* soup

poubelle *n.f.* trash bin

poule *n.f.* hen

poulet *n.m.* chicken

poupée *n.f.* doll

pourboire *n.m.* tip (money)

poursuivre *v.* to follow, to pursue

pourtant *adv.* however, yet, still

pourvu que *conj.* provided that; *see* Conjunctions and conjunctive locutions, §7.ff and §35.1

pousser *v.* to push, to grow; **pousser une barbe**/to grow a beard

pouvoir *v.* to be able, can; *see* §40.ff; *as a n.*, power

pré *n.m.* meadow

précieux, précieuse *adj.* precious

se précipiter *refl. v.* to rush

préciser *v.* to state precisely, to be precise

prédicateur *n.m.* preacher

prédire *v.* to predict

premier, première *adj.* first

prendre *v.* to take, to take on, to catch; *see* §40.ff and §41.; **prendre des billets**/to get (buy) tickets; **prendre garde**/to watch out for; **prendre ses jambes à son cou**/to run fast; **se prendre à** + *inf.*/to begin + *inf.*; for other idioms and idiomatic expressions with **prendre**, *see* §20.26

près *prep.* near; **à peu près**; *see* idioms with **à**, §20.2

présenter *v.* to introduce, to present

presque *adv.* almost

pressé, pressée *adj.* hurried, hurrying; **se presser**/to be in a hurry

prêt, prête *adj.* ready

prêter *v.* to lend

preuve *n.f.* proof

prévenir *v.* to warn

prévoir *v.* to foresee; **prévu, prévue** *adj.* foreseen, expected

prier *v.* to beg, to pray; **Je vous en**

prie/I beg you, You're welcome.
pris *past. part. of* **prendre**; *see* §39.24 and §39.51
se priver *refl. v.* to deprive oneself
prix *n.m.* prize, price
procédé *n.m.* process
prochain, prochaine *adj.* next
prochainement *adv.* soon
procurer *v.* to procure, to obtain; **se procurer** *refl. v.* to procure for oneself
prodigue *adj.* wasteful, prodigal, extravagant
prodiguer *v.* to lavish
produit *n.m.* product; **produit laitier**/dairy product
profond, profonde *adj.* deep
profondeur *n.f.* depth
proie *n.f.* prey
projet *n.m.* plan, project
prolonger *v.* to prolong
promenade *n.f.* walk; **faire une promenade**/to take a walk, to go for a walk; **faire une promenade en voiture**/to go for a drive; *see* idioms and idiomatic expressions with **faire**, §20.18
promeneur *n.m.* stroller, walker
promettre *v.* to promise; **promis** *past part.;* **promirent** *passé simple of* **promettre**
propos *n.m.* resolution; **à propos de**/concerning, regarding, having to do with; *see* idioms with **à**, §20.2
propre *adj.* own, clean; see Antonyms, §3
propreté *n.f.* cleanliness
propriétaire *n.* owner, proprietor
propriété *n.f.* property
protéger *v.* to protect
provoquer *v.* provoke
Prussien, Prussienne *n.* Prussian
puis *or* **peux** *v. form of* **pouvoir**; *see* §40.1
puisque *conj.* since; *see* Conjunctions and conjunctive locutions, §7.ff and §35.1
puissance *n.f.* power
puissant, puissante *adj.* powerful
puits *n.m.* well (for water, oil, mining)
pullover *n.m.* sweater
punir *v.* to punish
punissait *v. form of* **punir**
punition *n.f.* punishment
purent *v. form of* **pouvoir**; *see* §40.1 and §41.

Q

quai *n.m.* wharf, quay
quand même! all the same! even so!
quant à, quant au *conj. locution* as for
quartier *n.m.* quarter, section
quel, quelle *See* §1.12, §20.27, and §20.28
quelque chose *See* §20.29
quelque part *adv. locution* somewhere
quelquefois *adv.* sometimes
quelques-uns, quelques-unes *pron.* some
se quereller *refl. v.* to quarrel
qu'est-ce que & qu'est-ce qui *See* §29.26ff
queue *n.f.* tail; **faire la queue**; *see* idioms with **faire**, §20.18
qui est-ce qui *See* §29.26ff
quincaillerie *n.f.* hardware store
quitter *v.* to leave (a person or place); **se quitter**/to leave each other
quoi *pron.* what; *see* §20.6, §20.30, §29., §29.32
quoi que whatever
quotidien, quotidienne *adj.* daily

R

raccrocher *v.* to hang up (again)
raconter *v.* to relate; **se raconter**/to tell stories to each other
raffiné, raffinée *adj.* refined
rafraîchir *v.* to refresh
rafraîchissement *n.m.* refreshment
rageusement *adv.* in a rage
ragoût *n.m.* stew
raison *n.f.* reason; **avoir raison**/to be right; *see* idioms and idiomatic expressions with **avoir**, §20.6
raisonnement *n.m.* reasoning
raisonner *v.* to reason
ramasser *v.* to pick up
ramener *v.* to bring back
rang *n.m.* rank, row; **rangée** *n.f.* row
ranimer *v.* to revive
rappeler *v.* to recall; *see* §39.53 and §39.67; **se rappeler** to remember
rapport *n.m.* report; **rapporter** *v.* to report
rarement *adv.* rarely; *see* §2.ff
ras *n.m.* surface level; **au ras de la peau**/on the surface of the skin; **se raser**/to shave oneself
rassurant, rassurante *adj.* reassuring **Rassurez-vous!**/Rest assured!
rayon *n.m.* ray; **rayonnant, rayonnante** *adj.* beaming
rebâtir *v.* to rebuild

recevoir *v.* to receive; *see* §40.ff; **recevoir des nouvelles**/to receive news, to hear from
rechauffer *v.* to heat again, to warm up
recherché, recherchée *adj.* sought after
récit *n.m.* story, tale
reçoit *v. form of* **recevoir**; *see* §40.1 and §41.
recommencer *v.* to begin again, to start over again
reconnaître *v.* to recognize
recours *n.m.* recourse, resort
recouvrir *v.* to cover again
reculer *v.* to recoil, to step back
reçut *v. form of* **recevoir**; *see* §40.1 and §41.
redoubler *v.* to double again, to do again, to repeat
réfectoire *n.m.* refectory
réfléchir *v.* to think, to reflect
se réfugier *v.* to take refuge
regard *n.m.* glance; **regarder** *v.* to look at; **Cela ne vous regarde pas**/That is none of your business; **se regarder**/to look at each other, to look at oneself
règle *n.f.* rule; **règlement** *n.m.* rule, ruling
régler *v.* to regulate; *see* §39.68ff
régner *v.* to reign; *see* §39.68ff
regretter *v.* to regret, to be sorry
reine *n.f.* queen
religieux, religieuse *n., adj.* religious person
remarquer *v.* to notice, to observe
remède *n.m.* remedy
remerciement *n.m.* gratefulness, gratitude; **remercier**/to thank
remettre *v.* to put back, to replace, to submit, to deliver, to hand in; **se remettre**/to pull oneself together
remise *n.f.* **en état**/restoration
remonter *v.* to go back in time
remplacer *v.* to replace
rempli, remplie *adj.* filled; **remplir de**/to fill with
remporter *v.* to carry away, to win (a game in sports)
remuer *v.* to shake
renard *n.m.* fox
rencontre *n.f.* encounter; **aller à la rencontre de qqn**/to go to meet someone; *see* idioms with **à**, §20.2 and with **aller**, §20.5
rencontrer *v.* to encounter, to find, to meet
rendement *n.m.* yield, return, profit
rendez-vous *n.m.* meeting, date, appointment

rendre *v.* to return (something), to render, to make; **se rendre**/to go, to surrender; **se rendre compte de**/to realize; **rendu, rendue** *adj.* rendered, made; *see also* §20.38 and §39.–§39.50

renommé, renommée *adj.* famous, famed

renommée *n.f.* fame

renoncer *v.* to renounce

rénover *v.* to renew, to revive

renseignement *n.m.* information

renseigner *v.* to inform

rentrée *n.f.* return; **la rentrée des classes**/back to school

rentrer *v.* to go in again, to return (home); *see* §39.29

renverser *v.* to knock over, to knock down; **tomber à la renverse**/to fall backwards

renvoyer *v.* to send away

repas *n.m.* meal

réplique *n.f.* verbal reply

répliquer *v.* answer verbally

repos *n.m.* rest; **reposé, reposée**/rested; **se reposer**/to rest

reprendre haleine/to catch one's breath

représentant, représentante *n.* representative

représentation *n.f.* show, presentation (theatrical)

réputé, réputée *adj.* famous, reputed

résoudre *v.* to resolve, to solve

se ressembler/to resemble each other; **Qui se ressemble s'assemble**/ Birds of a feather flock together.

ressentiment *n.m.* resentment

ressortir *v.* to go out again; *see* **sortir**, §40.1

rester *v.* to remain, to stay

retard *n.m.* delay; **en retard**/late; *see* idioms and idiomatic expressions with **en**, §20.16

retenir *v.* to retain, to reserve

retirer *v.* to pull out, to withdraw; **se retirer**/to retire, to withdraw

retour *n.m.* return; **de retour**/back; **être de retour**/to be back; *see* idioms and idiomatic expressions with **être**, §20.17

retraite *n.f.* retreat; **à la retraite**/retired

retrouver *v.* to retrieve, to regain, to find again

réunion *n.f.* meeting, reunion

réunir *v.* to meet, to bring together, to reunite; **se réunir**/to join each other, to meet

réussir *v.* to succeed; *see* §39.44

revanche *n.f.* revenge

rêve *n.m.* dream

réveil *n.m.* awakening, waking, alarm clock

réveille-matin *n.m.* alarm clock

réveillé, réveillée *adj.* awakened

réveiller *v.* to awaken

se révéler *v.* to reveal oneself

rêver *v.* to dream; **rêveur, rêveuse** *adj.* dreamer

revins, revint, revînmes, revinrent *v. forms of* **revenir**/to return; *see* §41 and **venir** in §40.1

rhume *n.m.* cold (common cold, illness)

rideau *n.m.* curtain

ridiculiser *v.* to ridicule

rien *See* idioms and idiomatic expressions with **rien**, §20.31

rigueur *n.f.* rigor, severity, rigidity; **de rigueur**/required; *see* idioms and idiomatic expressions with **de**, §20.14

rinçage *n.m.* rinsing, rinse

rire *n.m.* laughter

rire *v.* to laugh; **rire dans sa barbe**/ to laugh in one's sleeve

rival, rivaux, rivale, rivales *n., adj.* rival, rivals

rive *n.f.* edge, bank (of a river)

robe *n.f.* dress

roi *n.m.* king; **Roi-Soleil**/Sun-King (Louis XIV)

romain, romaine *adj.* Roman

roman *n.m.* novel

ronfler *v.* to snore

roquefort *n.m.* name of a cheese

rose *n.f.* rose; *adj.* pink; **voir tout en rose**; *see* idioms with **en**, §20.16

roue *n.f.* wheel

rougir *v.* to blush, to turn red

rouler *v.* to move, to roll along, to roll, to drive

Roumanie *n.f.* Rumania

route *n.f.* road

royaume *n.m.* kingdom

ruban *n.m.* ribbon, bow

rude *adj.* rugged

ruelle *n.f.* narrow street

ruse *n.f.* trick, ruse

rusé, rusée *adj.* tricky

Russe *n.* (person); **le russe**/Russian language

S

sable *n.m.* sand

sac *n.m.* bag; **un sac à main**/handbag

sachez bien/know well, be informed

sage *adj.* wise; **la sagesse**/wisdom

sain et sauf/safe and sound

sain, saine *adj.* healthy, sound

sale *adj.* dirty, soiled; *see* Antonyms, §3.

salé, salée *adj.* salty

salle *n.f.* room; **salle de bains**/bathroom; **salle de conférence**/meeting room

saluer *v.* to greet, to salute

salut *n.m.* salutation, greeting, salute, salvation

sang *n.m.* blood; **sanglant, sanglante** *adj.* bloody, rare (meat)

sans *prep.* without; **sans cesse**/unceasingly; **sans doute**/undoubtedly, without a doubt

santé *n.f.* health

sauf *prep.* except

sauf, sauve *adj.* safe; **sain et sauf**/ safe and sound

saumon *n.m.* salmon

sauter *v.* to jump, to leap

sauvage *adj.* savage

sauver *v.* to save; **se sauver**/to run away

sauvetage *n.m.* rescue, saving

sauveur, sauveuse *n.* savior, rescuer

savon *n.m.* soap

scolaire *adj.* scholastic, school

séchage *n.m.* drying

sécher *v.* to dry

secouer *v.* to shake

secourir *v.* to help

secours *n.m.* help

Seigneur *n.m.* Lord

sel *n.m.* salt

selon *prep.* according to

semaine *n.f.* week; **la fin de semaine**/week-end

semblable *adj.* similar; **faire semblant**/to pretend; *see* idioms with **faire**, §20.18

sembler *v.* to seem; **il semble que**; *see* Impersonal expressions, §35.7

sens *n.m.* sense, meaning

sentiment *n.m.* feeling

sentir *v.* to feel, to smell, to sense; **se sentir**/to feel (health)

serrer *v.* to squeeze, to shake (hands)

sert *See* §41.

serveur, serveuse *n.* waiter, waitress

service *n.m.* favor, service

serviette *n.f.* napkin

servir *v.* to serve; **se servir de**/to use, to make use of, to help oneself to (something)

seul, seule *adj.* single

si *adj.* so; *as a conj.*, if, what if, whether; **si** is sometimes used instead of **oui**, meaning yes; *see* §24.

siècle *n.m.* century

siège *n.m.* seat

sien: le sien, la sienne, les siens, les siennes; *see* §29.35ff

siffler *v.* to whistle

signification *n.f.* meaning

signifier *v.* to signify, to mean

s'il te plaît/please (familiar form)

s'il vous plaît/please (polite s. and plural form)

silencieux, silencieuse *adj.* silent

singulier, singulière *adj.* odd

soie *n.f.* silk

soient *v. form of* être; *see* §39.81, §39.102, §40.1, §41.

soif *n.f.* thirst

soigné, soignée *adj.* cared for

soigner *v.* to care for

soigneusement *adv.* carefully

soin *n.m.* care

soirée *n.f.* evening

sois, soit *v. form of* être; *see* §39.81, §39.102, §40.1, §41.

sol *n.m.* dirt, ground

soleil *n.m.* sun; **le lever du soleil**/sunrise

somme *See* §23.1

sommeil *n.m.* sleep

sommet *n.m.* summit, height

songer (à) *v.* to think of, to dream of; *see* §39.42ff

sonner *v.* to ring

sort *n.m.* fate

sorte *n.f.* sort, kind; **de sorte que** *conj.* so that; *see* §7.ff and §35.1

sortir *v.* to go out; *see* §39.29 and §40.ff

souci *n.m.* care, worry; **se soucier**/to be worried, to be concerned

soudain *adv.* suddenly

souffler *v.* to blow, to puff, to prompt

souffrant, souffrante *adj.* ill, sick; **souffrir**/to suffer

souhait *n.m.* wish; **souhaiter**/to wish

soulier *n.m.* shoe; *see* Synonyms, §38.

soumettre *v.* to submit

soupçonner *v.* to suspect

soupe *n.f.* soup; **souper** *v.* to sup, to have supper

sourcil *n.m.* eyebrow

sourd, sourde *adj.* deaf

sourire *n.m.* smile

sourire *v.* to smile

souris *n.f.* mouse

soutenir *v.* to maintain, to uphold

se souvenir de *refl. v.* to remember; **Souvenez-vous. . .**/Remember . . .

souvent *adv.* often

soyons *v. form of* etre; *see* §39.81, §39.102, §40.1, §41.

spectacle *n.m.* theatrical show, presentation

station *n.f.* station; **station thermale**/spa, health resort

stationner *v.* to station, to park (a vehicle)

su *past part. of* savoir; *see* §40.1, §41.

sucré, sucrée *adj.* sweetened

sucreries *n.f.pl.* sweets, candy

suffire *v.* to suffice, to be sufficient; **suffise** *v. form of* **suffire; suffisamment** *adv.* sufficiently

suis *v. form of* être and suivre; *see* §39.81, §41.

Suisse *n.f.* Switzerland

suit *v. form of* suivre

suite *n.f.* continuation; **et ainsi de suite**/and so on and so forth; *see* idioms with de, §20.14

suivre *v.* to follow; **suivre un cours**/to take a course

sujet *n.m.* subject; **au sujet de**/concerning

superficie *n.f.* surface area

supérieur, supérieure *adj.* higher, superior

supermarché *n.m.* supermarket

supplier *v.* to beg

supporter *v.* to endure

supprimer *v.* to suppress

sur *prep.* on, upon; *see* idioms with sur, §20.32

sûr, sûre *adj.* sure

surcharger *v.* to overload, to overburden

sur-le-champ *adv.* quickly, at once, on the spot

surlendemain *n.m.* second day after, two days later

surnommer *v.* to give a surname to, to nickname

surprenant, suprenante *adj.* surprising

surprendre *v.* to surprise

surtout *adv.* above all, especially

survendre *v.* to charge too much, to overcharge

suspendre *v.* to hang

T

T.S.F. télégraphie sans fil/(wireless) radio

tableau *n.m.* painting, picture

tâche *n.f.* task

tâcher (de) *v.* to try (to)

taille *n.f.* size

tailler *v.* to trim

tailleur *n.m.* tailor

se taire *refl. v.* to be silent, to be quiet; **taisez-vous**/be quiet

tandis que *conj.* while, whereas; *see* Conjunctions & conjunctive locutions, §7. and §35.1

tant *adv.* so, so much, so many; *see* idioms with **tant**, §20.33

tape *n.f.* slap, hit, tap

taper *v.* to tap, to hit

tapis *n.m.* carpet

tapisserie *n.f.* tapestry

tard *adv.* late

tarder *v.* to be late, to delay

tardivement *adv.* late

tel, tels, telle, telles/such; **un tel garçon**/such a boy; **une telle fille**/such a girl; **tel que**/such as

téléviseur *n.m.* television set

télévision *n.f.* television; **la télé**/TV

tellement *adv.* so

tempéré, tempérée *adj.* temperate

tempête *n.f.* tempest, storm

temps *n.m.* time; **à temps**/in time; weather; *see* weather expressions, §37.

tenir *v.* to keep, to hold; **tenir à;** *see* §39.44; **se tenir debout**/to stand; **se tenir droit**/to stand erect, straight; **tenir le ménage**/to keep house; **tenir sa parole**/to keep one's word

tenter (de) *v.* to attempt (to)

terrasser *v.* to throw down to the floor, to the ground

terre *n.f.* earth, ground; **par terre**/on the floor, on the ground

terrestre *adj.* terrestrial, ground

tête *n.f.* head

thé *n.m.* tea

théâtre *n.m.* theater; **faire du théâtre**/to act on the stage

thermal, thermale *adj.* thermal; **une station thermale**/spa, health resort

tiède *adj.* warm

tiens *v. form of* tenir; **un tiens vaut mieux que deux tu l'auras**/a bird in the hand is worth two in the bush; **Tiens!**/Look! Here!

timbre-poste *n.m.* postage stamp

tirer *v.* to pull, to draw; **se tirer d'affaire**/to get along, to get out of a fix, to get out of trouble, to get out of a situation

tiroir *n.m.* drawer

tissu *n.m.* cloth, material

toile *n.f.* canvas

toilette *n.f.* toilet; **faire la to-**

ilette/to wash and dress oneself

toit *n.m.* roof

tomber *v.* to fall; **laisser tomber**/to let fall, to drop; **faire tomber**/to knock down; **tomber à la renverse**/to fall backwards

tonne: il tonne/it is thundering; *see* weather expressions, §37.

tortueux, tortueuse *adj.* winding

tôt *adv.* early

tour *See* §23.1

tourmenter *v.* to torment

tourner *v.* to turn

tourner autour du pot/to beat around the bush

tourner des films/to shoot films

tous *pron., adj., m.pl.* all; *see* idioms with **tous**, §20.34

tousser *v.* to cough

tout *n., pron., adj.m.* all; *see* idioms with **tout**, §20.35 and with **à**, §20.2

toute *pron., adj.f.pl.* all; *see* idioms with **toute**, §20.36

toutefois *adv.* however

trahir *v.* to betray

train *n.m.* train; **être en train de +** inf.; *see* idioms with **être**, §20.17

traître, traîtresse *n.* traitor

tramway *n.m.* trolley car

tranquille *adj.* calm, quiet

transport *n.m.* transportation; **le transport en commun**/public transportation

travailleur, travailleuse *n.* worker; *see* Antonyms, §3.1

traverser *v.* to cross; **la traversée**/crossing; **à travers**/cross, through; *see* idioms with **à**, §20.2

trentaine about 30

trésor *n.m.* treasure

trêve *n.f.* truce

tricher *v.* to cheat

triste *adj.* sad, unhappy; *see* Antonyms, §3. and Synonyms, §38.

tromper *v.* to deceive; **se tromper**/to be mistaken

trompette See §23.2

trône *n.m.* throne

trottoir *n.m.* sidewalk

trou *n.m.* hole

troupeau *n.m.* flock, herd

trouver *v.* to find, to think (opinion); **se trouver**/to be located; **trouver que**/to be of the opinion that . . .

tu *past part. of* **taire**; *see* **se taire**

tuer *v.* to kill

tue-tête *adv. locution* at the top of one's voice; *see* idioms with **à**, §20.2

U

unique *adj.* unique, only; **fils unique**/only son; **fille unique**/only daughter

uniquement *adv.* only, solely, expressly for

unir *v.* to bring together, to unite

usage *n.m.* use

usine *n.f.* factory

utile *adj.* useful; *see* Antonyms, §3.

utiliser *v.* to use

V

vacances *n.f.pl.* vacation; **les grandes vacances**/summer vacation

vache *n.f.* cow

vaincu, vaincue *adj.* conquered, vanquished

vaisselle *n.f.* dishware, dishes; **faire la vaisselle**/to do the dishes; *see* idioms and idiomatic expressions with **faire**, §20.18

valeureux, valeureuse *adj.* valorous

valoir *v.* to be worth; **valoir la peine**/to be worth while; **valoir mieux**/to be better, to be preferable

vapeur *n.f.* steam; *see* §23.2

vase *See* §23.1

vaut *v. form of* **valoir**

veille *n.f.* eve; **la veille de Noël**/Christmas eve

veiller *v.* to stay up late, to keep watch

vélo *n.m.* bike, bicycle

velours *n.m.* velvet

vendeur, vendeuse *n.* salesperson

vendre *v.* to sell

venir *v.* to come; **venir à**/to happen; *see* §40.; *see* **venir de** in §20.14

vent *n.m.* wind; **up coup de vent**/a gust of wind

vente *n.f.* sale

vérité *n.f.* truth; **en vérité**/in truth, truthfully

verni, vernie *adj.* shiny, glossy, patent leather

verre *n.m.* glass (drinking); **un verre de lait**/a glass of milk

vers *n.m.* verse, poetry

vers *prep.* toward; *see* §18.

vertige *n.m.* vertigo, dizziness

veston *n.m.* jacket, coat (of a suit)

vêtement *n.m.* clothing, clothes

vêtu, vêtue *adj.* dressed

veuf, veuve *n.* widower, widow

veut dire; *see* **vouloir dire**; *see also*

§20.38 and §39.–§39.50

viande *n.f.* meat

vibrer *v.* to vibrate

victoire *n.f.* victory

vide *adj.* empty; *see* Antonyms, §3.

vie *n.f.* life, living

vieil, vieille *adj.* old

vieillard, vieillarde *adj.* old person

vient de/has just; **venir de +** inf./to have just done something + past part.; **Elle vient de partir**/She has just left; *see* **venir de** in §20.14

vieux, vieil, vieille *adj.* old

vif, vive *adj.* alive, lively, active

vigueur *n.f.* vigor, strength; **en vigueur**/in force

villageois, villageoise *n.* village person, villager

ville *n.f.* city; **en ville**/down town

vin *n.m.* wine

vingtaine about 20

vint *passé simple of* **venir**; *see* §40.1 and §41.

violon *n.m.* violin

virgule *n.f.* comma

visage *n.m.* face

vit *v. form of* **vivre** *and* **voir**; *see* §40.1 and §41.

vite *adv.* quickly, fast

vitesse *n.f.* speed

vitre *n.f.* window pane

vitrine *n.f.* window (of a store); shop window

vivre *v.* to live

voeu *n.m.* vow, wish

voie *n.f.* road, way, track

voile *See* §23.1

voir *v.* to see; *see* §40.1 and §41.

voisin, voisine *n., adj.* neighbor, neighboring

voisinage *n.m.* neighborhood

voiture *n.f.* car, automobile; **faire une promenade en voiture**/to go for a drive; **en voiture!**/all aboard!

voix *n.f.* voice; **à voix basse**/in a low voice; **à haute voix**/in a loud voice, aloud; *see* idioms with **à**, §20.2

vol *n.m.* flight, theft, hold-up; **un vol à main armée**/armed robbery; **faire de vol**/to fly

volaille *n.f.* poultry

voler *v.* to fly, to steal

voleur, voleuse *n.* thief

volontiers *adv.* willingly

vouloir *v.* to want; *see* §40.; **en vouloir à qqn**/to hold a grudge against someone; *see* idioms with **en**, §20.16; **vouloir dire**/to mean; *see* §20.38 and §39.–§39.50

voûté, voûtée *adj.* arched

voyage *n.m.* trip, voyage; **faire un voyage**/to take a trip; *see* idioms with **faire,** §20.18

voyager *v.* to travel

voyageur, voyageuse *n.* traveler

voyelle *n.f.* vowel

voyons *imper. of* **voir** let's see, see here; *see* **voir** in §40.1

vrai, vraie *adj.* true, real; **à vrai dire**/to tell the truth, truthfully; *see* idioms with **à,** §20.2

vue *n.f.* sight

W

wagon *n.m.* freight car; **wagon restaurant**/dining car (on a train)

Y

y *See* idioms with **y,** §20.37

y compris/including

yeux *n.m.* eyes; **l'oeil**/the eye

Verbs used in idiomatic expressions

On the pages containing 50 verbs fully conjugated in all the tenses, I offer simple sentences using verbs and idiomatic expressions. They can help build your French vocabulary and knowledge of French idioms.

When you look up the verb forms of a particular verb in this book, consult the following list so that you may learn some common idiomatic expressions. Consulting this list will save you time because you will not have to use a standard French-English word dictionary to find out what the verbal idiom means. Also, if you do this, you will learn two things at the same time: the verb forms for a particular verb and verbal idioms.

Remember that all verbs in the French language are not used in idioms. Those given below are used very frequently in French readings and conversation. Some of the following entries contain words, usually nouns, that are related to the verb entry. This, too, will help build your vocabulary. I also include a few proverbs containing verbs because they are interesting, colorful, useful, and they help build your knowledge of French words and idiomatic expressions.

accuser, s'accuser to accuse, to accuse oneself
    accuser réception de qqch to acknowledge receipt of something
    Qui s'excuse, s'accuse. A guilty conscience needs no accuser.

acheter to buy, to purchase
    acheter qqch à qqn to buy something from someone

achever to achieve, to finish
    achever de faire qqch to complete (finish) doing something

adresser to address
    adresser la parole à to speak to, to direct your words to

agir to act, to behave
    agir à la légère to act thoughtlessly

aider, s'aider to help, to help oneself
    Aide-toi, le ciel t'aidera. Heaven helps those who help themselves.

aimer to like
    aimer (à) faire qqch to like doing something
    aimer mieux to prefer

aller to go
    to feel (health)   **Comment allez-vous?** How are you?   **Je vais bien.** I'm fine; **Je vais mal.** I'm not well; **Je vais mieux maintenant.** I'm feeling better now.
    aller à quelqu'un to be becoming, to fit, to suit someone
        Cette robe lui va bien. This dress suits her fine; **La barbe de Paul ne lui va pas bien.** Paul's beard does not look good on him.

aller à la pêche   to go fishing

aller à la rencontre de quelqu'un   to go to meet someone

aller à pied   to walk, to go on foot

aller au-devant de quelqu'un   to go to meet someone

aller au fond des choses   to get to the bottom of things

aller avec qqch   to match something

aller chercher   to go get

aller de pair avec. . .   to go hand in hand with. . .

aller en voiture   to ride in a car

aller sans dire   to go without saying;   **Ça va sans dire.**   That goes without saying.

Allez-y!   Go to it! Go ahead!

allons donc!   nonsense! come, now! come on, now!

Just for the fun of it, try reading aloud this play on words as fast as you can:
   Un ver vert va vers un verre vert. (A green worm is going toward a green glass.)

appeler   to call

être appelé à qqch   to be destined for something, to have a calling (vocation, career)

apprendre   to learn

apprendre par coeur   to memorize

arriver   to arrive

to happen   **Qu'est-ce qui est arrivé?**   What happened?   **Qu'est-ce qui arrive?**   What's happening? What's going on?
   Quoi qu'il arrive. . .   Come what may. . .

assister   to assist

assister à   to attend, to be present at   **Hier soir, j'ai assisté à la conférence des musiciens.**   Last night I attended the meeting of musicians.

avoir   to have

to have something the matter   **Qu'est-ce que vous avez?**   What's the matter with you?   **Qu'est-ce qu'il y a?**   What's the matter?

avoir. . .ans   to be. . .years old   **Quel âge avez-vous?**   How old are you?
   J'ai seize ans.   I'm sixteen.

avoir à + inf.   to have to, to be obliged to + inf.
   J'ai à vous dire quelque chose.   I have to tell you something.

avoir affaire à quelqu'un   to deal with someone

avoir beau + inf.   to be useless + inf., to do something in vain;   **Vous avez beau parler; je ne vous écoute pas.**   You are talking in vain (uselessly); I'm not listening to you.

avoir besoin de   to need, to have need of   **Vous avez l'air fatigué; vous avez besoin de repos.**   You look tired; you need some rest.

avoir bonne mine   to look well, to look good (persons)
   Joseph a bonne mine aujourd'hui, ne trouvez-vous pas?   Joseph looks good today, don't you think so?

avoir chaud   to be (feel) warm (persons)   **J'ai chaud; ouvrez la fenêtre, s'il vous plaît.**   I feel warm; open the window; please.

avoir congé to have a day off, a holiday from work or school **Demain nous avons congé et nous allons à la plage.** Tomorrow we have off and we're going to the beach.

avoir de la chance to be lucky **Ah! Tu as trouvé une pièce de monnaie?! Tu as de la chance!** Ah! You found a coin?! You're lucky!

avoir de quoi + inf. to have the material, means, enough + inf. **As-tu de quoi manger?** Have you something (enough) to eat?

avoir des nouvelles to receive news, to hear (from someone)

avoir droit à to be entitled to

avoir du savoir-faire to have tact

avoir du savoir-vivre to have good manners, etiquette

avoir envie de + inf. to feel like, to have a desire to **Madame Loisel a toujours envie de danser.** Mrs. Loisel always feels like dancing.

avoir faim to be (feel) hungry **As-tu faim, Fifi? Bon, alors je vais te donner à manger.** Are you hungry, Fifi? Good, then I'm going to give you something to eat.

avoir froid to be (feel) cold (persons) **J'ai froid; fermez la fenêtre, s'il vous plaît.** I feel cold; close the window, please.

avoir hâte to be in a hurry; **avoir hâte de faire qqch** to be anxious to do something

avoir honte to be (to feel) ashamed

avoir l'air + adj. to seem, to appear, to look + adj. **Vous avez l'air malade; asseyez-vous.** You look sick; sit down.

avoir l'air de + inf. to appear + inf. **Vous avez l'air d'être malade; couchez-vous.** You appear to be sick; lie down.

avoir l'habitude de + inf. to be accustomed to, to be in the habit of **J'ai l'habitude de faire mes devoirs avant le dîner.** I'm in the habit of doing my homework before dinner.

avoir l'idée de + inf. to have a notion + inf.

avoir l'impression to be under the impression

avoir l'intention de + inf. to intend + inf.

avoir l'occasion de + inf. to have the opportunity + inf.

avoir l'oeil au guet to be on the look-out, on the watch

avoir la bonté de + inf. to have the kindness + inf.

avoir la langue bien pendue to have the gift of gab

avoir la parole to have the floor (to speak)

avoir le cafard to feel downhearted (downcast), to have the blues

avoir le coeur gros to be heartbroken

avoir le droit de faire qqch to be entitled (have the right) to do something

avoir le temps de + inf. to have (the) time + inf.

avoir lieu to take place **Le match aura lieu demain.** The game will take place tomorrow.

avoir l'occasion de faire qqch to have the opportunity to do something

avoir mal to feel sick **Qu'est-ce que tu as, Robert?** What's the matter, Robert? **J'ai mal.** I feel sick; **avoir mal au coeur** to feel nauseous

avoir mal à + (place where it hurts) to have a pain or ache in. . . **J'ai mal à la jambe.** My leg hurts; **J'ai mal à la tête.** I have a headache.

avoir mauvaise mine to look ill, not to look well **Qu'est-ce que tu as,**

Janine?   What's the matter, Janine?   **Tu as mauvaise mine.**   You don't look well.

avoir peine à + inf.   to have difficulty in + pres. part.

avoir peur de   to be afraid of

avoir pitié de   to take pity on

avoir qqn   to get the better of someone

avoir raison   to be right (persons)

avoir recours à   to resort to

avoir rendez-vous avec qqn   to have a date (appointment) with someone

avoir soif   to be thirsty

avoir soin de faire qqch   to take care of doing something

avoir sommeil   to be sleepy

avoir son mot à dire   to have one's way

avoir tendance à faire qqch   to tend to do something

avoir tort   to be wrong (persons)

avoir trait à qqch   to have to do with something

avoir une faim de loup   to be starving

en avoir marre   to be fed up, to be bored stiff, to be sick and tired of something   **J'en ai marre!**   I'm fed up! I've had it!

en avoir par-dessus la tête   to have enough of it, to be sick and tired of it, to have it up to here   **J'en ai par-dessus la tête!**   I've had it up to here!

en avoir plein le dos   to be sick and tired of it

il y a. . .   there is. . ., there are. . .

il y avait. . ., il y a eu. . .   there was. . ., there were. . .

il y aura. . .   there will be. . .

il y aurait. . .   there would be. . .

il y a + length of time   ago   **Madame Duclos est partie il y a un mois.**   Mrs. Duclos left a month ago.

Il y a dix minutes que j'attends l'autobus.   I have been waiting for the bus for ten minutes.

Il y a lieu de croire que. . .   There is reason to believe that. . .

Il n'y a pas de quoi.   You're welcome.

boire   to drink
  boire à la bouteille   to drink right out of the bottle
  boire à sa soif   to drink to one's heart content

briller   to shine, to glitter
  Tout ce qui brille n'est pas or.   All that glitters is not gold.

casser, se casser   to break
  casser la tête à qqn   to pester someone
  casser les oreilles à qqn   to bore someone stiff (by talking too much)
  casser les pieds à qqn   to be a pain in the neck to someone
  se casser +   a part of one's body;   **Janine s'est cassé la jambe.**   Janine broke her leg.
  se casser la tête   to rack one's brains

changer   to change
  changer d'avis   to change one's mind, one's opinion;   **changer de route**   to

take another road;   **changer de train**   to change trains;   **changer de vêtements**   to change clothes

Plus ça change plus c'est la même chose.   The more it changes the more it remains the same.

chanter   to sing

faire chanter qqn   to blackmail someone

Mais qu'est-ce que vous chantez là?   What are you talking about?

chercher   to look for

envoyer chercher   to send for   **Je vais envoyer chercher le médecin.**   I am going to send for the doctor.

combler   to fill up, to fill in

pour comble de malheur   to make matters worse

comprendre   to understand, to comprise

y compris   including;   **y compris la taxe**   tax included;   **y compris le service**   service included

craindre   to fear

Chat échaudé craint l'eau froide.   A burnt child dreads the fire. (Literally, the French proverb refers to a cat but to a child in English.)

croire   to believe

Je crois que oui.   I think so;   **Je crois que non.**   I don't think so.

dire   to say, to tell

à ce qu'on dit. . .   according to what they say. . .

à vrai dire   to tell the truth

c'est-à-dire   that is, that is to say

dire du bien de   to speak well of;   **dire du mal de**   to speak ill of

entendre dire que   to hear it said that, to hear tell that;   **J'entends dire que Tina s'est mariée avec Alexandre.**   I hear that Tina married Alexander.

vouloir dire   to mean;   **Que veut dire ce mot?**   What does this word mean?

Dis-moi ce que tu manges et je te dirai ce que tu es.   Tell me what you eat and I will tell you what you are.

Qui l'aurait dit?   Who would have thought so?

disposer   to dispose

L'homme propose mais Dieu dispose.   Man proposes but God disposes.

donner   to give

donner à boire à qqn   to give someone something to drink

donner à manger à qqn   to feed someone

donner congé à   to grant leave to

donner du chagrin à qqn   to give someone grief

donner rendez-vous à qqn   to make an appointment (a date) with someone

donner sur   to look out upon;   **La salle à manger donne sur le jardin.** The dining room looks out upon (faces) the garden.

donner un cours   to give a course, to lecture

dormir   to sleep

dormir à la belle étoile   to sleep outdoors
dormir sur les deux oreilles   to sleep soundly

éclater   to burst
éclater de rire, rire aux éclats   to burst out laughing, to roar with laughter
éclater en applaudissements   to burst into applause

écouter   to listen (to)
être aux écoutes   to be on the watch, to eavesdrop

écrire   to write
de quoi écrire   something to write with

égaler   to equal, to be equal to, to match
Cela est égal.   It's all the same; It doesn't matter; It makes no difference.
Cela m'est égal, Ça m'est égal.   It doesn't matter to me; It's all the same to me.

endommager   to damage
C'est dommage!   It's too bad! It's a pity!

entendre   to hear
bien entendu   of course
C'est entendu!   It's agreed! It's understood!
entendre dire que   to hear it said that, to hear tell that;   **J'entends dire qu'on mange bien dans ce restaurant.**   I hear that a person can have a good meal in this restaurant.
Qu'entendez-vous par là!   What do you mean by that!
laisser entendre   to hint
entendre raison   to listen to reason
ne pas entendre malice   not to mean any harm

entendre parler de   to hear about, to hear of;   **J'ai entendu parler d'un grand changement dans l'administration de cette école.**   I've heard about a big change in the administration of this school.

envoyer   to send
envoyer chercher   to send for;   **Je vais envoyer chercher le docteur.**   I am going to send for the doctor.

être   to be
Ainsi soit-il!   So be it!
être à qqn   to belong to someone;   **A qui est ce livre?**   Whose is this book?
Ce livre est à moi.   This book is mine.
être à l'heure   to be on time
être à temps   to be in time;   **Nous sommes arrivés juste à temps.**   We arrived just in time.
être au courant de   to be informed about;   **Madame Beaupuy parle toujours au téléphone avec ses amies; elle est au courant de tout.**   Mrs. Beaupuy talks on the telephone all the time with her friends; she is informed about everything.
être bien   to be comfortable;   **Est-ce que vous êtes bien dans cette chaise?**   Are you comfortable in this chair?
être bien aise (de)   to be very glad, happy (to)

être bien mis (mise) to be well dressed; **Madame Paquet est toujours bien mise.** Mrs. Paquet is always well dressed.

être d'accord avec to agree with

être dans son assiette to be "right up one's alley"; **Ces problèmes de mathématiques sont très faciles; je suis dans mon assiette.** These math problems are very easy; they're right up my alley; to be one's cup of tea.

être de bonne (mauvaise) humeur to be in a good (bad) mood

être de retour to be back; **A quelle heure ta mère sera-t-elle de retour?** At what time will your mother be back?

être en bonne forme to be in good shape

être en état de + inf. to be able + inf.; **Mon père est très malade; il n'est pas en état de vous parler maintenant.** My father is very sick; he's not able to talk to you now.

être en panne to be broken-down, out of order (machine, auto); **La voiture de mon père est toujours en panne.** My father's car always has a breakdown.

être en retard to be late, not to be on time; **Le train est en retard.** The train is late.

être en train de + inf. to be in the act of + pres. part., to be in the process of, to be busy + pres. part.; **Mon père est en train de réparer le téléviseur.** My father is busy repairing the television set.

être en vacances to be on vacation

être en vie to be alive

être enrhumé to have a cold, to be sick with a cold

être hors de soi to be beside oneself, to be upset, to be furious, to be irritated, annoyed; **Je suis hors de moi parce que je n'ai pas reçu de bonnes notes dans mes études.** I'm upset because I did not receive good grades in my studies.

être le bienvenu (la bienvenue) to be welcomed; **On est toujours le bienvenu dans cet hôtel.** One is always welcome in this hotel.

être pressé(e) to be in a hurry

être sur le point de + inf. to be about + inf.; **Dépêchons-nous parce que le train est sur le point de partir.** Let's hurry because the train is about to leave.

être temps de + inf. to be time to + inf.; **Il est temps de partir.** It is time to leave.

De quelle couleur est (sont). . . What color is (are). . .? **De quelle couleur est votre nouvelle voiture?** What color is your new car?

Il était une fois. . . Once upon a time there was. . .

Quelle heure est-il? What time is it? **Il est une heure;** It is one o'clock; **Il est trois heures.** It is three o'clock.

y être to be there, to understand it, to get it; **Ah! J'y suis!** Ah, I get it! I understand it!

c'est ça! That's right!

étudier to study

à l'étude under study; **Le dossier de Monsieur Pompier est à l'étude.** Mr. Pompier's file is under study.

faire ses études à to study at; **Gervaise fait ses études à l'Université de**

Paris.   Gervaise is studying at the University of Paris.

Depuis combien de temps étudiez-vous le français?   How long have you been studying French?

J'étudie le français depuis deux ans.   I have been studying French for two years.

excuser, s'excuser   to excuse, to excuse oneself

Qui s'excuse, s'accuse.   A guilty conscience needs no accuser.

faillir   to fail, to miss

faillir + inf.   to almost do something;   **Le bébé a failli tomber.**   The baby almost fell.

faire   to do, to make

aussitôt dit aussitôt fait (aussitôt dit que fait)   no sooner said than done

Cela ne fait rien.   That doesn't matter; That makes no difference.

Comment se fait-il. . .?   How come. . .?

en faire autant   to do the same, to do as much

faire + inf.   to have something done;   **Ma mère a fait faire une jolie robe.** My mother had a pretty dress made;   **Mon père a fait bâtir une nouvelle maison.**   My father had a new house built.

faire à sa tête   to have one's way

faire attention (à)   to pay attention (to)

faire beau   to be pleasant, nice weather;   **Il fait beau aujourd'hui.**   It's nice weather today;   **faire mauvais**   to be bad weather

faire bon accueil   to welcome

faire chaud   to be warm (weather);   **Il a fait beaucoup chaud hier.**   It was very warm yesterday.

faire comme chez soi   to make oneself at home;   **Faites comme chez vous!** Make yourself at home!

faire d'une pierre deux coups   to kill two birds with one stone

faire de l'autostop   to hitchhike

faire de la peine à qqn   to hurt someone (morally, emotionally)

faire de son mieux   to do one's best

faire des châteaux en Espagne   to build castles in the air

faire des cours   to give courses, to lecture

faire des emplettes, faire des courses, faire des achats, faire du shopping to do or to go shopping

faire des progrès   to make progress

faire du bien à qqn   to do good for someone;   **Cela lui fera du bien.**   That will do her (him) some good.

faire du ski   to ski

faire du sport   to play sports

faire du vélo   to ride a bike

faire exprès   to do on purpose

faire face à   to oppose

faire faire   to have something made (done).   **Mon père fait peindre la maison.**   My father is having the house painted.

faire fi   to scorn

faire froid   to be cold (weather);   **Il fait très froid ce matin.**   It's very cold this morning.

faire jour to be daylight

faire la bête to act like a fool

faire la connaissance de qqn to make the acquaintance of someone, to meet someone for the first time, to become acquainted with someone; **Hier soir au bal Michel a fait la connaissance de beaucoup de jeunes filles.** Last night at the dance Michael met many girls.

faire la cuisine to do the cooking

faire la grasse matinée to sleep late in the morning

faire la lessive to do the laundry

faire la malle to pack the trunk

faire la queue to line up, to get in line, to stand in line

faire la sourde oreille to turn a deaf ear, to pretend not to hear

faire la vaisselle to do (wash) the dishes

faire le ménage to do housework

faire le tour de to take a stroll, to go around; **Faisons le tour du parc.** Let's go around the park.

faire les bagages to pack the baggage, luggage

faire les valises to pack the suitcases, valises

faire mal à qqn to hurt, to harm someone; **Ce grand garçon-là a fait mal à mon petit frère.** That big boy hurt my little brother.

faire mon affaire to suit me, to be just the thing for me

faire nuit to be night(time)

faire part à qqn to inform someone

faire part de qqch à qqn to let someone know about something, to inform, to notify someone of something; **Je leur ai fait part du mariage de mon fils.** I notified them of the marriage of my son.

faire partie de to be a part of

faire peur à qqn to frighten someone

faire plaisir à qqn to please someone

faire sa toilette to wash up

faire savoir qqch à qqn to inform someone of something

faire semblant de + inf. to pretend + inf.

faire ses adieux to say good-bye

faire ses amitiés à qqn to give one's regards to someone

faire ses études à to study at; **Ma fille fait ses études à l'Université de Paris.** My daughter is studying at the Univerity of Paris.

faire son lit to make one's bed

faire son possible to do one's best (utmost)

faire suivre to forward mail; **Faites suivre mes lettres, s'il vous plaît.** Forward my letters, please.

faire un cours to give a course, to lecture

faire un tour to go for a stroll

faire un voyage to take a trip

faire une malle to pack a trunk

faire une partie de to play a game of

faire une promenade to take a walk

faire une promenade en voiture to go for a drive

faire une question to ask (to pose) a question

faire une réclamation to make a complaint

faire une visite   to pay a visit

faire venir l'eau à la bouche   to make one's mouth water

faire venir qqn   to have someone come;   **Mon père a fait venir le médecin parce que ma mère est malade.**   My father had the doctor come because my mother is sick.

Faites comme chez vous!   Make yourself at home!

Que faire?   What is to be done?

Quel temps fait-il?   What's the weather like?

se faire faire   to have something made (done) for oneself;   **Ma mere se fait faire une belle robe.**   My mother is having a beautiful dress made.

falloir   to be necessary, must, to be lacking

Il faut. . .   It is necessary; one must. . .

Il ne faut pas. . .   One must not. . .

Comme il faut. . .   As it ought to be. . .

Peu s'en faut. . .   It takes only a little. . .

s'en falloir   to be lacking

Il s'en faut de beaucoup. . .   It takes a lot. . .

féliciter   to congratulate

féliciter qqn de qqch   to congratulate someone for (on) something;   **Je vous félicite de votre succès.**   I congratulate you on your success.

fermer   to close

fermer a clef   to lock

fermer au verrou   to bolt

hâter, se hater   to hasten

en toute hâte   in all possible speed, in great haste

importer   to matter, to be of importance

Cela n'importe.   That doesn't matter.

jeter   to throw

jeter l'argent par la fenêtre   to waste money

manger   to eat

de quoi manger   something to eat;   **Y a-t-il de quoi manger?**   Is there something to eat?

manquer   to lack, to fail, to be missing

manquer de + inf.   to fail to, to almost do something;   **J'ai manqué de tomber.**   I almost fell;   **Paul a manqué de venir.**   Paul failed to come.

manquer à sa parole   to go back on one's word

mettre   to put, to place

mettre   to put on (clothing);   **Mimi a mis ses souliers blancs.**   Mimi put on her white shoes.

mettre au courant de   to inform about;   **Tu ne me mets jamais au courant de rien!**   You never inform me about anything!

mettre de côté   to lay aside, to save

mettre en cause   to question

mettre en pièces   to tear to pieces, to break into pieces;   **Roger était si**

fâché contre Julie qu'il a mis sa lettre en pièces. Roger was so angry at Julie that he tore her letter to pieces.

mettre fin à qqch to put an end to something

mettre la table, mettre le couvert to set the table

se mettre à table to sit down at the table; **La cuisinière a mis la table et a annoncé: Venez, tout le monde; mettez-vous à table!** The cook set the table and announced: Come, everybody; sit down at the table!

montrer to show

montrer du doigt to point out, to show, to indicate by pointing

parler to talk, to speak

à proprement parler strictly speaking

adresser la parole à to speak to, to direct one's words at; **Ecoutez, le professeur va nous adresser la parole.** Listen, the professor is going to speak to us.

entendre parler de to hear about; **Avez-vous jamais entendu parler de cela?** Have you ever heard of that?

Il est bon de parler et meilleur de se taire. Speech is silver; silence is gold.

Ce n'est qu'une façon de parler. It's just a way of speaking.

partir to leave

à partir de from now on, beginning with; **A partir de cet instant, tu vas faire tes devoirs tous les soirs *avant de* regarder la télévision.** From this moment on, you are going to do your homework every evening *before* watching television.

passer to pass, to pass by

passer un examen to take an exam

passer chez qqn to drop in on someone

passer un coup de fil à qqn to give someone a ring (a telephone call)

plaire to please

s'il vous plaît (s'il te plaît) please

Plaît-il? What did you say? Would you repeat that, please?

pleuvoir to rain

pleuvoir à verse to rain hard

pouvoir to be able (to)

n'en pouvoir plus to be unable to go on any longer, to be exhausted; **Je n'en peux plus.** I can't go on any longer.

Cela se peut. That may be.

prendre to take

prendre garde de + inf. to avoid + pres. part., to take care not + inf.; **Prenez garde de tomber;** Avoid falling; **Prenez garde de ne pas tomber.** Take care not to fall.

prendre le parti de + inf. to decide + inf.

prendre un billet to buy a ticket

Qu'est-ce qui vous prend? What's got into you?

profiter to profit

profiter de   to take advantage of

proposer   to propose
L'homme propose mais Dieu dispose.   Man proposes but God disposes.

regarder   to look (at), to watch
Cela ne vous regarde pas.   That's none of your business.

rendre   to render, to return (something)
rendre hommage à qqn   to pay someone homage
rendre visite à   to pay a visit to

reprendre   to take up again
reprendre la parole   to go on speaking, to resume speaking
reprendre ses esprits   to regain one's senses

retourner   to return, to go back
être de retour   to be back;   **Madame Duval sera de retour aujourd'hui.**
   Mrs. Duval will be back today.

revoir   to see again
au revoir   good-bye

rire   to laugh
rire au nez de qqn   to laugh in someone's face
rire aux éclats   to roar with laughter

risquer   to risk
Qui ne risque rien, n'a rien.   Nothing ventured, nothing gained.

sauter   to leap, to jump
sauter aux yeux   to be evident, self-evident

savoir   to know
savoir bon gré à qqn   to be thankful, grateful to someone

servir   to serve
Cela ne sert à rien.   That serves no purpose.
se servir de   to use, to make use of;   **Ma mère se sert d'une machine pour
   faire la vaisselle.**   My mother uses a machine to do the dishes.

suivre   to follow
suivre un cours   to take a course;   **Je vais suivre un cours de francais
   cet été.**   I'm going to take a course in French this summer.
suivre un régime   to be on a diet
à suivre   to be continued

tomber   to fall
tomber à la renverse   to fall backward

traverser   to cross, to traverse
à travers   across, through

trouver   to find
Ne trouvez-vous pas?   Don't you think so?
trouver visage de bois   not to find anyone answering the door after knocking

tuer to kill

à tue-tête at the top of one's voice, as loud as possible; **Pour attraper l'autobus qui était en train de partir, Monsieur Duval a crié à tue-tête.** To catch the bus which was about to leave, Mr. Duval shouted at the top of his voice.

valoir to be worth

valoir mieux to be better (worth more), to be preferable; **Mieux vaut tard que jamais.** Better late than never.

venir to come

venir à to happen to; **Si nous venons à nous voir en ville, nous pouvons prendre une tasse de café ensemble.** If we happen to see each other downtown, we can have a cup of coffee together.

venir à bout de + inf. to manage, to succeed + inf.

venir de + inf. to have just done something; **Je viens de manger.** I just ate; **Tina Marie venait de sortir avec Alexandre quand le téléphone a sonné.** Tina Marie had just gone out with Alexander when the telephone rang.

vivre to live

de quoi vivre something (enough) to live on; **Je vais apporter du pain et du beurre chez les Duval parce qu'ils n'ont pas de quoi vivre.** I'm going to bring some bread and butter to the Duvals because they don't have enough to live on.

voir to see

à vue d'oeil visibly

voir de loin to be farsighted

voir tout en rose to see the bright side of things, to be optimistic

vouloir to wish, to want

en vouloir à qqn to bear a grudge against someone

vouloir dire to mean; **Que voulez-vous dire?** What do you mean?

vouloir du bien à qqn to wish someone well

Que voulez-vous?! What do you expect?!

Veuillez agréer. . . Please be good enough to accept. . . (This is the usual closing statement in a formal letter.)

References in this Index are to sections of the book indicated by the symbol § in front of a numerical decimal system. The abbreviation **ff** means *and the following*. In this Index, find the p. number of abbreviations used in this book.

Consult the French-English Vocabulary for additional § references.

Consult the French-English Vocabulary for additional § references.

Consult the French-English Vocabulary for additional § references.

A GUIDE TO PRONUNCIATION OF FRENCH SOUNDS

PURE VOWEL SOUNDS

Phonetic Symbol	French word	pronounced as in the English word*
a	la	at
ɑ	pas	father
e	été	ate
ɛ	ère	egg
i	ici	see
o	hôtel	over
ɔ	donne	bun
u	ou	too
œ	leur	urgent
Ø	deux	pudding
y	tu	fume
ə	le	ago

NASAL VOWEL SOUNDS

Symbol	French word	English word
œ̃	un	unguent
ɔ̃	bon	song
ɛ̃	vin	sang
ɑ̃	blanc	dong

SEMI-CONSONANT SOUNDS

Symbol	French word	English word
w	oui	west
y	huit	you eat
j	fille	yes, see ya later

CONSONANT SOUNDS

Phonetic Symbol	French word	pronounced as in the English word*
b	bonne	bun
d	dans	dong
f	fou	first, pharmacy
g	garçon	go
ʒ	je	measure
ʃ	chose	shake
k	café, qui	cap, kennel
l	le	let
m	mette	met
n	nette	net
ɲ	montagne	canyon, onion, union
p	père	pear
R	rose	rose
s	si	see
t	te	lot
v	vous	vine
z	zèbre	zebra

* English words contain sounds that only approximate French sounds.

NOTE: The colon sign : means that the vowel sound right in front of : is prolonged, as in Ro : z (rose).

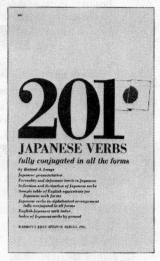